*American
Sea Power in
the
Old World*

American Sea Power in the Old World

THE UNITED STATES NAVY IN EUROPEAN AND NEAR EASTERN WATERS, 1865–1917

William N. Still, Jr.

Contributions in Military History, Number 24

Greenwood Press

WESTPORT, CONNECTICUT   •   LONDON, ENGLAND

Copyright Acknowledgments

Grateful acknowledgment is made to the following for permission to reprint material:

The National Maritime Museum, Greewich, England, photograph of the USS *Chicago*.

"Red Bill's Interpreter," *United States Naval Institute Proceedings* 5 (December 1928): 1117–18. Courtesy of the U.S. Naval Institute.

Rear Admiral Frederick J. Bell, *Room to Swing a Cat* (New York: Longmans, Green & Co., 1938), pp. 237–40. Reprinted by permission.

Library of Congress Cataloging in Publication Data

Still, William N
    American sea power in the old world.

    (Contributions in military history; no. 24
ISSN 0084–9251)
    Bibliography: p.
    Includes index.
    1. United States. Navy—History. 2. United
States—History, Naval. I. Title. II. Series.
VA55.S79   359'.00973   79–6572
ISBN 0–313–22120–0 lib. bdg.

Library of Congress Catalog Card Number: 79–6572
ISBN: 0–313–22120–0
ISSN: 0084–9251

First published in 1980

Greenwood Press
A division of Congressional Information Service, Inc.
88 Post Road West, Westport, Connecticut 06881

Printed in the United States of America

10   9   8   7   6   5   4   3   2   1

CONTENTS

ILLUSTRATIONS

PREFACE

Unquestionably the emergence of an industrial society is the dominant theme in American history from the end of the Civil War until World War I. This industrial growth is without parallel in modern history. When the United States entered World War I, the economy had reached the point where it could support the nation's war effort and that of its allies without much strain. This industrial expansion required a similar growth in American economic interests abroad and was characterized by the search for new markets, the acquisition of colonies, and the growth of foreign investments.

Traditionally, the United States has accepted the responsibility of protecting the interests of its citizens abroad, either by diplomatic means if possible or military deployments if necessary. For both geographical and political considerations, the navy was usually employed where force was desired.

The navy also changed in these years. The wooden sailers and steamers gradually disappeared to be replaced by steel warships. Although the United States Navy was the largest in the world in 1865, it soon declined rapidly and remained relatively small until shortly before the outbreak of World War I.

Throughout the period the navy proved adequate to carry out its responsibilities, including the protection of American interests abroad, as was shown most clearly in European waters, even during the years after the Civil War when the fleet consisted of obsolete wooden vessels. For this reason one might ask would these interests have been harmed or threatened if naval protection had not been provided? Clearly insofar as Western Europe was concerned the answer is no, for during the Franco-Prussian War and the Spanish crisis of the 1860s and 1870s, the belligerents and other national governments provided sufficient protection for American interests. But the European station also included the Mediterranean coast of Africa and the Near East, areas of constant political instability and frequent turmoil, and there naval vessels were needed. Consequently, during the fifty years covered by this study, American warships spent much more time in the eastern Mediterranean than elsewhere on the European station.

The Ottoman Empire was particularly sensitive because of significant American missionary interests and the explosiveness of the Eastern Question. Presidents from Andrew Johnson through Woodrow Wilson ordered the deployment of naval vessels in Turkish waters; Cleveland at one time seriously considered a naval demonstration that might have resulted in conflict between the two countries. Although the presence of American warships reassured resident Americans in the Ottoman Empire, it is doubtful that gunboat diplomacy greatly influenced the Turkish government. In most instances differences between the Ottoman Empire and the United States were settled, not by the presence of American naval vessels, but by the intervention of one or more of the European powers.

The United States was at peace during most of these years, but at the beginning and for a brief period in 1898, the nation was involved in conflict. In neither case did the presence of American warships in European waters play a major role in the wars' beginning, outcome, and aftermath. It is possible that the activities of American warships in the Near East were partly responsible for the United States and Turkey remaining at peace when Congress declared war on Germany in 1917. These vessels, however, were not factors in the decision to declare war.

Throughout the period the United States did not expect to fight a war in European waters, which explains the almost total neglect of military factors in the activities of the American warships. Although target firing and station keeping were routinely practiced, serious maneuvers were rarely conducted, and intelligence was gathered with little or no idea of fighting a European war. Information on ports, for example, would have been invaluable when the United States found itself having to move thousands of men to Europe in World War I.

The navy considered the European the most important of its foreign stations when it was first established. Nevertheless, it declined in importance, as American commitments expanded in other parts of the world, especially in East Asia and Latin America. Consequently, the European Squadron was weakened and finally abolished early in the twentieth century. Although strategic considerations played a major role in President Roosevelt's decision to abandon the station, its low priority was also a factor. The European station was not restored until the United States entered World War I. During the intervening years American naval vessels were deployed in European waters whenever the national government considered it necessary to do so.

Recently, the presence of American warships in European and Near Eastern waters has become increasingly important. The developing hostility between the United States and the Soviet Union in the post-World War II years added a new dimension to the responsibilities of American naval forces in

European waters. For the first time in peacetime they had a purely military mission. The instability that characterized the Near East during the nineteenth century and the early decades of the twentieth century has continued to the present. At the same time American interests in the area, both political and economic, have become increasingly significant. These responsibilities would have been considerably more difficult to carry out if it had not been for the normalizing effect of warships present in European and Near Eastern waters for over a hundred years.

This book is primarily an operational study, narrating the history of the deployment of American naval forces in a distant part of the world. It is not, however, a discussion of all naval activities that occurred in that area. For example, no effort has been made to include the work of the naval attachés, naval observers, inspection missions, and intelligence-gathering assignments, except when they relate to the operation of the naval units. Although it is not a diplomatic history, the navy's involvement in European waters between 1865 and 1917 was essentially for diplomatic reasons. Only at the beginning of this deployment, in 1898, and again in 1917 was the United States involved in war. American warships were present in European waters for decades before 1865, but their cruising responsibilities were generally confined to the Mediterranean. The European station was not officially established until the last year of the Civil War.

ACKNOWLEDGMENTS

There are three principal reasons this study was undertaken: (1) a suggestion by Dr. Robert Johnson of the University of Alabama, who wrote *Thence Round Cape Horn*, a study of a similar type about the Pacific station; (2) encouragement from Rear Admiral Ernest M. Eller, USN (Ret.), former Director of Naval History; and (3) the curiosity of the author, who spent nearly two years with the Sixth Fleet in the Mediterranean.

I am indebted to many individuals and institutions for aid in the preparation of this manuscript. I owe a tremendous debt to the staffs of depositories and archives in the United States and abroad. I would like to acknowledge the unusually generous help provided me by the Library and the Division of Naval History of the Department of the Navy and by the library of Christchurch College, Oxford University, England.

I wish to thank my colleagues, especially Charles Cullop, Herbert Paschal, Bodo Nischan, William Cobb, Herbert Rothfeder, and a former colleague, Gene Goll, for reading portions of the manuscript and making valuable suggestions or helping me with the translations of various records in German and French. Miss Francis Morris of the East Carolina University staff was invaluable in locating and obtaining essential materials on interlibrary loan, and Kelvin Hagelin assisted in the manuscript's final preparation. I wish particularly to acknowledge the assistance rendered by Mrs. Pat Augspurger, who worked long hours typing the final manuscript. Support for much of the research was provided by the East Carolina University Research Council. My wife, Mildred, as usual, aided me in innumerable ways to complete the work. Her encouragement and understanding made this volume possible.

THE NAVY AS AN INSTRUMENT OF POLICY: THE EUROPEAN STATION

1

A warship is a physical symbol of a nation's power in peace as well as in war. The deployment of warships on distant stations* in peacetime is an accepted axiom of naval strategy. A naval presence in foreign waters provides a number of advantages. It is available to respond quickly in case of a local threat to its country's interests. It can prevent war or limit it by acting as a passive force, demonstrating to other nations its ability to control the seas. It also acts as an instrument of diplomacy. Perhaps its chief value is that the naval presence becomes "normal," an accepted or traditional peacetime function. This point is illustrated by the reaction to the presence of Soviet and American warships in the Mediterranean. In recent years Soviet deployment of a naval force in the Mediterranean has provoked considerable attention and, from the United States and its European allies, concern. In contrast, the United States Sixth (task) Fleet, also stationed in the Mediterranean, attracts little attention. A major reason for the difference is that Soviet deployment of warships in foreign waters is a relatively recent strategy, whereas the United States has maintained naval forces on distant stations almost continuously since the early years of the nineteenth century.

The Mediterranean Squadron was the first of several squadrons established in various parts of the world, as the United States Navy adopted a peacetime policy of dispersing its warships on distant cruising stations. The station was founded in 1801 because of depredation on American commerce by the Barbary corsairs. Even after the Barbary wars ended in 1805, the flag continued to be shown in the Mediterranean. Two years later, however, the station was discontinued and the vessels called home because of the developing crisis with Great Britain. No American warships patrolled the Mediterranean until the war with Great Britain ended. In 1815 the station was reestablished because the Barbary states had taken advantage of the war to renew their attacks on

*"Distant stations" refers to forces operating in areas remote from home waters.

United States shipping. In May of 1815, Commodore Stephen Decatur led a squadron to the Mediterranean. The appearance of a naval force again persuaded the North African states to negotiate with the United States. Nevertheless, the inconstancy of relations with these states followed by the need to protect American interests in other parts of the Mediterranean world resulted in the station's becoming a permanent fixture in American naval policy. Until the outbreak of the Civil War in 1861, a naval squadron cruised in the Mediterranean, using as its winter headquarters and base Port Mahon, Minorca, leased from Spain.[1]

The Pacific, West India, Brazil, East India, Home, and African squadrons were also formed in the years before the Civil War. Although some squadrons would be absorbed and others would change their names, this operational pattern would continue up to the present.[2] The number and type of ships serving on the distant stations varied from year to year. The current importance of the station and the availability of ships and personnel were the major factors in determining a squadron's composition.

The fundamental mission of these squadrons has remained the same: to carry out the policies of the United States government. Generally, these policies have evolved around supporting American diplomatic, commercial, and military interests abroad. Support was at times simply showing the flag; at other times it involved a demonstration, intervention, "police action," or what became known as "gunboat" or "battleship" diplomacy. A recent authority defines gunboat diplomacy as the "use or threat of limited naval force, otherwise than as an act of war, in order to secure advantage, or to avert loss, either in the furtherance of an international dispute or else against foreign nationals within the territory or the jurisdiction of their own state."[3]

Gunboat diplomacy has become an accepted international practice, particularly as carried out by the great powers. Lord Palmerston as British prime minister once stated, "Diplomats and protocols are very good things but there are no better peace-keepers than well-appointed three-deckers."

Throughout the nineteenth century the United States publicly followed a policy of noninvolvement in the political affairs of other nations. In reality, however, this doctrine was never absolute. Leaders from Thomas Jefferson on recognized the right right to intervene in foreign countries in order to protect American lives and property. This policy has been based on the assumption that military intervention does not necessarily involve political penetration or interference.[4]

Frequently such actions were considered completely divorced from international relations. American authorities could see little contradiction in noninterference in political affairs of other nations and the protection extended to American economic and humanitarian interests. Yet these purveyors of Western materialism and values would ultimately contribute to sweeping social and political upheavals in the Near as well as the Far East. As Professor Braisted noted in his study of the U.S. Navy in the Pacific, "the lines between legitimate and illegitimate interference by the Navy in the domestic affairs of a friendly state was indeed difficult to determine."[5]

The crisis with the Ottoman Empire in the 1890s resulting in American naval demonstrations was completely separated from the broader international question of the future of the empire, not only by the American public but by the government as well. In this instance and in many others Americans, in the words of Professor Field, "conducted their police action less as nationalists than as self appointed agents of the international commercial society."[6]

Recent historical writing has emphasized not only the strong ties between American commercial expansion and naval policy but also the convincing argument that the navy's primary purpose in peacetime was the protection of American commerce,[7] particularly after the Civil War.

Secretary of the Navy Gideon Welles in his annual report for 1865 asserted that the navy should return to its role of "visiting every commercial port where American capital is employed. . . . The commerce and navy of a people have a common identity, are inseparable companions. Wherever our merchant ships may be employed, there should be within convenient proximity a naval force to protect them." Virtually every secretary of the navy has stressed the navy's responsibility for commerce protection, although not all have gone so far as Welles or as Paul Morton's declaration that the navy's basic mission was that of "the watchdog of American commerce everywhere on the high seas."[8]

Frequently in the 1870s and 1880s congressional debates over naval appropriations focused on this relationship. The continuing decline of the merchant marine after the war was a major factor in congressional parsimony towards the navy. Representative Samuel Cox in 1870 urged that the number of naval officers be halved: "we have no use for them so long as we have no commerce." Representative Cadwaller Colden Washburn of Wisconsin echoed these sentiments: "The Navy Department asked if they could not have an increase of thirty-five hundred men. . . . The Committee [on appropriations] after due consideration determined that there was no necessity for this additional force at this time. We have little or no commerce anywhere."[9]

Naval officers have also overwhelmingly recognized the transcendent importance of protecting and stimulating American commercial expansion. In 1878 Commodore Robert W. Shufeldt wrote a widely distributed essay entitled "The Relation of the Navy to the Commerce of the United States." Originally written as a letter to Congressman Leopold Morse of the House Naval Affairs Committee, he emphasized the interdependence of the navy and merchant marine and the importance of commerce to a nation's greatness.[10] His emphasis on trade would be repeated and greatly expanded upon by Captain Alfred Mahan in his *Influence of Seapower upon History* and other writings. Admiral Robert E. Coontz wrote in the 1920s: "The Navy is an investment to the nation in a way other than that of protecting trade. The Navy is a developer of trade."

Secretary Welles pointed out to Congress the advantages that American commerce could derive from naval officers who would be in a position to acquire useful information, "thereby benefiting commerce." It became standard practice for naval officers to include in their reports information concerning commercial activities and opportunities in ports visited. As both Karsten and Hagan clearly demonstrate, senior and junior officers not only were cognizant of the interdependence of commerce and naval power but also strongly endorsed it.[11]

There was one exception to the commerce-navy thesis in the post-Civil War years, and that lay in the European station. The expansion and protection of the American economy was not the primary responsibility of the European Squadron, although it had been important in the prewar years. It is true that trade with European countries grew in volume and importance during these years, but there was little danger to American shipping in European ports, other than that from economic weapons such as tariffs. Also, trade was negligible in Asia Minor and North Africa, the areas of potential danger within the European Squadron's cruising station.

The European Squadron was the successor to the Mediterranean Squadron. Established during the Civil War because of the Confederate threat to American commerce, it would generally continue to exist until early in the twentieth century. The United States naval force in European waters was weakened during the 1870s and 1880s by obsolete ships and later by naval policy that relegated the station to a low priority. From 1865 to 1904 the European Squadron was normally commanded by a rear admiral. The first of these was Louis Goldsborough, who assumed the command in the last months of the Civil War. The station was abandoned twice, briefly from 1889 to 1893 because of the limited number of available vessels and from 1905 until April 1917 because of the navy's decision to abandon its distant station policy. During these years, however, naval vessels were frequently deployed on special or detached duty in European waters.

The European station frequently became the target of congressmen who opposed naval expansion. Fernando Wood cried, "The Mediterranean Ocean! A Fleet there! How absurd! Sir, the American flag is driven from the Mediterranean." In 1870 Samuel S. "Sunset" Cox criticized the navy for the European Squadron's headquarters at Villefranche: "There is not an American merchant vessel east of Marseilles. . . . Our officers hobnob with broken down dukes and saunter into the operas. . . . Our people can rest assured that their European Squadron is naught else but a pic-nic for which they must pay the bills." What little commerce we have in the Mediterranean "is safe . . . as in Chesapeake Bay," Senator Charles R. Buckalew assured his colleagues. "I [do not] . . . think that it is necessary to keep up a large number of vessels for the purpose of national display."[12]

James E. Harvey, U.S. minister to Portugal, in 1869 recommended the elimination of the European squadron:

It [the squadron] might be still further reduced without the least incon-
venience because the principal duty now performed is of a ceremonious
and conventional character. . . . Commerce is protected mainly by
treaties, by the accepted conditions of public law applicable to it and by
the moral and material power of the flag. . . . A few men of war here or
there in no manner add to that protection however pleasant it may be to
see them in foreign ports. The Atlantic cable has sensibly affected the
sphere of activity and usefulness of the naval service abroad, for in case
of exigency, ships might be summoned from the United States and reach
a given point of duty as soon and perhaps even sooner than they could be
called from the north to the south of Europe.[13]

Few American diplomats shared Harvey's perceptive views, and one wonders
if even he would have so candidly expressed them if he had not been retiring at
the time he wrote these lines. In his *Innocents Abroad* Mark Twain suggests a
more typical attitude: "The arrival of an American man of war is a god-send to
them." The frequent appeals for a warship's visit were not altogether for
reasons of state. These visits in many cases represented the only contact bored
American diplomats in isolated posts had with the outside world.

Some naval officers also questioned the need for a squadron in European
waters. Commodore Shufeldt observed that "there is not a single reason, national or commercial, for the presence of an American squadron on the European Station." George Dewey wrote in his autobiography that "as we had no
commerce or interests to protect in Europe, and were unable to protect them if
we had, the presence of a squadron in European waters was perfunctory."[14]
The reduction of the squadron and its temporary withdrawal in the late 1880s
was at least partly a result of the belief that is was not needed. This belief was
generally correct, for only in the post-Civil War years and in the period immediately after the outbreak of World War I were U.S. warships called upon to
protect American interests in European and Near Eastern waters.

Much of the criticism was based on the erroneous assumption that American warships in European waters spent most of their time in cruising from port
to port or taking in elaborate fleet reviews, and their officers and crews in shore
visits and all the other social, military, and diplomatic trivia of "showing the
flag"—all standard fare, of course, at the taxpayers' expense. On the whole,
this was true in northern European waters and those parts of the Mediterranean firmly controlled by other, greater military and naval powers. In these
waters American naval presence played a subsidiary role.

Yet the European station was important. It included not only Europe proper
but the Near East and North Africa as well, and it was in these areas that naval
vessels were needed. During the fifty years covered by this volume, U.S. warships would spend more time by far in the eastern Mediterranean than in any
other part of the European station. Throughout these years the Near East

passed through one crisis after the other as the collapse of the Ottoman Empire, the "sick man of Europe," resulted in internal turmoil and external pressure from the "Great Powers." Political instability was equally present in the North African states. The potential danger to American interests persuaded administrations from U.S. Grant's through Woodrow Wilson's to deploy warships in these areas.

Although American economic interests, as mentioned earlier, were generally weak in the Ottoman Empire and the North African states, missionary interests were strong and widespread. This was particularly true in Turkey, where in 1870 the American Board of Commissioners for Foreign Missions supported some twenty stations, over a hundred missionaries, sixty congregations, some two thousand evangelical church members, and about two hundred schools with more than five thousand students. The Congregational Church spent more than four-and-a-half million dollars developing these missions. By the outbreak of World War I, there were more than a thousand missionaries, educators, editors, and doctors in the Near East, and in missionary philanthropy American Protestants were rivaled only by the French Catholics.[15]

The American missionary movement grew rapidly in the post-Civil War years and by the 1890s had assumed the proportions of a crusade. Whenever missionary interests abroad were threatened, religious and other organizations supporting these activities exerted pressure directly or through newspapers to persuade the Washington government to take action. The various administrations were certainly sensitive to this pressure, although it is impossible to say to what degree it influenced decisions.[16]

Probably this pressure was most effective in the "field." In the Ottoman Empire local American diplomats spent more time on problems related to missionary activities than on everything else and were vulnerable to pressure about them. The intransigence of Turkish officials made it virtually impossible to "solve" many of these problems; yet, time and time again, American diplomatic representatives were criticized for their inability to do so. Undoubtedly, most of them would have agreed with George Boker's sentiment that missionaries were "one of the major occupational hazards for diplomatic representatives in the Ottoman Empire."[17] It is not surprising that when missionary interests demanded naval protection they usually got it.

Missionaries and businessmen were not the only Americans who demanded protection. Professor Karsten suggests that naval diplomacy in European waters involved a greater degree of protection of individuals than was found anywhere else in the world,[18] and it certainly did in the latter part of the nineteenth and early twentieth centuries. In addition to the missionary and businessman, the tourist, the educator, and the American living abroad expected protection. During the Franco-Prussian War a warship was stationed at Nice as a "place of refuge" for the American colony along the French Riviera.

Americans living in Egypt were evacuated during the crisis of 1882, which led to the British bombardment of Alexandria. On 27 July 1868, Congress passed an act that extended to all American citizens, native-born and naturalized, the right of protection, a law that would seriously complicate relations between the United States and various nations. Turkey's definition of citizenship also frequently created diplomatic discord over the Jews in Palestine and the Armenians, and American efforts to extend protection to these nationals on more than one occasion required the presence of warships. U.S. diplomatic representatives in Asia Minor and North Africa overwhelmingly favored frequent visits by vessels of war, acknowledging that these calls were very effective in negotiating various issues with the local governments. Even the old wooden vessels were considered adequate for this purpose.

Throughout this period American naval forces in European waters were numerically inferior to those of the European powers, as was frequently the case in Near Eastern and North African waters as well. In a number of instances, these forces protected American interests along with those of their own country. However, the concerns of these governments were not in every case the same as those of the United States, particularly in the Ottoman Empire, where internal disturbance frequently resulted in political repercussions involving the great powers. U.S. policy usually was to maintain non-involvement in the political questions while protecting American citizens and their individual and group interests, especially as these powers were dilatory at times in providing protection. At Alexandria in 1882 an American force landed before other nations, including the British, to protect foreigners after the bombardment. However, this was the only case where a force was actually landed. In several instances threats of landing forces were issued and on a few occasions a small number of men were sent ashore for special duty (signals and the like); but commanding officers were aware of the possible ramifications of such an action. Thus, as Commodore Charles S. Boggs reported to the Secretary of the Navy in 1871, "The only real service (aside from the moral effect its presence might provide) a vessel of war could render to American citizens, in case of riot, or civil war, would be to serve as a place of refuge for them or to assist to remove an American vessel out of danger."[19]

The overseas squadrons had other responsibilities in addition to protecting American interests in various parts of the world. Gathering information was a major one. Periodic intelligence reports were considered routine for commanding officers. During the Franco-Prussian War the *Juanita's* captain was ordered to "gather . . . information concerning the strength, condition, and performance" of the French naval force blockading the German coast. Rear Admiral C. H. Poor, while commanding the North Atlantic Squadron, circulated among his officers a departmental general order instructing them to report "the naval force of all foreign powers on your station" in terms of tonnage, number of guns, and so on.[20]

   This intelligence responsibility held a high priority on the European station because of the rapid technological advances by British and continental navies, especially in countries where we did not have naval attaches. In 1888 Congress passed a law establishing military missions in foreign countries; and the first five were established the following year in Berlin, Vienna, Paris, London, and St. Petersburg.[21] Officers inspected ships, yards and stations, and weapons whenever they could. In 1869 the commanding officer of the European Squadron forwarded an enthusiastic report on experiments with Whitehead torpedoes conducted at Fiume, Austria.[22] In 1885, the squadron commander was reprimanded for the "unsatisfactory character of the intelligence reports which have been received from the European Station." In the letter, the naval secretary reminded him that "the office of Naval Intelligence was established in order that the Navy Department might be supplied with the most accurate information as to the progress of naval science and condition and resources of foreign navies."[23] When the European Squadron visited Trieste, Austria, in 1904, each ship was assigned certain intelligence responsibilities. For example, the *Olympia* was to concentrate on "coaling, docking, and repairing facilities"; the *Baltimore*, "the Austrian Navy in general—particularly the men-of-war now building here"; the *Cleveland*, the army and defenses of Trieste; and all ships, the social and political conditions of the country. The squadron intelligence officer requested that each officer devote at least one afternoon and one evening to intelligence work.[24]

   In general, however, intelligence gathering was clumsy. Much of the information came from published sources such as official reports and newspapers. There is no evidence that American naval vessels or officers shadowed or observed foreign warships while they were involved in maneuvers.

   Other tasks were performed by the warships operating in European waters. Training cruises were considered routine, particularly in the twentieth century. In the mid-1870s, the *Gettysburg* spent considerable time preparing sailing directions for the Mediterranean. Periodically, American warships carried art works and objects of historical and scientific value back to the United States. The *Gettysburg* carried the Obelisk from Egypt in 1878, the *Franklin* carried several pieces of art to Philadelphia, the *Guerriere* carried the anchor of the frigate *Philadelphia*, burned in the Barbary wars, from Tripoli in 1875. In 1897 the Navy Department ordered a vessel to Kronstadt, Russia, to pick up "geological specimens" for transportation to New York City. Warships carried the remains of John Ericcson back to Sweden in 1890 and John Paul Jones from France to the United States in 1905. Occasionally, the vessels were used to transport diplomats to and from their posts, but this was frowned upon by the Navy Department.[25]

   Americans have traditionally responded to other people's sufferings by offers of help in the way of money, food, and clothing. United States warships in European waters would frequently be called upon to carry out such relief.

The *Worcester* carried food to France for the starving Parisians after the siege of Paris was lifted during the Franco-Prussian War. The Irish famine in 1880 prompted the sending of the old *Constellation* with food; a similar effort was made during the Russian famine of 1891-92, but no suitable vessel was available. During the Messina earthquake of 1908 American vessels carried food, medicine, and building material. From 1914 until the United States entered the war in 1917, U.S. warships carried relief funds, food, clothing, and medical supplies to various parts of the Near East and were involved in evacuating refugees from the Ottoman Empire.[26]

During the latter part of the nineteenth century naval reviews and expositions became standard fare for European powers anxious to show off their new modern warships. American men-of-war usually joined in these festivities. In 1888, the European Squadron went to Barcelona, Spain, for an "exposition"; in 1892 ships from Spain, Italy, and the United States assembled at Cadiz to celebrate the four-hundredth anniversary of the discovery of America. In 1897, the squadron joined the powerful fleets from other nations at Spithead, England, for Queen Victoria's Jubilee celebration; and during the first decade of the twentieth century, American vessels participated in reviews at Kiel, Marseilles, Spithead, and elsewhere on various occasions.[27]

By the beginning of the twentieth century, European statesmen were far more interested in the activities of American warships in European waters than they had been forty years earlier. The presence of a small naval force had excited no unusual interest or suspicion on the part of the European nations, particularly in the 1870s and 1880s, when the wooden vessels of the U.S. Navy were looked upon with tolerance and a certain amount of amusement by Europeans.[28] There was also little likelihood of conflict. However, rumors that the United States was seeking a naval base or coaling station generated concern. Although no serious effort was ever made to acquire a base in European or African waters, periodically the idea of obtaining such a facility was investigated or mentioned.[29] The transition from sail to steam did suggest the necessity of a coaling station, but the policy of the navy in the post-Civil War years to continue stressing sails over steam cancelled this. As far as the European station was concerned, coal could be purchased locally; and since the possibility of war with a European power was discounted until late in the century, these facilities continued to be available. Early in the twentieth century the first oil burners were deployed in European waters, but again the policy was to requisition oil locally. In 1913 Standard Oil Company had stations at Bizerta, Tunis, and Port Said, Egypt, that provided fuel for American warships.[30]

Outside of the Ottman Empire the occasional visits by American warships were generally ignored by national governments. Local authorities, however, were usually pleased with visits by American warships because of their impact on the economy. When the *Lancaster* arrived at Cattaro on the Dalmatian coast in 1882, local officials got around the regulation that foreign warships were to obtain permission from Vienna to enter the port (which apparently the *Lancaster* had failed to do) by treating the American vessel-of-war as a ship in distress.[31]

The turn of the century witnessed a change in the attitude of European powers. No longer did they look with disinterest upon American ships in close proximity. American naval intervention in the Turkish imbroglio and the Armenian massacres followed by the Spanish-American War and the acquisition of colonies convinced European statesmen that the United States had apparently abandoned its policy of noninvolvement in international affairs outside the Western Hemisphere. What most concerned the European powers was the direction that this involvement would go. The U.S. was the X-factor, the unknown. They wanted American favors but at the same time were uneasy about the new world power's increasing interest in international affairs. Inevitably this was reflected in their attitude towards the presence of American warships.

The acquisition of colonies by the United States in the Caribbean and Asia had little direct effect so far as the navy's responsibilities in Europe were concerned. Yet, once again, the possibility that the United States might acquire a naval base in the Mediterranean or off the west coast of Africa stirred up alarm. This concern disappeared with the realization that the American government had little interest in bases outside the Caribbean and the Pacific.[32]

Throughout the period before World War I, American ships operating in European waters generally depended on local facilities for logistical support—not just fuel, but food, general stores, and ship maintenance and repairs as well. Supply ships and later colliers were periodically sent out from the United States, but at best they could carry only a limited amount. A supply depot was maintained at Villefranche for several years after the Civil War but was abandoned in the early 1880s as impracticable. Baring Brothers and Company of London were the navy's bankers in Europe. When the squadron and or ship commanders needed money, they were authorized to draw sight drafts on the company. However, squadron commanders rarely had the authority to draw out funds for entertainment. The department was quite parsimonious for this purpose, causing constant complaints. Rear Admiral Louis M. Goldsborough, who had the reputation of being a "tightwad," in 1865 bitterly assailed the department for expecting him "to stand the brunt of everything and this as a Rear Admiral upon the European Station with[,] in reality, the ridiculous compensation of $5,000 per annum—a compensation just equal to that of the head fireman of New York."[33]

London was also the city for the U.S. Dispatch Agency, which acted as a clearing house for all official correspondence passing between the State and Navy departments and the various diplomatic posts in Europe. It also handled all communications with American warships operating in European waters. The first transatlantic cable was completed in the 1850s. The proliferation of telegraph lines and cables by the end of the Civil War so accelerated communications that seldom were the squadron commanders or captains out of touch with each other or Washington. However, because of the expense of sending cablegrams, the bulk of communications continued to go by mail and the dispatch agency continued to play a major role in this system until well after World War I. In recommending the continuation of the agency, Rear Admiral John L. Worden wrote:

> From the very nature of [this] . . . command comprising a very large area of waters to be patrolled, a great number of ports to be visited, and the limited number of the squadron, it is necessary that all the vessels including the flagship, should be constantly on the move. By having an Agent easily reached by mail, or telegraph from any port, the Commander in Chief is enabled to be in communication with the commanding officers of the squadron much more readily and economically than if he were obliged to send letters or telegrams from one consul to another without any absolute certainty of their reaching their final destination. Again, if on occasion of emergency, it is necessary for the Department to communicate directly with any commanding officer, it is always possible to do so with only a minimum loss of time. Still more important is the fact that it would involve great expense for the Commander in Chief to keep the Department informed by telegraph of all his movements, while the Agent can almost always be informed by mail, and with little loss of time, and from knowing the Admiral's exact location can always forward immediately telegraphic orders from the Department."[34]

The wireless telegraph appeared early in the twentieth century, and although warships were being equipped with these instruments before World War I, their range was limited to a few hundred miles.

One would assume that the shift in communication from ship to telegraph between the Navy Department and the distant stations would have significantly affected the command relationship. "The cable spoiled the old Asiatic Station," Rear Admiral Casper F. Goodrich once declared. "Before it was laid, one really was somebody out there, but afterwards one simply became a damned errand boy at the end of a telegraph wire."[35] Before the Atlantic cable was in use, the slowness in communication meant that squadron and ship commanders had an unusual amount of discretion and responsibility. Frequently, commanding officers had to make important decisions without reference to Washington.[36] In fact, European Squadron commanders seldom recommended policy or decisions to the Navy Department. They simply took it upon themselves to initiate whatever action was considered necessary. Yet, their decisions in some instances would commit the government to a course of action it might not have chosen. Even after the completion of the Atlantic cable, this practice would continue, well into the twentieth century. In 1901 the Secretary of the Navy wrote, "The movement of ships in the [European] . . . Squadron is, to a very great extent, dependent upon the will of the Commander in Chief."[37] Nevertheless, a tendency did develop to refer major decisions to Washington.

Rare was the naval commander who considered himself qualified to report on foreign policy. Lieutenant Commander Stephen B. Luce, while in command of the *Juanita* on the European station, was one, however. The future founder of the Naval War College wrote in 1870, "constantly visiting foreign countries and being thrown among foreign officials of almost every grade, it seems to me that we officers of the Navy are peculiarly qualified to look upon all such questions with a single eye to the interests of our government; hence it becomes our duty to express an opinion upon such subjects as concern our foreign relations. . . ."[38]

In decisions affecting the distant squadrons, the State Department oftentimes played as important a role as the Navy Department. Although before World War I there were no formal procedures or established institutions to promote or produce cooperation between the military and diplomatic services, cooperation was a part of national policy. As Secretary of State William Seward observed in 1867, "There is no subordination of the Minister to the Commander of the Squadron; and no subordination of the Commander of the Squadron to a Minister."[39] The interpretation and effectiveness of the principle of cooperation varied widely. It has always been a paramount policy of the navy that the commanding officer of a vessel has sole and exclusive charge of his ship and that he cannot share or delegate any portion of this total responsibility. As Rear Admiral William L. Rodgers wrote, "The Navy Department has never placed its ships and officers under the direct orders and control of the Department of State." Admiral Colby Chester agreed: "American [naval] officers may be advised by the regular diplomatic agents abroad, but such agents cannot direct them what course to take. . . . They are responsible for their acts directly to the Commander-in-Chief, the President."[40]

The State Department on the whole accepted this principle. In general, naval ships responded to requests for assistance through the State Department and its officials. If a situation were considered sufficiently grave, American diplomatic representatives had authority to appeal directly to squadron and ship commanders. However, the minister or consul could only request. The naval officer had the responsibility of making the decision. In 1881, Secretary of State James G. Blaine requested "the propriety of . . . the Admiral of the European Squadron to occasionally notify our diplomatic and consular officers in the countries bordering the Mediterranean of the movements of the fleet in that sea and to extend to such representatives every proper assistance. It is not to be understood by this that the fleet movements are in any case to be subject to a Minister's direction, or to conform with his instructions."[41] Yet in several instances American diplomats were given some authority over the movements of warships. Henry Morgenthau, American ambassador to Turkey in 1914–15, directed the relief operations of American warships in Turkish waters, including their movements from port to port, apparently with the approval of Secretary of the Navy Josephus Daniels. Understandably, disagreements between naval and diplomatic officials occurred over this practice.

Such occasions, however, were the exception rather than the rule; cooperation was generally quite good. Diplomatic officials and naval officers abroad had to depend on each other for a variety of services. James Harvey, U.S. minister to Portugal in the immediate post-Civil War years, complained that the aid given by diplomatic officials to ships of war was "imperfectly appreciated." Harvey went on to list the types of assistance given: "He is the interpreter between the ships, the authorities, and the multitude of persons having business or other relations with them; he receives and distributes all their correspondence; he often makes large advances of money for their convenience, translates all documents, is charged with recovery of deserters, and is the absolutely needful person to consult in all matters of supplies and contracts."[42] One could add that he usually acted as host for visiting officers and, of course, had to smooth over difficulties that frequently arose between the naval force and local authorities.

The Navy Department has always emphasized the importance of respecting local customs, traditions, holidays, and observances. The playing of the host nation's national anthem by the ship's band became common in the post-Civil War navy. Musicians were frequently enlisted from European countries by ships operating in those waters. In some instances entire bands came from a particular country (Italians were preferred). There were occasional problems. Shortly after the end of World War I, the *Pittsburgh's* bandmaster was unable to locate the national anthem for Palestine (which did not have one, as Palestine was not an independent nation) as the vessel approached Haifa, so the band played "Lena, She's the Queen of Palestina."[43]

The firing of salutes was rigidly enforced and expected. Flag officers and dignitaries listened for the appropriate number of guns; if they were not forthcoming, formal protests were made. On more than one occasion the absence of proper respect so offended national sensibilities that it took the governments involved to work out the difficulties.[44] On at least two occasions salutes had rather startling results. In 1834 the frigate *United States*, in exchanging a salute with the French ship of the line *Suffren*, sent one shot through the side of the French vessel, killing one seaman and seriously wounding five others. The gunner had forgotten to remove a shot from one of the guns. Six years later the *Cyane* upon entering Naples harbor passed an English squadron and fired a salute, as it was Queen Victoria's birthday. Unfortunately, the salute frightened a pair of horses pulling a carriage along the sea road, and they jumped over a cliff. The occupants, however, escaped without injury.[45] Rear Admiral Casper Goodrich recounts the story of a Russian general at Kronstadt who, after receiving a fifteen-gun salute from the *Lancaster*, shouted, "The enemy is upon you—commence firing!" Fortunately the matter was straightened out before the Czar's gunners responded.[46]

Honors between warships are not always rendered by gun salutes, which are reserved for special occasions; they are also exchanged by the ancient custom of manning the rail. Captain Allan Bosworth includes in his book *My Love Affair with the Navy* a story about the *Arizona* at Constantinople in 1919. As she passed a British warship, the rails were manned. Later the British promptly manned the rails again when the American ship drifted by, dragging her anchor. The *Arizona* steamed back to her anchorage, and as she passed the British ship the sailors were once more piped to the side.[47]

Quarantine was a common problem for vessels of all nations throughout the world. Fear of cholera was so strong that ships were frequently isolated for periods of time running up to weeks before being cleared by a health official. In 1866 the *Shamrock* entered Malaga, Spain, where she was promptly placed in strict quarantine and ordered to leave immediately. Her commanding officer was told that the vessel, which had recently arrived from New York, would not be allowed to stay at the Spanish port because of rumors of an outbreak of cholera in the United States. Thanks to the Atlantic cable the American consul was able to gain assurance that there was no epidemic of cholera in the United States, and the vessel's quarantine was lifted.[48] The practice was universal, however, and frequently disrupted cruising schedules.

"The Mediterranean Station is the only one on which officers do not rejoice on receiving orders from home." So wrote a young officer to his future bride in 1859.[49] Although this was obviously an exaggeration, it nevertheless expresses the attitude of thousands of naval officers from the time the first American warships were deployed on foreign stations until the present. As Rear Admiral Stephen B. Luce wrote, "a European cruise was considered the most desirable sea duty in the Navy."[50]

For many officers professional interest was the attraction. John Dahlgren considered it to be the best training grounds for a naval officer: "the constant activity and habitual experience in handling a ship in close proximity to the shore, the entering and leaving all kinds of harbors, the contact with the finest ships of England and France, gives at once a standard for comparison, and one to strive to excel." Commodore Matthew C. Perry considered command of the Mediterranean Squadron as the "most desirable" in the Navy.[51]

For the majority, however, the allurement was "good liberty." For social events and pleasant ports, European cities were considered unsurpassed by most officers and enlisted men. "To be ordered to a ship on the European Station was simply to be included as a member of a perpetual yachting party," wrote one officer in a chapter of his published memoir entitled "How we apples do float! Sure is an Honor taking tea with the nobility of Brittany—the uniform does wonders over here."[52]

A common but unpleasant feature of a naval unit's visit to a port were the altercations involving sailors. Ordinarily nothing more than fist fights or drunken brawls, the affairs occasionally were more serious. In 1910, the London *Times* wrote that the riotous behavior of American bluejackets from the Atlantic fleet visiting French ports amused more of Europe, but outraged France. In Cherbourg and Brest actual rioting occurred between the local inhabitants and the sailors.[53]

For some reason American sailors in European waters had more trouble in Italian ports than elsewhere. In 1894 bluejackets from the flagship *Chicago* complained of difficulties in Venice. In 1913 Neapolitan newspapers deplored the fights and incidents caused by men from American warships visiting Naples. In 1906 the captain of the *Maryland* wrote the Navy Department, condemning Palermo as a liberty port. "As to the conditions on shore in regard to giving liberty to the crew of a large ship," he reported, "I am of the opinion that they are worse than in any other city of large size in all the Mediterranean. . . . Immediately on landing, the men were surrounded by gangs of harpies, and thieves, who followed them about wherever they went. . . . There were brawls in which our men were the aggressors, but there were several attempts by the Sicilian thugs to cut and slash the men when they would not yield their money. The local police were not at hand as a rule."[54]

Officers were not immune. In 1902 four drunken officers from the *Chicago* on liberty in Venice became involved in a brawl with local inhabitants and damaged a restaurant. Although the officers were arrested, tried, convicted, and sentenced to prison terms by an Italian court, George L. von Myer, U.S. Ambassador to Italy, obtained a special pardon from the king. The European as well as the American press generally condemned the disorderly conduct of the *Chicago's* officers; the *New York Times* referred to it as one of the "fruits of Imperialism." Although a court of inquiry recommended that the men be court-martialed, the squadron commander disapproved, and the incident was dropped.[55]

There is little doubt that the overwhelming majority of American sailors visiting European ports behaved satisfactorily. Nevertheless, unfortunate incidents can seriously damage the image of the United States, and have. A recent letter by an American in Venice printed in the Naval Institute *Proceedings* illustrates this:

> While many of the crew members are well behaved, a large number appear not to be; there is a lack of the right discipline which seems to be apparent in other navies which visit Venice. . . . A goodwill visit probably should not have too many casualties resulting from it. It is said that a visit last year cost two dead and one seriously injured (by stabbing) at least. The local newspaper suggested that in each case the cause could be traced to a surfeit of drink.[56]

Drinking was (and is) always a problem. George Dewey mentioned it when he was executive officer on the *Kearsarge* in 1865. Admiral Coontz blamed it on the fact that a large percentage of the enlisted men were foreigners.[57] More than likely it was simply the availability of an inexhaustible supply of cheap alcoholic beverages.

Robbery and petty thievery were quite common, although not as prevalent as the drinking problem. A British officer recalled that, while dining with a Turkish official, he observed an unusual number of attendants standing behind the chairs. When he inquired about this, the host replied that "some American sailors had been dining not long before, and a few of the gold spoons were subsequently missing."[58]

It is meaningless to generalize about the attitudes of the people in the countries comprising the European station toward the presence of American warships. These attitudes varied widely, as did those of their governments. To generalize about the attitude of American sailors in European waters toward people of different nations and races is equally difficult. Karsten's observation that the officers of the period had the same prejudices as most American travelers is probably correct. There was great admiration for the English in particular and for the European people in general.[59] At the same time, the ethnocentric sailors showed little respect for the inhabitants of the North African and Near Eastern countries. At best these people were considered "semicivilized." Mahan's messmates had little political sophistication and less social sensitivity. There was little or no awareness of the nationalistic movements in the Ottoman Empire and North Africa. They seldom saw any contradiction between their oft-repeated injunction against meddling in political affairs and the protection (at times leading to armed intervention) extended to American merchants and missionaries.[60]

Naval officers understood and approved of the protection extended to some businessmen abroad, but frequently they felt differently where missionaries were concerned. They were not aware of the relationship between missionary activities and the nationalistic movements in the Ottoman Empire, but they were aware that missionary influence was the reason that they were so frequently on duty in Turkish waters. They believed that in most cases naval vessels were called upon to protect not the missionaries but the people whom the missionaries were working with—the Christian minorities, especially Armenians.[61]

In European ports, officers were usually granted entree into upper-class social events. Balls, dinners, and parties were common occurrences, particularly in England and along the French Riviera. American ships reciprocated by holding gala events to which the local elite as well as officers from other visiting warships were invited.

Enlisted men were not so fortunate. As organized recreation was rare, they were generally left to find their own. Boat races were common not only between boats belonging to a particular vessel but also between vessels and with boats of other nations.[62] Ball games and organized tours were quite as prevalent then as today. Nevertheless, enlisted men did not look upon a tour in European waters with the enthusiasm of the officers.

As established before the Civil War, normal ship rotation on foreign stations occurred every two to three years. In 1873 the European squadron commander reported that he had failed in his efforts to persuade the crews of the *Shenandoah* and *Brooklyn* to reenlist. By calling for volunteers from the *Brooklyn* before she returned to the United States, however, he extended the *Shenandoah's* tour for another year. When the *Shenandoah* returned to the United States, she had spent three-and-a-half years on the station, logged more than twenty-six hundred miles, and visited more than fifty ports.[63]

During the last decades of the nineteenth century, filling a ship's complement was difficult, and a majority of the ships were manned by foreigners. Even the popularity of the European Squadron did not commend it to enlisted personnel. In 1872 the sailors in the squadron came from thirty-five nations. Sixty percent of the enlisted men in 1878 were foreign-born. Admiral Goodrich mentioned that on one of the ships, a maintopman placed on a gangway a placard reading, "English spoken here."[64] In the 1890s efforts were made to recruit more native-born Americans. Although the percentage of foreign-born declined, commanding officers up to World War I would have the authority to enlist foreigners if "citizens of the United States" could not be obtained.[65]

GOLDSBOROUGH, FARRAGUT, AND THE ESTABLISHMENT OF THE EUROPEAN SQUADRON

2

On 12 April 1865, Rear Admiral Louis M. Goldsborough broke his flag on the steam frigate *Colorado* at anchor in New York harbor. Goldsborough was under orders to take command of American naval vessels in European waters, with the *Colorado* as his flagship. Rumors had persisted for several months that he was to receive the command, although he was not a favorite of Secretary of the Navy Gideon Welles. When Goldsborough was up for promotion, Welles mentioned in his diary that "[he] had not a single qualification, but size, belley, and lungs." Admittedly rather large (estimates from 300 pounds up), he nevertheless was qualified to command the squadron. He spoke French and Spanish fluently and was the senior officer in the navy, having been commissioned a midshipman in 1812. He also had served creditably, if not brilliantly, during most of the Civil War. Goldsborough commanded the North Atlantic Blockading Squadron when the Confederate ironclad *Virginia* attacked and destroyed units of this squadron in Hampton Roads. In September of 1862 he asked to be relieved because of newspaper criticism and the separation from his command of several vessels to form a river flotilla. From then until his appointment to the European Squadron, he performed administrative duties in Washington.[1]

He was a well-known figure in the navy partly because of his immense size (6'4" in height) and "red, red beard" and also for what one officer called his eccentricity in deportment. To junior officers "his manners [were] somewhat rough, so that he would almost frighten a subordinate out of his wits. . . ." One tale is told that on a Sunday morning while at anchor in Gibralter, the *Colorado's* chaplain began his sermon by bowing his head and saying "The Lord is in his Holy Temple," when Goldsborough violently flung open his cabin door and bellowed, "Hold on chaplain, hold on. I'll have you to understand that the Lord is not in his Holy Temple until I get there."[2] Even his good friends wrote disapprovingly of his intemperate nature: "He seems . . . to have wanted

Rear Admiral Louis M. Goldsborough, commander of the European Squadron, 1865–1867. *Courtesy of the United States Department of Navy.*

patience and amenity with officers; they complain very much of his imperious temper. . . ." Yet to his contemporaries he was an able officer. Rear Admiral Samuel F. DuPont wrote that "there is no one who is going to be made an Admiral who could aid the Government in all those matters connected with the national defense of the country than he is. . . ."[3] DuPont's faith would be put to the test; for the European Squadron would not be, as one newspaper correspondent reported, a "show fleet" but would face serious problems concerning the Civil War. In fact this was a major factor in the decision to reestablish the squadron.

The Navy Department decided to reactivate the European station sometime between the fall of Fort Fisher on 16 January and the end of February 1865.[4] The exact date is unknown. Welles' diary ignores the decision; although he does mention on the day after the surrender of Fort Fisher that in a cabinet session Secretary of State William H. Seward "thought there was little now for the Navy to do. . . ." On 1 February a newspaper correspondent wrote to Major General Benjamin Butler that Goldsborough would command it. At the end of the month the State Department notified its legations in various European countries of preparations to send a squadron under Goldsborough's command.[5]

The reasons that the squadron was established are apparent enough. The Civil War was clearly nearing its conclusion, and Seward was not far from wrong when he expressed the opinion that there was little for the navy to do in home waters after the fall of Fort Fisher. Only three major ports remained in Confederate hands, and one of these, Charleston, would surrender before the month was out. Wilmington, North Carolina, would hold out until the twenty-second of February; but with the capture of Fort Fisher, few vessels would be needed to effectively close that port to blockade runners. Galveston, Texas, was also closed but would not surrender until 2 June. Several Confederate warships (including ironclads) in the James River were defending Richmond and up the Red River in Louisiana.

Welles, however, apparently agreed with the secretary of state that the threat from Confederate naval vessels in European waters was more important. The devastating successes of the *Alabama* and other commerce cruisers obtained in Europe had been a constant headache to Lincoln's government. By 1865 these vessels were either destroyed or, like the *Shenandoah*, no longer in European waters. The one exception was the steam sloop-of-war *Rappahannock*. Originally in the Royal Navy, she was secretly purchased for the Confederate navy, and after barely escaping seizure she was forced into Calais, France, because of defective machinery. Although the French government later stationed a gunboat across her bow and in other ways effectively prevented the vessel from leaving port, American diplomatic and naval authorities still feared that she would be able to slip out.[6]

The Confederate navy had also attempted to acquire ironclad warships in

Europe. These efforts were generally frustrated by Seward and American diplomats in France and England. However, the *Stonewall*, a seagoing iron-clad ram built in France, did successfully elude the Americans as well as French officials and was commissioned in the Confederate navy. After taking on stores and provisions in Quiberon Bay, she got under way for Madeira but ran into a storm that forced her into Ferrol, Spain, for repairs. She was discovered there in late January 1865 by the Union warships *Niagara* and *Sacramento*.

The senior American naval officer in European waters at this time was Commodore Thomas T. Craven of the *Niagara*. Welles considered Craven "a good officer though a little timid and inert by nature."[7] This "timidity" would later led to Craven's court-martial for allowing the *Stonewall* to escape. Even before the commodore reached the Spanish coast, he was appealing to the Navy Department for reinforcements. On 5 February he asked for additional vessels; and nine days later John Bigelow, U.S. consul general and minister in Paris, wrote Seward, "I doubt if Craven feels entirely confident of his ability to meet the *Stonewall* single-handed." Bigelow's suspicion proved correct. On 20 February Craven expressed to the American consul general his fears if the Confederate ram should attempt to escape: "If she is as fast as reputed to be in smooth water, she would be more than a match for three such ships as the *Niagara*. So, sir, you will readily perceive I am placed in a most unenviable predicament, and that our only chance for cutting short her career rests upon the possibility of detaining her here until such time as our government sees fit to send out the necessary re-enforcements."[8] Craven evidently wrote in a similar tone to Welles; for the Secretary recorded in his diary, "He says he is 'in an unenviable and embarrassing position.' There are many of our best naval officers who think he has an enviable position. . . ."

Craven was told that he could expect no immediate help, although American diplomatic officials in Europe were informed of the decision to send a squadron in the near future. On 27 February and again on 13 March Seward advised the chargé d'affaires in Madrid that because "many vessels of our Navy are now engaged repairing damages," the squadron ordered to European waters probably would not arrive "early enough for a contingency in the case of the *Stonewall*." However, Welles did agree to send the *Kearsarge*, then at Boston, to reinforce Craven's small force.[9] Even this was a little late; for on 24 March, the *Stonewall* sortied from Ferrol; and after Craven declined to engage the ram, she coaled in Lisbon and disappeared into the Atlantic.

In proclaiming their neutrality in the American Civil War, both Great Britain and France required belligerent naval vessels to depart from their ports within twenty-four hours after arriving, "except in case of stress of weather or of . . . requiring provisions or things necessary for the subsistence . . . or repair."[10] Horatio Perry, the chargé in Madrid, would later write several dispatches to the State Department implying that the navy could have prevented the *Stonewall's* escape if reinforcements had been sent. Welles defended his actions by pointing out that intelligence from American representatives abroad had been confident that the vessel would never fall into Confederate hands; and even if she did, she was unseaworthy. He also stressed that "no great advantage could have been gained by sending an adequate force abroad . . . as [the *Stonewall's*] movements could not well be controlled under the twenty four hour rule."[11] The *Stonewall's* Confederate career was brief, however. She reached Havana, Cuba, in May; and the news of the Confederacy's collapse resulted in her seizure by Cuban authorities.

When Admiral Goldsborough in the *Colorado* sailed from New York on June 21, the *Stonewall* was no longer a problem; but there still were Confederate warships at large, possibly in European waters. His orders were to "seize and send into port any of the rebel vessels that you may find out of neutral waters, especially the *Rappahannock, Shenandoah,* and *Tallahassee.*" At the insistence of the State Department his orders explicitly instructed him to avoid entering "any port, unless absolutely necessary," where belligerent privileges had been extended to the Confederacy "or where naval honors are by governmental authority withheld from the flag of the United States." He was also forbidden to "exchange any of the customary courtesies with the foreign officials [of the nations extending belligerent privileges to the Confederacy] whom you may meet. . . ." After obtaining from the State Department a list of European nations that still extended belligerent rights to the Confederacy (England, France, Spain, Portugal, and the Netherlands), he protested to the Assistant Secretary of the Navy, Gustavus Fox:

> I find myself in effect confined as to Ports to those which lie in Belgian and Hanover. . . . I can visit it would seem no place to the Southward of Belgium, unless absolutely necessary within the limits of my command, nor even in fact the islands, except the Azores in going over. I urge no complaint whatever at these restrictions. . . . Only I want to be assured that at the time my instructions were considered, the fact of the attitude of Spain, Portugal, and the Netherlands, was present to your mind. I know very well it is more than probable that in a short time all the above powers—England and France included—will take back the concession of belligerent rights to the South.[12]

When Goldsborough finally sailed only the Netherlands had withdrawn belligerent rights to the Confederacy.[13]

Goldsborough would also be handicapped by the "twenty-four-hour rule." Not only did this rule provide some protection for Confederate warships, but also it made Union naval efforts to capture them most difficult. The French were the most pliant in interpreting the "rule." The *Rappahannock,* for example, was allowed to remain in Calais nearly sixteen months. After the decision was made to send a large naval force to European waters, Seward in

March 1865 opened negotiations with France, Great Britain, and other nations to reopen their ports to American vessels-of-war. Two days after Robert E. Lee surrendered, Lincoln issued three proclamations, one of which demanded free access to foreign ports for U.S. warships.[14]

The French and British governments generally followed the same policy in matters concerning the American Civil War. For example, both governments had delayed in withdrawing belligerent rights, including various neutrality rules, from the Confederate States, even after it was apparent that the South was collapsing. On 20 May, however, the French government informed the American minister in Paris that they were no longer enforcing the twenty-four-hour rule on American vessels; nine days later they officially announced that they no longer considered a state of war to exist in the United States. Unfortunately, because of a disagreement with the French foreign office over the right of American warships to search neutral vessels, Goldsborough was not notified of the French action until 18 June.[15]

The British were slow to follow the French lead. On 2 June Lord Russell informed the United States Government that belligerent rights to the Confederacy had been withdrawn, but with the curiously inconsistent proviso that any Southern warship in a British port should "have the benefits of the prohibition heretofore enforced against their being pursued within twenty-four hours by a cruiser of the United States lying at the time within the same port. . . ." Seward was irritated, and he persuaded President Andrew Johnson to continue a policy of refusing to carry out the "customary courtesies" to British naval vessels. The secretary of the navy opposed what he considered a petty rejoinder that would handicap naval operations, but his protests were ignored. Fortunately, no serious problems occurred over this disagreement, although British restrictions on American vessels in their ports were not withdrawn until October 1865.[16]

On 18 July 1865 the *Colorado*, some twelve-and-a-half days out of Fayal in the Azores, and nearly a month out of New York, dropped anchor at Flushings, in the Netherlands. The flagship was joined by the *Frolic*, but the other three vessels in the European Squadron were in British waters. Although the war was over, British procrastination over the "twenty-four-hour rule" made it necessary to keep warships patrolling these waters. Because the *Tallahassee* and *Rappahannock* were in Liverpool, the *Sacramento, Niagara,* and *Kearsarge* maintained station off the southern coast of England. Late in August this force was reduced to one vessel; the *Niagara* was detached from the European station and the *Sacramento* ordered elsewhere, leaving the *Kearsarge* to continue observing Liverpool. In October, when it became obvious that the two Confederate vessels had been interned by the British Government, the *Kearsarge* was withdrawn and joined the flagship at Lisbon.

Goldsborough was making plans for the squadron to enter the Mediterranean. The winter season was approaching, and as in the past the admiral expected to establish headquarters somewhere in that sea for the noncruising months. He had been under orders to keep his vessels out of the Mediterranean until "all possible disturbances resulting from this war are dispersed," but in late September the Navy Department cancelled this order, and he was allowed to search for a suitable rendezvous. The tender *Frolic* was ordered to survey various harbors. Six ports in France, Spain, and Italy were examined, and three of these, Genoa, Leghorn, and Villefranche, were recommended. The *Frolic's* commanding officer reported from Genoa that "here as everywhere in Italy a strong desire is manifested by the officials, and others, to have a portion of the squadron at this port for the winter."[17] The selection of a headquarters for the squadron generated considerable interest in the cities that were being contemplated, not only among the officials and businessmen who would profit from the location of a naval force in their community but also among American diplomats as well. It was a common practice for consuls to take on business interests on the side. Two former naval bases, Port Mahon and Spezia, were not examined. The American consul at Nice protested the latter port's exclusion in a letter to the admiral, mentioning that a petition was being forwarded to the State Department by "citizens" of the city.

Goldsborough selected Villefranche on the southern coast of France, the region today known as the Riviera. "The climate of Ville Franche," he wrote to Welles, "is excellent, whereas that of Spezia or Leghorn is not so regarded.... Genoa, at best, is but a small artificial port." He mentioned other factors such as an abundant supply of fresh provisions and coal, official permission for gunnery practice and infantry drill, the absence of other naval squadrons, and the use of government moorings.[18] His second choice was Genoa, but he considered its harbor too crowded. The major factor in his decision may have been personal reasons. He was extremely anxious to bring his wife and invalid daughter out to join him, and he considered Villefranche's climate to be much more suitable than that of all the other ports examined. As a matter of fact he emphasized climate in all of his correspondence concerning the establishment of a winter headquarters.[19] The whole question proved meaningless. His family never joined him (his daughter died while he was in Europe), and Villefranche was not to be his headquarters.

The American minister to Portugal was James Harvey, a former newspaper reporter and close friend of Seward. Harvey was anxious to have Lisbon designated the squadron's headquarters. When Goldsborough left Lisbon in November to enter the Mediterranean, he informed the American minister of his plans to winter at some port in that sea. Harvey immediately protested to Seward. Lisbon, he wrote, "may not offer as many agreeable attractions as those of Italy," but "if the squadron now in Europe has been detailed with a view of protecting our citizens, commerce and interests abroad, they will be far better served by the presence of these ships where they may be practically serviceable and readily reached, than in a sea difficult of access and egress with indifferent and artificial harbors, and remote from the ordinary channels of communication." Harvey also urged that naval forces were needed along the Iberian coast because of the threat of revolution in Spain. When word of Goldsborough's selection of Villefranche reached him, Harvey referred to the port in a letter to Seward as "a pleasant resort for invalids where the Admiral had established himself."[20] Shortly afterwards the State Department informed the minister that Lisbon, not Villefranche, was to be the squadron's headquarters. Harvey's protest may have been a factor in the decision, but the major reason was the expansion of the squadron's cruising area.

Goldsborough's announcement of his determination to winter at Villefranche passed en route an order from the Navy Department to make Lisbon his base for the winter. "The move is rather unexpected," the admiral wrote his wife, adding, "the place is good enough as to climate and security of anchorage, but it is rather dismal on the score of society."[21] This order was the result of a decision not to reestablish the African Squadron. Instead, the Brazilian and European Squadrons would divide its responsibilities. The cruising station for the European Squadron would include not only the Atlantic coast and islands off the coast but also the Mediterranean Sea, the African coast as far south as St. Paul de Loanda, and the adjacent islands (the Azores, Madeira, the Canaries, and Cape de Verde). St. Paul de Loanda (in Portuguese Angola) was selected as a joint coaling depot for the two squadrons.[22]

Goldsborough was promised additional vessels "as will enable you to discharge . . . [your] additional duties and responsibilities," but they never arrived. When he assumed command of the squadron, it was composed of five vessels: the flagship *Colorado*, frigate *Niagara*, sloops-of-war *Sacramento* and *Kearsarge*, and the side-wheel tender *Frolic*. The *Niagara* and *Sacramento* were shortly ordered home and replaced by the sloops *Canandaigua* and *Ticonderoga*. Although there would be other replacements during Goldsborough's tour, the size of the squadron would remain constant, at least in part because of the rapid decrease in the number of commissioned vessels after the war. In 1864 Secretary Welles was a big navy advocate, proudly proclaiming the naval force assembled up to that time as the "most powerful national navy in the world." He even seriously considered a naval program that would put and keep the United States on a par with Great Britain. But before the war was over, he reversed himself. A recent biographer suggests that the secretary abandoned it because he feared that the nation was heading for an economic disaster.[23] Even before Lee's surrender, he ordered to northern ports all purchased vessels in need of repairs and shortly afterwards directed the blockade squadrons to cut their strength in half. In January 1865, the ships of the blockading squadrons numbered 471 and carried 2,455 guns. By the end of the year, they numbered 29 and carried 210 guns.[24] Although Welles in his 1867 annual report mentioned that 238 ships of all types were in commission, only 103 were in active service; and, of this number, 56 were assigned to the 6 squadrons stationed in foreign waters. The decline in numbers did not end here but continued year after year as ships were sold or broken up.

Early in February 1866 the squadron rendezvoused at Lisbon. This concentration was brief, however, for Goldsborough was under orders to visit "as early as practicable . . . each port of importance." Within a few days after anchoring in the Tagus, the ships of the squadron scattered for various ports; but the flagship remained at anchor. The admiral wrote his wife, "I have been excessively busy ever since my arrival here. . . . Commanding a squadron of vessels in these times is no joke in the way of labor."[25]

Goldsborough had hoped to take his entire squadron on a tour of northern European ports. This was not possible, however, because of a new policy announced by the Navy Department. Welles wrote in his annual report: "In pursuance of the system of active operations adopted by the Department when reestablishing the Foreign squadrons lengthy anchorages and cruising collectively have been avoided." Goldsborough had received orders in April to send his vessels out "independently and continuously," but to no port north of Denmark.[26] This was really not a new policy, for squadrons had rarely operated as a unit before the Civil War—and rarely would they operate as a unit before the Spanish-American War. Goldsborough wrote his wife that "by the time this ship and the others reach Lisbon in May, it will be found that . . . at least seventy . . . ports will have been visited by the different vessels of the squadron. This result will, I think and hope, gratify the Department."[27]

The department was probably "gratified," but it was more concerned by Goldsborough's efforts to protect American interests in areas where unrest existed. In January 1866 a revolution broke out in Spain, and the U.S. minister to Portugal requested that American warships should be sent to the Spanish coast.

During the middle decades of the nineteenth century, Spain was consumed by dynastic quarrels, chronic disorders, and instability, at times approaching anarchy. The country was ruled by Queen Isabella, a foolish, frivolous, impulsive, and impatient young woman who had ascended the throne in 1843 at the age of thirteen. Her reign was characterized by increasing financial difficulties, scandals, and chaotic government. Unrest was widespread, periodically leading to disorders and revolts. In January, an insurrection broke out that, although unsuccessful, dragged on for several months. American interests in Spain at this time were minimal; nevertheless, on 11 January, Goldsborough ordered the *Frolic* to Barcelona and the *Kearsarge* to Malaga and sailed with the flagship to Cadiz. The revolt was quickly suppressed, and the American warships were withdrawn at the end of the month. At the request of the United States minister in Madrid, however, Goldborough agreed to keep one vessel "close by" for emergencies.[28]

On 14 June 1866 war broke out between Austria and Prussia over the Schleswig-Holstein controversy. Within a few days most of the German states lined up in support of Austria, while Italy allied herself with Prussia. Golds-borough ordered the *Ticonderoga* to the Adriatic, the *Canandaigua* to the Elbe and Weser, and the *Swatara*, which had recently arrived from the United States, to Bremerhaven. He informed Fox at the Navy Department that as soon as the *Colorado* was reprovisioned (she was in Lisbon at the time), "my present purpose is to return with her, for a while at least, to the Mediterranean, for if the cutting and slashing now going on in Europe is to bring any of our citi-zens into trouble, I want to be at hand to apply the remedy. If the war had not broke out, I should have gone to the North of Europe, but now the Adriatic and Italy will probably be the scene of warm work."[29] The war, as the name "Seven Weeks' War" implies, was brief. On the day that Goldsborough was writing to Fox, the Austrian army was decisively defeated at the battle of Sadowa (Königgrätz), and that country sued for peace. Three weeks later the Italian fleet was defeated by the Austrian fleet near Lissa, bringing to a close the active fighting between those two nations. By September vessels of the Euro-pean Squadron had resumed their normal cruising duties.

During the final weeks of 1866 Goldsborough would again order American vessels into Italian waters. The initial occasion was the discovery of John Har-rison Surrett in Rome. Surrett, one of the conspirators in Lincoln's assassi-nation, had fled to Canada and then to Europe, where he was discovered as a Zouave in a unit of the papal army. Rufus King, United States representative to the Papal States, requested that a warship be sent to Civitavecchia to carry Surrett back to the United States. The request was promptly granted, and the *Swatara* was ordered to Civitavecchia, although Goldsborough was not informed why a vessel was "urgently" needed.[30] Before the *Swatara* reached the Italian coast, Surrett escaped his captors and fled to Alexandria, Egypt, only to be recaptured there within a few weeks. The *Swatara* was then sent to Alexandria. On 8 January 1867 the warship, with Surrett on board, sailed for the United States under strict orders to touch at no port unless absolutely necessary.[31]

For several months after the Surrett affair, Goldsborough kept a vessel at Civitavecchia. The *Frolic* relieved the *Swatara*, and the admiral periodically rotated his vessels because of the unsettled conditions in Rome following the close of the war between Italy and Austria, the withdrawal of French troops from papal territory in December 1866, and the invasion by Garibaldi's troops.[32] The last vessel was withdrawn in June 1867, shortly before Golds-borough relinquished command of the squadron.

While providing naval protection for American interests in Europe, Golds-borough did not neglect the far corners of his station. In the spring of 1866 the *Kearsarge* was ordered to visit various ports along Africa's eastern coast. The ship got only as far as the coal depot at Sierra Leone when it had to return to Lisbon because of an outbreak of yellow fever.[33] Goldsborough made no effort to send another vessel to the eastern coast of Africa, but early in 1867 the

American commercial agent at Gaboon requested that a warship be sent there to "aid in suppressing the slave trade." The Navy Department passed the request on to the European Squadron, but nothing was done about it.

Goldsborough also sent a vessel to visit the Ottoman Empire. In August 1866 the commanding officer of the *Ticonderoga* requested permission from the Turkish government to pass through the Dardanelles. His request was at first denied on the grounds that it would violate the Treaty of Paris of 1856, which formally reaffirmed the closure of the Straits to foreign warships "of more than 800 tons measurement and . . . more than 150 feet in length." The United States was not a signatory of the 1856 treaty but had signed a treaty with Turkey in 1830 that gave American commercial vessels freedom of passage. However, nothing was said of warships. The problem of the right of passage for U.S. vessels-of-war first arose in 1858 when the fifty-gun steam frigate *Wabash* visited Constantinople. European diplomatic representatives protested her visit, and no further requests were made until 1866.[34] Jay Morris, the American minister in Constantinople, was then able to obtain permission for the *Ticonderoga* to pass through the Straits. There is no evidence that the representatives of the major European powers protested the visit, probably because they recognized the disinclination of the United States to become involved in the Eastern Question.[35]

The Eastern or Near Eastern Question, as the fate of the disintegrating Ottoman Empire was called, was one of the most critical as well as complex diplomatic problems in the nineteenth century. The empire encompassed a vast area at the opening of the century, including the entire Near East, Turkey, the Arab world, and even most of northern Africa. To most observers it was not a question of whether the empire would break up, but of who would inherit it. One force that was slowly tearing it apart was nationalism, the Greeks, Bulgarians, Serbs, and others struggling for independence. Religious differences complicated the situation; for not only were many of these nationalities Christian under a Moslem government, but they provided an excuse for foreign intervention. For nearly three-quarters of the nineteenth century, four European powers, Great Britain, France, Austria, and Russia—the "Great Powers"—vied with each other over Turkey. Near the end of the century a united Germany would enter the rivalry, primarily for commercial advantages.

The traditional policy of the United States was noninvolvement as far as the Eastern Question was concerned. As Secretary Seward told the French minister, he was glad to leave to Europe "the disentangling of the Turkish knot."[36] In reality, however, this country was frequently involved, partly because of American interests in the Ottoman Empire and partly for humanitarian reasons. Although American commercial relations were limited and fluctuated considerably from decade to decade, they nevertheless remained profitable, particularly in Smyrna and Constantinople. In 1855 the latter city witnessed the weekly arrival of an American ship bringing rum, flour, and sugar.[37] It was to protect this commerce from piracy that the Mediterranean Squadron cruised the Archipelago during the Greek War for Independence. In the decades after the Civil War, however, American commercial activities declined.[38]

Although American commercial relations were relatively unimportant, missionary interests were quite significant. Joseph L. Grabill, in his recently published book, *Protestant Diplomacy and the Near East: Missionary Influence on American Policy, 1810–1927*, found that American Protestant missionaries and philanthropists had more influence than other interests on United States policy with the Near East from the mid-nineteenth century through World War I.[39]

From a modest beginning of two American missionaries in 1823, the mission field in the Ottoman Empire expanded until by 1885 more than two hundred American citizens were engaged there in operating mission stations, schools, and hospitals. The two principal American missionary bodies that carried on this work were the Presbyterian Board of Foreign Missions and the American Board of Commissioners for Foreign Missions (Congregationalist). After the Civil War the field was divided; the Presbyterians concentrated in Syria with their center at Beirut, and the American Board took Turkey proper with its center in Constantinople. From the beginning they made little effort to convert Moslems; instead they concentrated on the Christian minorities. For this reason the Sultan's government was generally tolerant toward the missionaries and their activities.

The Sultan's Moslem subjects, however, were not always so tolerant, and clashes did occur.[40] These incidents resulted in demands for protection, both diplomatic and naval. By 1850 the U.S. government had come to acknowledge that its primary purpose in sending warships to Turkish waters was the protection of American missionary interests.[41] Inevitably, as the missionary demand for warships increased, diplomatic and naval officials began to react in a hostile fashion. Louis Goldsborough, when in command of the corvette *Levant* in Turkish waters in 1853, called them "blackguards" and damned the "turbulent, disturbful, dirty, Missionaries!!!"[42] With some validity an American diplomat to Turkey would later write that "since 1815 the United States had maintained a Mediterranean Squadron mainly to wrestle concessions from the Turks in favor of American Missionaries."[43]

American interests in Turkey were affected by the absence of warships during the Civil War, as commerce nearly disappeared. When several American missionaries were murdered in 1862, the French navy offered the protection of a warship. With the end of the war, diplomatic officials as well as missionaries began to clamor again for naval vessels.[44]

In the summer of 1866 a revolution broke out on Crete, an Ottoman possession. It occurred because of Turkish misrule, the failure of successive harvests, and perhaps most importantly, the desire of the Cretans to unite with Greece. Despite official pronouncements of noninvolvement, American diplomatic representatives in the Near East generally were philhellenic, particularly E. Jay Morris, minister to the Ottoman government, and William J. Stillman, "an aesthetically-minded journalist and amateur archaeologist," who was consul on the island.[45] In November 1866, both Goldsborough and Secretary of State Seward received dispatches from Morris, Stillman, and the American consul at Piraeus, Greece, requesting that a warship be sent to evacuate "the suffering women and children on Crete" to Greece. The admiral declined, but forwarded the request to Washington for "direction."[46] On December 25 Seward wrote Morris, "This Department fully approves of the course adopted by the consul [Stillman]. . . . Admiral Goldsborough will be directed to send a vessel of war to that island for the purpose indicated." Understandably, Stillman concluded that a warship would be sent to help evacuate the refugees. The American consul went so far as to inform the Cretans of this, and a large number of women and children assembled on the coast to await the warship's arrival. The expected vessel failed to appear, however, and Morris' and Stillman's frantic appeals were without result. Goldsborough, who was still without orders, continued his refusal to send one, pointing out that "it is, I think, far beyond my authority to detail a vessel for the purpose in view, to act in defiance of the local authorities, for I, at least, must bear in mind that we are at peace with Turkey."[47] Finally, on 16 March, the *Canandaigua* arrived in Suda Bay. Goldsborough had decided to send a vessel to the island and to remove the women and children, if permission could be received from local officials. Permission was refused, however, and a few days later the American vessel departed.

By this time it was clear that a "misunderstanding" had occurred. On 21 March 1867, Welles wrote Seward:

> The views expressed and the position taken by Goldsborough meet the approval of this Department, and are in conformity with its instructions. . . . Our Naval officers were expected to consult and co-operate with our officials and accredited representatives abroad, but when these representatives invoke them to do unauthorized acts, and appeal to them officially, in the name of humanity, to disregard neutral obligations, there arises a question how far such representatives or authority shall be respected. . . .[48]

Later Welles would recommend to the president at a Cabinet meeting that Morris should be recalled, for, the naval secretary observed in his diary, Morris has "made himself busy in trying to induce our naval officers to . . . interfere in this insurrection."

Seward apparently concurred in placing the blame on Morris. He later censured the minister for sending a report that (so Seward insisted) gave the erroneous impression that the Turkish government would give permission for an American warship to assist in evacuating Cretans from the island. Yet the secretary of state himself was at least partly responsible for the blunder, as he had informed Stillman that a vessel would be sent and apparently never retracted that statement. This omission may have been a result of Seward's efforts to obtain permission from the Turkish government, although he was aware that Russian and British warships had already evacuated some Cretans without Turkish authorization.[49] This may also explain why Seward apparently never requested the Navy Department to order a vessel to Crete. Goldsborough never received such orders, and Welles certainly implies this when he wrote in his diary, "sent [Seward] the correspondence which had passed between Admiral Goldsborough and E. J. Morris. . . . The latter has been urging Admiral G. to send a ship to Candia . . . Morris justifies himself on the ground of assurance from the Secretary of State."[50] Goldsborough was never authorized to send a vessel, and when one was sent, it was on his own responsibility.

In July 1867, Congress passed a resolution of sympathy for the inhabitants of Crete, and shortly afterwards Admiral Farragut (who replaced Goldsborough) ordered the *Swatara* to the eastern Mediterranean under orders to once again investigate the possibility of removing refugees from Crete. As before, the answer was negative. The *Swatara* then departed for Piraeus; and Commander William Jeffers, her commanding officer reported, "I find that we have no interest whatever in this island, there being no American residents, nor trade."[51] The Cretan revolution would drag on until 1869 before finally being suppressed; but outside of a brief visit by the *Ticonderoga* in 1868, the European Squadron stayed clear of the island.

Relations between the United States and the Ottoman Empire had traditionally been friendly, but the Cretan question and the enormous publicity given to Assistant Secretary of the Navy Gustavus Fox on his visit to Russia clearly annoyed the Turks. As the commanding officer of the *Ticonderoga* reported on the occasion of that vessel's visit to Constantinople in 1866, the American minister was greatly pleased "at my arrival and considers the visit of the ship particularly well timed because the suspicions of the Turks have been recently excited by our friendly demonstration towards the Russians. . . ."[52] The *Ticonderoga's* visit corresponded with Fox's trip to Russia, but whether this was planned is not known. American officials were certainly aware of the long-standing enmity between the two countries.

In 1863 a Russian squadron visited American harbors. It was popularly and erroneously believed that Czar Alexander II had sent the warships out of sympathy to the Union cause. In April 1866, Alexander narrowly escaped assassination, and Congress passed a joint resolution of congratulation on his escape. At the recommendation of Seward, the president reluctantly agreed to the selection of Assistant Secretary of the Navy Fox to convey the resolution to St. Petersburg. Welles in his diary suggests that Seward selected Fox—admittedly a surprising choice—in order to embarrass him. On the other hand Fox himself may have manipulated his selection, although he had lost considerable influence (including a possible admiral's commission) upon the death of Lincoln.[53]

Fox, at his request, received permission to sail in the double-turreted monitor *Miantonomah*. Her sailing created considerable excitement both at home and abroad, for no monitor up to that time had crossed the Atlantic. Accompanied by the paddle steamers *Augusta* and *Ashuelot*, she reached Queenstown, Ireland, on 15 August 1866. The British admiral in command asked Fox, "Did you cross the Atlantic in that thing?" Fox replied that he had, indeed, to which the admiral retorted, "I doubt if I would."[54] From there the *Ashuelot* departed for Lisbon, while the *Miantonomah* and the *Augusta* sailed to Portsmouth and then to Cherbourg, France. In the middle of July the two vessels entered the Baltic, and after brief stops at Copenhagen and Helsingfors (Helsinki), reached Kronstadt, Russia. They accepted Russian hospitality for six weeks, then visited Stockholm, Kiel, and Hamburg. During the winter months the two vessels cruised in the waters of southern Europe and the Mediterranean, temporarily attached to the European Squadron. Fox, however, was not on board. He spent this time touring various European countries investigating naval facilities. On 2 May the ships (with Fox again on board the monitor) left Naples for the return trip to the United States.[55]

While in Europe, Fox informed Goldsborough that Farragut was to be offered command of the European Squadron. Goldsborough told his wife that if Farragut accepted the command, he should return home in the summer of 1867; if not, he expected to remain in command another year.[56]

The cruise had been an unhappy one for Goldsborough. He had hoped to bring his family out to join him, but in the spring of 1866 his daughter's health began to fail, and she died in May of the same year. The blow was a severe one, as she was his only remaining child; and his many letters to his wife in the following months were taken up with reminiscences of her. He continued to press his wife to join him, but she decided against it after the death of their child. Deeply disappointed, but resigned to her decision, he wrote her, "at any rate if the Secretary will not permit you to come with me on board this ship, . . . it is on the whole better for you not to come." At his urging she had petitioned the naval secretary for permission to accompany the admiral on board his flagship, but the request was refused. One can imagine his chagrin when Farragut arrived to take command of the squadron with his wife in residence on board the *Franklin*.

In 1867 Goldsborough was sixty-two and ready to be relieved of his command.[57] He began to fear that it would be extended. "Farragut," he wrote his wife, "is a full admiral and full admirals do not command squadrons." Wishfully he added, "If I could have you on board this ship with me, I would be willing to remain out a year longer, but otherwise I am not. . . ."

In the spring, Goldsborough's impatience to get home as quickly as possible was accentuated by a controversy with Welles over his retirement. He was slated to retire in 1867, having served some fifty-five years in the navy. Golds-borough decided to challenge the date on the dubious grounds that he had not received orders for sea until four years after his appointment. Welles refused to rescind the order, and Goldsborough's wife, the daughter of former Attorney General William Wirt, began gathering support from influential politicians. The matter was to be turned over to Andrew Johnson in June, and Golds-borough was anxious to be relieved of the European command in time to inter-vene personally with the president. He did not make it; nor as a matter of fact was it necessary, for Goldsborough was allowed to remain on active duty for another four years.[58] His final four years in the navy were spent in Washington, D.C., performing various administrative functions for the department. Four years after his retirement, he died.

In May, Goldsborough received word from the Navy Department that Far-ragut would relieve him at Cherbourg. By the end of June, the squadron had assembled at Lisbon. Leaving the *Shamrock* and *Swatara* there, Golds-borough took the remainder of the squadron to Cherbourg, arriving on July 7th. The admiral's obvious impatience to give up the command caused him to be-come involved in a verbal clash with James Harvey, the irascible minister to Portugal. Harvey had requested that the squadron remain in Lisbon for a few days, as he was involved in negotiations with the Portuguese government over the imprisonment of certain American citizens. He felt that the presence of American warships during the negotiations would add weight to his argu-ments. Goldsborough refused, because of his determination to be at Cher-bourg when Farragut arrived. With justifiable irritation, Harvey wrote Goldsborough, "I have been greatly surprised by your refusal to give me the least aid and co-operation. . . . I had supposed that the squadron in Europe had been sent here especially for the protection . . . of our citizens. . . . It would seem. . . . that I have not been correctly informed. . . ."[59] Harvey protested to the State Department, but nothing came from it, possibly because this was not the first or the last altercation between the minister and the navy.[60]

On Bastile Day, 14 July 1867, the steam frigate *Franklin*, with Farragut on board, arrived in the harbor of Cherbourg and was saluted by the European Squadron. The following day Farragut relieved Goldsborough of his com-mand.

Admiral David G. Farragut was the most famous naval officer of his day. His spectacular victories at New Orleans and Mobile during the Civil War had won for him fame not only at home but abroad as well. Admiral Lord Clarence E. Paget, while in command of the British Mediterranean Squadron, met Far-ragut and referred to him as a "remarkable man."[61] Yet his appointment to the European command surprised many. He was sixty-two years old, a full ad-miral, and not in good health (although Dr. Oliver Wendell Holmes who saw him a few months before his appointment wrote that "he was the gayest, heartiest, shrewdest old boy you ever saw. . . .").[62] Welles does not say in his diary why he appointed Farragut to command the squadron, but the reasons seem obvious. He was the most prestigious officer, and there was no chief of naval operations in those days; the European Squadron was at that time still the most important command; it was a traditional appointment for a senior officer about to retire; and Farragut clearly wanted it.

Farragut spent the first week of June 1867 in Washington as a guest of Secretary Welles, where he received his orders and then journeyed to New York to hoist his flag on the steam frigate *Franklin*. Shortly before sailing, he gave a "Grand Ball" on board the flagship. Among those attending was President Johnson. Farragut had accompanied the president the summer before on his political tour in the Midwest, and at one time had been rumored as Welles' successor. Johnson rewarded Farragut by personally waiving the naval regulations that prevented wives from cruising with their husbands on warships. Mrs. Farragut and the wife of the *Franklin's* captain accompanied their husbands on the flagship when it sailed for European waters.[63]

As undoubtedly the navy and state departments anticipated, Farragut's seventeen-month tour was one triumphal visit after the other to various European countries.[64] He was received with honor by royalty everywhere he went; newspapers vied with each other in speculating about the diplomatic objectives of his visits. At one time English papers reported erroneously that the admiral was avoiding the British Isles, and the *British Army and Navy Gazette* suggested that his men would be well received and that such a visit might smooth over some of the differences between the two countries.[65] Farragut did finally visit Britain, with apparently little effect on relations between the two countries.

Farragut spent very little time in Lisbon, the designated winter headquarters of the squadron. Fortunately, during his tour no serious problems required attention. However, because of continuing unrest and disorder the *Ticonderoga* and *Swatara* were ordered to remain in Italian and Cretan waters respectively throughout 1867. The *Guard* was left at Lisbon as store ship. The remainder of the squadron usually sailed with the *Franklin*—probably a violation of naval policy concerning cruising responsibilities.

Farragut began his grand tour after relieving Goldsborough in July 1867. From France he sailed for St. Petersburg. Then on 3 September, the American squadron anchored off Waxholm, Sweden, about fifteen miles from Stockholm. This was followed by a brief visit to Copenhagen and a month's stay in England. While the warships anchored at Gravesend on the Thames, Farragut inspected various naval installations and was wined and dined in London. He then went to Portsmouth and Plymouth before sailing for Lisbon early in October. After three weeks spent at the squadron's rendezvous, he sailed via Gibraltar for the Mediterranean. On 5 December, the *Franklin* arrived off the old Spanish city of Carthagena, and from then into the winter months of 1868 the admiral visited various Mediterranean ports. In the spring he returned to Lisbon, then sailed to the Netherlands, and back to England; finally, in the middle of July, the *Franklin* turned towards the Mediterranean again—destination Constantinople.

On 10 August, Farragut arrived at Constantinople. He made the trip through the Dardanelles on the tender *Frolic* while the American minister attempted to persuade the Ottoman government to allow the *Franklin* to enter the straits. The size of the flagship was such that if she were permitted to enter the straits without special permission, it would be a violation of the treaty of 1856. When the minister was informed that exceptions were permissible only in favor of royalty, he replied that "if Admiral Farragut were not a prince of the blood, he was at least a naval officer of such pre-eminent fame and achievements that the sovereigns of Europe had treated him with princely honors. . . ."[66] Permission was granted, but probably not because of Farragut's eminence.

There is no evidence to indicate that Farragut's visit was anything more than an extension of his goodwill tour to the eastern Mediterranean. Nevertheless, most observers were convinced that his visit had definite diplomatic overtones. Turkish officials, concerned over the Cretan insurrection and the possibility of American intervention, suspected that Farragut's visit had something to do with that crisis. Rumors had been rampant for some time that the United States desired Suda Bay as a naval base and was willing to cooperate with the Cretans, the Greeks, or perhaps the Russians for this purpose.[67] The Reverend Cyrus Hamlin, missionary, educator, and the founder of Roberts College in Constantinople, gave Farragut credit for persuading the Turkish government to allow the college to be built. In his memoirs he also mentioned an interview with a Turkish official who was convinced that the admiral was sent to investigate affairs in Crete.[68]

There is nothing in the records of the navy and state departments to suggest that Farragut was under orders to investigate Suda Bay as a possible American naval base. Yet on 21 May 1868, Sir Henry Elliott, British ambassador to the Ottoman Empire, reported to the Foreign Office: "[I have] been able to ascertain the undoubted existence of . . . a plan as well as that of a recent report made by Admiral Farragut of the ability of the Insurgents to continue their resistance . . . for an indefinite period. If I am not misinformed, Admiral Farragut dwelt upon the capabilities of Suda Bay as a naval station."[69]

Farragut left Constantinople for Greece in September, after three weeks of receptions, banquets, and the like. His brief stop there certainly did nothing to ease the minds of those who feared U.S. intrigue over the Crete problem. He was enthusiastically greeted upon arrival at Piraeus by a crowd of Cretan refugees and by the mayor of the port, who appealed to him for assistance in the insurrection. Charles K. Tuckerman, the newly appointed minister to Greece, was quite open in his support of the Cretans and even suggested to Seward that they would eagerly place themselves under the American flag.[70]

Again, there is no evidence that Farragut expressed any opinion on the situation in Crete or the acquisition of a base in the eastern Mediterranean.

After leaving Greece Farragut made only two stops before departing for the United States. He visited Trieste in the Adriatic and stopped at Gibraltar to take on coal and to exchange personnel with the ships that were remaining on the European station. On 18 October 1868, the *Franklin* left for the United States, and for all practical purposes Farragut's active service in the navy came to an end.

3

The rumors of American interest in acquiring a naval base or depot in the Mediterranean were not without foundation. When the station was reestablished, however, the Navy Department returned to its prewar policy of designating a winter rendezvous for the squadron. Lisbon was so chosen in 1866.

No shore facilities of any kind were established at Lisbon. The navy's logistical policy at that time was to utilize floating storeships anchored at the designated rendezvous. The policy was inefficient, although the navy considered it economical. Merchant vessels were chartered to replenish the storeships from the United States. Any delay in their crossing the Atlantic, whether from a breakdown in machinery or from being becalmed or quarantined, affected the squadron's operations. Rear Admiral Henry Erban, while in command of the European Squadron, mentioned how once an accident to a supply ship had delayed his departure from a port for nearly a month.[1] The squadron's replenishment needs frequently determined cruising schedules. Routine cruises to distant parts of the station were usually brief, as any extended tour created serious logistical problems.

Dry stores and machinery parts were usually brought from the United States. "Articles of a perishable nature" such as bread and fresh provisions could be purchased locally. Later selected nonperishable items such as paint were added to that category, but only under the stipulation that the purchase price was less than what the same item would cost in the United States. Occasionally a supply ship brought more than the squadron could use. In 1861 the storeship *Supply* was authorized to sell its cargo of flour in England, "as . . . [the European Squadron] had more flour than . . . [it] knew what to do with."[2] The department later modified its policy, allowing storeships to rendezvous with the units of the squadron in various ports.

Coal was contracted for with local merchants. American diplomatic representatives (usually consuls) frequently arranged the matter, and in many cases

they received a commission for this service.[3] In 1867 a dispute broke out between the U.S. minister to Portugal, J. E. Harvey, and the Navy Department
over a coal contract. A Portuguese businessman by the name of J. Abecassis
travelled to Washington and obtained a contract with the department to provide some 500 tons of coal to vessels of the European Squadron. When he received word of this transaction, Harvey immediately protested to the State
Department that Abecassis was "an Israelite trader," a "keeper of a tavern,"
and "notoriously hostile to us during the war." The minister also complained
that he was not consulted "as prescribed by . . . standing relations."[4] Harvey's
protests were forwarded to the Navy Department, where they were answered
by the chief of the Bureau of Equipment and Recruiting. He pointed out that
Abecassis's price was lower than that of other dealers. "The Bureau is led to
believe," the report concluded, ". . . that there has been a powerful influence
exerted to induce Mr. Harvey to interest himself in a matter which as he states,
'the Legation has no concern whatever.' " In endorsing the report and for-
warding it to the State Department, Secretary of the Navy Welles added,
"Commanders of vessels are instructed to consult with consular representatives and to act upon the suggestion of the consul if it shall appear to the interest
of the naval service to do so, but not otherwise. This precautionary direction to
commanding officers does not, as Mr. Harvey and the consul suppose, pre-
clude the Department from making contracts, issuing or sending supplies of
any kind to any port."[5] Harvey's protest was futile. Not only did Abecassis's
original contract remain intact, but he received additional ones periodically.
Admiral Farragut was informed of Abecassis's contract and that, since his
coal was cheaper, it was "desirable to have our cruisers coal at Lisbon, when it
does not interfere with the movement of your command."[6]

Harvey refused to give up. Until he left the legation in the summer of 1869,
he continued to complain bitterly of Abecassis's contract and of what he considered to be the navy's mishandling of the case. In one report he accused Abecassis of making exorbitant charges for certain work performed (probably for
loading the coal in ship's bunkers, for which he was paid extra). Commodore
Joseph Smith, chief of the Bureau of Equipment and Recruiting, who became
increasingly irritated at Harvey, as the dispute dragged on for month after
month, replied that if, as alleged, "exorbitant charges have been made, with a
view of defrauding the government," it was surprising that the admiral in command of the squadron was unaware of the "fraud." Nor had the minister
informed the admiral so that an investigation could be made. Welles, who was
also becoming annoyed at Harvey's persistence, wrote in his diary that "the
monopoly of trade has been long previously enjoyed by certain American officials, who gave the trade to favored parties and received therefore a high commission. . . . I have little confidence in Harvey who was a mercenary
correspondent here prior to the commencement of the Rebellion. . . ." Welles
informed Seward that "without entering into the personal feelings of Mr. Har-

vey . . . the denunciation of Mr. Abecassis as a 'Jew' and 'adventurer' who once kept a common tavern fails to convince me that he is unworthy of our trust.'"[7]

Harvey denounced Abecassis to Rear Admiral William Radford, when he assumed command of the squadron early in 1869: "It is my duty to inform you that . . . flagrant imposition and frauds in different forms have been practiced in the purchase of supplies and work done for the U.S. Navy at this port through the intervention of a person named Isaac Abecassis. . . ." Welles received a copy of the minister's letter and wrote Seward that he "cannot but regard this letter as an impertinent interference in the affairs of the squadron" and that the "needed supplies will be procured in [a] . . . manner [deemed] . . . most advantageous to the . . . Government, regardless of the . . . prejudices of Mr. Harvey." Welles also instructed Radford to ignore Harvey.[8] One of Harvey's last acts as minister to Portugal was to reiterate his complaint that the navy had refused to investigate his charges against Abecassis. He even carried his crusade against Abecassis back to the United States. In December 1869, a resolution was introduced in the House of Representatives requiring the Navy Department to furnish that body with all records concerning the Abecassis contract. The matter was laid before the House Committee on Appropriations, where it was buried in spite of the remarks of Representative Cadwallader C. Washburn of Wisconsin, who accused the navy of "great irregularities" on contracting for coal on foreign stations.[9]

In August 1869, Admiral Radford was instructed by the Bureau of Equipment and Recruiting to coal his vessels from Lisbon as "it desires to have the contract dated [completed] as soon as possible." This may have been because of Harvey's return to the United States and the possibility of a Congressional investigation, but more than likely it was a result of the recent change in policy concerning fuel economy on ships. Nevertheless, a year later the coal had not been used up and again the bureau requested the admiral to coal his vessels at Lisbon "whenever possible."[10]

In 1871 the department decided to return to its previous policy of purchasing coal on the open market, and Abecassis's bid for another contract was turned down. "The Bureau does not intend at present to make further contracts or agreements with any parties, . . . for the supply of coal as it prefers that coal shall always be bought . . . when needed and not at any one port."[11] However, well into the twentieth century the Abecassis brothers continued providing American naval vessels that entered Lisbon with coal and other supplies.[12]

After the spring of 1869, in one respect the coal issue declined in importance. The Navy Department, in an economy move, issued a general order ". . . [to] use . . . steam . . . [only] under the most urgent circumstances [and] . . . to do all . . . cruising under sail alone. . . ." In conclusion, commanding officers were warned that they were expected to report to the department "every occasion where it is necessary . . . to use steam."[13] One naval officer later wrote that "to burn coal was so grievious an offense in the eyes of the authorities that for years the Captain was obliged to enter in the Logbook in *red ink* his reasons for getting up steam and starting engines." For example, in November 1869, Admiral Radford informed the department that he used steam to take his flagship to Malaga as quickly as possible "in consequence of information received . . . from the U.S. Consul . . . that a collision was momentarily expected between the people and the troops and as I had been wind bound for a week. . . ."[14]

The amount of coal allotted to the European Squadron declined steadily for several years. For the 1874–75 fiscal year, the squadron received $50,000 to purchase coal. The admiral reported to the secretary of the navy that this amount "will allow the *Congress, Alaska,* and *Juanita* to be filled with coal three times and the *Franklin* twice during the year without leaving margin for contingencies. . . ."[15]

Although machinery may have been used infrequently, it did break down or need repairs occasionally. There were no American repair facilities in European waters; instead, the squadron had to depend upon European yards. Goldsborough was authorized to send his vessels to Cadiz or Farrol. Later Gibraltar would become the major repair center for American warships.

Even before the Civil War American diplomatic representatives from time to time tried to interest the government in acquiring a naval base in the Mediterranean.[16] A naval depot was established at Spezia, Italy, in 1848, with a naval agent as storekeeper in charge. Although some repair work was done there, it was primarily a supply depot and was abandoned during the Civil War. In the spring of 1866 the American consul at Spezia urged the reestablishment of at least a coal depot there. The Navy Department was not interested, probably because the Italian government had determined to locate a naval station there. For several years George P. Marsh, American minister to Italy, tried to find another suitable location, but his efforts were ignored by Washington officials.[17]

In May 1866, Stillman, the American consul in Crete, wrote to Seward strongly recommending the acquisition of that island as the site of a naval base. He mentioned that the Cretans had approached him with the idea, because there was a widely circulated report that the United States desired to purchase an island in the Levant.[18] The British ambassador probably had knowledge of this communication when he reported Admiral Farragut's interest in Suda Bay as a naval station. The Russian government also showed interest in the possibility of an American naval base in Crete. Minister Morris in Constantinople reported that Count Ignatiev, the Czar's representative to the Porte, expressed approval that the U.S. desired to purchase an island in the Levant "to be used as a commercial and naval depot." Russian encouragement was probably prompted by the effect that such a development would have on British policy in the Mediterranean. Britain's support of the Ottoman Empire had successfully blocked Russian designs in the Near East. Relations between the U.S. and Great Britain continued to be strained, while Russia and the United States were apparently developing stronger ties. In this circumstance American presence in the Near East would benefit Russia in a crisis with Great Britain and Turkey. In fact the presence of a Russian squadron in New York in 1863 would be repeated in the Mediterranean if the United States acquired a base.[19]

Seward was not opposed to the idea. Historians generally agree that his imperialistic outlook was strongly motivated by a determination to establish American commercial supremacy in all parts of the world including the Levant. He considered England the major rival. Seward undoubtedly instinctively understood the interdependence of naval power and commerical supremacy.[20] Secretary of the Navy Welles also recognized the need for overseas bases. In one communication he wrote:

> On former occasions and elsewhere, I have expressed my convictions, in consequence of the revolution which steam has wrought in naval warfare that it will be essential that our government should possess at important points on the great ocean highways suitable stations for coal and general supplies. Without such stations we shall be unable to maintain the naval supremacy to which our country . . . is entitled.

But he went on to point out that the "acquisition of such stations involves a change of policy on the part of our government for which the people may not be fully prepared, and it is therefore a question whether it would be judicious to commence this change of policy in the Crecian Archipalago, which is remote from the great lines of commerical naval intercourse."[21]

When Welles alluded to the acquisition of overseas bases as a "change of policy of our government," he was of course referring to the traditional reluctance of the United States to expand overseas. Nevertheless, both he and Seward were interested in acquiring strategic military outposts abroad. Welles wanted naval stations, but "in quarters . . . more important to our navigating interest." From the end of the Civil War until they retired, both secretaries pursued policies designed to obtain overseas bases. There is little evidence that they collaborated; in fact, Welles was deeply suspicious of Seward's policies.

Although the naval secretary was clearly not interested in establishing a naval base in the eastern Mediterranean, he did not rule out altogether a station or depot in European waters. In December 1866, Goldsborough was ordered to give his views "relative to the selection of a suitable place for a coal depot in the Mediterranean." Three months later Welles informed the State Department that the "Bureau [of Equipment and Recruiting] is now engaged in the investigation of the subject of establishing *permanent* [author's italics] coaling depots, with the view of selecting the most desirable and accessible localities on the several cruising stations. . . ."[22]

The news that the government was actively seeking naval bases abroad prompted a number of suggestions from American diplomatic representatives. Crete, an unnamed island off the western coast of Africa, and even the Cape Verde Islands were recommended. A French company sought to obtain permission from the Greek government to purchase a site in that country and lease it to the United States for ninety years.[23]

European newspapers reacted with alarm at the report that the United States was seeking such a base. A French journal considered such efforts to be undesirable interference with the interest of European powers, and a French-language newspaper in Constantinople agreed with this sentiment. It further asserted that "we are not ignorant of the attempts of the United States at this time to obtain a new point of supply and refreshment in the Mediterranean."[24] The French press were only voicing the uneasiness of their government. A question from the French minister in Washington brought a denial from Seward. Nevertheless, French suspicions of such a design by the United States would persist for years.

The Navy Department decided against establishing a base for the time being in European waters. Goldsborough recommended against the idea, and the Bureau of Equipment and Recruiting endorsed his disapproval. Seward reluctantly agreed. Apparently influenced by European (primarily French) reaction, he recognized that such a radical change in policy would inevitably project the United States into European affairs, a possibility he wanted to avoid.[25]

To those who were most conscious of its potential value, the American diplomatic representatives, an American military installation in the Old World remained an attractive goal. Periodically the State Department would receive confidential correspondence urging such a project. For over two years (1873–1875) Michel Vidal, the American consul at Tripoli, investigated and made lengthy reports concerning the suitability of Cyrenaica for a naval base.[26]

In 1873 another proposal by a French company ("Franco-American Company") to obtain territory in Greece and lease it to the United States for a naval base was passed on through the American minister in Athens to the State Department. "Political difficulties . . . render it impossible for the two governments of Greece and the United States to negotiate a direct concession of this character. . . . hence it appears . . . advisable to arrange through an intermediaire. . . ." The writer of the letter does not specify the "political difficulties." Although the State Department passed it on to the secretary of the navy, no action was taken.[27]

The following year representatives of yet another French company approached George Boker, the American minister in Constantinople, with a scheme. He was informed that the company had secured a concession of land on Bab el Mandeb, the strait uniting the Indian Ocean with the Red Sea, and

were willing to sell it to the United States as a "coaling, watering, and provi-
sioning station for our fleet." As Boker expected, Secretary of State Hamilton
Fish was not interested. In a private letter to Fish, Boker wrote, "I supposed
that you would poke fun at me for proposing to you the purchase of Bab el
Mandeb, but as the affair was seriously offered to me by a French company,
and pressed upon my attention by the Russian Ambassador, I thought it my
duty to lay the matter before you. . . ." The minister then quipped, "If the late
Mr. Seward was permitted to furnish the United States with a refrigerator, why
should not you provide an oven?"[28]

The attitude of the French government towards American naval penetration
into the Mediterranean changed with the overthrow of the Second Empire.
Relations between France and the United States had deteriorated rapidly
during the American Civil War and had remained at a relatively low point
during the remainder of Napolean III's reign. However, during the early years
of the Third Republic, French opposition to American involvement in the
Mediterranean declined, possibly because the French were trying to improve
relations with the United States or because they felt that American involvement would block British designs in that area. It may also have been because of
the American-Russian detente and the desire of some for France to join Russia
and the United States in a "triple entente."[29] What is undeniable is that after
1869 Villefranche, on the French Riviera, became the winter quarters and
depot for the European Squadron.

Ulysses S. Grant was inaugurated as president in 1869, and Gideon Welles
was replaced by Adolpe E. Borie, a genial Philadelphian merchant. Borie, not
particularly interested in the position, resigned after only four months. The department during his brief tenure was actually run by Vice Admiral David D.
Porter. It was Porter, in his efforts to reorganize the navy, who made extensive
changes in the logistical support for the foreign squadrons. In May 1869, for
"reasons of economy" squadron commanders were ordered to shift from
floating storeships to store facilities ashore. The European Squadron commander recommended Spezia, "as the presence of this squadron is more likely
to be required in the Mediterranean than elsewhere."[30] The department at first
favored Spezia but abandoned it when the Italian government decided to construct a naval base there. Syracuse was offered as an alternative, but was not
acceptable. Lisbon, the squadron's winter rendezvous, was not considered acceptable either, because the squadron commander reported that American
ships paid more than British vessels for provisions procured in the Portuguese
port.

In February 1870, Rear Admiral William Radford, the European Squadron
commander, wrote to the department that, after an interview with the prefect of
Nice, he was recommending Villefranche. His reasons were reminiscent of
those of Admiral Goldsborough, who had advocated the small French port
some five years before. The department approved Radford's recommendation,

and in March he arranged to lease a warehouse. The agreement was informal, however, and "rest[ed] solely upon the good feeling and 'politesse' of the French government." Clearly, relations between the two countries would determine the continued availability of the facility. For thirteen years, the logistic support base of the European Squadron remained, to all intents and purposes, limited to a rented warehouse on the French Riviera.[31] Although not officially designated as such, Villefranche would replace Lisbon as the squadron's winter headquarters and would continue so for many years, even after the storehouse was removed.

The European Squadron's fleet surgeon on several occasions tried without success to persuade the Navy Department to establish a hospital or medical facility at Villefranche. The navy's policy for years had been to retain the ill on board its ships unless they contracted a "dangerous" disease such as typhoid. They were then landed and placed in a hospital in whatever port the vessel was in or the next port of call. The fleet surgeon in 1874 reported that he placed "dangerously affected patients . . . in hotels, where they could remain under my control."[32]

Outside of sporadic visits to Villefranche to replenish, the squadron's only lengthy stay in its rendezvous occurred during the winter months. This had become standard practice during the early years of the Mediterranean Squadron when the fierce winter gales made routine port-to-port cruises hazardous, and it continued in the post-Civil War years.

During the winter months the ships followed a relaxed schedule. With the exception of normal shipboard maintenance, minor repairs, and in-port routine, very little was done. Rear Admiral John C. Howell, when in command of the squadron in the early 1880s, found it so difficult to carry out various drills and training exercises that at the beginning of the cruising season he took the squadron to Port Mahon. "This is the best port in the Mediterranean for ship and boat exercises," he reported to the department. "The town being . . . dull, possess[es] no attractions for officers or men and exercises of all sorts are cheerfully undertaken, in order to relieve the dreary monotony. . . ."[33]

Villefranche's harbor is an excellent one, although it looks more like a semicircular cove if one enters from the seaward side. The town has always been picturesque to the American sailors with its beach and its buildings, speckled with pink, yellow, and white villas. In the background, the towering Maritime Alps stretch to the East and West. During the 1870s and 1880s, the permanent population numbered only about a thousand persons, although it expanded considerably during the winter season. Many of the naval officers had their wives and families with them, taking up residence in the town or nearby. All in all, Villefranche was the most popular liberty port in the Mediterranean.

A few miles away, approximately an hour's ride by trolley, was Nice, a much larger city and the most fashionable resort on the Riviera. Unfortu-

The USS *Richmond* and USS *Franklin*, units of the European Squadron, at anchor in the harbor of Villefranche, France, in 1872. *Courtesy of the United States Department of Navy.*

nately, the water off Nice was shallow, and vessels drawing more than fifteen feet had to use Villefranche. For this reason Villefranche was considered the port of Nice. Although warships from many nations anchored there frequently, in the last decades of the nineteenth century only the United States used it as a station. Because of its semipermanent status, the American flagship was always moored to buoy one, the inshore buoy, that was so close one could almost "throw a biscuit on shore."[34]

Nice ran a close second to Villefranche in popularity as a liberty port. "We have had such a nice time in Nice it is a bore to be anywhere else," one young officer wrote home in 1879. Another declared, "This place is given up to gaieties—there is nothing like it in our fashionable places, nor in fact anywhere else in the World."[35]

A major reason for this popularity was the presence of a large number of English and American expatriates and tourists who apparently were just as enthusiastic for the sailors as they were for the city. One officer declared "that it was the presence of Anglo-Americans. . . who made Nice a paradise. . . . Elsewhere in the Mediterranean, the good people who speak, think and act English are few in number. . . . It is therefore revealing no secret to confess our love for Nice, or to admit our admiration for the man who recommended the harbor of Villefranche. . . ." A newspaper correspondent remarked in 1872 that Americans were the most "prominent of the foreign population [in Nice]. Prices have gone up. . . . Hotel keepers depend upon Americans for their customers. . . . The uniform of American naval men is better known than the hat of French soldiers. Nice is a navy yard without the odor of pitch and tar. . . ."[36]

For officers the social season was lively, with theater parties, whist parties, church parties, and dancing parties, as well as sight-seeing tours. "The whole city is alive with dancing parties," one officer exclaimed. "All the hotels give hops and even the pensions where there are large parlors. Four tonight, two last night, and some tomorrow. . . ." The same officer wrote a month later, "Although I haven't sought it, I see a great deal of Nice people, and dine out several times a week. Offers of seats at operas, rooms at two houses, dinners . . . and now and then ceremonies. I am having a splendid time and don't go over to Monaco and don't owe a cent."[37] Commander Cornelius Schoonmaker wrote his father, "You can go to a breakfast, an afternoon reception, a dinner and a ball, all in the same day, and you can do it every day of the week almost, if one's constitution will stand it. . . ." With obvious relief he wrote, "I am rather glad we are going away."[38]

The ships were usually there during Mardi Gras. "This is Ash Wednesday and every one has quieted down after the most hilarious Carnival that the Nice people ever saw before. . . . The 23, 24, and 25 [of February] were devoted to the Carnival, the first I ever witnessed and I assure you I never had a jollier time." This was written by a Marine officer who, after describing the various parades, added, "I was dressed as an old worm during the procession."

It became the custom for the flagship to hold weekly receptions or matinees—popular affairs, especially with the foreign colony. A correspondent reported in 1872 that "on Friday the Admiral and officers of the *Wabash*
'received.' The noble frigate was from two to five devoted to dance and flirta-
tion, to music and luncheon—and such a luncheon." It was customary
throughout the navy for a ship's officers to elect one to be mess officer. The
planning of social functions was usually one of his responsibilities. The *Lancaster's* mess officers in 1878 described a reception:

> About 300 invitations were sent out, and nearly 250 people came. The
> deck was covered with flags and the liveliest flowers, and they danced
> from 2 to 6 o'clock. About half past 4 all came down to our nicely
> carpeted wardroom, and partook of a colation. The usual sandwitches
> [sic], chicken salad, cakes, ices, and punch. The people delighted in
> coming on board, altho it is not unusual for the women to get a little af-
> fected by the motion of the boats coming off from shore. . . . The crowd
> was so dense in the wardroom that it was troublesome attending to so
> many. . . ."[39]

Occasionally members of Congress voiced their disapproval of the social attractions of Villefranche to the American navy. They were most critical of its
proximity to Monte Carlo and its gambling casino. The gambling casino did
attract many of the squadron's officers. The number drawn to the whirling
roulette wheels was probably very small, if for no other reason than their
meager salaries. Nevertheless, it was a problem for the squadron commanders. Admiral William E. Le Roy banned gambling at Monte Carlo and
threatened to "quarantine" any who disobeyed the order. Admiral Samuel R.
Franklin admitted that he had to discipline some of his officers for visiting the
casino too frequently, but he opposed moving the squadron's headquarters
elsewhere because of it. Commander Schoonmaker insisted that "the worse
thing about Nice is the Monte Carlo gambling place at Monaco. . . . it does
much harm."[40]

The Navy Department generally agreed with Schoonmaker's opinion, primarily because of the adverse publicity it gave to the navy; and on at least three
occasions, it seriously considered ordering the squadron's headquarters
moved from Villefranche.[41]

In January 1875, Rear Admiral Daniel Ammens, chief of the Bureau of
Navigation, wrote a confidential memorandum to Secretary of the Navy
George M. Robeson recommending the elimination of the storehouse at Villefranche, and added that "vessels should not be permitted to visit Villefranche
at all except en route. . . . The custom of 'wintering' and especially at Villefranche is believed to be very injurious to the *morale* of the service. It causes
officers of all grades to bring or send out their wives and families. . . . Villefranche is in the immediate vicinity of the most noted gambling place in

Europe. . . . Not only do the families of officers crowd Villefranche, but the vessels of war also, in spite of regulations in port, and in transit. . . ."⁴² Although Robeson apparently did nothing about the report, his successor, Richard Thompson, did order that the headquarters be moved to Lisbon. No explanation was given. The State Department, which was requested to seek permission from the Portuguese government for the port's use, was simply informed that the decision was made "for the best interest of the Naval Service." The squadron commander was told that it was done "after due deliberation, and for reasons deemed conclusive. . . ."⁴³ The *Army and Navy Journal* in its 10 November 1877 issue called gambling the reason for the decision.

Whatever the reason, the decision was a most unpopular one with the officers and men of the squadron. Rear Admiral John L. Worden, in command of the squadron at that time, strongly protested the move, pointing out that for the past six months the squadron had spent most of its time in the eastern Mediterranean and more than likely would be required to spend considerable time there in the future. "With the depot of stores at Lisbon . . . twenty-five hundred miles distant from the Eastern Mediterranean," he wrote, "vessels cruising anywhere on the Station except in the Atlantic where no commander, I think, deemed it important often to send ships, would find it quite impracticable to obtain their supplies from [Lisbon]." The admiral also argued that Villefranche was a better anchorage, that the officers and men much preferred the French port, and, surprisingly, that the gambling establishments in Lisbon were worse than those at Monte Carlo.⁴⁴

Worden's strong opposition to the proposed new rendezvous may have had some effect, for in April 1878 the department informed him that the change was "temporarily suspended." Nevertheless, the Navy Department still wanted the squadron out of Villefranche. In May the State Department was requested to seek the approval of the Italian government to use Spezia. Apparently, the attempt to establish a depot there earlier had been forgotten. Spezia was an Italian naval base, and the Italian government suggested that Leghorn "would be more convenient."⁴⁵ This was not acceptable, and the idea of moving the squadron's headquarters was dropped.

Five years later, Secretary of the Navy William Chandler reopened the removal issue. William Chandler considered the French Riviera, and particularly Villefranche, detrimental to the United States Navy. During his term as naval secretary, he expended a great deal of effort to remove the European Squadron from that place. His papers in the Library of Congress contain several anonymous letters and reports that describe the presence of American vessels there in most critical terms. For example, in 1883 one such letter stated: "It would be well if you sir while in power could personally know the scandal and derision brought upon the American Navy by the spectacle every winter, of a squadron moored at Villefranche for weeks, for the sole apparent purpose of giving a series of dancing parties." Later Chandler would use nearly identical words in reprimanding the commanding officer of the European

Squadron. Chandler was strongly influenced by Commodore Shufeldt, whom he appointed chairman of the naval advisory board in 1882. Shufeldt favored eliminating the European Squadron altogether.[46]

In November 1882, Chandler informed the bureaus of his decision to close the supply depot at Villefranche. They were ordered to have the stores inventoried and disposition made for their removal. The naval secretary ordered the closing of a number of yards and stations in the United States, but the Villefranche facility was the only one on a foreign station.[47]

Not surprisingly, Chandler's decision encountered opposition in the navy. The squadron commander, Rear Admiral James W. A. Nicholson, objected, as did some of the bureau chiefs. Admiral Smith of Provisions and Clothing strongly objected: "It is nothing to say that I think it is unwise," he informed Chandler. "It is something to say that I have yet to hear a valid argument. . . . That there should be some way to supply our vessels abroad whether sailing singly or in squadrons, with home productions, I assume to be an admitted fact." The admiral argued that "storeships" had been tried and given up as inefficient. Many necessary stores and equipment could not be purchased locally except by paying exorbitant prices. He also pointed out that the British navy used the system of establishing storehouses in various parts of the world. Admiral Smith had missed the point, however. Chandler was not going to abandon the entire system of storehouses abroad, but just the one at Villefranche, which he no longer considered necessary as the squadron itself was not necessary.[48]

On 20 July 1883, the storehouse at Villefranche was ordered closed, as soon as the stores could be removed. Admiral Charles H. Baldwin, who replaced Nicholson, was at Hamburg with the *Lancaster* but left immediately for Villefranche, arriving there in the middle of August, where he was joined by the remainder of the squadron. The ships were loaded "to utmost capacity" with stores; the *Quinnebaug* filled her gundeck to the point where it was impossible to handle the guns. The remainder of the stores were sent by chartered steamer to the United States.[49]

Although the squadron was not ordered to abandon its winter rendezvous at Villefranche, the naval secretary did try to reduce the community's attractiveness to many officers. The same month that Chandler directed the closing of the storehouse (July 1883), he issued what became known as the "woman order." Officers attached to vessels on cruising service, particularly on distant stations, were expected to leave their families at their "normal and fixed place of abode," in other words, at home. He warned that any officer who disregarded this injunction would be liable to removal from duty. In explaining this order he wrote to the commander of the Asiatic Squadron:

> You will advise all officers who have relations on the station to send them to a fixed place of abode elsewhere and after you have been there two months will advise me what officers have failed in that regard to meet the

expectations of the Department. It is folly to deny that the presence of families does not affect the movement of ships or the devotion to duty of the officers. I, myself, have visited the largest ship in the Navy, finding the Admiral and Captain absent with ladies, their wives, of course, and the ship in command of a lieutenant commander, at that very date reported to me by both Admiral and Captain as incompetent. It makes little difference to the ships whether the officers are away for good or bad purposes, the injury to the vessel's management and discipline is the same. . . .[50]

The origin of the practice of bringing families abroad is unknown, but in the European Squadron it had become quite common by the 1830s. There was little or no opposition to it before Chandler. On the other hand, on occasion captains received permission to carry their wives as passengers on their vessels to and from the United States, and from port to port. In some instances wives were actually taken on board for the duration of a cruise. Naval secretaries were generally reluctant to grant such privileges, but the political prominence of many officers and their families usually prevailed upon a secretary to grant such a request.[51]

Rear Admiral Goldsborough, while in command of the squadron after the Civil War, told his wife that he would have his flagship's upper deck cabin enlarged if she would join him; she never did. Although Welles opposed it, President Johnson allowed Mrs. Farragut and the flag captain's wife to sail on the *Franklin* with their husbands to Europe. Later the *Frolic* was sent to Stettin to carry the two ladies to Kronstadt to avoid "a very tedious railway journey."[52]

On 26 June 1875, the *Army and Navy Journal* carried a letter from a naval officer concerning the "presence of women and children as residents in our national vessels":

It is but a short time since a watch officer in one of the numerous "family ships" of the Navy on descending from the deck to indulge in his . . . meal found the steam heater in the vicinage of his seat at the wardroom table occupied as a species of patent drier for sundry small articles known as "diapers," emitting odors, which, if not in the highest degree appetizing, were at all events peculiar! . . . In one of the ships on a certain foreign station a few years since nearly every married officer in the ward-room mess had his wife double bunked on board at some period of the cruise. . . . It is said that during summer months the ward-room of this vessel at gray of dawn presented a sight both novel and amusing. Ladies' stockings hanging over the backs of chairs, corsets and flannel petticoats, false braids, crinoline and mayhap, patent articles for beautifying the person, scattered about in much admired disorder. . . .

The London *Army and Navy Gazette*, quoting this letter, pointed out that in the British navy regulations against such practices were strictly enforced. It went on to say: "The *Franklin* and the *Congress* of the European squadron are 'full of women' and it is said that the Captain has three daughters on board the latter."[53] One officer mentioned in a letter to his wife that junior officers "were rather glad" when the wives decided to travel by land from one port to another so that they could use the vacated rooms. Another declared that the whole thing was greatly exaggerated for "the officers are older and dislike women on board ship as a general rule."[54]

Rear Admiral Thomas O. Selfridge, Jr., referred to his tour with the European Squadron as "almost like yachting," since it was evidently rather common for naval vessels to serve as private yachts for the social convenience of captains and their families. During certain seasons (called the winter or "gale" season by commanding officers and the "party" season by others), it frequently became difficult for the department to move ships from unofficial headquarters such as Yokohama, Rio, and Villefranche, where the families tended to congregate.[55]

In 1881 Rear Admiral D. M. Fairfax sought permission to take his family on board the flagship when he assumed command of the European Squadron, "the privilege having been extended in other cases," but was curtly refused. He subsequently asked to be relieved of the command and retired from the service. The embittered admiral revealed to the newspapers what happened, and the publicity that followed persuaded Secretary of the Navy William Hunt to issue an order forbidding women from residing or being carried as passengers on board naval vessels.[56]

Early in January 1885, Secretary Chandler received an anonymous letter from a supposed American resident of the Grand Hotel in Nice. This letter accused unnamed officers from the *Lancaster* of denouncing publicly a recent order from the Navy Department sending the vessel to the Congo and claiming that the order was given because Admiral Earl English and his officers had ignored the order about wives and families in foreign ports. The officer also allegedly said that the *Lancaster* would not leave Villefranche until the "season was over." On the basis of this letter, Chandler ordered English to interview the *Lancaster's* officers and forward to him the name of the one responsible for the statement. In accordance with what was considered to be standard procedure in a matter involving a ship's crew, the admiral passed the order on to the commanding officer, who made an investigation and reported that all of his officers denied making such a statement.[57]

On 3 March, Chandler wrote English angrily accusing him of not carrying out his order to "interrogate directly all the officers of the *Lancaster*." "The original error," he informed the admiral, "was in taking the vessels to Villefranche for the purpose of instituting a series of social affairs, entertainments, and exposing the officers to the vices of Nice and Monaco contrary to the decided policy of the Department which no one understood better than yourself."[58] English was then ordered to the command of the South Atlantic

Squadron (the old Brazil Squadron), which was at the time considered the least desirable of the foreign stations.

English reacted strongly to the naval secretary's actions. "Neither she [*Quinnebaug*] nor the *Lancaster* were ordered to Villefranche for any social purpose whatever," he wrote Chandler. He also defended Villefranche: "It is, in my opinion, decidedly the best port on the whole station. . . . I have yet to learn that any of my predecessors, who repeatedly made it their winter quarters, ever occurred the displeasure of the Department for so doing." Finally, he defended the social activities of his officers: "The entertainment on board the *Lancaster* consisted merely of afternoon Receptions . . . [held] once in two weeks. . . ." English's letter arrived after William Whitney had replaced Chandler as secretary of the navy; in spite of efforts by various officers (including Rear Admiral Fairfax), the order was not changed, and English left for the South Atlantic Squadron.[59]

The press on both sides of the Atlantic followed the controversy with a great deal of interest. On 7 February, the New York *Times* condemned Chandler's actions. In an article entitled "The Wicked Wives of the *Lancaster*," the paper remarked with tongue in cheek,

> It has frequently happened that the wives of the officers of the Mediter-
> ranean Squadron have visited ports where the vessels were lying. These
> wives have even been seen to meet their husbands and converse with
> them, and it can be proved that on several occasions they have induced
> their husbands to spend their time ashore in their company instead of
> spending it in gambling saloons or in general dissipation. Such a state of
> things was too terrible to be allowed to exist. It threatened not only the
> morality of our naval officers but the safety of our ships.

Another paper asserted that a "gross injustice" had been done to Admiral English and the *Lancaster's* officers. "As to the reception which so disturbed the soul of the Secretary," it said, "we learn that the only receptions on board the *Lancaster* were those given by the officers of the ship, and the presence or absence of their wives had nothing whatever to do with them being given."

On the whole, most newspapers as well as naval officers were critical of Chandler's order. There were exceptions, however, several senior officers congratulated the naval secretary for it.[60] Chandler's successor rescinded the order a few months after taking office, and the custom of wives following their husbands to distant stations has continued to the present.[61] Also, the European Squadron once again observed the social season in Villefranche, and the matinees were resumed with their usual popularity. Rear Admiral Samuel R. Franklin, who replaced English in command of the squadron, justified them: "It gives me pleasure to grant them every facility for visiting the ships. . . . In the low state of our merchant marine just now, it is about the only way they can experience the pleasure of seeing our flag in foreign waters."[62]

Villefranche survived as a rendezvous despite Chandler's disapproval, but only for a few years. In 1889 the station itself was abandoned. The administration of Benjamin Harrison, which came to power in 1889, was committed to overseas expansion, and Secretary of the Navy Benjamin Tracy played a prominent role in this policy. The naval secretary was primarily interested in obtaining coal and supply depots beyond American territorial limits. There was little concern, however, for seeking naval facilities in European waters. When Whitelaw Reid, the American minister to France, approached the State Department about a coaling depot in the Azores, Secretary of State James G. Blaine responded, "There are only three places that are of value enough to be taken that are not continental. One is Hawaii and the others are Cuba and Porto Rico. . . ."[63] The naval secretary agreed, advising the president against going beyond the Western Hemisphere in the Atlantic.

To many naval officers the 1870s and 1880s were the nadir of the United States Navy. It may well be, as some writers have suggested, that the navy of the post-Civil War years was adequate so far as its peacetime responsibilities were concerned, but it was handicapped because of the decline in the number of commissioned vessels, a decline that continued throughout the period.[64] In spite of this fact, however, the European Squadron's responsibilities increased during these years.

In 1871, Secretary of the Navy George M. Robeson wrote in his annual report that the number of vessels available for duty on the distant stations, "forty three (43) . . . [is] too small in number, and too weak in character, force, and condition to perform the service required."[1] After 1865 an increasingly parsimonious Congress, at least where naval affairs were concerned, began to reduce appropriations. This was not the result of antimilitarism, but a result of the usual demobilization of armed forces in the United States at the end of a conflict and also a general lack of interest in the navy, both officially and in the public media.[2] To most members of Congress it seemed that the navy evidently could carry out its assignments, including distant cruising, without significant increases in appropriations. Unfortunately, it became more difficult to maintain, much less increase, the number of vessels in commission. Members of Congress also began to suggest that distant squadrons were an unnecessary luxury. In 1867 Congress passed a resolution to inquire into "reducing our foreign squadrons to the number of ships and guns that were in service before the war." The following year, during a debate over naval appropriations, Senator George F. Edmunds of Vermont said, "Now, we all know that the Navy, since the necessity of maintaining the blockade and chasing pirates has been over, have only had a holiday season. . . . I think that we can indulge in a little less gala parade on the ocean and lay up more of our vessels. . . ." Representative Samuel S. "Sunset" Cox echoed these sentiments in the House: "There is not an American merchant vessel east of Marseilles; but our squadron has its rendezvous at Nice or Ville Franca. They spend our money lavishly, and we pay it—in gold! . . . The cruise is for three years; so that at the end of that time the Government will have paid out for the purpose of letting its officers and their families see Europe, $2,355,000. . . . Our people can rest assured that their European Squadron is naught else but a picnic for which they must pay the bills."[3] The foreign squadrons were not withdrawn, but in the face of Congressional retrenchment they could not be strengthened either. Commodore C. R. R. Rodgers, chief of the Bureau of Yards and Docks, in some despair, wrote that "the Department is at its wits end to find vessels fit to go to sea, to relieve those now abroad."[4]

In 1873 there were only thirty-eight ships in commission that were considered seagoing. Eight years later, of 140 vessels in commission, all but 31 were unserviceable, and the remainder were in constant need of repair. By 1884 the United States ranked twelfth in quantity among the world's fleets and probably below that in quality. In fact, the greatest weakness of the navy during these years lay not just in the number of vessels in commission but in the lack of a modernization program that incorporated the important changes in naval technology. The annual report of the secretary of the navy in 1882 noted that of 2,664 guns mounted on the various vessels, 2,233 were smooth-bore muzzle loaders. The decline of the navy during this period is an oft-repeated tale of obsolete wooden vessels carrying obsolete guns with auxiliary sail. Some new vessels were added to the navy, but as one authority has recently stressed, they were obsolete in design and armament when they were built.[5]

Naval officers, particularly those serving on the European Station, became increasingly conscious of their obsolete ships. One officer in the *Marion* wrote from Villefranche: "The harbor here has ten immense foreign ships of war. . . and we with our unpainted sides make a sorry figure . . . it makes me sorry to think we are such small potatoes compared to them. . . ." An ensign joined the flagship *Trenton* (one of the vessels built in the 1870s) at Gibraltar and described his letdown: "I cannot tell you how disappointed I am in the *Trenton*. I had hoped to get at least on board a ship of war which might at least be not sneered at in the comparison of our ships with those of foreign navies—but alas! The *Trenton* is a failure comparatively. . . . So help me Bob if I can respectably do it, I am not going to sea in a United States man of war until one is built fit to be called such."[6] The *Trenton* did have electric lights, the first U.S. man-of-war to have that convenience.

The European Squadron was affected by the navy's decay. Although it remained the most powerful of the distant squadrons in the 1870s, it declined in numbers from eight ships in 1871 to five in 1873. By the mid-1880s it had dropped to two. Throughout most of this period the squadron was severely taxed in its responsibility of protecting American interests in a cruising station that included Europe, the Near East, and a large portion of coastal Africa. These were years of war and revolution in Western Europe and the Near East, and the drive by European powers to partition Africa was just getting into full swing. Late in August 1868, the United States minister to Spain, John P. Hale, wrote to Seward, "We are on the eve of some important movement in Spain." Minister Hale's premonition proved correct. Less than a month later, on 18 September, Admiral Juan Bautista Topete y Carballo issued a manifesto denouncing the existing regime and called for revolution. The revolution that followed was so successful that within two weeks Queen Isabella fled into exile, a constitution was promulgated, and a search was initiated for a new ruler. This search not only was responsible for continuing unrest in Spain, but also was the immediate cause of war between France and Prussia. The European Squadron, only recently returned from Farragut's Near Eastern cruise, was ordered to Spanish waters. The *Franklin* went to Barcelona, the *Frolic* to Cadiz, and the *Swatara* to Malaga. Captain A. M. Pennock was temporarily in command of the squadron at this time. He had been Farragut's flag captain and took the command when Farragut left for the United States in October 1868. Then in March 1869, Rear Admiral William Radford relieved Pennock. The command had been offered to Vice Admiral David D. Porter, but he declined it because of "ill-health." His health was not good, but Welles was convinced that Porter preferred remaining in command of the Naval Academy because of his increasing interest in political affairs.[7] On 10 August 1870, Radford was relieved by Rear Admiral Oliver S. Glisson. Neither Radford nor Glisson were well known outside naval circles, but both were respected by their contemporaries in the service. Radford, a Virginian, was in command of the *Cumberland* when she was destroyed by the Confederate ironclad *Virginia* in Hampton Roads. He later commanded the *New Ironsides* and at the end of the war led the James River division of the North Atlantic Blockading Squadron. Glisson was in command of the League Island Navy Yard when he received orders to the European Squadron. One of Glisson's officers wrote that "Glisson plays the Admiral with moderation and respectability— much more so than many men thought to be his superior. . . ."[8]

Throughout the winter of 1868–69, while Pennock was in command, the squadron remained in Spanish waters; the only trouble occurred when a small party of Americans were fired upon during street fighting in Malaga and had to take refuge on board the *Swatara*.[9] Admiral Glisson hoped to resume normal cruising when he assumed the command in the spring, but the outbreak of a revolution in Cuba forced him to keep most of the squadron in or near Spanish waters. Incidents involving American merchant vessels in Cuban waters resulted in some concern in Washington that the two nations were drifting toward a possible conflict. One British correspondent wrote that the "existing unsatisfactory relation between Spain and America" and the "unsettled state of Spain" caused the British Mediterranean Squadron to cancel a cruise to Malta in order to remain at Gibraltar.[10] In the spring of 1870 the number of warships retained in Spanish waters was reduced, and when Admiral Radford relieved Glisson in August, he reported that in the future he would keep only one ship along the Spanish coast.[11] However, even this vessel was removed in the fall of 1870 with the outbreak of war between France and Germany.

The Franco-Prussian war resulted from the efforts of Otto von Bismarck, the Prussian chancellor, to unify Germany. Convinced that only a conflict with France would accomplish his goal, he manipulated the controversy over the vacant Spanish throne into the desired war. In July 1870, the war broke out.

The *Army and Navy Journal* remarked that we had no alternative but to send warships into the Baltic Sea and North Sea to protect our commerce. However, only one vessel was deployed in those waters, and even this was delayed over a month because of an outbreak of smallpox in the squadron. On 26 August, Commander Stephen B. Luce in the screw sloop-of-war *Juanita* was ordered to Helgoland and then to cruise off the mouths of the Elbe and Weser, but not to penetrate the French blockade. In addition to the responsibility of protecting American commerce, Luce was to gather intelligence about the "strength, condition, and performance" of the French fleet.[12]

In September, the French vessels abandoned the blockade, and the *Juanita* entered Wilhelmshaven. A few days later the *Plymouth* arrived at Kiel. The two American vessels were the first to report the blockade lifted. This was the first time that American warships had entered a German port since 1867. Although the northern waters were in the European squadron's station, the ships rarely ventured that far north.[13]

The war went badly for France from the beginning, and the European Squadron had to concentrate many of its vessels on the French coast. Late in September the *Juantia* left the Baltic and entered Le Havre. Luce reported that there were several American merchantmen in the harbor and American property in the city worth over two million dollars. He later wrote, "the presence here of an American man of war has had far more moral effect than I could have believed possible. . . ."[14] By mid-September the German army had destroyed most of the French opposition in front of it and had reached the outskirts of Paris. Before the German investment of Paris was complete, thousands had fled, including the representatives of foreign governments. The one exception to this was the U.S. minister, Elihu Washburne.

At Washburne's request, the Navy Department continued to concentrate the European Squadron in or near French waters. The *Shenandoah* was sent to Antwerp, the *Plymouth* to Bordeaux, the *Guerriere* to Marseilles, and the *Franklin* to Villefranche. Evidently the Prussian government became uneasy over the presence of American warships in French ports, for Baron Gerolt, the Kaiser's minister in Washington, requested in an interview with Secretary of State Hamilton Fish that the "naval force of the U.S. be not turned to encourage France to resist fair terms of adjustment." Fish, who mentions this remark in his diary, does not give further details to explain the Prussian's odd request.[15]

The complications arising out of the Franco-Prussian War strained the squadron's limited resources. When rioting broke out in southern France, after the overthrow of Napoleon III's government, vessels had to be sent to Nice and Marseilles. The squadron commander reported to the Navy Department that

during the winter it was necessary to keep vessels stationed at Marseilles and Nice. At Nice because there was a large American colony very

many of whom were invalids, demociled there, who clamored for a vessel
of war and who were alarmed at the idea of being left for a day without a
place of refuge in time of trouble. At Marseilles because the Consul was
in a chronic state of alarm, although but two American families, his own,
and that of a ship chandler were residents of that port, and there was not a
single American flag flying in the harbor. . . .[16]

To further tax the squadron, vessels were required in other European countries.

When French troops were withdrawn from Rome, where they had been
since 1867, the American minister, fearful of an outbreak of rioting, requested
the presence of a warship in Italian waters. In November 1870, General
Daniel Sickles, U.S. minister to Spain, wrote to Admiral Glisson that he
feared "serious disturbances" would break out over the coming election of a
ruler and asked that the squadron "or at least a part of it" be stationed "where
I can communicate with the commanding officer. . . ."[17] The *Brooklyn* was
ordered to Cadiz, and the minister was promised that additional vessels would
be sent when needed.

In 1870 the Navy Department decided to divide the European Squadron,
and to redesignate it the "European Fleet." That portion deployed in the
Mediterranean was designated the "Mediterranean Squadron" with a commodore in command. Presumably, the admiral would command the division of
the "Fleet" operating along the Atlantic coast of Europe. Apparently this reorganization came about because the department feared that the admiral
would not be able to handle the squadron effectively if problems developed at
the same time in the Mediterranean and along the Atlantic coast. A divided
command, it was felt, would decrease the communication problem and provide
far more effective use of the individual vessels.

Commodore I. R. Mullany was appointed to command the Mediterranean
Squadron. In February 1871, Mullany wrote to Rear Admiral Charles S.
Boggs that he had received the assignment some four months before; but he still
was awaiting instructions "defining any position, limits of command, etc."
These instructions were supposed to come from the Navy Department.[18]

Rear Admiral Boggs had relieved Glisson of the fleet command in January.
He opposed the reorganization, considering it impractical. As he wrote Mullany, "there are but two vessels . . . now in the Mediterraean, out of which to
form a Mediterranean squadron." Perhaps a more candid reason was that
Boggs himself preferred to remain in the Mediterranean with his flagship. With
some reluctance Boggs did agree that, during his absence from the Mediterranean, Mullany would command the vessels left there.[19] At that time the admiral with the *Franklin* was at Villefranche while Mullany in the *Richmond*
was at Marseilles.

Mullany was understandably unhappy with the arrangement: "I am constrained to say that I cannot feel that I should be deprived of the command of a

squadron, when the Department ordered assigning me one. . . . I therefore respectfully ask that the vessels in the Mediterranean (irrespective of the flagship) may be assigned to my squadron." This arrangement was clearly unthinkable, and Boggs simply ignored the request. The admiral's obvious refusal to implement the department's instructions did not result in a sharp response from his superiors. No effort was made to see that the order was carried out, more than likely because of the difficulty of controlling the distant squadrons from Washington.

Mullany did command the Mediterranean vessels briefly while Boggs was in the Atlantic. In July 1871, the *Guerriere* ran aground in Italian waters and was badly damaged before she could be floated free. Mullany, who was under orders to sail to the United States, did not investigate the accident but instead left with the *Richmond* for England. When Boggs found out, he ordered Mullany back to the Mediterranean to conduct a court of inquiry concerning the *Guerriere* incident. "The efforts of Commodore Mullany to run away from the Commander in Chief, caused at least a ten day delay in ordering the Court of Inquiry," Boggs confided to his brother and added, "I say ran away and *neglect his duties* is self evident."[20] The European commander threatened to report Mullany to the department, but if he did, it had little effect. Three years later Mullany was promoted to rear admiral and appointed to command the North Atlantic Squadron. When Mullany did leave the European station, the idea of a two-squadron "fleet" was abandoned.

One reason that the department favored dividing the squadron was to persuade Admiral Boggs to concentrate the bulk of his force (presumably including the flagship) along the western coast of Europe. Boggs, like most of the squadron commanders, preferred the balmy Mediterranean to the bleak North Sea. In accordance with prevailing policy to allow squadron commanders as much discretion as possible in cruising schedules, there was hesitation about ordering him to leave the Mediterranean. Nevertheless, in January 1871, Secretary Robeson wrote "the interests of our countrymen on the northern part of the European Station particularly at this time when war prevails between two great powers . . . require that some of our ships of war should be constantly in that quarter. . . ." Boggs was also gently reprimanded for keeping most of his vessels in the Mediterranean. The admiral defended his actions:

> to answer the requirement of all the consuls upon this Station would necessitate the presence of the whole United States Navy. . . . I beg the Department to believe that in my disposition of the vessels of this fleet, I have acted according to the best dictates of my judgment. . . . Grave events have succeeded each other with such startling rapidity . . . that it was impossible always to have the right ship in the right place, but when difficulties were anticipated, or as soon as possible after the intelligence of trouble was received, a vessel has been dispatched to the threatened point without delay. . . .

In conclusion, the admiral expressed his belief in the futility of protecting American interests under existing conditions: "The only real service (aside from the moral effect its presence might provide) a vessel of war could render to American citizens, in case of riot or civil war, would be to serve as a place of refuge for them. . . . Landing an armed force would certainly bring on a conflict with one party or the other. . . ."[21] Boggs clearly recognized the dilemma he faced in trying to protect American interests, a dilemma that would face commanders of all the foreign squadrons.

In the fall of 1871, Rear Admiral James Alden came out in the *Wabash* to relieve Boggs.[22] Alden, a fifth-generation *Mayflower* descendant, was unanimously liked and respected in the navy. He was with both Farragut and Porter during the Civil War. He led the van in Farragut's sortie at Mobile Bay and was with Porter in the attack on Fort Fisher. Porter said that Alden had more tact and less temper than any other officer in his fleet. Welles characterized him as a "sycophant and courtier" but liked him and appointed him Chief of the Bureau of Navigation after the war. A Confederate naval officer and former U.S. naval officer called him "a good seaman, a skillful, courtly and accomplished officer," but Rear Admiral Samuel R. Franklin referred to him as a "pleasant fellow, but somehow, he never seemed to me to be serious about anything. It always appeared to me that he regarded life and all there was in it as an immense joke."[23] Nevertheless, he took his duties seriously, and junior officers seldom saw him crack a smile through his bushy black moustache.

Thje steam frigate *Wabash* had served as Rear Admiral Samuel Du Pont's flagship while he commanded the South Atlantic Blockading Squadron during the Civil War. Although not as large as the *Franklin*, which had been the flagship of the European Squadron since Farragut relieved Goldsborough, she was a good "sailor" and representative of the type of vessel that carried the flag in the various overseas squadrons.

When Alden took command of the squadron, the European situation was beginning to ease. The Franco-Prussian War had ended with the signing of the Treaty of Frankfort in May; by the fall of 1871 France had completed the metamorphosis from empire to republic; and Germany and Italy were finally unified nations.

Even relations with Great Britain improved with the settlement of the *Alabama* claims. Diplomatic difficulties that had developed during the Civil War, particularly over depredations by Confederate raiders, had continued to plague the two nations afterwards. At times the possibility of war worried the statesmen of both countries. In 1869, when the Senate rejected the first attempt to settle the claims, Lord Clarendon reported to Queen Victoria, "There is not the slightest doubt that if we were engaged in a Continental quarrel we should immediately find ourselves at war with the United States."[24] The deadlock between the two countries continued into the summer of 1872, presumably because the United States demanded compensation for losses suffered during the war. Irresponsible talk of possible conflict resulted in a sharp fall in prices on both the American and the British stock exchanges.

The European Squadron, which had spent the winter months at anchor in Villefranche, was ordered to remain there indefinitely, for what reason no one, including Alden, was sure. One correspondent wrote, "The European Fleet is here waiting for something to turn up, whether for a war with Spain, England, or a new Admiral." General William Tecumseh Sherman on a tour of the world had expected to accompany the *Wabash* on its scheduled visit to ports in the eastern Mediterranean. He was left stranded in Naples for several weeks because of Alden's orders. In disgust he wrote to Admiral Porter, "You can imagine my surprise and mortification. . . . There are six ships lying at anchor—have been three months . . . and I am denied the use of one. There is surely no war, or rumor of war here—of course we can have a naval war with Spain or England if we wish it but there is no occasion for one and the keeping [of] our ships shut up in Ville Franche is a timid, weak, bad policy. . . . poor Spain is to be pitied not provoked. . . . So is England." Sherman also described some British ironclads that he saw at Malta: "much superior to ours . . . *Wabash* a baby alongside some of them."[25] The British Admiralty agreed and was so confident of naval superiority in a war with the United States that it gradually reduced its squadron in American waters between 1869 and 1873. The First Lord wrote confidentially to Earl Russell that "the Americans have nothing with which they could think of crossing the Atlantic to attack us. . . ."[26]

Looking back at the growing disparity between the two navies, it seems a little ludicrous that Alden was holding fleet maneuvers off the southern coast of France with his six wooden vessels. With some pride he reported to Secretary Robeson that "while none of us ever had any experience in fleet sailing, . . . yet the evolutions were on a general thing performed . . . highly satisfactory."[27] Early in July Alden was allowed to assign his ships to various cruising stations, but he was warned to prepare for rapid concentration if necessary.

This need, so far as possible trouble with Great Britain was concerned, disappeared after the summer of 1872. A tribunal meeting in Geneva awarded the United States a total of $15,500,000 in damages for the *Alabama* claims and the British government reluctantly accepted the decision.

In June 1872, Alden with four ships of the squadron stopped off at Lisbon to take on coal before making a cruise in northern European waters. While he was there the American minister to Spain, General Daniel Sickles, requested that the squadron remain at Lisbon for a few days. Without elaborating, he wrote, "it will probably help in the disposition of some important questions I am now urging on this government." Alden sailed with the *Wabash* but left three vessels in the Tagus with orders not to sail until Sickles agreed. The admiral also promised to visit a Spanish port with his entire fleet in the near future.[28]

In the fall of 1872 Alden sent the bulk of his squadron to the eastern Mediterranean because of trouble in the Ottoman Empire. Early in 1873 the admiral prepared to follow with his flagship when he received a dispatch from Sickles: "Important to American interest that you come to Barcelona with Fleet." The Spanish ruler had just abdicated, and the American minister feared another outbreak of unrest. Alden, however, was convinced that the Turkish situation was more pressing. Leaving only one vessel on the Spanish coast, he sailed eastward and did not return to the western Mediterranean until shortly before he was relieved of the European command.

An outbreak of anti-Christian rioting in Constantinople and Beirut was the reason the European Squadron hurried off to the Near East. The American minister to the Ottoman Empire, George Boker, under missionary pressure, appealed for warships, and Admiral Alden dispatched the *Congress* to the eastern Mediterranean followed by other units of the squadron shortly afterwards.

The *Congress* was ordered to Constantinople. Minister Boker applied to the Turkish government for permission for the American vessel to pass through the Straits, but the request was denied. After Admiral Farragut's flagship, the *Franklin*, had visited the city in the fall of 1868, the Ottoman government had circulated a note to the representatives of the foreign powers, including the United States, that in the future only light vessels (under 800 tons) would be allowed to enter the Dardanelles.[29] The *Congress* was considerably larger than 800 tons.

For some time the Straits question had been under discussion by American and Turkish officials. In November 1870, Alexander II of Russia, taking advantage of the Franco-Prussian War, announced the abrogation of the Black Sea clauses of the Treaty of Paris of 1856, which had neutralized that inland sea. British concern over this, along with Russian desires to reopen the Straits, led to a convocation of European powers in London in the spring of 1871. Earlier the Russian minister in Washington sounded out Secretary of State Hamilton Fish's attitude towards the Straits question and asked whether the newly appointed minister to Russia had any instructions on this question. Although Fish answered negatively, within six months he was instructing the American minister in Constantinople to do anything he could unofficially "to facilitate the opening of the Dardanelles."[30]

Fish was clearly sympathetic to the Russian position relative to freedom of passage. He was shocked and angered, however, when the Russian minister informed the Czar that in case of an Anglo-Russian war, the U.S. would be willing to send a naval force into the Black Sea in support of Russia and that because of the "*Alabama* case," an alliance with Russia would be welcomed. Fish publicly denied the minister's declaration, which caused the American government little embarrasment.[31]

Considerable correspondence passed back and forth in 1871 between Washington and Constantinople concerning the Straits question, and Fish reiterated that it "is under serious consideration." Nevertheless, when the European powers meeting in London reaffirmed the principle of closure of the Straits, the United States generally accepted it. In a note to the American minister in Turkey in May 1871, and again two years later, Fish outlined what has been recognized as the American policy towards the Straits question until after World War I:

> The abstract right of the Turkish Government to obstruct the navigation of the Dardanelles even to vessels of war in time of peace, is a serious question. The right, however, has for a long time been claimed and has been sanctioned by treaties between Turkey and certain European states. A proper occasion may arise for us to dispute the applicability of the claim to United States men-of-war. Meanwhile it is deemed expedient to acquiesce in the exclusion.[32]

The frigate *Guerriere* was refused permission to enter the Straits in June 1871. The *Army and Navy Journal* referred to this as a "test case." If so, it illustrates the fact that the United States had no intention of challenging Turkish closure of the Straits.[33]

This policy was made explicitly clear when the *Congress* was refused permission. Minister Boker notified the State Department of this decision, and mentioned that he was surprised at the request for permission, as he had received no instructions concerning the proposed visit. The Ottoman government was also surprised and evidently alarmed, for military forces at the entrance to the Straits were alerted to prevent any attempt to force the Straits by an American warship. Blaque Bey, the Turkish minister in Washington, made an unusual Sunday morning call on Secretary Fish at his home. The minister was assured that the request was unauthorized. Fish then called a hurried meeting with the Secretary of the Navy, where a dispatch was drawn up and later sent off to Admiral Alden: "Don't dare to send ships to Constantinople. Must not ask permission for passage through the Dardanelles."[34] The European Squadron commander had not known that authorization was required from the State Department to seek passage through the Straits. He was under orders to send warships into Turkish waters to protect American interests, and Constantinople was one of the scenes of anti-Christian rioting.

As an anticlimax to this affair, two weeks later a shot was fired across the bow of a French steamer as she approached the Straits. The ship's captain sent a boat ashore and discovered that the senior Turkish officer there believed the vessel to be an American warship attempting to force the Straits. Fish was understandably alarmed over this incident: "While the U.S. . . . is disposed to respect the traditional sensibility of the Porte as to that passage, the shot which it is supposed may have been intended for a National vessel of this Government might . . . have precipitated a . . . serious complication."[35]

George Boker, in Constantinople, was equally alarmed. To make matters worse, the coded telegram he received from the State Department informed him that the *Congress*'s visit was authorized. The minister, however, asked for a clarification and discovered that the original dispatch had been incorrectly coded, making "it read in precisely the contrary sense which its writer intended." Boker, a personal friend of Fish, admonished him to instruct the clerk "to write the cipher in Roman capital letters, marking the space distinctly between each group of ciphers . . . as the correct transmission of telegrams in cipher is a matter of grave importance."[36]

Boker was a well-known playwright, poet, and man of letters. A Quaker, he was unusually sympathetic to the Turks and instinctively opposed a policy of threatening force to back up diplomacy. When a minor incident occurred at Beirut, the American consul there sent a telegram to the secretary of state, "Redress refused. Order gunboat to Alexandretta." When his rather peremptory message was ignored, he sent what can only be described as an impudent demand to his superior: "I trust . . . that the Department will so represent the matter to the Hon. Secretary of the Navy, that he may order a ship of war to visit this coast soon, and take time enough to visit the ports of Haifa, Acre, Tyre, Sidon, Tripoli, Latakia, Mersine, and Alexandretta so that the local government shall for once in their lives, see an American war vessel, and desist in their attempts to overawe our citizens. . . ."[37]

In a confidential letter to Fish, Boker wrote:

> We have a young idiot of a Consul General at Beirut who gives me a great deal of trouble. . . . On the slightest show of a disagreement with the Turks he at once arrays himself in decided hostility to the authorities, bullies, threatens, demands . . . talks like an ass about sending for the whole American fleet, and deports himself generally like a madman. From his last despatch to me, I perceive that not long ago he without consultation with me, telegraphed to the Department to send a gunboat to Alexandretta. Such mid-summer madness I never heard of. The occasion warranted nothing of the kind, and I trust that hereafter, you will neither be startled nor moved to action by any request that Mr. Hay may make of you, until you have consulted with me.

Evidently, "Mr. Hay's" indiscretions did not cease, for the Turkish government made an official complaint. In reporting this to Fish, Boker wrote that "whenever Mr. Hay gets into a difficulty with the Turkish authorities, he utters the following threats: In mild cases, he threatens to send for a gunboat, in grave cases for a frigate, and in very aggravated cases, for the whole American fleet."[38]

Boker might deplore the necessity for requesting the presence of American warships in Turkish waters, but he found himself increasingly obligated to do so. Anti-Christian unrest and riots occurred periodically during his tenure in Constantinople, and he apparently felt that he had no other recourse but to appeal for naval protection. He even suggested stationing permanently a warship in Constantinople. In a personal note to Fish pointing out some of the difficulties that he was having with Ottoman officials, Boker wrote: "My brother ministers tell me that I must bully; but what would be the result of that course if my threats were disregarded, for I have no means of power. All the other nations keep a gunboat, or stationnaire as it is called, in the Bosphorus permanently."[39] Fish was not interested; and even if he had been, there is not the slightest possibility that the Turkish government would have approved it. Boker also tried to persuade Admiral Alden to station units of the European Squadron permanently in the eastern Mediterranean, but increasing tension with Spain prevented it.

Admiral Alden returned to Villefranche with his squadron in the spring of 1873, having spent nearly six months in the eastern Mediterranean. In June he was relieved of the European command by Rear Admiral Ludlow Case. When Alden sailed for home, he took three of the squadron with him. Within a month an additional vessel was detached, leaving Case with four ships to carry out the squadron's responsibilities. One of the vessels, the *Shenandoah*, was in Spanish waters, left there by Alden when he sailed east. In July the American warship was at anchor in Cadiz when word was received that a Spanish naval mutiny had occurred at Cartagena, where two warships seized by the mutineers were headed for Cadiz.

A conference of commanding officers of various foreign warships in the port took place. At first a majority of the officers agreed to order the Spanish vessels to anchor outside the harbor if they should appear. This was discarded when diplomatic representatives warned them that such action might endanger foreigners in the city. One of the Spanish vessels did enter the harbor, and the *Shenandoah's* captain, Charles H. Wells, wrote later that he "should have been delighted to have captured her. . . . I had my guns cast loose on the side she passed."[40] Robley D. Evans, later admiral and at that time the *Shenandoah's* navigator, states in his memoir *A Sailor's Log* that the "council" of foreign commanding officers requested Wells to blow up the Spanish vessel if it attempted to enter the harbor, and that Wells agreed and actually anchored close to her. There is no evidence to support Evans' statement; and if Wells did indeed agree to this action, it was never carried out. Wells, however, did engage in certain unneutral acts such as giving refuge to Spanish officers. Sickles protested to Admiral Case and also requested him to concentrate the entire squadron in Spanish waters. The admiral refused unless so "directed by higher authority," but he did order the *Wachusett* to Barcelona. At Sickles' insistence, "higher authority" did so order. On 4 August, during a cabinet meeting, President Grant agreed to order the entire squadron into Spanish waters, "instructing the commanders of the vessels that they would be expected to offer protection to American citizens and property, but that they should not voluntarily interfere between the contending parties."[41]

Case arrived at Barcelona on 15 August and immediately ordered the *Wachusett* to Cadiz and the *Shenandoah* to Cartagena. The admiral cautioned his ship commanders (particularly Wells) not to intervene in the insurrection. "Our policy as a neutral," he wrote, "is one of peace and we have no right to interfere." Wells came very close to disobeying these instructions. He allowed a number of Spanish naval officers to come on board his ship for a brief period and later followed one of the Spanish warships out of the harbor. When Case questioned these actions, Wells hastened to reply that he followed the Spanish ship only in case she "committed any act of piracy."[42]

Case had discretionary authority to disperse the squadron whenever he considered that the Spanish situation had eased enough to justify it. With the exception of the *Shenandoah*, wisely ordered to the North African coast before Wells committed additional indiscreet actions, the squadron remained on the Spanish coast until early November 1873. At that time he received a dispatch from Washington to return to Villfranche immediately and await orders. A war with Spain was likely, and the American warships cleared Spanish waters quickly.

The rebellion against Spanish rule in Cuba, which had broken out in 1868, had resulted in a number of incidents involving American interests; property was destroyed, merchant vessels seized, and filibustering expeditions organized. The American public, sympathetic to the Cuban cause, began to agitate for intervention. For month after month, the Spanish government made promises to improve the Cuban situation, but nothing came of them. On 15 October, an exasperated Secretary Fish warned the Spanish government "that the present state of things cannot last. Our patience and endurance are sorely tried."[43] In less than a month Fish's prognostication became a reality when an American steamer, the *Virginius*, was captured by a Spanish cruiser near Cuba with a large party of revolutionists and a cargo of arms on board. On 7 and 8 November, fifty-three passengers and crew members, including the American captain, were summarily shot as pirates. It was the news of this which caused the Navy Department to hurry the European Squadron out of Spanish waters. The squadron remained at Villefranche only long enough to take on coal and provisions before sailing for Key West, Florida.

American naval strategy did not encompass the possibility of having to fight a war outside the western hemisphere. The distant squadrons were not normally prepared for this eventuality. Needless to say, the European Squadron was far too weak to challenge Spanish naval power in home waters. Cuba was the decisive point, and it was therefore decided to concentrate naval forces as close to the island as possible.

Early in January 1874, the European Squadron rendezvoused at Key West with other squadrons and vessels, altogether totalling five frigates, fourteen smaller wooden vessels, six monitors, and assorted auxiliaries. Admiral Case, as senior officer present, was placed in command of this combined naval force.

Rear Admiral George A. Scott, in command of the North Atlantic Squadron, which included Key West in its cruising station, was somewhat chagrined at this. However, he was allowed to go on an independent cruise with his flagship, and as she passed the *Wabash*, a band played a popular tune, "Ain't I glad to get out o' the wilderness, Get out o' the Wilderness, Get out o' the Wilderness. Yes . . . I . . . am."[44]

Gradually the force concentrating at Key West was built up as vessels were taken out of ordinary at the Brooklyn Navy Yard, placed in commission with hastily assembled crews, and hurried south. The yard's workmen toiled night and day getting them ready for duty. Nevertheless, there was little official desire for war. Even Admiral Porter remarked that he favored exhausting every diplomatic channel before resorting to armed conflict. It was obvious to him that Spanish naval power was superior to that of the United States.

Fortunately, the crisis passed surprisingly fast. Neither government wanted war, and even while the naval force was assembling at Key West, Secretary Fish was working out an amiable though somewhat unsatisfactory agreement with Spain. It provided for compensation to the families of the executed Americans but provided nothing for the Cubans.[45]

Although the crisis had eased even before the European Squadron arrived from Europe, the Department decided to hold it temporarily in American waters. On 7 January, Case was ordered to take his "fleet" to the sheltered waters north of the Tortugas and conduct "fleet evolutions" and "steam fleet tactics." For nearly two months the "fleet" carried out tactical exercises, including gunnery practice, torpedo attacks, ship-to-shore landings, and other training maneuvers. The results were far from satisfactory. It was discovered that the navy in every respect had deteriorated since the Civil War. Apparently, newspaper criticism persuaded the navy to cancel a number of the exercises and disperse the force. Admiral Case, with his flag on the *Franklin* (the *Wabash* was ordered to the yard for an overhaul), and with the *Congress, Alaska*, and the *Juanita*, returned to European waters in early May 1874.[46]

So far as the navy was concerned, the *Virginius* affair and the resulting naval concentration clearly illustrated to what extent the fleet had declined since the end of the Civil War. As the *Nation* observed, "The huge wooden screws which we send cruising around the world . . . and which are paraded in newspapers as terrible engines of war, are almost useless for military purposes. They belong to a class of ships which other governments have sold or are selling for firewood."[47] Commander Foxhall A. Parker informed a congressional committee that the fleet assembled at Key West was composed of "antiquated and rotting ships." Before returning to European waters, Admiral Case stopped off briefly in Havana. The *Franklin* anchored near the Spanish flagship, and one young officer later commented that the American vessel was a "handsome ship, but none of her IX-smoothbores could send a shell through the armor plate of the Spaniard."[48]

Trouble with Spain did not end with the settlement of the *Virginius* crisis. In fact it lingered on for nearly two more years. The European Squadron had to resume patrolling Spanish waters because of frequent outbursts of unrest. The bloody Cuban insurrection dragged on in spite of repeated efforts by the American government to bring about a settlement. In one final and futile effort Secretary Fish attempted to persuade the six principal European powers to bring diplomatic pressure against Spain to end the Cuban war. In order to add a cutting edge to this pressure, United States naval vessels were deployed once again close to Cuba. Winter quarters for the force was established at Port Royal, South Carolina. Two ships in the South Atlantic Squadron were ordered to Key West "for fleet exercises." On November 13, the commanding officer of the European Squadron was ordered to send the *Congress* and *Juanita* to Port Royal and take the *Franklin* and *Alaska* to Lisbon to await further orders. He was also told to "act as if on your own authority and without attracting attention if possible."[49]

The New York *Herald* in its 18 November edition editorialized, "Is this Whiskey or War?" It certainly was not war, and although Europe gave what Thomas Bailey called a "chilly reception" to Fish's proposal, Spain made enough concessions to end the crisis. Probably Fish's venture in "gunboat diplomacy" had little effect on the final outcome. In reporting the news that two vessels of the European Squadron had been ordered to Lisbon, a Madrid newspaper ridiculed the squadron: "It is composed of five old wooden vessels."[50]

The *Army and Navy Journal* suggested that these "little Flareups or war excitements every year or two although somewhat expensive, prove of material benefit to our Navy."[51] Presumably the writer was referring to the dubious benefits of concentrating the various vessels and squadrons for fleet exercises. It also would affect the distant stations. When the *Congress* and the *Juanita* sailed for Port Royal, the European Squadron was reduced to three vessels, of which only one continued cruising activities. In January 1876, the *Alaska* was ordered to the West coast of Africa because of tribal unrest in the interior of Liberia, and from there she sailed to the United States. The flagship *Franklin* returned home in the summer of 1876, having been in the squadron for three years. By the fall of 1876 the squadron had been reduced to one third-rate wooden sloop-of-war, the *Marion*.

The squadron commander at that time was Rear Admiral John L. Worden of *Monitor* fame. Worden, a native of New York, became a midshipman in 1834 and later graduated from the naval school at the Philadelphia Navy Yard. In April 1861, he was arrested in Alabama while returning from delivering secret orders to Pensacola. Held seven months by the Confederates, he was ill when exchanged and assigned to the *Monitor*. In the engagement with the *Virginia*, Worden was blinded by an explosion. Although he recovered the use of one eye, his face was permanently scarred. He joined the European Squadron after serving as superintendent of the Naval Academy.

Worden was distressed at the weakened state of the squadron. In October 1876, he appealed to the department for additional vessels: "As to the force now under my command," he wrote, "the Department is aware that it consists of one . . . vessel . . . the *Vandalia* . . . not yet arrived in the Station, and the *Marion* is at present at Genoa under repairs to her machinery. . . ." For two weeks the *Marion* was in the yard, and there were no American warships cruising European waters. Worden went on to stress his inability to protect American interests. The department responded that the *Trenton*, a recently completed wood steam frigate, would be ordered out as his flagship.[52]

Worden had also objected strongly to the Navy Department's decision to move the squadron's headquarters from Villefranche to Lisbon, a decision that was abandoned because of developments in the Ottoman Empire. As Secretary of the Navy Richard W. Thompson wrote the State Department, "Eastern affairs . . . make it inexpedient for the present to order a change." By the fall of 1877 Worden had concentrated his entire squadron in the eastern Mediterranean with temporary headquarters at Smyrna.[53]

THE NEAR EAST, AFRICA, AND THE DECLINE OF THE SQUADRON

5

In the spring of 1876 an insurrection broke out in the Balkan states of Bosnia and Herzegovina against Turkish rule. In the months that followed, European powers failed in their efforts at mediation and the disorders spread. When they reached Bulgaria, Turkish soldiers carried out reprisals, which caused the deaths of thousands of inhabitants. In May, while the foreign ministers of Russia, Austria, and Germany were meeting in Berlin to work out a joint policy concerning the developing crisis, disorders occurred in Salonica, resulting in the murder of the French and German consuls. Four days later rioting in Constantinople led to the overthrow of the Grand Vizier.

Horace Maynard, who had replaced Boker as U.S. minister to the Ottoman Empire, immediately telegraphed for naval protection. Admiral Worden replied that only the *Franklin* was in the Mediterranean, and her engines were under repair. The admiral at first was reluctant to commit his only vessel on station unless absolutely necessary, but when orders were received from the naval secretary to sail at once, repairs were rapidly finished; the vessel's captain hurried back from leave in Paris, liberty was cancelled, and the *Franklin* left Villefranche forty-eight hours later.

Worden took advantage of the crisis to urge reinforcing the squadron. However, the Navy Department did not respond to this request. A penciled note on the back of the incoming telegram stated simply, "We have no ships available at present," and added "our opinion that an increase of force is not absolutely necessary."[1] Ironically, shortly after Worden reached Salonica, he received a routine message from the Navy Department ordering the *Alaska*, his only other vessel (at that time in the Atlantic), home, leaving him the *Franklin*. A week later the squadron did get another vessel. The steam sloop *Marion* was ordered out shortly after the House of Representatives passed a resolution requesting the president to furnish information concerning steps taken to protect American citizens in the Ottoman Empire.

At Salonica Worden found the city calm. Leaving the *Franklin* anchored among warships from other powers, he went by commerical steamer to Constantinople for a conference with the American minister. Worden decided to remain with his vessel in Turkish waters. His decision was based on his conversations with Maynard as well as a number of letters he had received from alarmed missionaries. In August the *Marion* arrived, and Worden immediately sent her to Constantinople. Maynard took advantage of the presence of the *Marion* to repeat his request for a stationnaire. The *Franklin*, however, was ordered home in September; and in spite of Maynard's objections, the *Marion* was withdrawn from the Ottoman capital.

In October the crisis deepened with the imminent possibility of war between Russia and Turkey. Once again Worden pleaded for more ships: "The Department is aware that the squadron . . . consists of one third-rate vessel, the *Marion* . . . at present at Genoa under repair to her machinery. . . . Should it seem to be necessary for me to proceed in person to the East there is no ship in the Station in any way suitable for such purpose." The department promised him two additional vessels, the *Vandalia* and *Trenton*. The *Vandalia* arrived at the end of November, but the *Trenton* would not arrive until the following March. Before they arrived, however, Worden's predicament became ludicrous. At one point while the *Marion* was undergoing one of her many repairs, he had hoisted his flag on a hotel in Nice. It became something of a joke to the French who referred to it as "l'amiral Suisse."[2]

In spite of pleas from various diplomatic officials in Europe and some pressure from the State Department, the navy was unable or unwilling to heavily reinforce the squadron. There were only thirty-seven vessels (including eleven monitors with the North Atlantic Squadron) in commission with the various squadrons; and there is no question that the European Squadron had declined in importance, a decline that would continue for nearly two decades. In the spring of 1875 when the squadron was reduced to three vessels, the *Army and Navy Journal* suggested that the squadron was as large as it needed to be. "It is seldom there is any occasion for interference for the better protection of our countrymen or their interests, and a large force there is not important. . . . It may be desirable to show the flag occasionally, to remind our neighbors that we still have a Navy afloat."[3] The Navy Department undoubtedly agreed with this conclusion.

The *Vandalia* arrived and was sent to Constantinople. The State Department, however, had decided not to pursue the idea of a permanent station ship at the city, but did urge the stationing of two vessels on the Syrian coast, where they could be reached from the Ottoman capital by telegram "in case their presence should be deemed necessary." Worden opposed leaving vessels permanently on the Syrian coast but did send the *Marion* there. The *Vandalia* remained in Constantinople for four months (later replaced by the *Gettysburg*), and the *Marion* stayed for seven months on the Syrian coast.

On 24 April 1877, Russia declared war on Turkey. Under orders from Washington, Worden concentrated the entire European squadron in Turkish waters. The *Vandalia* returned to Constantinople to relieve the *Gettysburg*; the *Alliance* was stationed off the Syrian coast; and the *Marion* and *Trenton* went to Smyrna. The *Trenton* was the newest ship in the United States Navy, a 3,900-ton frigate mounting thirteen 8-inch converted rifles and two Gatling guns, with a top speed of fourteen knots. Although a wooden vessel and no match for the modern vessels of the European powers (and Turkey as well), she was still a more respectable flagship than the squadron had rated for sometime.[4] The *Gettysburg* was not actually a unit of the European Squadron but was on special surveying duty in the Mediterranean. At Worden's request, she was temporarily attached to the squadron and relieved the *Vandalia* in Constantinople, while the latter vessel underwent repairs. She was detached when the *Vandalia* returned to Constantinople.[5]

In June the *Dispatch* arrived on special assignment with the legation at Constantinople. Formerly the steamer *America*, she had been attached to the Washington Navy Yard performing duties such as transporting the secretary of the navy and other government dignitaries and towing monitors. In announcing her arrival, Maynard mentioned that she was "assigned for duty as a stationnaire to the Legation." However, neither the State Department nor the Navy Department agreed with this designation, simply stating that the vessel was in the Ottoman capital "for service auxiliary to the Legation," which may have been a subterfuge to forestall any possible opposition from the European powers. Whatever the reason, the *Dispatch* remained in Constantinople for nearly two years, until the end of the Russo-Turkish War.[6]

The *Dispatch* was used to transport the minister as well as his military attaché to various places. On one of these occasions she carried the minister to Volo in the Aegean to investigate an incident involving American missionaries. Upon arriving at the port, it was discovered that the "outrage" consisted of tomatoes thrown at two missionaries some three months before.[7] The primary mission of the *Dispatch*, as well as the other American vessels at Constantinople, was to act as a refuge in case rioting broke out in the city. Commanding officers, however, were warned not to land armed parties. During the *Dispatch's* twenty-four months in the Sultan's capital, no occasion arose that required the utilization of the vessel as a place of refuge.

The State Department was surprised at the willingness of the Turkish government to allow American warships passage of the Straits, not only because of the treaty of 1856 but also because relations between the two countries had deteriorated. The Ottoman government had protested the reports and activities of Eugene Schuyler, the consul general at Constantinople, as well as those of American missionaries and even the minister himself. More than likely the presence of a Russian naval squadron in American ports during the winter of 1877 as well as the concentration of the European Squadron in Turkish waters contributed to this situation. Rumors of a secret agreement between the United States and Russia by which the American navy would participate in the war against Turkey reached the Turkish capital.[8]

In October 1877, Rear Admiral William E. Le Roy relieved Worden. Le Roy had served as fleet captain of the European Squadron under Farragut and had commanded the South Atlantic Squadron before receiving the European command. Widely known in the navy as "Lord Chesterfield" because of his dogmatism on "good breeding and gentlemanly bearing," he was characterized as "a great stickler for etiquette and red tape, nervous and easily excited," but popular with his officers.[9] Le Roy retained the *Trenton* as his flagship.[10]

In December the fall of Plevna to Russian forces opened the way for an attack on Constantinople. As the Russian army advanced, the Turks appealed to the European powers for mediation and to Russia for an armistice. The British, alarmed over the threat to the city and the Straits, prepared to send a fleet with or without Turkish approval. As the city became choked with refugees, Maynard requested that the *Trenton* be ordered there. "Situation critical," he informed Le Roy. The admiral replied that the *Trenton* was undergoing repairs, adding, "as our ships stationed at Constantinople cannot at any time do more than afford an asylum to our citizens . . . and as their presence merely in the Bosphorus can scarcely be expected to influence the course of events in the Capital, the *Dispatch* . . . would seem to be sufficient." He did agree, however, that, if the minister considered it absolutely necessary, repairs on the flagship would be halted and the vessel ordered to the threatened city.

The *Trenton*, at anchor in Smyrna harbor, made ready to sail. The officer in command of the flagship's marine detachment wrote his wife: "We are still here as you can see, altho today the caterers of the messes were ordered to have their stores on board in six hours, so as to be prepared to sail somewhere immediately. Where no one except the Nabob knew, so it was treated as a great secret. I went on shore . . . returned to the ship to dinner, by which time the matter of sailing had ceased to be a nine days' wonder."[11] In fact she did not go to Constantinople.

Late in January 1878, Russia finally accepted Turkey's plea for an armistice, but the arrival of a British fleet in the Sea of Marmara threatened to prolong and broaden the conflict. Although an Anglo-Russian war was averted when the British naval force made no move to steam on to Constantinople, Greece decided to take advantage of her traditional enemy's plight and declared war on Turkey in February.

Admiral Le Roy's small squadron of five vessels was stretched to its limit trying to protect American interests. The *Marion* was sent to the Piraeus, where plans were worked out to evacuate a few American citizens from Greece if necessary. In March, Le Roy in the *Alliance* temporarily relieved the *Marion* while the latter vessel evacuated some non-Americans from Volo.[12]

To further discomfort the admiral, former President U. S. Grant arrived in the eastern Mediterranean on his round-the-world tour. The *Vandalia* was sent to Alexandria to carry Grant and his party to Smyrna. Later the *Dispatch* was ordered to carry them to Constantinople. At a time when the eastern crisis was on the verge of boiling over into a full-scale European war, American diplomatic and naval officials as well as representatives of various countries (including the belligerent and potential belligerent) were having to take time to entertain the former president. While the *Vandalia* sailed through Turkish waters, Grant sat in a deck chair and read Mark Twain's *Innocents Abroad*. In Greece the Parthenon was illuminated in his honor, and in Turkey the Sultan presented him with four Arabian horses. He left oblivious of the crisis.[13]

With the signing of the Treaty of San Stefano between Russia and Turkey (ratified 23 March), the Near Eastern crisis eased. U.S. naval vessels were gradually withdrawn from Turkish waters; by early 1878 all of them, including the *Dispatch*, had left. The withdrawal was temporary, however, for at the request of the American legation in Constantinople, the *Wyoming* was ordered there in May, only to be replaced in a few weeks by the *Quinnebaug*.

For some time Minister Maynard had planned a tour to explore the commercial potential in the Black Sea. The project was delayed by the war and then by a leave of absence in the United States, but in 1879 he received permission to use a naval vessel for the trip. The *Quinnebaug* was placed at his disposal, but the Turkish government refused to allow her to enter the Black Sea. This may have been because of her size or, as Maynard believed, because of European commercial opposition.[14] For whatever reason Maynard finally obtained permission for the *Wyoming* (a smaller vessel) to enter the Black Sea. For three weeks during August 1879, the vessel carrying the minister and guests (including the president of Roberts College) toured various ports. Unfortunately Maynard's report excited little commercial interest in the United States.[15]

As a matter of fact American commercial interest had become negligible in the eastern Mediterranean. Samuel "Sunset" Cox, minister to Turkey in the 1880s, wrote, "Our flag is never seen on the Bosphorus, except from our [the legation's] launch."[16] In 1876–77, Turkey ordered U.S. goods valued at $4,677,517.68, but nearly half of this total was ammunition destined for the Turkish armies during the Russian war. The bulk of the remainder was oil. At the same time American customers imported attar of roses, opium, and bazaar items valued at only $167,000.[17] The U.S. lost most of the petroleum trade in the 1880s to Russia. In May 1880, Rear Admiral John C. Howell, who relieved Le Roy in command of the European Squadron, wrote: "The *Nipsic* will be left to look out for American interests in the East. I only wish that there were more American interests to look out for; but we have almost entirely lost our Eastern trade and American vessels are as rare as black swans."[18] Stephen B. Luce, who was on board the *Nipsic* on one cruise to Near Eastern waters, recounted the remark of a British official at the presence of American warships in an area where we had so little trade: "I declare . . . you Americans are the most impertinent people in the world. . . . What possible interest has America in Constantinople, that you should keep a ship of war here?"[19]

American commercial interests may have declined, but missionary activities did not. On 4 August 1880, the State Department received a telegram from the legation in Constantinople that a "Reverend Mr. Parson," an American missionary living in a village near the Gulf of Ismid, had been murdered. The minister requested a warship, but none was available—the *Wyoming* was at Leghorn undergoing repairs; the *Nipsic* was in the Aegean investigating rumors of pirates; and the *Quinnebaug* was at Southampton waiting for machinery parts. Even if the latter vessel had been available, Admiral Howell wrote, the Turks would refuse permission for her to pass through the Straits. However, as a result of missionary pressure in the United States, the *Nipsic* was ordered to Constantinople in September.[20]

By the time the *Nipsic* arrived, three suspects had been arrested, tried, found guilty, and hanged. The *Nipsic* remained at anchor near the Golden Horn for several months. At first the crew believed that the ship would be relieved immediately by a smaller vessel, but as the weeks dragged by, this optimism disappeared. The *Nipsic's* captain, Cornelius M. Schoonmaker, wrote to his father on 30 October, "as you see by the heading we are still in this place and . . . are a regular stationnaire—it is becoming very tiresome." A month later in some exasperation, he told his sister, "I am glad to see in the American papers that the moral effect here of this ship is so good. *I did not know it before. I hope we will be sent somewhere else as our reward.*" By December he had evidently become reconciled to remaining indefinitely in Constantinople: "There is no news of our departure," he wrote his mother, "and I do not expect any for sometime. . . . I can get along very well here for it really does not make so much difference to me where the ship may be . . . but it is hard for those officers who have their families out in western Europe."[21]

Schoonmaker was not being completely honest with his mother, for he disliked Constantinople and was relieved to receive orders taking him out of the Bosphorus. His dislike was shared by a surprisingly large number in the European Squadron, especially junior officers. This is at least partly explained by the unsettled conditions at that time in Turkey and the reluctance of commanding officers to grant liberty. A marine officer on the *Vandalia* complained in 1877, "Doubtless you want me to tell you of our cruise. So far it has been a failure. Captain Henry B. Robeson has developed himself into a petty despot . . . lights out at 11, no boats, no liberty, but plenty of work on Sundays. . . ."[22] Liberty was granted, but harassment by Turkish officials was not uncommon. Drunken sailors were frequently treated harshly by officials, because Turkey was Moslem. Occasionally incidents of a more unusual nature occurred. One night two engineers from the *Quinnebaug* were returning to the ship when they were arrested by Turkish sentries, marched to a building at some distance from the harbor, confined for several hours, and finally released. It later came out that they were accused of waving handkerchiefs at the Sultan's harem, a serious offense.[23] Generally, however, the Turks were quite hospitable. Minister Cox recounts the entertainment offered the officers and men of the *Kearsarge* when that famous vintage ship visited Constantinople. It included not only banquets for the admiral, his staff, and officers of the vessel, but dinner for the crew as well. For the duty section, dinner was sent out to the ship.[24]

Smyrna was considered a more pleasant place, but even this city of cypress and fig trees became tedious after several days. Part of the problem was the humdrum of inactivity while anchored in port. Like Constantinople, liberty was infrequent in Smyrna, primarily because of the constant threat of plague. When granted, it was confined to the city because of the lawless bands that roamed the countryside. The infrequent liberty did not concern one officer: "We get on first rate in the mess, and there has been no trouble between any of us . . . and we have plenty of fun during the day. . . . This is the best thing for our contentment, and no one has much of a leaning to go on shore." But he went on to complain that "our cooking is horrible, and I live on ship's bread. . . . We get plenty of nice game . . . but it is literally ruined in cooking. We weigh ourselves every month, and many of us have greatly increased in weight. It must be from the climate as we don't eat much and the drinking is almost exclusively red wines and beer. I never saw a more abstanmus [sic] set of Navy people together. . . ."[25] In a statement that probably expressed the general sentiment of his shipmates towards duty in the Near East he wrote: "One year of the cruise is over, and . . . it has been more *Asiatic* than European. . . . We laugh in derision at the idea of this being considered a European cruise, as so much of our time has been spent in Asia Minor, where ones eyes soon wearies of the everlasting sameness of camels, donkeys, and Turkish fezzes."

The Eastern Question continued unabated during the decade of the 1880s and 1890s during the timid rule of Abdul Hamid. Relations between Turkey and Britain deteriorated during the period, while relations with Russia improved. There was little political reform, but the Sultan's inefficient despotism resulted in remarkably little internal unrest. Nevertheless, minor incidents prompted missionary and diplomatic interests to ask repeatedly for naval protection; and in spite of the visible decline in American sea power in European waters, warships continued to make frequent cruises in the eastern Mediterranean.

In 1881, General Lew Wallace replaced Maynard as minister to Turkey. Wallace, a high-ranking officer in the Civil War, was the author of the well-known novel *Ben Hur*. Appointed by President Garfield supposedly to gather information for a new book, his tenure was generally routine. However, on several occasions he felt constrained to call on the navy for assistance. One minor incident occurred when an American citizen in the town of Volo was assaulted, and a plow ordered from the U.S. was seized by a custom's official. At the minister's request a warship was sent to demand redress, but Wallace's correspondence is silent as to the result. One can only assume that it was settled satisfactorily.[26]

In 1883 an attempt to assassinate an American missionary strained Turkish-American relations. Wallace's efforts to persuade Turkish officials to do something about the harassment of missionaries were futile. After one such attempt he wrote, "The Sublime Porte and I have been in a quarrel. . . . The head of the concern . . . got in a tantrum, and I had to give him a speciment [sic] of my bull dozing faculty." Wallace, who at first apparently developed a friendly relation with the Sultan, became so angry that he demanded warships to force a passage through the Dardanelles and bombard the capital if his demands were not met. He followed this with a recommendation that diplomatic relations be broken off. Secretary of State Frederick T. Frelinghuysen ignored both suggestions. Nevertheless, the European Squadron was ordered to Turkish waters. President Henry O. Dwight of Roberts College probably played a major role in this by utilizing the American press to demand naval protection.[27]

"The influence of this may be good," Secretary Frelinghuysen wrote Wallace. Nothing, however, came from it. The *Quinnebaug* did visit Constantinople, while the flagship *Lancaster* (too large to pass through the Straits) and a smaller vessel cruised along the Syrian coast. The squadron's weakness did nothing to help Wallace, who wrote his brother, "our government is in no condition to assert its rights in the Mediterranean." Wallace had been forewarned; for when he went to the State Department to receive instructions before journeying to Constantinople, the secretary of state told him that he would have a problem similar to those of his predecessors: "to maintain American prestige without visible evidence of military power. . . ."[28]

In February 1885, the *Quinnebaug* was once again ordered to Turkish waters, "exactly what for no one knows," one officer exclaimed in disgust. Lieutenant Charles Sperry, in informing his father of the orders, wrote, "I believe that the wayward Turks are accused of having roasted either a stray missionary or possibly boiled a stray consul over his rosy kitchen fire and we are supposed to proceed to Constantinople and wring satisfaction from the Sultan."[29] He later discovered that the American minister desired to tour the Syrian coast. Wallace's only comment in his autobiography was, "The *Quinnebaug*—what a name for a ship." Sperry later wrote that the cruise was like a pilgrimage, as they primarily touched ports associated with Christianity. "For the last week or two the ship's Bible has been going the round of the ward room as if it were a new novel."[30] The warship with the minister on board also stopped at Alexandria, for the Sultan considered most of North Africa to be a part of the Ottoman Empire.

In 1870 a Moslem fanatic murdered a Christain in Tunis. Rumors spread among the foreign residents that a local Jihad, a religious war against infidels or nonbelievers, was imminent. The American consul appealed to the commanding officer of the European Squadron for naval protection; and the sloop of war *Juanita*, commanded by Stephen B. Luce, was sent there. Because of unrest in Spain, Luce was ordered to remain in Tunis ten days and if no trouble occurred to go on to Malaga. The city remained relatively calm during the vessel's stay, more than a week beyond the allotted time. Luce later concluded his report that the *Juanita's* presence was used by foreign representatives to force the Tunisian government into revoking a recent decision to raise import duties.[32]

Two years later a native employee of the American consular agent in Bizerta was murdered; and when the local officials procrastinated in bringing to trial those arrested, the consul requested a warship. The State Department thought the matter serious enough to request the Navy Department to order the entire European Squadron to Tunis. Secretary of State Fish also informed the naval secretary that "if the show of force should prove to be insufficient . . . further measures . . . will then be [considered]. . . ." The American consul, alarmed over the possible effect an entire squadron would have on relations with Tunis, requested that the orders be delayed. He was then able to persuade the Tunisian government to hold the trial, and the squadron's orders were cancelled.[33] One is left with the impression that the consul exaggerated to the State Department his difficulties, only to discover that his misrepresentation might make matters worse. One also wonders what "further measures" the secretary of state was referring to. We had little interest in Tunis to threaten a naval demonstration, and yet we did the same thing two years later in Tripoli, with even less.

The reorganization of the distant stations at the end of the Civil War resulted in the expansion of the cruising grounds of the European Squadron to include the African coast as far south as St. Paul de Loanda in Portuguese Angola. For a few years a coal depot was maintained at Loanda for both the European and South Atlantic Squadrons, but it was abandoned when the coal became useless. During the postwar years, American involvement in the "Dark Continent" was limited. There was little commerce, and missionary activities were minimal. In 1866 less than 1 percent of U.S. exports went to Africa. Twenty years later the total amount destined for Africa was only $3 million, still far less than 1 percent. In the late 1870s and 1880s some interest developed in the commerical possibilities in Africa, but even this was primarily confined to tropical Africa. American missionaries were scattered from Alexandria to the Cape of Good Hope, but their number was small; and until the mid-1880s, most of them were in Egypt.[31] Despite the fact that American interests in Africa were slight, units of the European Squadron made regular calls in North African ports and periodically answered appeals for naval protection.

The American consul in Tripoli was Michel Vidal, a former newspaper editor, organizer of the Republican party in Louisiana, and congressman from that state. The appointment of Vidal was unfortunate. His overweening and self-opinionated attitude alienated the European community, and even more importantly, his vocal opposition to slavery antagonized Tripolitan officials. Vidal was an energetic diplomat whose trips to various parts of Cyrenaica convinced him of the unlimited commercial opportunities in northern Africa. His correspondence to the State Department strongly advocated the establishment of a naval base there and ultimately the seizure of the entire coastal area.[34] Vidal's recommendations excited no interest among American officials, although at that time the newspaper articles by William Stanley were attracting a great deal of interest in Africa. The consul's machinations came to a grinding halt in 1875 when he became the center of what one historian has described as an opéra bouffe crisis.[35]

Vidal had leased a magnificent villa overlooking the Mediterranean, a short distance from town. A sailor from a Turkish gunboat anchored nearby entered the house searching for a light for his cigarette. A servant observing him became frightened and screamed. Vidal then chased the sailor to the beach where he encountered an officer from the Turkish ship. The American consul, highly excited, evidently shook the officer's shoulders. The following day Vidal was summoned to appear before a court and ordered to apologize to the Turkish admiral for disrespect to his officer. Vidal on his part demanded reparation for breaking and entering his house. He later reported that the sailor was searching for his dispatch book. The impasse that followed resulted in a situation that became increasingly tense as the people, inflamed by local newspapers, took up the argument. On 10 August, Vidal appealed to the State Department for naval protection.[36]

American response to this request was so abrupt and decisive that European diplomats in Tripoli feared the outbreak of war. Apparently there was a breakdown in communications involving the assistant secretary of state (Fish was on vacation), the secretary of the navy, the European Squadron commander, and Captain Earl English, in command of the first warship to arrive in Tripoli. The State Department would later insist that the navy was requested to send a vessel there only to investigate and report. However, the *Congress*, under English's command, was at Corfu when orders were received to sail without delay for Tripoli and, in the words of one officer, to "exact ample reparations." The *Hartford*, on her way home from the Asiatic station, was diverted to join the *Congress*, and the steam sloops *Alaska* and *Juanita* at Southampton were ordered to stand by if needed. The State Department recognized the effect of the naval orders, but by then it was too late.[37] Departmental officials would later argue that the peculiar relationship between the United States and Tripoli, a dependency of Turkey, justified the naval demonstration. The *Army and Navy Journal* agreed, pointing out that "the moral effect of a visit from our Navy is the only thing the State Department can rely upon to maintain the respect of the Tripolitan authorities. If a U.S. consul in any of the enlightened countries should be insulted, diplomatic correspondence would be resorted to, but with Tripoli, a dependance . . . the State Department knows of only the way just carried out."[38]

The *Congress* was the first to arrive; when Captain English sent an officer ashore to consult with the consul, he was greeted by a restless crowd that followed him to the consulate shouting (as later translated by the consul's secretary), "Go on pig, go on hog!" A company of marines and a Gatling gun were then landed but remained on the beach. The Pasha later apologized for the demonstration but adamantly refused to apologize to Vidal.

In spite of the obvious weakness of his force (two old wooden vessels after the arrival of the *Hartford*), English did not hesitate to present what amounted to an ultimatum to the Pasha and backed it up by clearing for action. Both ships were anchored with their guns trained on the city's fortifications. Fortunately the Pasha gave in and went in full uniform to the American consul's residence and formally apologized. "The consul . . . not a forgiving turn of mind, demanded that . . . dirt should be eaten, but [English] . . . put an end to the business," one officer later remembered. The *Congress* with Vidal and his family on board for "safe keeping" sailed the following morning.[39]

Tripoli was claimed by the Ottoman government, a relationship that the United States tacitly recognized. In reality, however, the Pasha was treated as an independent ruler. The State Department as well as Vidal completely ignored Maynard, the American minister in Constantinople, during the Tripolitan crisis. Maynard learned of it only through the newspapers and was forced to maintain an embarrassing silence when the Turkish minister of foreign affairs demanded an explanation. "As you will perceive I am wholly in the dark," he wrote the State Department.[40]

The affair was an unfortunate example of unnecessary "gunboat diplomacy," which did nothing to benefit American prestige in Africa or Europe. As the *Congress*'s executive officer later wrote, "Those of us who knew the real facts in the case were not very proud of the whole performance."

The United States had virtually no involvement in Morocco in the latter half of the nineteenth century. No mission field was established there, possibly because of the hostility of the natives, who were overwhelmingly Moslem. Trade was negligible; and as one authority has stated, the interest of the United States rested upon the commercial possibilities of the future.[41] Nevertheless, an American consul had been in residence in Tangier since the latter part of the eighteenth century. The United States was also one of the powers that had been granted the right of extraterritoriality by the Moroccan government.

Briefly, extraterritorial jurisdiction was granted in Mohammedan countries because foreigners, non-Moslems, were considered outside the law. Moslem governments allowed foreigners to settle their own disputes and also granted the right of protection not only to foreigners but also to natives in the employ of foreigners. This "right" was gradually enlarged and abused when various consuls extended the right of protection to Christians and native Jews for commercial reasons. The American consul in Tangier reported in 1888 that some eight hundred persons enjoyed the protection of the United States. He mentioned a village near Tangier where the approximately three hundred inhabitants refused to pay taxes on the ground that they were an American colony; they claimed this right because the village provided beaters for boar hunts organized by the consulate.[42] The Moroccan government disliked extraterritorial jurisdiction but could do little about it. In order to back up this "protection," American consuls frequently requested warships to visit Moroccan ports. For that reason Moroccan ports were called on as a normal part of the European Squadron's cruising duties. In 1880, the *Quinnebaug* touched Moroccan ports and her commanding officer reported that "intelligent persons in all the ports are unanimous saying that protection is necessary."[43]

Egypt, with its fabulous remains of antiquity, had long been attractive to Americans. In the 1850s, missionaries sponsored by the United Presbyterian Church established themselves all the way from Alexandria to far up the Nile. Trade in the post-Civil War years was slight, but growing, especially in the importation of American arms.[44] Tourists were numerous, and a small American colony had grown up in Cairo. The most important members of this colony were a number of ex-Union and Confederate officers who had been recruited into the Khedive's military service. The best-known was General Charles P. Stone, who became chief of the Egyptian Staff.

Diplomatic relations were similar to those with Tripoli. Although Egypt was technically a part of the Ottoman Empire, the United States had treated it as an independent nation. Consuls were appointed without consulting Constantinople, although the American minister to Turkey frequently included Alexandria in touring the ports of the Ottoman Empire.[45] Inevitably, the minister was involved in problems relating to Egypt. The completion of the Suez Canal in 1869 catapulted Egypt into a position of importance to the European powers. In 1876, Khedive-Ismail was unable to pay interest on a debt, and both France and Great Britain jointly took control of Egypt's finances. Because of Ismail's ineptitude, growing foreign influence, and Egyptian nationalism, discontent culminated in an outbreak of riots in June 1882.

In late 1881, the American consul general to Egypt requested a warship because of the "very unsettled condition[s]. . . ." Secretary of the Navy William M. Hunt agreed, and orders were sent to the European Squadron to provide a vessel. If these orders had been carried out to the letter, some navigational difficulties might have been encountered, as the vessel was ordered to Cairo rather than Alexandria.[46]

The squadron at that time was commanded by Rear Admiral James W. A. Nicholson, a dour New Englander who had commanded the monitor *Manhattan* in the Battle of Mobile Bay. The European Squadron was his first flag command afloat.[47] Nicholson assumed command of the squadron in September 1881, but because of President Garfield's assassination, the usual change of command ceremony was called off.

Nicholson's flagship was the wooden screw sloop-of-war *Lancaster*, probably the best-known ship in the post-Civil War navy, excepting the *Hartford*. Commissioned in 1857, she had been flagship of the Pacific Squadron during the Civil War and flagship of the South Atlantic Squadron for several years after the war. She received extensive modifications in the late 1870s, including a huge bronze ram bolted to her bow. Casper Goodrich, who served in her before and after the modification, compared this to putting "spurs on a snail."[48]

Nicholson gained the reputation of being a strict disciplinarian, a stigma that was responsible for his nickname "War horse." He alienated many officers and men in the European Squadron by frequently revoking weekend liberty as a result of some fault discovered during weekly inspections. He also did not get along with the commanding officer of his flagship, Captain Bancroft Gheradi, one of the most popular officers in the navy. An unpleasant situation was created when officers on the flagship were invited to dine with the admiral or the captain, depending upon one's loyalty. Nicholson also made diplomatic blunders. On one occasion, James Russell Lowell and several British officers came on board the *Lancaster* for lunch at Nicholson's invitation. Apparently the admiral had forgotten, for no preparations had been made. They were finally invited by the officer of the deck to the wardroom. In a later incident, the Greek government lodged a protest with the State Department for what was called "rudeness" on the part of the admiral to the Greek royal family. All in all, Nicholson's tour of duty with the European Squadron was not a happy one, and he left it an embittered man.[49] At the same time, because of the Egyptian crisis in 1882, Nicholson received more publicity in the United States than any other officer in command of the squadron since Farragut.

In June 1882, rioting in Egypt left some fifty Europeans dead and hundreds of others fleeing the country as rumors of anti-Christian massacres began to spread. The entire European Squadron (four vessels) was ordered to Egyptian waters to join warships from other nations converging on the hapless country. The *Galena* and *Nipsic* arrived early in June followed by the *Quinnebaug* and *Lancaster* two weeks later. The admiral was at Cadiz preparing for a northern cruise when orders reached him to concentrate the squadron at Alexandria.

On 30 June, Nicholson reported that he was giving refuge "not only to Americans but to all persons of any nationality asking protection whose country has no vessels of war in port." He added that there were only six Americans in Egypt.[50] Actually more than fifty Americans (mostly missionaries) were at that time residing in Egypt, and within two weeks nearly all would be on board one of the vessels in the squadron. Even before Nicholson arrived on the *Lancaster*, the American vessels were providing refuge for non-Americans. The *Galena*, which arrived first, was swamped with refugees, and her com-

manding officer decided to hire an Italian sailing ship to take care of the over-
flow. The *Quinnebaug* arrived on 1 July, and within twenty-four hours fifty-
eight had come on board. "I was cruelly afraid of a fifty-ninth," Captain
Whitehead wrote, "but we were fortunate in removing the expectant mother
without damage. I coralled them all in the poop, French, Italians, Greeks,
Turks, Syrian, and . . . in the whole lot we had three Americans, two missionaries and a judge. . . . [A] fine time I had particularly at night when the poor
little children raised a row."[51] Fortunately, the weather was good, and awnings
were spread to accommodate many of them topside. By the middle of July
more than 250 refugees were congregated on Nicholson's ships.

The American consul at Alexandria, who later wrote an account of the
crisis, described the harbor, which had become packed with warships and commerical steamers:

> Steamers of various nations were constantly coming and going, generally
> sailing away loaded with refugees. . . . There were then no docks ap-
> proached by steamers at which passengers could be landed and
> embarked. Hence, the waters were covered with small native boats going
> to and from the vessels. . . . The beautiful weather, the bunting displayed
> by the numerous ships, the activity of the native boatmen, made joyous
> by their increased business and indifferent to the future, gave the whole
> scene the appearance of a gala-day without a suggestion of impending
> disaster.[52]

Not all were impressed by the colorful native boatmen. A marine mentioned in
his diary that the "bumboats [were] so annoying that we turned steam fire
hoses on them."

Admiral Nicholson added to the illusionary scene by informing the warships present, as well as the American consul, that his squadron would commemorate July Fourth. On that day the assembled warships—over forty in
number—dressed ship and at noon fired salutes. When the American consul
informed the Egyptian government of the observance, the Khedive protested
that the "firing might provoke a conflict, and that the Arabs might run away."
Lieutenant Colonel Challé-Long, ex-Union and ex-Egyptian army officer and
at that time acting American consul, later wrote that he responded, "Don't you
think that at this moment it would be a good thing if the natives did run
away?"[53]

In Constantinople the Sultan was alarmed over the Egyptian situation, especially the prospect of armed intervention by foreign powers. He refused to
cooperate in any kind of joint effort with a European nation, but he did ask the
American minister as the representative of a "disinterested power" to help
settle the dispute between Great Britain and Egypt. Although the State Department agreed and Wallace was willing, nothing came from it, probably
because the British government had already decided on armed intervention.[54]

On 9 July, Nicholson was informed unofficially (official notice was given the American consul the following day) that the British squadron was preparing to bombard the forts at the harbor's entrance. By the evening of the tenth the last Americans on shore except General Stone and his family had boarded the American vessels; and they, along with the warships and merchant vessels of neutral nations, stood outside the harbor. One officer in the *Lancaster* noted that "when we passed the *Monarch* [the British flagship] the band and guard were up and crew mustered." The American vessels anchored approximately a mile beyond the British squadron but within clear view of the harbor.[55] A correspondent from the New York *Herald* cabled that Nicholson threatened to return fire if any of his vessels were hit, but there is no corroboration of this in the naval records.

For forty-eight hours (11 and 12 July) the British squadron bombarded the forts. During the afternoon of the twelfth the Egyptians asked for a truce, which was granted after the forts were evacuated. Not only were the forts abandoned, but the city as well, leaving it wide open. British losses were six killed and twenty wounded; Egyptian, approximately 115 killed and from 350 to 400 wounded. Shortly after the firing ceased, the American flagship *Lancaster* steamed through the British squadron, her band playing "God Save the Queen," and was received with "continuous cheers and 'Hail Columbia.' "[56] In this way a "disinterested nation" rendered honor.

Throughout the night of 12 July, sailors on board the American vessels observed large sections of Alexandria in flames. On the thirteenth, Colonel Challé-Long made three trips into the city to reopen the consulate, but without success. The city was in chaos with crowds of looters roaming the streets. At that time the British had not landed a force and would do so only after various neutral nations sent detachments ashore. The British government, including Admiral Sir Beauchamp Seymour, in command of the British squadron, was later criticized for the delay in landing troops to preserve law and order. The reasons for this delay (more than twenty-four hours) are not known; possibly, as one writer has suggested, it was to demonstrate that Great Britain was not contemplating an occupation. A British observer later wrote that it was "the landing of the American marines [that] forced the hand . . . of Admiral Seymour."[57]

At Challé-Long's request, Admiral Nicholson agreed to send a force ashore to help restore the consulate. The Khedive acquiesced and asked, according to the admiral, that the Americans aid in restoring order and putting out the fires. Nicholson evidently made the decision on his own; he had no discretionary instructions from Washington concerning such an eventuality. Although there were precedents for such an action, Nicholson must have known that his decision would create concern in Washington.[58]

On 14 July, shortly after 10:00 A.M., the *Lancaster*, followed by the *Quinnebaug* and *Nipsic*, got under way and stood into the harbor. The ships were dressed in honor of Bastille Day with the French flag at the main. By 3:00 P.M.

a detachment of bluejackets and marines—nearly 150 and two Gatling guns—had landed under the command of Lieutenant Commander Caspar Goodrich. Their objective was the American consulate located on the Grand Square in the center of the city, and it took them nearly three hours to wend their way to it along hot and smoke-filled streets filled with debris. Goodrich would later write that the only trouble he had came from the hundreds of cats that followed his detachment. During the night the Americans occupied the consulate, and patrols were sent out, but no trouble developed. Captain Henry C. Cochrane, who commanded the marines, wrote in his diary that they arose on 15 July at 5:15 in the morning, "after passing a . . . night fighting fleas and mosquitos, listening to falling walls, crackling flames, howling dogs, meowing cats, noisy sentinels, [and] loquacious Greeks."[59] According to Long the Americans spent that day fighting fires. In his diary he credits them with saving a number of buildings, including St. Mark's Episcopal Church and the Palace of Justice as well as the consulate. The only casualty was a slightly burned marine, although nine others were sent back on board under arrest, probably for intoxication.[60]

With the landing of small contingents from the warships of other neutral nations, as well as the British, the American force was reduced to twenty-five men.[61] On 20 July, Nicholson reported that all the refugees had been disembarked, and the force ashore was reduced to five men. Two days later the admiral sailed with the *Lancaster* and *Nipsic* for Villefranche, leaving the *Quinnebaug* in the harbor.

Admiral Nicholson was commended for his actions by the British, Dutch, Norwegian, and Swedish governments. In the United States, however, his actions became the subject of controversy, which ultimately led to a Congressional investigation. Although much of the trouble stemmed from exaggerated and erroneous newspaper accounts, Nicholson himself was partly to blame. Incidents such as saluting the British squadron after the bombardment contributed to the widespread rumors that the admiral had landed a military force to cooperate with the British. His actions were supported by the secretaries of the navy, state, and most naval officers. One officer wrote to Secretary of the Navy William Chandler, "I hope you will stand by Admiral Nicholson in his conduct at Alexandria. He is not a favorite in the Navy (or of mine) but he seems to have acted just as he should. . . ."[62] The investigating committee approved his actions.

The unrest in Egypt spread along the North African coast and alarmed Americans, who inevitably demanded naval protection. Nicholson considered the Egyptian situation the most pressing and refused to weaken his force there until ordered to do so by the Navy Department. Late in July the *Galena* was detached to patrol the North African coast from Tripoli to Morocco. No serious disturbances occurred, and early in August, the *Galena* was withdrawn.[63]

The growing influence of various European powers in North Africa in the 1880s did not stabilize the area. As a matter of fact, the sharpening rivalries among these powers for control of various ports generated more unrest among the natives. Although the United States tried to remain aloof from the European imperialistic struggle, Americans continually found themselves involved, primarily because they were Christian and white. Hence, units of the European Squadron were frequently called upon by diplomatic representatives when American subjects or interests were threatened.[64]

On 10 March 1883, a "Red letter day in the European Squadron," declared Captain Cochrane, Admiral Nicholson was relieved of the command by Rear Admiral Charles H. Baldwin. Cochrane wrote in his diary:

> Lieutenant Commander Course and Lt. Paul both remarked that Admiral Nicholson said yesterday that he left the navy without regret, that he did not care anything for anybody in it and did not know that anyone cared anything for him. . . . Admiral Nicholson came on deck in citizens clothes with a blue cape and uniform cap. Soon after he put the latter under his arm and walked ashore. When he left the ship he looked at the small array of blue jackets about a half dozen and said "good bye lads."[65]

Admiral Baldwin, a native of New York City, entered the navy in 1839. According to Goodrich, he was "a courteous gentlemen and an officer of distinction." Baldwin had little opportunity to distinguish himself on the European station, and about the only noteworthy event of his brief tenure (slightly over a year) occurred when he took the *Lancaster* to Kronstadt and journeyed to Moscow to take part in the coronation of Alexander II.

In 1884 Baldwin was replaced by Rear Admiral Earl English, who had served as chief of the Bureau of Equipment and Recruiting for five years before assuming the European command. With twenty-six years and seven months, English had more active sea service than any other senior officer in the navy. Although his years as bureau chief were marked by frequent clashes with Secretary Chandler over appointments, he was popular with both officers and men and was considered one of the "ablest seamen in the Navy." English requested the European command months before it became vacant, probably because of his disagreement with the naval secretary.[66]

In December 1884, five months after taking command, English was ordered to send the *Kearsarge* to the mouth of the Congo River. She was to survey the area and determine a "healthful point well situated for a commerical resort . . . not already lawfully appropriated by another power." In February English was ordered to take his flagship to join the *Kearsarge*. Referring to the Berlin Congress meeting at that time Chandler wrote: "In consequence of the very general interest felt in regard to the political and commercial situation along the Congo, it is believed that the position taken by our Government will be strengthened by the presence in the vicinity for a time of the Commander in Chief of the Naval Forces on the European Station."[67]

The latter decades of the nineteenth century witnessed a tremendous drive by European powers to partition Africa, an imperialistic movement that has been called one of the most disruptive forces in modern history. This movement did not attract Americans until the late 1870s.

In 1878 Commodore Robert W. Shufeldt stopped off in various West African ports while on a round-the-world cruise. Shufeldt, who was a strong advocate of American commercial expansion, recommended the establishment of consular service in West Africa, Liberia, and Fernando-Po, a small island that is part of Guinea today.[68] The Congo region attracted President Chester Arthur and Secretary of State Frelinghuysen. President Arthur in his annual message in December 1883 suggested cooperation with other nations in opening up the Congo region. Thus when the European powers held a conference in Berlin in 1884 to discuss the Congo, Arthur appointed a delegate, John A. Kasson, to it. Kasson discovered that several nations had sent naval vessels to the area and recommended that the United States do the same,[69] which prompted the sending of English's small force to the region.

"African fever" did not result in American involvement in the Congo or West Africa. Admiral English's report on the Congo was generally negative, and the Democratic administration of Grover Cleveland that followed that of Arthur was disinterested in the whole idea.[70]

In the spring of 1885, Rear Admiral Samuel R. Franklin relieved English in command of the squadron and broke his flag in the *Pensacola*. Franklin, a somewhat pompous officer, had commanded the flagship *Franklin* in the squadron a decade before. The *Pensacola* was a stately old veteran of the Civil War that had been fitted out as a flagship with such features as a fireplace in the captain's cabin. She was commanded by George Dewey, who at first got along with Franklin, but the boredom of inactivity later led to quarrels. On 4 June 1886, Dewey wrote a friend, "tomorrow [Commander William A.] Marshall goes to Constantinople with Admiral Franklin. . . . I shall miss him very much, the other not so much." Again on November 17, he wrote, "The Admiral and I each live in our cabin and are on . . . official terms. . . . I can stand it if he can, as he returns next August."[71]

In August 1886, Rear Admiral James A. Greer replaced Franklin. Greer's two-and-a-half-year tour ended with the temporary abandonment of the station in 1889. In the spring of that year the *Quinnebaug* was ordered home after a record cruise of eight years with the European Squadron. In November the *Lancaster* left, leaving Greer with only one vessel, the *Enterprise*. A month later Greer hauled down his flag, and the *Enterprise* sailed from Lisbon for New York.[72]

The decision that led to the breakup of the squadron was made by Benjamin Franklin Tracy, who became secretary of the navy in March 1889. He apparently decided to disband the squadron soon after taking office. There simply were not enough vessels to go around; and the other foreign stations, particularly the Pacific and Asian, were considered more important. A number of naval officers agreed with this. Commodore Shufeldt, in testimony before Congress, pointed out that European governments and navies would maintain order, and the vessels in the squadron would provide more useful service elsewhere. George Dewey was also critical of displaying ships in European waters: "As we had no commerce or interests to protect in Europe, and were unable to protect them if we had, the presence of our squadron in European waters was perfunctory."[73]

Yet naval protection was needed in Asia Minor and North Africa, areas that were in the European Squadron's cruising station, and even the old wooden vessels were adequate for this. One could not always depend upon European navies either. The British waited more than twenty-four hours after the conclusion of the bombardment of Alexandria before sending a landing party ashore, a considerable time after the American force landed to protect lives and property. Perhaps the solution was in redefining the cruising station, excluding the Northern European countries; but this was not done nor evidently considered. When the station was reactivated in 1893, it was because of the need for naval protection in Asia Minor.

THE NEW NAVY AND THE TURKISH CRISIS, 1889–1895

6

The *Enterprise*'s departure from Lisbon in 1889 symbolized the end of the old navy and the beginning of the new. As Admiral Greer left the wooden-hull screw sloop-of-war for the last time, he could see the steel-protected cruisers *Atlanta, Boston*, and *Chicago* anchored in the stream nearby.

Recent historical writing has clearly demonstrated the effect commercial expansion had on naval reform. When Rutherford Hayes in 1880 made the first important plea by a chief executive since 1865 for a large navy, he was undoubtedly influenced by the fact that in the previous decade, 1870–1880, American exports had increased more than 200 percent.[1] By the early 1880s, it became increasingly clear that a large segment of the population favored naval expansion. Labor and religious groups, as well as what William Appleton Williams called "metropolitan expansionists" and agricultural businessmen all demanded naval reform. In 1881 William A. Hunt, President James Garfield's secretary of the navy, appointed a board of naval officers to advise him as to the types and numbers of ships that should be recommended to Congress. In 1883, on the basis of the board's recommendation, Congress authorized the construction of four steel ships, *Atlanta, Boston, Chicago*, and the dispatch vessel *Dolphin*. Although modest and conservative, this was the beginning of the "steel navy." During the next six years thirty additional vessels of various classes from battleships to tugs would be authorized.

In April 1889, the *Chicago*, the last of the original protected cruisers, was commissioned. The cruisers, along with the gunboat *Yorktown*, were then designated the "Squadron of Evolution." Secretary of the Navy Benjamin Tracy, who wanted to show off the new vessels, ordered the squadron to European waters. Rear Admiral John G. Walker, who was appointed to the squadron's command, was told that it was to be a shakedown cruise. Nevertheless, Tracy considered leaving it in Europe for an extended period. At Lisbon, the "archives relating to the European Squadron" were transferred to the flagship from the *Enterprise* shortly before she departed for the United States. The plan was abandoned later because of personnel problems (the enlistment of many of the men was to run out during the summer) and because the naval secretary decided to send the squadron to South America.[2] In June 1890, the squadron took on stores at Gibraltar and left for Brazil. Admiral Walker reported to Tracy that "much interest [has] . . . been manifested [in Europe] in the . . . re-establishment of American naval power."[3] The European press did comment on the new American warships, but in all candor, by European naval standards they were virtually obsolete when launched.

Tracy made no immediate attempt to replace the squadron in European waters. Suitable vessels were unavailable, not only for the European station but for others as well. His policy until he left office was to shift vessels from one station to another as they were needed. The *Baltimore* carried the remains of John Ericsson back to Sweden in 1890 and cruised in the Mediterranean for several months. The Navy Department ordered the cruiser to Chile early in 1891 when a revolution broke out there.[4] In the fall of 1890 two vessels were detached from the South Atlantic Squadron and ordered to the Mediterranean, where both Spain and Italy were celebrating the four-hundredth anniversary of the sailing of Columbus to the New World. In December, the cruiser *Newark* was ordered to take the recently appointed American minister to Constantinople. Because of her tonnage, the *Newark* was not allowed in the Straits, and the Sultan's yacht was sent to carry the new minister from Smyrna to his post.[5]

When Tracy left office in March 1893, the European station had not been reestablished. However, Hiliary Herbert, Tracy's replacement as naval secretary did so shortly afterwards.[6] Herbert's decision was a result of several factors. In the first place, modern warships were available. The decrepit, obsolete wooden vessels of the old navy were rapidly disappearing, as new steel vessels were commissioned. There were nineteen ships in commission, ranging from gunboats to battleships less than six years old, when Herbert was sworn in. Six more were scheduled to be completed during the year. The naval secretary announced in his annual report for 1894, "I have decided to put into operation a policy which will keep a number of cruising vessels sufficient for the ordinary needs of naval policy on each of six stations, viz: North Atlantic, South Atlantic, North Pacific, South Pacific, Asiatic, and European."

Herbert also advocated the creation of a large battleship navy. He based his arguments not only on defensive needs but on an expanding commercial empire as well. European markets would play a prominent role in this expansion. American farm exports to continental markets soared during the early 1890s, partly as a result of crop failures in Europe. Although there was an overall decline in manufactured goods exported to Europe, paper products made gains, along with iron and steel. In 1893 the American consul in Barcelona wrote that approximately fifteen million dollars' worth of goods (primarily cotton, petroleum, and staves) were imported from the United States to that port annually, nearly five million more than from any other nation. Admiral Henry Erban reported to the Navy Department after he returned from a cruise in Turkish waters that American trade at Mersin and Alexandretta was constantly increasing.[7] Big-navy advocates both in Congress and the navy were constantly linking commercial expansion to naval protection. Yet, there was little need for American naval protection in continental ports, and trade elsewhere in the cruising grounds of the European station was negligible.

Perhaps the most plausible cause for the station's reestablishment was one suggested by the New York *Times*, that is, trouble in the Ottoman Empire involving American missionaries. Although the problem was certainly not new, it had gained momentum in the winter of 1892–93, when an American educational institution at Marsova was sacked and burned. The American Board of Commissioners for Foreign Missions in Boston demanded reparations, and the U.S. minister in Constantinople was informed that President Grover Cleveland considered the incident "of a critical nature. . . ." Shortly after this the Navy Department ordered the cruiser *Chicago*, carrying the flag of Rear Admiral Henry Erban, to the Mediterranean. The arrival of the cruiser in Queenstown, Ireland, in July marked the reactivation of the European station.[8]

Erban was a "bluff and hearty sea-gob," a true deep-water sailor of the old school. Nicknamed "Bully" by the blue jackets because of his "John Bull" appearance, he was a big man with white, spikey side-whiskers. Although jovial most of the time, he was also impatient and quick-tempered. On the eve of the Civil War, when a junior officer, he had an altercation with a prosecessionist officer that culminated with their grappling as they rolled down a staircase at the Pensacola Navy Yard. Erban was a native of New York City and quite proud of it. An officer who served under him said that he looked down on anyone who did not come from *the city*. He told one officer that he expected to be buried in Trinity Cemetery in New York City and added, "I'll be in damn fine company, too!"[9]

Erban had a long and distinguished career behind him, having entered the navy in 1848. During the Civil War he served with Farragut on the Mississippi River and later commanded various vessels including monitors. After the war he held the usual assignments, rotating from shore to sea duty and back to shore duty again. In 1893 he was in command of the New York Navy Yard and was in line for a sea command when ordered to the European Squadron.

Erban would command the squadron fourteen months, and except for the growing crisis in the Near East, there was nothing to prevent what should have been a pleasant last command afloat before retirement. Generally, it was; but a serious estrangement between the admiral and the captain of his flagship marred the tour. The captain was Alfred Thayer Mahan, whose book *The Influence of Sea Power upon History* had brought fame if not fortune to the author. Mahan's career had not been particularly noteworthy until he was assigned to the Naval War College in 1885. Five years later his monumental study on sea power was published. This was followed two years later by *The Influence of Sea Power upon the French Revolution and Empire*. These volumes received immediate acclaim abroad where they were translated into various languages, including German and Japanese. Mahan had hoped to remain on shore where he could continue writing, but the Chief of the Bureau of Navigation, Commodore Francis M. Ramsay, ordered him to sea. Mahan tried various avenues to get his orders changed, but to no avail, and with some bitterness he assumed command of the *Chicago* in May 1893.

Erban would have had trouble getting along with Mahan under the best of circumstances. The admiral's brusque, good-humored nature contrasted rather sharply with the captain's courteous but cold and formal manner. There was the awkwardness created by Erban's commanding a squadron of only one ship most of the time. Early in September, Mahan commented to his wife, "As admiral there is practically nothing to do except visiting on this ridiculous station; so he is kind of supernummery captain. He [complains] . . . about trifles and talks ship. . . ."[10] Erban was certainly aware of Mahan's aversion to going to sea. Mahan may have lacked confidence in his own seamanship. His frequent drills convinced one officer that the captain was obsessed with fear of a collision. An American diplomatic official recalled in a conversation that he had with Mahan that "he frankly confessed that as a real sailorman he was a failure. . . ."[11] On 11 November 1893, the admiral wrote to Mahan, criticizing him for not "give[ing] that attention to the details of the ship that is required both by the Regulation and by the custom of the service." He went on to say that he had to do many things through the executive officer rather than the commanding officer. During the first months of the cruise there were a number of incidents concerning shiphandling, discipline, and other matters that probably contributed to Erban's sending in a poor fitness report on the *Chicago*'s captain.[12] Mahan soon heard about it and demanded a court of inquiry. Inevitably, the relationship between the two on board ship deteriorated. On one occasion, in a heated exchange, Erban angrily told Mahan that "if you are dissatisfied, you have only to apply, and I will send you home by the next steamer."[13] Although Mahan obviously wanted to go home, he could not do so under the cloud of a poor fitness report, which had already been leaked to the press. Mahan was not relieved of his command, and Erban's successor would later write a very favorable report on the captain. Although Erban's report on Mahan may have been too strong, it seems only fair to point out that the captain did nothing to help himself. His letters to his wife clearly indicate his disinterest in the cruise, his command, and the details of running a ship.

The *Chicago*'s cruise became a triumphal tour for Mahan. European leaders recognized and praised him as the world's foremost naval scholar, and everywhere he went they entertained him. Queen Victoria welcomed him to

The USS *Lancaster*, flagship of the European Squadron, 1881–1888. *Courtesy of the United States Department of Navy.*

dinner at Buckingham Palace; Lord Roseberry, the Prime Minister, privately entertained him; naval clubs gave him luncheons; the British Admiralty held a banquet for him; and Oxford and Cambridge both conferred honorary degrees upon him. Erban attended many of these functions, but it was clear who the celebrity was. The admiral, however, carefully disguised his feelings about playing second fiddle to a subordinate. On 6 September, Mahan wrote his wife, "So far I think the European Squadron wears less than the others. The everlasting visiting is a nuisance and a distraction but often helps matters by breaking the monotony."

This "monotony" was broken before the year was out when Erban received orders to visit the Near East as soon as possible. On 30 November, Mahan informed his wife, "the Admiral told me today that he wanted to leave Nice early in January where for I don't know. I gather he has received some orders from the Department and he spoke of an 'interesting trip'. . . . I take little stock, but it [is] all in the cruise which wears steadily away."

In April 1893, President Cleveland appointed Alexander Terrell from Texas, an ex-Confederate, to be minister to Turkey. Terrell's efforts to solve the problems that confronted him in Constantinople proved to be just as frustrating to him as to his predecessors, and in due time he too turned to what had become a traditional remedy, naval support.

For several months after first reaching Constantinople, the American minister attempted unsuccessfully to collect an indemnity promised by the Turkish government for the destruction of a building belonging to American missionaries by local police. As so frequently occurred, promises were made but not kept. In addition to that, he was having increasing trouble over the treatment of naturalized Americans of Turkish origin. The problem was not a new one; but in the last decade the number of Ottoman subjects, particularly Armenians, who immigrated to the United States and after receiving American citizenship returned to Turkey, had grown significantly. Turkish law did not recognize the naturalization of Ottoman subjects after 1869 without the consent of the Turkish government. Naturalized Americans returning to the Ottoman Empire were subjected to a variety of harassments, including arrest, and the U.S. minister found it impossible to protect them. Yet, as Secretary of the Navy Herbert wrote in his annual report, as the United States had accepted these people "we assume[d] the responsibility of protecting them, in many cases against their former governments."[14]

On 29 November 1893, the State Department passed on to the Navy Department a request from Terrell for a warship to "hover about Smyrna," which he felt would "help American diplomacy greatly." The *Chicago* was then ordered to the east. This news prompted Terrell to recommend a course of action: "Periodically," he wrote, "the Turk must be reminded that our Government is weary with his methods. . . . In my opinion the duty of protecting American citizens and at the same time avoiding trouble here . . . can be reconciled, if just before the arrival of the *Chicago* at Smyrna, his minister in Washington be informed that arbitrary imprisonment must cease. . . ." He followed this up two weeks later with the optimistic assertion that "if [the *Chicago*] . . . were not anchored in the harbor of Smyrna . . . our applications at the Porte would not be treated with conspicuous civility." The American minister had discovered that the Ottoman government was apparently susceptible to gunboat diplomacy. An official of the Turkish foreign office once candidly admitted that American diplomats were always regarded with favor because their diplomacy was simple and direct, "consisting only of threats to send for American warships whenever they wanted anything done."[15]

The *Chicago* was supposed to arrive early in January, but she was delayed first at Nice for stores to arrive from the U.S. and later at Naples because of boiler problems. When the ship failed to arrive by the beginning of February, Terrell's patience wore thin. He wrote Admiral Erban urging him to sail for the east without delay: "The moral influence of your presence . . . cannot be overestimated." To the secretary of state he telegraphed, "Palace alarmed. . . . Our warship in the Mediterranean and your talk with Turkish minister alarm them. This I know absolutely." In what was evidently an impulsive afterthought he concluded, "Have they not been dancing at Nice long enough with the Nobility of France." Terrell either was not aware of or did not give credence to the reasons offered by Erban for the delays. He wrote Secretary of State Walter Gresham, complaining that "if these boats had been in the Eastern Mediterranean when we had interests to protect, instead of remaining at anchor for two months amid the festivities of Nice and Villefranche, I would have accomplished everything you desire."[16]

Erban's reply did nothing to sooth the minister's feelings. Apparently unperturbed by Terrell's anxiety, the admiral replied calmly that he did not know when the *Chicago* could sail. Terrell must have read with astonishment Erban's pronouncement that if he were needed in Constantinople, someone else would have to foot the bill—the navy would not do it, and he could not afford it. If such a trip were made, he would be accompanied by six or seven officers, two orderlies, a coxswain, and a twenty-one-piece band. "Unless provision be made for our proper entertainment during the time such a visit would require, it will be impossible for me to make it." Terrell had not requested such a trip, nor did he later, to Erban's obvious disappointment. If Erban's reply was not enough, the minister was reprimanded by the secretary of state for his criticism: "The remark with which your telegram of the 6th concludes is out of place and not courteous to the officers of the *Chicago*."[17]

Gresham's reprimand made little impression on Terrell. On 20 February he again urged Erban to expedite his movement to the east: "Half the moral effect on the Turks has been lost by the publication in the Paris *Herald* of your future movements," he scoldingly observed. A week later he was informing the secretary of state that there was absolutely no truth in a newspaper story implying that he had threatened the Turkish government with a war vessel. "I have never remotely intimated a resort to force," a statement that even to Gresham must have sounded strange. Terrell had many times made it quite clear why he desired the presence of a naval vessel. The Ottoman government was clearly not deceived, for the *Chicago* finally arrived at Smyrna on 2 March.

The warship proceeded to visit the principal Turkish ports and then, after remaining in Near Eastern waters for nearly a month, returned to the western Mediterranean. Erban wrote in his report of the eastern cruise that all the detained naturalized American citizens had been released before the *Chicago* arrived. He also observed that much of the trouble was caused by Armenians who went to the United States and later returned to Turkey. They were frequently involved in what the Turkish authorities considered subversive activities, and many were arrested. Unfortunately, "genuine American citizens" were occasionally caught up in the web. Erban felt that Terrell had overreacted and that the difficulties could have been cleared up by diplomacy without the presence of a warship.[18]

In June the *Chicago* reached England, where Erban received word that he would be relieved in September by Rear Admiral William A. Kirkland. During the intervening months the warship visited ports in the British Isles and northern Europe. As a showcase of the new American navy, she made a favorable impression on foreign observers—this despite the masts and yards that gave her the appearance of a remnant of the old navy. The New York *Times* reported that "the era of good feeling which has followed the cruise of the flagship *Chicago* in European waters is likely to be prolonged. . . . It is likely that next year, or maybe this, will witness more and greater honors to the United States through its naval representatives in European waters."[19]

On 6 September 1896, Admiral Erban hauled down his flag on the *Chicago*. The wardroom gave him a farewell champagne party, after which he donated the balance of his wine store to the junior officer's mess. Mahan, who was not invited to the party and who was clearly relieved at Erban's departure, wrote his wife, "Erban let down his flag today and went ashore. He was slopping over, a thing which always rasps me, particularly when it follows a jollification and champagne. . . . One hates to see tears after wine." A week later he informed his wife that Kirkland "came on board yesterday looking much the same, but has shaved his chuks leaving only mustache and a painted chin."[20]

Kirkland was a veteran of some forty-five years in the navy, having entered Annapolis in 1850. A North Carolinian, he refused to follow his state into secession and remained on foreign station with the Brazilian and East India squadrons until 1864. During the last six months of the war he was captain of the monitor *Winnebago* in the Western Gulf Blockading Squadron and was present at the surrender of Mobile. Following the end of the conflict he received command of the iron paddle-wheel steamer *Wasp* in the South Atlantic Squadron. The Paraguayan war was going on, and the *Wasp* spent most of the

Rear Admiral William A. Kirkland, commander of the European Squadron, 1896–1897. *Courtesy of East Carolina University Manuscript Collection, Greenville, North Carolina.*

time in the River Plate. Kirkland, according to the squadron commander, was particularly well qualified for the command, "for he spoke Spanish and the dialects of the river like a native . . . and was a skillful diplomatist as well as a gallant officer."[21] His diplomatic finesse was not as apparent while in command of the European Squadron, and as a matter of fact, this remark seems incongruous with his character.

Kirkland was a colorful figure. He was known throughout the fleet as "Red Bill" because of his sandy hair, florid complexion, and fiery nature. He was, according to his grandson, not only an iconoclast but "something of a rebel," whose sharp tongue kept him frequently in hot water with superiors. He had a "foghorn" voice and salty language, for as Yates Sterling said, "he was in no sense the drawing room type." Mahan, who in many ways was so dissimilar, got along with Kirkland. Nevertheless, even he was apprehensive about Kirkland's commanding the squadron. "He is irascible, profane and gouty—a warm heart, but that is of little account when the temper is violent and uncontrolable [sic]," Mahan confided to his wife.[22]

There were some similarities so far as personalities were concerned between Kirkland and his predecessor. Mahan grudgingly admitted it, although he insisted that Kirkland was more "manly and masculine." At first Mahan was uneasy about the new commanding officer's attitude toward him; he feared that Erban would "poison the new one against me." His fears, however, were unfounded, as Kirkland clearly admired the author of the *Influence of Sea Power*. He tore up a memorandum from Erban about Mahan and later wrote a very complimentary letter to supplement his fitness report.[23] Apparently the attitude of the new admiral came as something of a surprise to Mahan, a change that was at first difficult for him to accept. On 13 September, he wrote "[Kirkland] appears disposed to leave much more in my hands than did Erban, but on the other hand he is a much more . . . decided man than the other, and may be worse if I make mistakes." On 5 October, he observed that

> Kirkland has not been on board more than three weeks and has been very nice to me, although I've indications of an impatient temper which may become uncomfortable. . . . He seems disposed to make a companion of me. . . . asks me to walk with him, etc. Of course, for one of my reserve . . . and temper . . . , this has its inconvenient side . . . he walks slowly whereas I go fast. He is besides extremely profane, to a degree distasteful to me; but I am determined . . . to avoid any occasion of coldness or dislike.

Kirkland was in poor health, which may explain in part his frequent outburst of temper. On 21 November, Mahan told his wife that the Admiral "suffers much gout and has so drenched his stomach with _____ [?] that it is in very bad condition. He is continually upset and is somewhat worried especially for fear less any thing should hinder his promotion. . . . The Admiral is mainly dominated by the desire to reach a climate where his gout will give him less trouble and now fancies Algiers." The *Chicago* was visiting various British ports at the time Mahan wrote, and they did go to Algiers in December, where she remained until relieved by the *San Francisco* two months later. Although the last months had certainly been more pleasant than the first so far as his relationship with his commanding officer was concerned, Mahan had not enjoyed the cruise. The hoisting of the huge homeward-bound pennant—some 380 feet in length—to the main truck must have gladdened his heart.

Kirkland had hoped for a quiet cruise, but this was not to be. Shortly after breaking his flag on the *Chicago*, he outlined an itinerary that included the more pleasant ports in the Mediterranean. He ignored the eastern part, which prompted Mahan to remark to his wife, "No Levant, but I fear he may be ordered to go there." Mahan's prediction was correct, but by the time the admiral's presence was required in the Near East, the *San Francisco* had relieved the *Chicago*. In December, the U.S. minister in Constantinople was informed that Kirkland would be "requested" to send a vessel to the Turkish coast as soon as one was available. The cruiser *Marblehead* was then ordered from the Caribbean to refit at Norfolk and join the European Squadron as soon as possible. The *Army and Navy Journal* noted that she was particularly well suited for duty in Turkish waters because of her light draft.[24] The vessel displaced only 2,094 tons and frequently was described as a "gunboat" or "peace cruiser," because she was deliberately designed for peacetime service. However, the *Marblehead* would not arrive in European waters until March 1895.

In the meantime, because of Terrell's demands, Kirkland reluctantly agreed to take the *San Francisco* to the Near East. The admiral refused to accept the possibility that there was any urgency or even necessity for the cruise and was determined to make it as brief and painless as possible. The flagship got underway from Algiers on 28 February and went first to Alexandria. After spending a week there, giving the officers and men time to visit Cairo and the pyramids, she entered Turkish waters and spent several days at anchor in Jaffa, Syria. Since there seemed to be no trouble, Kirkland ignored the other major Ottoman ports, spent a few days at Piraeus, Greece, and left for Italy. More than likely, notification from the secretary of the navy early in March that he was to represent the United States at the ceremonies opening the canal at Kiel, Germany, in June was a factor in his hurried departure. Nevertheless, there can be little doubt that he was unenthusiastic about the cruise in the eastern Mediterranean in the first place.

The brevity of his visit did not go unnoticed. The American consul at Beirut expressed bitter disappointment that the *San Francisco* failed to visit that port. He was particularly irritated because the State Department had assured him that the warship would do so. The consul also wrote the admiral but received no reply. Terrell in delineating his distress mentioned his "feeling of dread should the Admiral's boat [sic] continue to avoid the coast when our people express their fear of an approaching massacre."[25] The State Department was receiving similar reports from missionaries. Reverend Judson Smith, executive secretary of the American Board of Commissioners for Foreign Missions, in an appeal for naval protection, emphasized the missionaries' growing fear of a renewal of the Armenian massacres.

The Armenians, some one to one-and-a-half million, were scattered throughout the Ottoman Empire. Most lived in the high mountains and elevated plateaus of eastern Asia Minor. They were a minority and, primarily because they were Christians, a badly oppressed minority.[26] In the middle of the nineteenth century the Armenians came under the influence of a cultural revival. Newspapers and schools were established, and many young Armenians were educated abroad. Gradually there developed a national movement that ultimately had as its major objective autonomy for the Turkish Armenians. At first the Armenian nationalists hoped for international assistance, but by the 1880s they were moving towards revolution. From 1890 on disturbances between Turks and Armenians were frequent, culminating in August 1894, when a rising in the Sassun district was put down with the slaughter of thousands of Armenians. Public outcry in Europe led to an investigation, which solved nothing. The Turkish government, with some validity, declared that they had suppressed a revolution, and at the same time they insisted that there had been no massacre. A commission of representatives from France, Russia, and Great Britain recommended certain reforms, but as usual the Sultan vacillated. By the spring of 1895 it became apparent that without coercion Abdul Hamid had no intention of carrying out the reforms recommended by the powers. Nevertheless, Great Britain was the only one of the powers willing to use force.[27]

The American missionaries were concentrated primarily in the Armenian districts. In February 1895, a missionary stationed at Smyrna wrote to Judson Smith, warning of the possibility of renewed violence. He mentioned that the missionaries were evidently suspected of "encouraging [the Armenians] . . . in their efforts towards a revolt." He then appealed for naval protection.

> I do not know how much influence a word from you would have at Washington, but if it might be the means of sending to this point one or more gun-boats flying the Stars and Stripes, I believe it would do more to modify the feeling of this government towards American interest in Turkey than any amount of diplomacy. But a visit should not be merely a hasty flying visit, but so much of a stop as to the Turks, would *mean business*. . . . The wholesome influence of such visits cannot be questioned, for news of a gunboat in the Smyrna harbor is carried at once far into the interior. . . . We feel that we are neglected, almost ignored, at present.[28]

Finally, he informed the executive secretary that when the *Chicago* visited Smyrna in 1894, Admiral Erban told him that he would recommend the establishment of a naval station there.[29]

In a letter to the secretary of state, Judson Smith expressed his interest in such a naval station, but the suggestion was politely ignored until the New York *Herald* carried an article about it. Undoubtedly the information was supplied by the board, for the *Herald* mentioned not only Smith's letter but Erban's supposed recommendation as well. The State Department immediately consulted with the secretary of the navy, who responded that it was "contrary too the practice of this government to establish naval stations abroad on account of the great expense incident to their maintenance."[30] The matter was then dropped.

Although Judson Smith was not successful in his efforts to persuade the government to locate a naval base in the Near East, his power was felt in Washington. As a matter of fact it would be difficult to exaggerate the influence that missionaries, through their home boards, had on American foreign policy in the 1890s. It was strong at least partly because of the evangelism of Dwight Moody and his converts, who began advocating the saving of souls not only in America but throughout the world. Josiah Strong was perhaps the best known of the evangelists who advocated the establishment of a missionary frontier abroad. A Congregational minister and prolific writer, he wanted to Christianize the world, a goal that he considered inevitable because of the superiority of the Anglo-Saxon race. Strong and other religious leaders began to link the missionary movement with economic expansion. One of the missionaries in Syria recognized this when he identified the commercial interests of Smyrna as a justification for establishing a naval station there. Missionary fervor reached its peak during the 1890s and the early years of the twentieth century. Humanitarianism, nationalism, and imperialism provided the framework by which the missionary movement gained public support.[31]

It was in this context that the American missionaries in Turkey worked to mold public opinion as well as public policy. These missionaries, of course, had been under the watchful care (including naval protection) of the United States government for many years, but the Armenian crisis created a situation that for the first time seriously threatened the traditional policy of noninvolvement in Turkish internal affairs. To be sure, immigrant Armenians played a part in this change, but the leadership was provided by ministers, missionaries, and church boards. There were few commercial interests, and no imperialistic design to speak of. In 1892 at least nine-tenths of the work of the U.S. legation in Constantinople dealt with missionary affairs. Lloyd Griscom, the American chargé d'affaires to the legation in Constantinople in the 1890s, wrote, "Trade between the United States and Turkey was negligible; the Legation's real purpose was to protect and advance the interest of the hundreds of missionaries scattered throughout the country—an American in Turkey was practically synonymous with missionary."[32]

The power of missionaries in the Ottoman Empire was so great that they could literally "make or break" U.S. diplomatic representatives there. During the last decade of the nineteenth century, the missionaries in Turkey became the greatest single factor shaping the course of American-Turkish relations. As Griscom emphasized, "Even the head of our State Department used to quake when the head of a Bible society walked in." Understandably, when Judson Smith requested in March 1895 that warships be sent to Turkish ports, Gresham and Herbert heeded his request.

Admiral Kirkland and the *San Francisco* arrived at Palermo, Italy, in late March 1895, and there he received a peremptory order from the department to return immediately to Turkish waters. Within a few days he learned that the *Marblehead*, en route to Gibraltar, was ordered to join him in the Near East. The *Marblehead* was to go to Beirut and the *San Francisco* to Smyrna. Herbert ordered the admiral to investigate the "alarming apprehensions. . . in regard to the massacre of Christians in Turkey." If his investigation proved sufficient ground for concern, he was to inform Turkish officials "that it is the intention of this Government to afford full protection to its citizens." The combination of Terrell's warnings and pressure from the influential missionary board in Boston had had their effect.[33]

The orders irritated Kirkland. He wrote Mahan, "They couldn't find time to send us word at Athens that we were wanted in Smyrna but waited till we got here [Palermo]—now we have to turn round and go back—the round trip is only some 1600 miles." Eight hours after receiving the orders, the *San Francisco* steamed for Smyrna.

On 5 and 6 April, American newspapers carried news of the dispatch of warships to Turkish waters. The New York *Herald* headlined the story on 6 April: "A massacre threatened—United States war vessels ordered to Turkish waters immediately." In Washington, Mavroyeni Bey, the Turkish minister, demanded an explanation from the State Department, "in view of the friendly relations which unite the two Countries." In normal diplomatic double talk he was assured that the visit was a friendly one. In a following exchange of notes American officials admitted to him that they were being sent to investigate whether there were just grounds for "the apprehension of insecurity of life and property which our citizens in that region have expressed."

The ever-suspicious Turks distrusted the friendly nature of this visit when American newspapers repeatedly suggested that the ships were being sent there because of the Armenian troubles. Ottoman officials apparently suspected that the real reason for the American naval force was to join European powers in bringing pressure to bear on the Sultan over the Armenian problem. The Sultan told the German ambassador that he was astonished at the appearance of a warship "with the alleged purpose of saving the inhabitants of Asia Minor who were under American protection from an approaching massacre." He went on to say that "this unfounded rumor must have been put about by the Armenians in order to revive the sympathy of the Powers and especially of America."[34] In note after note, the Turkish government continued to insist that the missionaries were in no danger, that adequate protection was being provided them, and that the warships were not needed. The American government, however, refused to recall the vessels, pointing out that under its treaty rights naval protection could be provided its citizens and their interests: "abstaining from intermixture in the internal matters of other states, this government . . . so acting can alone be the judge of the occasion therefore, and may not be called upon to account for the course it may consider wise or necessary."[35]

The *San Francisco* arrived at Smyrna on 11 April. While Kirkland conferred with the Turkish governor, the ship's officers gathered intelligence from the city's inhabitants. The admiral was so belligerent in his interview with the governor that even the missionaries were alarmed. One missionary described it to Judson Smith: "He [the admiral] was exceedingly gruff and dictatorial in his first interview with the governor, telling him he had come to protect the Americans and threatening vengeance if he should allow any evil to befall them; and when the governor asked him when it would be convenient to receive him on board, and remarking, 'I suppose you have Easter tomorrow,' the Admiral replied, 'we have no Easter, but cannon.' "[36] A number of years later the ship's paymaster described this visit and the "diplomatic" role played by Lieutenant Aaron Ward who acted as interpreter:

Now I ought to say that Admiral Kirkland did not have a bit of use in the world for a Turk, and he was pretty sore at this time over the Armenian massacres. He would have like permission from his government to waltz into the harbor of Constantinople and blow that town flat to the ground, and what's more he often said so right out loud so that he could be heard. "Ward," said Admiral Kirkland, "you can tell that beady-eyed individual across the table—he looks as if he had murder in his heart like all the rest of his tribe—that if I had my way about it I'd keel-haul every blithering mother's son of a Turk that wears hair. You tell him that, Ward," and the admiral gazed as graciously as you like at the pleased-looking vali. "The august admiral," translated Ward, bowing to the vali, "desires me to tender to your excellency the assurances of his most devoted consideration." The vali hereupon bowed his thanks and smiled. "Did you tell the curmudgeon that, Ward?" inquired the blunt old admiral. . . . "All right," continued Admiral Kirkland. "Now you can just tell him that if these massacres continue I'll be swuzzled if I won't some day forget my orders, or at any rate get away from cable communications, and find some pretext to hammer a few Turkish towns. Tell him that, Ward—tell the black-browed runt that, Lieutenant, if you'll be so kind," and the admiral with his face wreathed in a gracious self-satisfied smile, bowed respectfully in the direction of the vali. "The most august admiral," said Ward to the Turk, "desires me to convey to your excel-

lency the hope that your present station is one of unending happiness for
you and your family. . . ." The conversation went on in this way for about
an hour and a half [before the vali took his leave]. . . . On the following
day Lieutenant Ward went ashore on some personal business. He ran
smack into the vali. . . . The vali beckoned pleasantly Ward to approach
him. "My boy," said the vali, in perfect, liquidly fluent, and bubbling
English such as Ward had never before heard a Turk use, "My boy, will
you be good enough to say to the gracious Admiral Kirkland for me that I
regard you not only as an interpreter of inestimable value, but as a gifted
diplomatist, as well."[37]

Although the anecdote is more than likely an exaggeration, it is the kind of
incident that "Red Bill" was known for. Kirkland's visit impressed Thomas R.
Gibson, the American consul at Smyrna: "He not only carried out the orders
of the Department in his [negotiations with] . . . the Turkish officials, but he
made such an impression by his characteristic and commanding manner as to
allay the fears of Americans in particular and of Christians in general."[38] What
effect, if any, it had on the Turkish officials is not mentioned.

Kirkland cabled his report to the Navy Department. He saw no evidence of
"a massacre of Christians," and no evidence that such might occur in the
future. The admiral was convinced, as he bluntly informed the secretary, that
the governor of Massachusetts "is as much liable for the murder of settlers by
the Apaches as the Governor of Smyrna for the murder of the Armenians by
the Kurds."[39]

Meanwhile the *Marblehead* arrived at Beirut, having steamed 2,000 miles
from Algiers in less than a week. She was commanded by Captain Charles
O'Neil, who entered the navy in 1861 as a volunteer enlisted man and retired
in 1904 as a rear admiral in charge of the Bureau of Ordnance. Shortly after the
Marblehead arrived in Beirut harbor, O'Neil called on the Turkish governor
and informed him of his orders to protect American citizens. According to
O'Neil, who later wrote an account of his eastern Mediterranean cruise,[40] the
governor in some surprise replied, "Have you seen or heard any thing amiss?
Your men have been on liberty too. Is there anything wrong?" "I had to say,"
O'Neil wrote, "we had not seen or heard anything wrong, and he replied 'I
assure you, if a Musselman mule kicks a Christian, they call it a Turkish massacre!' " O'Neil's report strengthened Kirkland's conclusions that the missionaries were in no immediate danger; an opinion concurred in by the British
consul in Beirut when he reported to his superior in Constantinople that an
American warship had arrived. The consul added, however, that the "presence of the ship of war will have good moral effect."[41] As far as the American
missionaries were concerned, he erred badly.

The American Board of Commissioners for Foreign Missions and Judson
Smith were duly informed of the results of Kirkland's investigation. It did nothing to placate the board, which was being bombarded by communications from

angry missionaries. The Reverend Harrison Dwight wrote from Constantinople: "The ships of war have come upon the coast, have reported that they see no missionaries in danger of massacre, but see plenty of smiling and sensible Turks ready to entertain them, and this being the case they are making ready to depart for the Holstein Canal. So much for the great naval demonstration of the U.S. Government." Dwight wrote again after talking with Terrell. He pointed out that the newspaper announcements of the warships under way for Turkey alarmed the Sultan as well as Ottoman officials along the coast, but that their anxieties disappeared after conferring with Kirkland and his officers. Dwight also stressed that the quick withdrawal of the ships convinced the Turks that President Cleveland believed that the missionaries had deceived him.[42] Another missionary compared Kirkland's investigation to that of a "transient tourist who skirts along the coast and never sees a missionary. . . . The admiral had no opportunity to investigate and much less had he any desire to investigate." However, he saw the admiral and was not impressed: "[He was a] Godless, profane, vulgar fellow. . . . we were all much chagrined and disappointed. . . . the Admiral was angry that he was ordered from Palermo back to Smyrna . . . and he had no kind words for the missionaries or for any other Americans. If the American Navy has no better admirals than Admiral Kirkland they will gain little credit in foreign ports. . . ."[43]

Kirkland was equally unimpressed with the missionaries, blaming them for what he considered to be unnecessary cruises to the Near East. In reports to the Navy Department he strongly opposed the stationing of a naval force in Turkish waters. These reports, which were published by the press, inevitably brought down upon his head the wrath of missionaries and their families, clergymen, and others who had been following the Armenian troubles. To make matters worse, he also publicly criticized the missionaries. The New York *Times* quoted him as calling them a "bad lot," and Kirkland as much as admitted it to Mahan when he wrote, "I met several liars and sons of bitches in the east, not all of them outside the limits of the Church," and added, "I left them a first class reputation to maligne and guess they'll—some of them— make a riffle at it. . . ."[44] The mounting public criticism caused by these intemperate remarks resulted in Secretary Herbert's demanding an explanation. Kirkland's reply did not disavow the published statements, but merely stated, "I have authorized no person to circulate the opinion credited to me by the newspapers."[45] The naval secretary was not satisfied with this response—nor was Cleveland, who was under pressure to relieve Kirkland from the command.

While the admiral's name was being bandied around from "pillar to post" in the United States, he represented his country at the most important naval review ever held. In March 1895, the United States received an invitation to the celebration commemorating the opening of the Kaiser Wilhelm Canal at Kiel, Germany, today known as the North Baltic Sea Canal. Construction had been started in 1887. At Kirkland's request two additional warships were temporarily added to the European Squadron, the armored cruiser *New York* and the recently commissioned cruiser *Columbia*. In late May the squadron of four ships assembled in Southhampton and then steamed to Copenhagen. There Kirkland shifted his flag to the *New York*, and on 15 June the squadron entered Kiel Bay, passing between two long lines of German warships.[46]

German efficiency was apparent throughout the ceremonies. Each ship (more than eighty warships were assembled in the beginning, and later the number was increased to 116 from nineteen countries) had a numbered buoy with the flag of the nation she represented mounted on top and was connected by telephone with the shore. In contrast to a naval review held a few years before in New York at which the vendors, salesmen, and others had exploited foreign warships, the German government purchased everything needed and resold it to the warships at a designated price.

The two-week-long celebration was a profusion of ceremonies and entertainments—banquets, balls, receptions, hunting expeditions, boat races, firework displays, sham battles and maneuvers by the German fleet, and a review of all the warships present by the Kaiser on board the royal yacht. The center of attention was Wilhelm II, the German emperor, who spent much of his time cruising around the harbor in an eight-oared galley. He made frequent and unexpected visits to the foreign warships, including the *New York*. At night the ships were illuminated by hundreds of electric lights outlining their hulls, masts, funnels, and even flags. The flagship carried a huge illuminated shield of the United States.[47]

Not all was fun, however. The squadron's officers were assigned intelligence duties. Officers from each of the four ships had vessels of designated nations to inspect and write detailed reports on. For example, the *New York*'s officers were responsible for intelligence reports on the warships of England, Italy, and Russia.[48]

The United States had hoped to make a favorable impression by sending two of its most modern warships. Although the vessels, particularly the *New York*, received considerable attention, including a minute inspection by Wilhelm, the much larger German, British, French, and Russian naval forces attracted most of the attention. Because most of the official representatives of the countries present were senior to Admiral Kirkland, the Americans frequently were at the tail end of the ceremonies and entertainments. Robley D. Evans, the *New York*'s captain, in disgust later called Kirkland a "baby admiral" and suggested that an officer more senior in rank should have been sent.[49]

After the ceremonies ended, the European Squadron dispersed. The *Columbia* and *New York* returned to the United States via Great Britain, while the *San Francisco* and the *Marblehead* went to Kronstadt. From there the squadron—once again two vessels—went to Stockholm, Christiania, Norway, and finally to Gravesend, England. The *San Francisco* arrived at Gravesend for minor repairs on 27 July, and the *Marblehead* a week later. The *Marble-*

head was scheduled to enter drydock for minor repairs and maintenance, but received orders to the Near East before this could take place.

On 9 August 1895, newspapers carried a report that an American school in Tarsus, Turkey, had been attacked and "looted" by a mob. Under pressure from missionary interests, and without confirming the incident's authenticity with minister Terrell, Richard Olney, the new secretary of state, requested the navy to send a warship to the Turkish coast.[50] Two days later Herbert ordered the *Marblehead* to get under way as soon as the cruiser had completed taking on coal. In informing Terrell of this action, Assistant Secretary of State Adee justified it on the grounds that the visit by "[a]... European [squadron]... a few months before had produced good effect." Terrell forwarded the results of his investigation of the incident to Washington, disclosing that the incident had been nothing more than a quarrel between one of the school's employees and several Turks and that the "attackers" had been arrested for trial.

It was too late to order the *Marblehead* back to Gravesend, as she was already in the Mediterranean beyond recall. The State Department informed the navy that the cruiser was no longer required in Turkish waters but that she might be needed there in the near future.[51] The Turkish minister in Washington, who had protested the decision to send a warship, was told that the cruiser was simply on a routine visit to various Mediterranean ports. The note also rather cheekily requested that she be allowed to visit a Turkish port. The *Marblehead* by this time had reached Algiers, where she received orders to Spezia, Italy, for docking and painting.[52]

The missionary-educator whose employee was attacked, in what Terrell called an "outhouse," protested the decision not to send the warship and emphasized that the vessel was needed immediately and "permanently." "I fully believe," he warned, "it is the only thing that can avert serious trouble here."[53] The missionary's alarm was justified, although the presence of an American warship would have made no difference. Less than two weeks after he wrote the warning, the massacre of Armenians broke out again, this time starting in Constantinople and spreading into the provinces. Within a few days, more than 10,000 had been killed.

The European powers led by Great Britain had continued throughout the summer months searching for a solution to the Turkish problem. Britain followed its traditional policy of collaborating with the other powers, particularly Russia and France, but Russia opposed any action that would upset the status quo. Lord Salisbury, the British foreign secretary, seriously considered using force, which included sending a fleet through the Straits, if the Sultan continued to reject their demands for reform. This action was not implemented because of strong Russian opposition, a circumstance well known to the Turks. But the outbreak of violence in Constantinople threatened subjects of the powers, and in the middle of October, the Sultan reluctantly announced the acceptance of various reforms.[54]

In the meantime the outbreaks once again placed the Cleveland administration under heavy pressure to send naval forces into Turkish waters. On 6 October, Terrell cabled the State Department that the missionaries in the interior provinces were in some danger, but that he could not advise them to evacuate to the coast until naval protection was provided. Two days later he informed Washington that the British ambassador had requested his government to send warships to Turkish ports to provide refuge if needed. The following day the *Marblehead* was ordered to the Gulf of Alexandretta.[55] The three-day delay cannot be explained. The *Marblehead* was already in the Mediterranean, there for just such an eventuality. It is possible that the State Department was waiting for more information from Terrell. If so, the news of the British ambassador's request must have been the stimulus that persuaded the president to act.

On 21 October, the cruiser arrived at Mersin, the only seaport of any importance along the southern coast of Asia Minor. Captain O'Neil described it as a "dirty uninteresting little town with a mixed population of Turks, Armenians, Greeks, and a few foreigners." Although a railroad did run from the port to Tarsus and Adana in the interior, where American missions were located, at that time most of the transportation to those places was by camel.

O'Neil conferred with the American consul and among other things was told that the Tarsus incident during the summer had been more serious than disorderly conduct growing out of an argument between a missionary's employee and several Turks. He was told that the missionary himself had been assaulted. Although this information was not consistent with Terrell's report of the incident or newspaper accounts, O'Neil was convinced that the consul was telling the truth and wrote a formal demand to the governor that the "offenders be apprehended and punished." This was done without consulting the American minister in Constantinople, Kirkland, or his superiors in Washington. According to O'Neil the judge who had earlier tried the case and dismissed the charges was fired, while the accused were retried, convicted, and awarded prison terms. He later wrote, "How much our presence had to do with the result is hard to say; but probably, a good deal."[56]

For the next month, the *Marblehead* cruised up and down the coast of Asia Minor, O'Neil frequently going on shore to interview missionaries and Turkish officials. He even went inland to Tarsus, Adana, and other places where American missionaries and their institutions were located. O'Neil was apparently effective in his diplomatic endeavors. He got along with the missionaries and with Turkish officials as well. One missionary wrote him, "I am superlatively happy to tell you that we have had no sort of annoyance, nor so far as we know, have any of our people suffered any, since the Vali had [the] opportunity of pondering your sagacious suggestions. If he would only secure you for his private secretary." The American consul at Beirut lauded O'Neil's "firm but courteous course" in dealing with Turkish officials, and added, "such a man is not only an honor to the United States Navy, but he makes friends for himself and his country wherever he goes."[57] O'Neil became deeply interested in the activities of the missionaries, donating to their institutions and corresponding at length with them long after his ship had departed from Turkish waters. The impression O'Neil made was quite the opposite to that made by Admiral Kirkland, and "Red Bill" reaped the consequences of his faux pas.

On 22 October, the New York *Daily Tribune* headlined its evening edition "KIRKLAND ORDERED HOME." The paper reported, "a sensation in naval circles today to the announcement that Rear Admiral William A. Kirkland . . . had been detached from duty and ordered home." The decision was not wholly unexpected, as rumors to that effect had been floating around for several days.[58]

Kirkland had been the center of controversy for months. Missionaries and their home boards denounced him in newspapers and letters to President Cleveland. What angered them the most were not his public remarks about the missionaries themselves, but his opposition to maintaining a naval force in Turkish waters. He had also provoked the religious community by his supposed mistreatment of a chaplain. According to a newspaper correspondent, while at Kiel, the admiral in front of assembled officers, ordered the *San Francisco's* chaplain to go below as he was out of uniform. The chaplain later filed an official letter of complaint with the secretary of the navy and provided the press with copies of his letter. Finally, Kirkland had become embroiled in a controversy over a letter that he wrote to Felix Faure, newly elected president of France, congratulating him on his victory. On 21 July, Kirkland had written Mahan, "I was *astonished* to receive a letter from the Secretary . . . a most insulting letter of reprimand for mixing up with the affairs of France and endangering the Peace of Europe. Some of these times I'll show you my answer. Its the worst dose I ever gave any of those fellows and is a socker. I don't think the Department will publish it and I am laying back, with my bristles up, waiting for the next move." The next "move" was a demand from Herbert for a copy of the letter he wrote to Faure. Kirkland refused, suggesting that the French president be requested to provide a copy. The admiral also demanded that the reprimand be removed from his service record, and when the naval secretary ignored him, he appealed to the president.[59]

Most newspapers sympathized with the admiral. "Rear Admiral Kirkland ought to feel like a good boy pretty soon," the New York *Daily Tribune* noted sarcastically, "he has already been reprimanded twice by an infuriated Secretary, and if Mr. Herbert can keep up his present gait the admiral before the month runs out will have reprimands to burn. . . . This would be funny if it were not so pitiful and trumpery. There is something almost humiliating in this spectacle of the Navy Department . . . frittering away its time in pretty nothings." The *Army and Navy Journal* suggested with caustic humor that "if [the

French president] should refuse to furnish the letter Admiral Kirkland might be ordered to bombard one of the French ports. This would be fitting the punishment to the crime."[60]

There is little doubt that Kirkland had become an embarrassment to Cleveland and, perhaps more important, a political liability to the Democratic party. Missionary interests in the United States had become politically powerful. The Christian Alliance alone claimed to represent 15,000,000 "members of the Christian churches in America." It was more than likely this power that persuaded the president to change commanders of the European Squadron. Considering the fact that the squadron's principal mission at that time was the protection of those missionaries that Kirkland criticized, there was really little choice. On 17 October, the Bureau of Navigation prepared a memo on the correspondence concerning the controversy, presumably at Herbert's request. Four days later the decision was made to relieve Kirkland. As the *Army and Navy Journal* concluded, "the indiscretions by Admiral Kirkland in the matter of the missionaries would appear to be the chief occasion for relieving him of the command. . . . The letter to the President of the French Republic might have been passed over, for the only Frenchmen who vote in this country are the few who have been naturalized. . . . but to shock the religious sentiment of the United States is to commit the unpardonable sin. . . ."[61]

7

THE TURKISH CRISIS, 1895–1897

In November 1895, Acting Rear Admiral Thomas O. Selfridge, Jr., arrived at Le Havre by mail steamer to assume command of the European Squadron. His flag was hoisted on the *San Francisco*, which sailed immediately to join the *Marblehead* in the troubled Ottoman Empire.[1] Selfridge, whose father retired from the navy as a captain, graduated from Annapolis in 1853 at the head of his class, the first officer to receive a diploma from the Naval Academy.[2] He spent the entire Civil War period on active duty and had the dubious distinction of having two ships sunk under him—the *Cumberland* under the *Virginia's* guns in 1862 and the river monitor *Cairo* sunk by a Confederate torpedo several months later. "He has lived a good while for a young man," a fellow officer noted about Selfridge's Civil War career.[3]

Selfridge was an excellent officer, but his "by the book" or no-nonsense attitude was at times considered to be excessive by subordinates. As a squadron commander he personally examined the ships' logs, and when a discrepancy was found, the commanding officer would be reprimanded. Even spelling was corrected. He constantly wrote his commander expressing disapproval of any actions that deviated even slightly from regulations. He personally conducted weekly inspections of the vessels under his command, writing long, detailed reports of their condition. Should one man fail inspection, he would cancel liberty for the entire ship's crew. On one occasion he went into a detailed explanation of how to clean and paint the *San Francisco*, because "I do not approve of the manner painting is done and paint work is treated." He constantly harassed his commanders about coal consumption. Although the regulation requiring that the amount of coal used be recorded in the ship's log had been abolished years before, Selfridge demanded daily coal reports, including explanations for the quantity expended. The admiral's concern over fuel was justified while his squadron operated in the eastern Mediterranean; locally procured coal was expensive.[4] While Selfridge was in command, the squadron would spend most of its time in Turkish waters.

When Selfridge assumed command of the squadron, he was ordered to the Ottoman Empire to "personally investigate and report fully on the danger to American missionaries," virtually the same orders given to his predecessor.[5] The missionaries certainly thought they were in danger. Selfridge's arrival in Europe coincided with a new outbreak of terror against the Armenians. The Sultan's promised reforms of 6 October did not materialize; rather, within forty-eight hours after Abdul Hamid had given his word, reports reached Constantinople of serious trouble in Anatolia. In the following weeks thousands of Armenians met their deaths, along with the destruction of hundreds of houses and even entire villages.

As the seriousness of the Armenian massacres became clearer, the British again took the initiative in appealing for international cooperation. Early in November, Count Agenor Goluchowski, the Austrian foreign minister, agreed. He suggested joint naval action, including forcing the Straits by a combined European fleet if necessary. Already an English squadron had rendezvoused in the eastern Mediterranean, and both Austria and Italy sent warships into Turkish waters. Once again any concerted action against the Sultan quickly collapsed when Russia, followed by France, announced opposition to it. Goluchowski then withdrew his proposal. He lacked a genuine interest in the Armenians, but he was motivated by his fears of an Anglo-Russian agreement over Constantinople.

Lord Salisbury had to deal with two interrelated problems: the Armenian massacres and the possibility that Russia might take advantage of the trouble in the Ottoman Empire to seize Constantinople and the Straits. On 18 December 1895, Salisbury wrote Viscount Goschen, the first lord of the Admiralty, "The Eastern question may be summed up thus. It is impossible to mend the lot of the Armenians without coercing or deposing the Sultan. It is impossible to get at the Sultan without quarrelling with Russia, Turkey, France, and (now) Austria. So there is no practical course open at present."[6]

In contrast to the European powers, the United States was not concerned with the Turkish question except where it affected its citizens. But the presence of the American missionaries irrepressibly drew the nation further into the crisis. President Cleveland wanted to avoid becoming involved. When Terrell visited him, Cleveland instructed the American minister to "*Keep me out of trouble over yonder, and protect the Missionaries.*" This task proved impossible because of its incongruity.[7] The absence of important commercial interests in Turkey, the growing problem with Great Britain over Venezuela and with Spain over Cuba, and the general economic condition at home were all considered more important to the president. He lacked interest in an aggressive policy as far as the Turkish situation was concerned, yet in the fall and winter of 1895–96, intervention by force became a definite possibility.[8]

In the middle of November 1895, mission stations and schools as well as missionary residences were looted and burned at Marash and Harput. Although American missionaries were not bodily harmed, several were apparently fired upon and property damage was extensive. The news of the violence visibly increased the pressure on the Cleveland administration. In Turkey, American diplomatic officials forwarded petitions to the State Department. Missionaries flooded the country with appeals and petitions, personal letters to the mission board, to newspapers, church congregations, influential individuals, and government officials. John S. Kennedy, a wealthy New York philanthropist and Democrat, forwarded to Cleveland a number of letters he received from missionary-educators in Turkey.[9] The Reverend Harrison Dwight wrote Judson Smith, "I wish that you would stir up the newspapers to force our Government to send a ship here. . . ." Religious and business leaders organized rallies in New York, Boston, Baltimore, Chicago, and other cities. Religious journals like the *Independent*, the *Congregationalist*, the *Baptist Philadelphers Commonwealth*, and the *Methodist Western Christian Advocate* began to demand intervention by force.

Terrell himself strongly advocated the deployment of naval vessels in Turkish waters, including the Golden Horn; and his recommendations were no less militant than those of the missionaries. Early in November he wrote glowingly of a conversation held with the French ambassador, M. Paul Cambon. According to Terrell, Cambon approved the use of naval vessels to "persuade" the Turkish government to settle the Armenian problem.

> He [Cambon] freely expressed the opinion that it was not so much an irrepressible Mussulman populace whom Christian powers should try to impress with their earnestness, as the authorities governing (or neglecting to govern) from Constantinople. "If I were the American Minister," said the ambassador, "I should inform the Turkish authorities that my government would hold them directly responsible for the safety of every American in the Ottoman Empire." (This is language which I had already used at the Porte . . . as shown in my despatches) "and I should wish to have a naval force accessible to which I could point in order to back up my words."[10]

The French, who opposed intervention by the European powers, had no objections to American intervention. This, they believed, would in no way upset the prevailing balance of power and at the same time might ease the Armenian difficulty.

On 27 November, Terrell cabled the State Department that a "fleet" was necessary before the Turkish government would pay "under the muzzle of its guns" for the damage to missionary property. He even mentioned an ultimatum. Expressing similar sentiments a few days later, the American minister recommended that any demand for damages be delayed until "your Department is in condition to enforce compliance. . . ." He reiterated his conviction that the Turkish government would ignore United States demands "until a naval force compels it." In a concluding statement that was as rash as the one Reverend Dwight made a few days later, Terrell wrote, "If an American Squadron with [England's] . . . consent, unexpectedly rushed the Dardanelles and held the Porte under its guns, it would be the surest way of obtaining indemnity for the past and security for the future." Like most proponents of gunboat diplomacy, he believed that such action would not bring on war with the Ottoman Empire. "A calm survey of the situation," Assistant Secretary of State Adee was told, "convinced me that this Government must be compelled to protect our missionaries through fear."[11]

Terrell's messages to the State Department were, if anything, only slightly less hysterical than those of missionaries published in the newspapers. He frequently included lurid accounts of pillage and wholesale slaughter of Armenians, generally taken from information provided by the missionaries. He also recommended that the missionaries be advised to evacuate their inland missions and concentrate in the coastal towns where they would come under the protection of American warships. Cleveland agreed, and the European Squadron commander was ordered to station his vessels along the Syrian coast.[12]

At the same time, however, Admiral Selfridge reported finding little evidence that the missionaries were in danger. When he arrived with the *San Francisco* at Alexandretta, Syria, he learned of the destruction of mission property at Marash and Harput. A warning was sent to the Turkish governor holding him responsible for American lives and property, but the admiral remained convinced that the missionaries were exaggerating their peril. In later reports to the Navy Department, after his ships had visited various ports along the coast, he reemphasized his conviction that no immediate danger to missionaries existed, virtually the same opinion that Kirkland had arrived at the year before.[13] Nonetheless, the admiral requested reinforcements.

The Cleveland administration's response to the increasing demand for involvement in the Turkish crisis was cautious. A third cruiser, the *Minneapolis*, was ordered to join the European Squadron,[14] and the Sultan was petitioned to allow one of the American warships to pass through the Dardanelles to Constantinople, at the urging of the missionaries and the recommendation of Selfridge and Terrell. "Other Governments," the American minister wrote, "have . . . boats on which their people could take refuge, ours have none." When the request was denied, angry American residents in the Ottoman capital signed a petition urging that the denial be defied. Reverend Harrison Dwight, an influential missionary, in a note to the American minister asserted that the Sultan had no right to refuse the request: "only courtesy deters our Government from passing the Dardanelles when it chooses." Terrell forwarded Dwight's note and the petition, but even he balked at such action. "To attempt to force the Dardanelles with a war-ship would be madness. . . . If its passage was resisted it would mean war."[15]

On 2 December, Cleveland sent his annual message to Congress. Although it devoted as much space to the Turkish crisis as to the Venezuelan situation, the tone remained restrained. He emphasized that no American lives had been lost, although property had been destroyed; that the naval vessels were there to gather information and act as a place of refuge for American citizens.[16]

In the following weeks this position changed. He began to seriously consider sending strong naval reinforcements into Turkish waters and landing a force from these ships if necessary. This change in policy resulted from Terrell's recommendations, the appeals from religious groups, and perhaps more important, increasing political pressure on him to take a stronger stand.[17]

Inevitably the Turkish problem became embroiled in American politics. Republicans criticized the Cleveland administration for its failure to respond to missionary appeals. Members of Congress began to recognize the political sensitivity of the issue. Representative George A. Boutelle of Maine, who had several missionaries from his district serving in Turkey, wrote Olney, requesting that additional naval vessels be sent to the eastern Mediterranean. Senator Orville Platt of Connecticut asked that a warship be stationed at Alexandretta, because a company from his state had a large business interest there. Olney passed it to naval secretary Herbert with an attached note: "I would like to suggest for your consideration the importance of doing what is desired," he wrote in endorsement. Wilkinson Call of Florida demanded in a Senate speech cooperation with other powers in "suppressing the cruelties perpetuated on an innocent people." Senator George F. Hoar of Massachusetts, the home state of the foreign mission board, was particularly jingoistic. He wired Cleveland of his support in whatever action the president might take against the Turks, who, for all he cared, could be treated "as pirates or common enemies of the human race." However, his colleague from Massachusetts, Henry Cabot Lodge, rejected a policy of active intervention in Turkey. "We have no political interests . . . [there]," he wrote to a correspondent, "and our consistent policy has always been to hold entirely aloof from the affairs of Europe."[18] On 10 December, Senators Call and Hoar introduced resolutions calling on the administration to prevent by peaceful negotiations, or by force of arms if necessary, the cruelties inflicted on the Armenians.[19]

Nine days later Admiral Selfridge was ordered to concentrate his squadron at Alexandretta, to take on board all Americans, and if necessary to "land a force." Alexandretta was selected because the city of Marash, some ninety miles inland, was considered the point of greatest danger. Selfridge's reply made it clear that he considered the whole idea ludicrous. He only had approximately 3,000 men (including a few dozen Marines) to man his vessels, and Marash was a ten-day journey, "there being for a large part of the way nothing but bridle paths."[20] The plan to land a force was discarded, but the squadron did drop anchor off Alexandretta to await the arrival of missionaries from the interior.

The New York *Times* suggested in its 20 December issue that the decision to remove the missionaries immediately was prompted by the fear that the Venezuelan crisis with Great Britain might lead to war, and the European Squadron would be bottled up in the Mediterranean. Nothing has been found to substantiate this. The Venezuelan problem had become a crisis when Cleveland sent a special message to Congress on 17 December, reviewing the boundary controversy between Venezuela and Great Britain, and in short, announcing that the United States would determine the boundary and enforce it by force if necessary. This message was delivered *two days* before Selfridge was ordered to land a force at Alexandretta. Probably the timing was coincidental. As Cleveland did not expect war with Great Britain, the European Squadron was not even alerted. Nevertheless, for several weeks—until the latter part of January 1896—Cleveland was faced with two potentially explosive situations.

Joseph Chamberlain, British secretary of state for colonies, suggested to Lord Salisbury the idea of a joint naval demonstration against Turkey as a means of distracting American attention from the Venezuelan issue. On Christmas Eve he wrote the prime minister:

> I think there is a possibility of getting good out of evil.... Would it be possible to communicate to the American Government some of the reports about massacres and cruelties and appeal to them to join us in a naval demonstration.... The demonstration might take the form of cutting him [Turkey] off from Arabia and from Crete—or even of forcing the Dardanelles.... Here is the proper destiny of the two Nations—not to cut each other's throats but to bring irresistible force to bear in defense of the weak and oppressed.... The mere fact of their alliance for such a Mission would settle the question and bring the Sultan to his knees.... In the stir created by such an alliance the Venezuelan difficulty would be lost sight of.[21]

Although Chamberlain advocated the idea again a few days later, Salisbury evidently showed little interest in it. This was at least partly because, as he wrote the first lord of the Admiralty, "In Armenia I have been told by the Cabinet practically to sit still; and in America, I can obviously do nothing else except sit still."[22] Salisbury did not approach Thomas Bayard, the American ambassador, about Chamberlain's proposal at this time. However, Lord Playfair, a liberal peer and a distinguished scientist, wrote Bayard on 13 January 1896 about it. Playfair may have been sounding out the ambassador and the American government for Salisbury in this way, as he performed such a role for the prime minister in the Venezuelan boundary dispute. There is no record that Bayard passed the idea on to Olney. The ambassador received a letter from a British subject who signed his name "A Glasgow chappie," which in part said, "All friends of humanity were looking forward ... to see the fleets of

Britain and America engaged in putting an end to the horrible Armenian atrocities."[23] Although Cleveland's administration did not consider cooperating with the British, it did seriously consider some sort of naval demonstration.

Early in January 1896, newspapers carried stories that a powerful fleet of American warships would be concentrated in Turkish waters. The Sunday, 5 January, edition of the New York *Herald* included an entire page on this "naval demonstration." The article suggested that the North Atlantic Squadron, at that time anchored in Hampton Roads, was under orders to sail for the Mediterranean and that other squadrons, including the Asiatic, would assemble there. Other newspapers carried similar stories. The New York *Times* headlined its account, "May coerce the Sultan." In the following days the press seethed with rumors. Even the usually authoritative *Army and Navy Journal* reported on 11 January that "We have absolutely reliable authority . . . that the administration has prepared a plan of campaign against Turkey."[24] Both the New York *Herald* and *Times* were critical of a naval demonstration. The *Herald* asked in one editorial, "Is jingoism again Rampant?" The *Times* said, "We can see no immediate need for sending even a single ship to say nothing of a fleet to reinforce Admiral Selfridge's command." The *Herald* warned that, because of the Cuban situation, warships were needed in the western hemisphere. The *Army and Navy Journal* pointed out that the Cuban, Venezuelan, and Turkish problems clearly demonstrated the need to strengthen the navy.[25] The *Herald* also asked, "Has Mr. Cleveland completely lost his head owing to the unprecedented ebullition of jingoism."

The navy was taking certain measures that can be construed as war preparations. Admiral Selfridge requested all intelligence on the Turkish fleet, "In view of possible complications." Shortly before Christmas in 1895, Rear Admiral Francis M. Bunce, in command of the North Atlantic Squadron, made a hurried trip to Washington. The squadron's scheduled cruise to the West Indies was cancelled, and most newspapers blamed the change on the Turkish crisis. On 2 January, Bunce ordered his ship commanders to make a detailed list of "fittings and articles" that would "unnecessarily endanger the officers and crew when under fire. . . ." Three days later, orders were issued for instructions in "arranging the knapsacks, etc., of the landing force. . . ."[26] The *Army and Navy Journal* later outline the preparations by the navy:

It is not generally known, but it can be stated authoritatively that this program was an extremely extensive one and meant business. In the first place, it contemplated the consolidation of practically the entire Navy at one of four places, Smyrna, Alexandretta, Beirut, or Candia. . . . In order to take Candia it would require an army of about 15,000 men. This was considered the best point of attack, not excepting Smyrna. It was pointed out that it is a splendid strategic point, and its capture would have created consternation among the Turkish officials and brought about instant compliance with our demands. It was suggested that it would be well enough to take Smyrna, but the danger of a land attack in case of occupation was urged as an argument against this plan. It is even stated that a place of supplies at some point adjacent to Turkey was selected, which the Department intended to stock with coal, ammunition, and provisions for the ships. Had Turkey not shown herself to be more anxious to protect American interests, and had Russia not entered into her agreement with the Sultan, there is every reason to believe that a lively struggle would have taken place between the United States and Turkish Navies. . . .[27]

It is, of course, possible that the whole thing was a ploy; that no armed intervention was contemplated, and that it was designed to frighten the Turkish government into settling the Armenian trouble. One might argue with much validity that such an intervention outside the western hemisphere was so contrary to traditional American policy as to be unthinkable. Many historians have never considered the Turkish crisis to be serious. It is equally possible that the navy was being readied in case of trouble with Great Britain over the Venezuela boundary dispute. However, neither Cleveland nor Richard Olney, his secretary of state, wanted or expected war with Great Britain.

Olney also did not contemplate war with Turkey; he simply looked on a solution to the Near Eastern situation the same way he approached the Venezuelan boundary controversy. He was responsible for the strong position taken on the Venezuelan matter and equally responsible for the aggressive policy adopted towards Turkey. A vigorous policy of direct action was the type of diplomacy he preferred. If, as a number of historians have suggested, Olney was convinced that vigorous diplomacy in the Venezuelan affair would aid his political party in the coming election, certainly the same was true of the Turkish problem.[28]

Yet Olney seriously considered armed intervention. Assistant Secretary of State Adee wrote, "Mr. Olney came very near directing a demonstration against Alexandretta to collect our demands, but he was distrustful at the way the European powers would take it." On 23 January 1896, a medical missionary recently returned from the Ottoman Empire had an interview with the secretary of state. During the course of conversation the secretary asked, "Suppose this country should send a fleet there to demand an indemnity from Turkey for the losses of property that [the missionaries] have suffered in these riots?" The missionary replied: "It would be hazardous." Olney later said, "The Government means to insist upon the indemnity, but in doing this it might be necessary to bombard a Turkish port, which would jeopardize the lives of the missionaries in the interior."[29] The apparent contradiction can be explained by the fact that Olney did not believe armed intervention with limited objectives would precipitate war.

Congress was also making warlike gestures. The New York *Herald* reported on 9 January that the Senate Foreign Relations Committee devoted its first meeting of the new year to "Armenian affairs." Turkey continued to play a prominent part in this committee's discussions for the next two weeks. On 22 January Senator Shelby Cullom, chairman of the Foreign Relations Committee, introduced a concurrent resolution calling upon the signatories of the Berlin Treaty to use whatever means were necessary to halt the violence and offering reassurance to Cleveland of congressional support in any appropriate measure that he might adopt. After two days of debate in which one senator, William P. Fyre of Maine, urged that American warships "sail up the Dardanelles and plant themselves before Constantinople," the resolution was adopted. Debate in the House was more vigorous. Representative Henry G. Turner of Georgia questioned giving approval for any action the president might decide on, including bombarding "the whole Turkish coast. . . ." Charles S. Grosvenor of Ohio and James A. Walsh of New York agreed that the resolution was too weak. "It should advocate protecting our citizens even if it means going to war," Walsh insisted. William F. Hepburn moved we sever diplomatic relations with the Ottoman Empire. Alexander Hardy of Indiana recommended that the North Atlantic Squadron riding at anchor in Hampton Roads sail at once for Constantinople.[30] The resolution passed.

The *Nation* reported that there was more debate over the Armenian resolution than over the Venezuelan correspondence. It went on to chastise Congress for abandoning the Monroe Doctrine and denounced that august body for standing behind the president even if "vigorous action were required." Sending a fleet, it said, would accomplish nothing. *Harper's Weekly* referred to the resolution as "raving bluster" and an "instance of the puerile levity with which foreign affairs are treated in Congress." The London *Times* said the resolution had the support of the American people, but the Vienna (Austria) *Pester Lloyd* remarked that "it sounds like a warning, or, indeed a lesson, given by America to the European powers." The New York *Herald* reported that Parisian papers were devoting considerable attention to what they called a new departure in American foreign policy. The *Journal des Debats*, the *Herald* wrote, "regrets that Europe has not some sort of Monroe Doctrine to protect it from the meddling of the United States in purely European affairs." The French minister of foreign affairs later said that he now looked upon increasing American design in Europe as the equivalent of the "yellow peril."[31] Bayard wrote to Cleveland from London that in regard to the Armenian question there seemed to be an insanity on both sides of the Atlantic, and "some of the propositions reported from the United States would wrap the world in flame if carried out."[32]

Whatever action the Cleveland administration had contemplated was abandoned in late January or early February because Admiral Selfridge's reports continued to stress that the missionaries were in no immediate danger and that the use of force would clearly endanger them. However, he did admit that, if a powerful naval force would pass through the Dardanelles, it might result in a "restoration of peace . . . at the Cannon's mouth."[33]

The missionaries themselves refused to cooperate. In contrast to expectations, few missionaries left their missions and homes for the coast and evacuation. One missionary angrily wrote, "We don't want warships as a refuge. . . rather for defense and redress." Minister Terrell observed that the missionaries recognized that "the most secure place in the Ottoman Empire is always on the Mediterranean coast . . . [but they claim] that the moral force exerted by the presence of a naval force in the eastern Mediterranean extends far in the interior." Reverend Dwight wrote Terrell explaining that the missionaries refused to withdraw because of a principle: "In brief, this principle is that a great American enterprise, and not merely the lives of its agents, is the interest for which protection has been invoked. . . . Our business [which he enumerated as schools, hospitals, and 'a large publishing and bookselling business'] is of sufficient financial importance to warrant the somewhat persistent demands which we ask for protection from the United States Government." Terrell forwarded Dwight's explanation to Olney. Exasperated at the missionaries' determination to remain in what he considered "fearful peril," he wrote the secretary of state, "Can it be that there is a hope that the United States may be *forced*, by the sacrifice of our missionaries, to resort to armed intervention."[34]

Throughout the spring of 1896, missionary interest continued to put pressure on the Cleveland administration to provide more naval protection. The missionaries had become increasingly critical of Terrell, convinced that he opposed naval protection. When Terrell came home on leave in March, Reverend Dwight quickly followed. Shortly after reaching the United States, Dwight passed on his misgivings about the American minister to a number of influential supporters. He also wrote Secretary Olney that Turkish officials were convinced Americans would "submit to almost any arbitrary aggression," as the United States government would not increase the number of warships in Turkish waters and send a naval vessel to Constantinople. In April, representatives of various missionary and religious organizations formed a committee, which met with Cleveland and Olney to demand more naval protection. When Terrell was informed of this, he commented that the missionary cry in 1896 was "for gunboats along the coast to aid in propagating the religion of love." Actually the missionaries insisted that their appeals had been misunderstood. They did not want armed conflict, as this would endanger their work (and themselves), nor did they favor abandoning their missions and leaving the country. They simply wanted adequate naval protection, refusing to recognize that this might result in exactly what they wanted to avoid. They stressed their viewpoints in meetings with Terrell and Selfridge and in communications with their home boards.[35]

With the missionaries backing away from their saber rattling, it is not surprising that the idea of intervention in Turkey began to lose its priority. Undoubtedly the other diplomatic and domestic problems that faced the administration at that time, as well as the possibility of complications with European powers, had an effect. By the middle of February 1896, Postmaster General William L. Wilson could write in his diary that the Cuban situation was the only diplomatic problem that "causes anxiety." The postmaster general also mentioned in his diary that the Sultan "has refused our request for the entrance of the *Bancroft* into . . . Turkish waters."[36] While debate raged in Congress over the Armenian resolutions and the newspapers reported the details of a powerful naval demonstration, State Department officials had quietly petitioned the Ottoman government to allow a small warship to be stationed at Constantinople.

The major powers had for many years maintained a "stationary ship," usually of small size, at the "disposal of their diplomatic representatives." American officials in Turkey and missionaries had long urged this action and during the 1870s the gunboat *Dispatch* was maintained there for nearly two years. However, Ottoman officials insisted that the right of a station ship was granted only to those nations that signed the Straits Convention of 1856 and the Berlin Treaty of 1878, and the United States was not one of these. In December 1895, Terrell requested permission for one of Admiral Selfridge's vessels to pass through the Dardanelles, which was refused. On 4 January, the State Department instructed the minister to request permission for the 800-ton gunboat *Bancroft* to be stationed at Constantinople as a dispatch boat. The British ambassador in Constantinople reported that Terrell "demanded" permission for a stationnaire and that the United States would break off diplomatic relations if this was refused. The American minister denied this, but did inform the Porte that refusal would be considered an "unfriendly act."[37] The Ottoman government at first curtly rejected the request but later agreed to reconsider, probably because of the threatened naval demonstration. It seems clear, however, that Turkish officials had no intention of allowing an American warship at Constantinople without approval from the major powers. Caught in an apparent dilemma between the threat of a naval demonstration on one hand and the "protectorship" of the European powers on the other, the Porte simply allowed the matter to drag on indefinitely.

On 5 February, the British ambassador informed Salisbury that Terrell had requested his support. "The matter was privately discussed yesterday at the Ambassador's meeting," he wrote the foreign secretary, "and most of my colleagues appear inclined to admit that the contention of the American minister was not unreasonable . . . that it was not intended to exclude the other powers from the privilege of keeping vessels for the service of their mission. . . . The Austrian Ambassador, however, stated that he had a most decided objection to the proposal. If the privilege was granted to the United States it would at once be claimed by the other powers and if every country had a war vessel in the

Bosphorus he could no longer consider that the closure of the Straits was maintained."[38] Austria's warning concerning the Straits virtually doomed any possibility of receiving the powers' approval. This attitude also ended any chance that Terrell had of gaining Turkish approval. Even a final half-hearted effort to obtain permission for the *Bancroft* to remain at Constantinople for a limited period was unsuccessful. Later Olney would attempt to enlist Russia's support by way of St. Petersburg, but months would pass before the Czar's government responded.

During the winter months of 1895–96, while the hubbub over a naval demonstration occupied attention, the European Squadron remained at anchor in Smyrna. In February, the *Marblehead* was sent to Naples for overhaul while the *Minneapolis* made brief visits to Alexandretta and Mersin. The flagship continued at Smyrna where the admiral had telegraphic contact with Constantinople and Washington. Selfridge persevered in his insistence that the missionaries were in no serious danger and that his vessels were serving no useful purpose confined to Turkish waters. He also believed that the assembled naval forces from other countries had done little to alleviate the Armenians' suffering. "After all," he wrote Herbert, "the Turks are accustomed to the assembling of war ships on their coasts for display."[39]

The admiral informed Terrell that he was going to assemble the squadron in April off Mersin in order to carry out tactical maneuvers. After that, one vessel would be left in the eastern Mediterranean, and the remainder of the squadron would be withdrawn. Selfridge did not inform the minister that he planned to leave Turkish waters in order to attend the coronation of Czar Nicholas II of Russia. Herbert had decided early in March to send Selfridge and so informed the admiral. However, the visit was not approved until after a cabinet meeting in the middle of April. Cleveland, aware of the potential political repercussions of removing the vessels from the Near East, reluctantly approved it.[40] More than likely Cleveland hoped that the presence of units of the U.S. Navy during the coronation ceremonies would persuade Nicholas to give his blessing to an American stationnaire at Constantinople. What effect, if any, it had on Russia's later consent is not known.

Early in May the squadron (without the *Marblehead*) sailed for Kronstadt. There the admiral and many of his officers journeyed to Moscow, where they participated in the pomp and pageantry surrounding the coronation of the last Romanov ruler of Imperial Russia.[41] The squadron remained a month in Russian waters and then visited Denmark and England before returning to the eastern Mediterranean in August.

While the squadron was on its northern tour, the little *Marblehead* returned to her lonely vigil in Turkish waters. Although there was violence in the Ottoman Empire during these months, most of it was in the interior. The *Marblehead* investigated a number of minor incidents, and on one occasion her presence probably resulted in a missionary's being released from jail.[42] There was no letup in the missionaries' demands for additional naval protection, including the return of the European Squadron, but after their earlier failure to persuade Cleveland, they had little hope of success. Dwight wrote Judson Smith in late July, "I doubt the possibility of moving our Government to do anything for us. The withdrawal of the fleet when it was known that the Turks would misinterpret this withdrawal, and the return of Mr. Terrell . . . gives the impression here that our Government has decided to abandon the missionaries to their fate." Terrell, however, did agree that the squadron should be ordered back to Turkish waters as soon as possible.[43]

In August 1896, two incidents sent the squadron back to the eastern Mediterranean. Early in the month a number of naturalized Americans were arrested at Aleppo on a charge of disloyalty to the Ottoman government. Then, on 26 August, a group of Armenians seized the Ottoman Bank in Constantinople. The immediate result was the massacre of several thousand Armenians in the capital and the renewal of unrest in the provinces. On the day before the second incident occurred, Selfridge (at that time in Southhampton) was ordered to send one of his two remaining vessels accompanied by the flag to Turkey. "Condition of affairs . . . is very bad," he was informed. The admiral sent a second vessel but refused to go himself. He excused this action on the grounds that his information based on reports from the commanding officer of the *San Francisco* (she had replaced the *Marblehead* in June) indicated that conditions were not that serious; second, the flagship *Minneapolis* needed an overhaul. In what can be described as a disregard of the Navy Department's instructions, he announced that he would visit Queenstown, Ireland, and then sail for the east about 20 September.[44]

Later Selfridge submitted to the naval secretary a lengthy report criticizing the policy of deploying the European Squadron in Turkish waters for extended periods. He repeated the argument that American interests were primarily missionary interests, located "wholly . . . in the interior, beyond the protection election approaching in November, Cleveland could not afford to antagonize the missionary interests by weakening the naval force in Turkish waters. Three months later (after McKinley's election), the squadron was withdrawn from the eastern Mediterranean.

The August violence also stimulated efforts to gain the Sultan's approval for of a man-of-war." He agreed that the Turks disliked the "native Christians," but they "respect[ed] foreigners." Finally, he recommended stationing one vessel at either Mersin or Alexandretta, eight miles apart and the "gateway[s]" to the missionary centers in the interior. "There is no trouble in any part of Asia Minor, that is reached from the Mediterranean Sea," he wrote, "and I have every reason to believe that this will continue." A month later he again requested that the squadron be withdrawn, included reports from his commanding officers, and asked that they be laid before the president.[45] Selfridge's perspective observations and recommendations were ignored. With an stationing the *Bancroft* in Constantinople. After a delay of several months, the Turkish government finally denied the American request to allow the gunboat to pass through the Dardanelles. This decision was no surprise to the State Department. In April, Olney had enlisted the help of Clifton R. Breckinridge, the American minister in St. Petersburg, in trying to persuade the Russian government to intercede with Turkey. Olney was quite aware of the relationship between the two countries. When Breckinridge reported his failure, Olney responded, "The Turk is at this time entirely in the hands of Russia and the . . . despatch boat will be permitted to pass through the Dardanelles when Russia says the word, and not before."[46] In August, Olney was informed that the Czar's government had finally given "the word."

On the same day (25 August) that Selfridge received orders to return to Turkish waters, Terrell was instructed to approach the Russian ambassador regarding a stationnaire. Surprisingly, the Russian ambassador agreed to cooperate but suggested secrecy. The application should be withheld until the *Bancroft* actually arrived at Smyrna, then together they would request her admission. As Terrell unfolded the scheme to the secretary of state, he would then go to Smyrna, board the gunboat, and "come on the boat up the Straits." The reasons for Russia's reversal as well as the ambassador's concern for secrecy are unknown. Perhaps they were in some obscure way involved in the efforts of Count Nelidov (the ambassador) to persuade his government to seize the Straits.

The State Department was enthusiastic, and even the navy entered wholeheartedly into the ploy. It received top priority. The vessel was hurriedly recalled from a "middy" cruise in Chesapeake Bay; officers and crew were assigned, and she paid a brief visit to the yards for modifications, the most important of which was to enlarge her coal bunkers for extended cruising. All of this was supposed to be done in secrecy, although William McAdoo, the assistant secretary of the navy, admitted that "it was quite impossible to have the ship put in a trunk and carried out of the country without the knowledge of anyone."

On 28 August, McAdoo notified Olney that "a moment ago the New York *Herald* correspondent came in here and asked me point blank if [the *Bancroft*] . . . had not orders to go to Constantinople. I positively denied this, and informed him that no orders of any kind had been issued to her (which is true). . . . I am satisfied that they ascertained nothing." McAdoo's optimism was ill-founded. The following day both the *Herald* and the New York *Times* reported that the *Bancroft* was destined for Constantinople. Recriminations followed, with the assistant secretary insisting that only his aide and the chief of the Bureau of Navigation knew the vessel's destination. The Turkish minister reminded the State Department that his government had not changed its policy so far as the Straits were concerned.[47]

The publicity (much of it exaggerated) surrounding the decision to send the

Bancroft to Constantinople once again generated rumors of American armed intervention in Turkey. Newspapers played up the possibility, and religious journals and leaders strongly endorsed it, but it was the foreign press that became most excited. On 14 October a Reuter's Agency story out of Constantinople created headlines in many European newspapers. The story, which was full of half-truths, announced that the American minister was to go on board the *Bancroft* when she arrived in Smyrna. The vessel would then force her way to Constantinople if necessary. The 15 October issue of the Liverpool *Post* carried the headline, "The Eastern Crisis: Active American Intervention: Determined to Force the Dardanelles." The Westminister *Gazette* exclaimed "United States and the Dardanelles: A Sensational Story." Nevertheless, most British papers tended to discount the story. The Sussex *Daily News* called it "purely sensational . . . utterly without a vestige of Truth . . . decidedly ludicrous." The Manchester *Courier* regarded it as a "Presidential election rumor." The London *Times* wrote, "The American policy of abstention from European quarrels unbroken for 100 years is not to be overthrown in a quixotic attempt to keep order in Armenia," and suggested that such a policy would mean war, a "policy . . . without any visible prospects of popular support."[48]

The publicity was also responsible for renewed interest in Anglo-American naval cooperation in the Near East. The chief architect was again Chamberlain, the colonial secretary, who had tried to interest Lord Salisbury in the idea earlier. For several years close cooperation, including an alliance, had been discussed on both sides of the Atlantic. Prominent Americans such as Andrew Carnegie and Alfred Mahan used the "Blood is thicker than water" argument to promote the idea of such an alliance. Even the Venezuelan difficulty was used to demonstrate the need for solidarity between the two nations.[49]

Chamberlain was in the United States conferring with American officials about the Venezuelan boundary dispute when violence broke out again in Turkey. On 19 September, he wrote Olney suggesting the idea of Anglo-American cooperation to solve the Armenian question. Cleveland was consulted and agreed that a qualified approval should be given to the colonial secretary. "It is hard to restrain one's self on this cursed Turkish question," the president told the secretary of state, "but we must do so I suppose. Of course you will not repel the idea he advances any more decidedly than necessary. . . . We don't want *him* to have any excuses for saying that we are in the least unmindful of the duty that rests upon us—even if his country is backward in doing hers." Olney then informed Chamberlain that "if . . . England should now seriously set about putting the Armenian charnelhouse in order there can be little doubt that the United States would consider the moment opportune for vigorous exertion on behalf of American citizens and interests in Turkey. . . . It would support such demands by all the physical forces at its disposal."[50]

Nothing came from it. Salisbury may have been informed, but if so, he made no effort to follow it up. As Professor Langer suggests, Salisbury was much more interested in Russian cooperation. At the time of the exchange of letters between Olney and Chamberlain, the prime minister had an opportunity to negotiate directly with the Czar. As before, the Russian government opposed joint armed intervention but did agree to cooperate in another attempt to persuade the Sultan to adopt needed reforms. The massacres did cease, but little was accomplished beyond this.[51]

Cleveland was probably just as happy that nothing came from his qualified endorsement of cooperation. He did hope that relations between the United States and Great Britain would improve, but the election of 1896 was imminent, and he was aware that public demand for intervention had declined considerably. The *Bancroft*, however, was under way for the eastern Mediterranean, and her ultimate destiny was far from settled.

Long before the vessel arrived at Smyrna, Terrell had given up hope that the scheme would work. He blamed its failure on the publicity. The Porte had been forewarned, and it came as no surprise when the Russian ambassador withdrew his support. The American minister blamed it on Anglo-American relations. "As for us," he wrote, "I fear that our country has ceased to be either warmly or seriously taken into account by Russia. . . . So long as we were considered a menace to England, we were important. But we grew closer to that power. . . ." When the Sultan told Terrell personally that the *Bancroft* would not be permitted to pass through the Straits (officially Terrell had never applied for her admission), the American minister informed Olney that he would not apply for permission "until thoroughly satisfied that the Russian Ambassador would . . . [waive] all his objections, for the Sultan would not hesitate to refuse me if convinced that his refusal would not be disagreeable to Russia."[52]

The *Bancroft* arrived at Smyrna in the middle of October, having required a month to make the passage from New York. She joined the vessels of the European Squadron already at anchor in the harbor. In a letter which demonstrates a surprising lack of knowledge about the controversy surrounding the *Bancroft*, Admiral Selfridge wrote brusquely to Terrell inquiring why permission for the *Bancroft* "to visit Constantinople" had not been obtained. In reply the American minister pointed out that he had not been ordered to request permission but advised that the vessel be retained at Smyrna. Selfridge agreed and held his entire squadron in the harbor until a decision was made about the gunboat.[53]

The United States still hoped to gain permission. The secretary of state responded to a Turkish plea for assistance in preventing the landing of "foreign revolutionaries" that the United States was powerless to do anything to Constantinople because of the absence of a warship. Terrell went even further, saying with tongue-in-cheek that if the Ottoman government so desired, he would be happy to request the stationing of a small vessel of war in the Turkish capital to prevent the "landing [of] undesirable" elements. Not surprisingly,

Ottoman officials did not reply. The American minister persisted, however, right up to the time that he resigned and left for the United States. Early in April 1897, shortly before his departure, he was notified that permission would be granted, if requested, for the *Bancroft* to make a brief visit to Constantinople. The visit never took place. War broke out between Greece and Turkey, and the units of the European Squadron, including the *Bancroft*, were deployed along the coast of Asia Minor.[54]

The squadron had remained at anchor in Smyrna harbor until early December, when news of renewed violence persuaded the admiral to send his vessels to various Ottoman ports. Shortly after Christmas the flagship *San Francisco* left for Genoa to undergo repairs; the *Bancroft* and *Cincinnati* returned to Smyrna, while the *Minneapolis* patrolled along the coast of Asia Minor.[55] The flagship lingered in the western Mediterranean for three months, including a month at Villefranche, while the rest of the squadron did yeoman duty along the Turkish coast. One of the *Minneapolis*'s officers complained that "we have not once lifted our anchor since we came here [Mersin] nearly two months and a half ago." Early in March, Selfridge informed the department that he would return to the east as soon as a general court-martial session was completed.[56] By the end of the month the *San Francisco* was again riding anchor at Smyrna.

The inauguration of William McKinley in March brought in John Long as Secretary of the Navy. On 8 April, Selfridge wrote the new secretary a very optimistic report about conditions in Asia Minor: "The situation is more encouraging than I could have hoped. Our missionaries in the interior . . . do not write with any apprehension of future disturbances." The admiral hoped that Long would agree to withdrawing the squadron from the Near East. Although missionary pressure in the United States had declined, those serving in the field were still requesting naval protection.[57] Any chance for the withdrawal of the squadron ended with the outbreak of the Greco-Turkish War on 17 April.

Two days later Long informed Selfridge that the protection of American subjects was his principal mission, adding that the "disposition of . . . forces would be left to his discretion." The admiral probably read more in this than the secretary intended. It seems highly improbable that Selfridge would have been allowed to weaken his force in the east, for McKinley was actually considering strengthening it. Theodore Roosevelt, the inexperienced but energetic assistant secretary of the navy, wrote that he "wished to heaven we were going to order the White Squadron to pass the Dardanelles," but this may have been typical Rooseveltian verbalism. In a memorandum to McKinley, he advised against sending one of the new battleships to the Mediterranean, "unless we intend to make a demonstration in force, in which case we should send certainly three or four armored vessels." He recommended dispatching the cruiser *New York* or *Columbia* if reinforcements were required.[58]

Yet Selfridge continued to advise reducing his force in Turkish waters. On

23 April, he wrote Long in language almost identical to a report to Herbert the year before, recommending leaving two ships of his squadron in the eastern Mediterranean. A week later he announced that one of the European powers (he did not mention which country, but it was probably Great Britain) had agreed to take under its protective umbrella Hellenic subjects in Asia Minor. He informed the Navy Department that, as this action would drastically reduce the possibility of serious disturbances, he was leaving for Venice "where I shall inspect the *Minneapolis*." The department reacted immediately and told him to remain in the east. Selfridge stubbornly refused to give up: "The Department can hardly realize the paucity of American interests in the Levant," he complained in reply, and he repeated his earlier arguments for reducing the force deployed in Turkish waters.[59]

Selfridge was displeased because he had not been selected to represent the navy at the Queen's Diamond Jubilee to commemorate Victoria's sixtieth year of reign. Although this was not the reason for his unremitting efforts to leave the eastern Mediterranean, however, it was certainly a contributing factor.[60] The naval secretary informed him that because his presence was needed in the east another officer was chosen.

Ironically, the squadron was reduced in May when the *Minneapolis* and the *Cincinnati* were ordered home, and only one vessel, the *Raleigh*, was sent as a replacement.[61] The squadron's reduction came about because the brief war between Greece and Turkey ended on 19 May with the signing of an armistice. Not only the two cruisers departed from Turkish waters, but also the flagship, leaving the gunboat *Bancroft* to watch over American interests.

The *San Francisco* left the eastern Mediterranean in order to investigate an incident at Tangiers, Morocco. The incident was minor. An employee of a naturalized American citizen was assaulted and robbed; and although the money was recovered, the American consul demanded an indemnity and the arrest of the guilty. Admiral Selfridge was ordered to enforce the consul's demands. The *San Francisco* arrived at Tangiers on 8 July and, after conferring with the consul, Selfridge sent the Moroccan minister of foreign affairs a sharply worded note calling for the receipt of $55,000 for "damages" and an apology to the consul. "The patience of the United States is exhausted, and unless . . . [the above conditions are met] I give your Excellency fair warning that I have the necessary force . . . to collect such claims." The *San Francisco* then left for northern Europe, leaving the recently arrived *Raleigh* to make sure that the warning was heeded.[62] The admiral's peremptory ultimatum had its desired effect, for the Moroccan government complied with the demands. One wonders what the bill would have been if the individual involved in the incident had been killed. This incident is a good illustration of the type of "gunboat diplomacy" that discredited the United States. Selfridge disapproved the presence of a warship, not because the incident was so trivial but because it was an example of how American officials abused treaty rights by allowing "natives" to claim "American protection."[63]

In September 1897, the *San Francisco* and the *Raleigh* joined the *Bancroft* in the eastern Mediterranean. There had been no outbreak of violence since the previous spring; however, the American government had demanded that Turkey pay for damage to missionary property during the 1895 trouble. It was hoped that a return to gunboat diplomacy might persuade the Turks to settle these claims. For months the vessels remained at anchor in Smyrna. The dull routine was occasionally broken by patrols along the coast and by brief trips to an Italian port for "rest and relaxation." The only unusual event occurred when the *Bancroft* was fired on by Turkish batteries at the entrance to Smyrna Bay. The Ottoman authorities apologized, claiming the gunners mistook the gunboat for a Greek vessel, a probable explanation as the incident occurred at midnight.[64]

In August the long-suffering Terrell had been replaced as minister to Turkey by James B. Angell, a former president of the University of Michigan. Angell found that he had no more success than his predecessor in solving the problems with Turkey. In December, he concluded that the Ottoman government would delay indefinitely without pressure. He recommended two possibilities: breaking off diplomatic relations or a naval demonstration. Even after the outbreak of war with Spain in the spring of 1898, Angell continued to call for the use of a naval force "to rattle the Sultan's windows." In August 1898, he urged the seizure of the customhouse at Smyrna, "which would succeed without the shedding of a drop of blood."[65] McKinley, however, opposed a naval demonstration and used the Cuban crisis and war as a convenient excuse to ignore Turkey. Oscar Straus, Angell's successor and a personal friend of the president, said that McKinley feared another *Maine* incident and "lost sleep over the Turkish situation."[66] Straus was opposed to coercion and wrote in his diary, after being appointed to the Ottoman post, "the President agreed with me entirely and said "I shall be guided by you, I shall support you. . . . no vessels will be sent to Turkey unless you demand them and only then will any be sent."[67] Straus requested none, and even the small squadron in European waters was withdrawn shortly before the outbreak of the Spanish-American war.

United States naval policy towards Turkey during the Armenian crisis of the 1890s was a failure. The pressure of naval forces, and even the threat of a naval demonstration, failed to persuade the Ottoman government to settle various differences with the United States. Several years would pass before the Sultan would agree to pay an indemnity for the destruction of American property during the massacres.

Although missionary property was destroyed, no American missionaries were injured or lost their lives. Was the presence of warships or the threat of coercion responsible for this? Certainly the missionaries thought so, yet naval vessels could provide little protection for the missions in the interior far beyond the range of their guns. In fact some contemporaries, including missionaries, actually feared that a naval demonstration might result in a massacre of foreigners. When the British prime minister urged such a demonstration, the German minister to Russia pointed out that the ships would "always come too late to rescue foreigners from a massacre in Constantinople."[68]

On the other hand, would the Ottoman government have allowed the missionaries to remain in Turkey if the United States had not exerted pressure through sea power? Probably not. Ottoman officials were aware of the influence of these people and blamed them for much of the Armenians' unrest.

Historians have stressed the effect that the Venezuelan and Cuban crises had on the building of the new navy in the 1890s, but the role of the Turkish crisis has been ignored.[69] Nevertheless, in the congressional debates that led to the passage of the naval appropriations act of 1896, the Armenian trouble was emphasized along with the Cuban and Venezuelan problems as justification for battleship construction.[70] Assistant Secretary of the Navy Roosevelt lobbied hard for the battleships. Characteristically, he wrote, "Spain and Turkey are the two powers I would rather smash than any in the world." He certainly got his chance with Spain.

THE NAVY AND THE
EUROPEAN POWERS,
8   *1898–1910*

At least two years before the outbreak of war with Spain, the navy had formulated plans for such an eventuality. In the summer of 1896 Lieutenant William W. Kimball of the Office of Naval Intelligence prepared a plan designating the Caribbean as the main theater and liberating Cuba from Spanish rule as the major objective.[1] The plan also provided for an attack on the Philippines and on the Mediterranean coast of Spain by a reinforced European Squadron. Naval strategists later gave some thought to modifying the plan, including an attack on the Canary Islands by the combined European and Asiatic squadrons. Although this was not adopted, they did agree to the establishment of a naval base near the Spanish coast as quickly as possible.

Theodore Roosevelt was convinced that war with Spain was inevitable and desirable. As assistant secretary of the navy he favored Kimball's plan and worked to implement it. Roosevelt's influence with President McKinley along with naval secretary John Long's ill health and disinterest in running his department placed the assistant secretary in an unusually strong position. In September 1897, while dining with the president, he outlined what he thought should be done if war were imminent. Among other recommendations, he advocated sending a flying squadron of cruisers to harass the Spanish coast. In November, he again summarized his ideas, this time in a letter to Lieutenant Kimball: "I would have our squadron in European waters consist merely of the *Brooklyn, New York, Columbia*, and *Minneapolis*; and of course, I should have this, as well as the Asiatic squadron, under the men whom I thought ought to take it into action."[2] He was successful in putting a man of his choice in command of the Asiatic Squadron, but not so successful with the European Squadron.

Admiral Selfridge's tour in command of the European Squadron was scheduled to end in August 1897, but the department agreed to allow him to remain until he reached the age of statutory retirement early in 1898. Competition for the few flag billets available was at times fierce, and aspiring naval officers frequently sought political help. Captain John A. Howell, commandant of the League Island Navy Yard, sought the support of William E. Chandler of New Hampshire, an influential Republican member of the Senate Committee on Naval Affairs and former secretary of the navy. Chandler agreed to back him for the European Squadron command. In return Howell promised to include the senator's son on his staff.[3] Chandler then approached naval secretary Long about Howell. Roosevelt became alarmed when he discovered that the Bureau of Navigation favored giving Howell the Asiatic Squadron. The assistant secretary was determined that that coveted command would go to Captain George Dewey. Roosevelt wrote to Chandler agreeing that Howell should have a squadron, but not the Asiatic. "By the way," he queried Chandler, "is not Commodore Dewey a friend of yours? I have been trying to get him the Asiatic Squadron." At the same time, Roosevelt pressured Long to disapprove Howell for the European command. The weary secretary replied, "I note your criticism. Possibly they are in a measure true, but they are all alike. . . ." There was no need for Long to point out Chandler's interest. Howell received the command.[4]

Selfridge was not slated to haul down his flag until early in February 1898. During the final months, the deepening crisis with Spain affected the squadron's deployment. As early as August 1897, Selfridge informed the department that the squadron was holding frequent torpedo drills and gun practice in case of war with Spain. On 11 January, the department ordered him to retain men whose enlistments were about to expire. A week later he was instructed to take the squadron to Lisbon, "in view of recent events . . . in Cuba. . . ." Selfridge, however, relinquished the command before the squadron reached Lisbon. On 2 February, Howell relieved Selfridge at Villefranche. That afternoon the squadron, consisting of the *San Francisco* and the *Bancroft*, departed for Lisbon,[5] while the gunboat *Helena* remained in the Mediterranean.

The Spanish minister in Washington assured his government that this movement was for no "other purpose than for its effect upon jingoes . . . [and] vote[s] in Congress." The American vessels in Lisbon were going on a northern cruise, he informed the foreign minister. Actually the commodore hoped to make a northern tour, but after the destruction of the *Maine* in Havana harbor, he was ordered to remain in Lisbon with his vessels coaled and ready for action.[6]

In January Roosevelt had urged Secretary Long to order the gunboats *Bancroft* and *Helena* out of European waters because of their vulnerability. The secretary hesitated issuing the orders until the *Maine* incident forced his hand. They finally sailed for the United States early in March. Shortly after they were detached, Howell was instructed to take his one remaining vessel to England and there place under convoy several merchant vessels that secretly had been loaded with ammunition. The convoy sailed on 26 March and arrived in New York two weeks before war broke out.[7]

The war was fought primarily in the Philippines and the Caribbean. In the Philippines, the Asiatic Squadron under Commodore Dewey destroyed a Spanish naval force in Manila bay and then established a blockade of the city. In the Caribbean, the North Atlantic Squadron under Admiral William Sampson blockaded Cuba and Puerto Rico and annihilated the Spanish fleet in the Battle of Santiago Bay. While this was going on, the navy was preparing to extend operations into European waters.

The prewar Kimball plan envisioned the deployment of naval forces along the Spanish coast; shortly before hostilities commenced, Roosevelt recommended sending a flying squadron of cruisers to the Mediterranean Sea. "The squadron should start [for the Mediterranean] the hour hostilities begin," he urged Long. "We especially want to keep the Spanish cruisers at home to prevent depredation on our coast."[8] This operation was shelved when Admiral Pascual Cervera disappeared into the Atlantic, headed for the western hemisphere with a Spanish squadron. In the middle of June, the "War Board" or "Strategy Board," an advisory body of ranking naval officers, recommended the dispatch of a striking force of battleships to the Mediterranean. Intelligence had been received that a Spanish naval force was preparing to sail for the Philippines by way of the Suez Canal.[9]

The battleships never sailed. A Spanish squadron had left Cadiz en route for the Philippines, but because of fueling problems it went no further than the Suez. Early in July, Long instructed Admiral Sampson to detach his armored ships for the proposed sortie. Sampson strongly objected to weakening his blockading force, and by the time his objections were overruled, it was too late. The Battle of Santiago Bay had taken place, and the Spanish government had asked for an armistice. The negotiations that led to the armistice led to the cancellation of the operation early in August.[10]

The Spanish-American War convinced even the most skeptical European statesmen that the United States had arrived as a world power. Lord Salisbury in a speech shortly after the war said that "it is the first year in which the mighty force of the American Republic has been introduced among the nations." This sentiment was echoed in the British press. Blackwood's *Edinburgh Magazine* commented that "unless all signs deceive, the American Republic breaks from her old moorings, and sails out to be a world power." In Paris, George Picot of the Institut de France wrote, "No illusion is possible; the equilibrium of the world is moving westwards." Jules Cambon, the French minister to the United States, warned his government that the Spanish-American War constituted a turning point in world history and that continental powers would have to cooperate to prevent Anglo-American domination of the world.[11]

Historians generally acknowledge that the end of the war with Spain was a watershed in American history—not that we immediately became a world power, for we had long been one before 1898, nor did it end our traditional policy of isolation, for the United States would continue to make no formal commitments or entangling alliances with foreign nations. But there was a change. Although the American people would refuse to recognize it, no longer could the United States escape the obligations of a world power. Equally important, the European nations recognized this as well. This change would affect the United States Navy, particularly its units operating in European waters.

The European Squadron was not reestablished immediately after the war. Nearly three years passed before a permanent force could be stationed in European waters. Trouble along the Pacific coast of South America and the Philippines Insurrection absorbed so many vessels that other areas, including Europe, were neglected.[12]

Nevertheless, American warships did cruise to the Old World during these years. No sooner was the war over than requests reached the Navy and State departments for visits; some were simply for "courtesy calls," others were "show the flag" requests, usually from American diplomatic officials. The diplomatic calls came primarily from officials in Africa and the Near East, areas that had traditionally required the presence of American warships. Because of the Philippines Insurrection a number of vessels plied the Mediterranean to and from the Far East. Dewey returned on the *Olympia* in the summer of 1899 and made visits to Trieste and Villefranche, where he was enthusiastically received. The majority of American warships visiting European ports during these years, however, were on training cruises. In 1900, the *Dixie, Alliance, Topeka, Wilmington, Vicksburg, Prairie, Essex,* and *Monogahela* made brief trips to Europe, followed in 1901 by the *Lancaster* and *Hartford*.[13] Although naval vessels had occasionally made training cruises to Europe before, these trips became common practice in the twentieth century, particularly the "middy cruises."

In 1901 the European station was reestablished. For some time the State Department had been urging the navy to do so, but not until the spring of 1901 were vessels available for this duty. In May the Navy Department announced that the Asiatic Squadron was to be greatly reduced. Two of the vessels, the cruiser *Albany* and the gunboat *Nashville*, were ordered to European waters. Then in June, the cruiser *Chicago* was withdrawn from the South Atlantic station and also sent to Europe. Rear Admiral Bartlett J. Cromwell, in command of the South Atlantic Squadron, received orders to hoist his flag on the *Chicago* and reactivate the station.[14]

There is some confusion as to the exact date the European station was officially activated. The annual report of the secretary of the navy for 1901 gives 19 July—the date the *Chicago* arrived in European waters. Yet on 2 March 1901, four months earlier, Rear Admiral Frederick Rodgers, as "Commander-in-Chief, U.S. Naval Forces European Station," reported his arrival at

Gibraltar on board the battleship *New York*.[15] A week later Rodgers received orders to proceed immediately to the Asiatic station. There is no record that Rodgers was officially designated as commander-in-chief of the European Squadron; yet the admiral continued to use this title without challenge from the Navy Department until he left the Mediterranean. With the entry of the *New York* into the Suez Canal in early April, only the training ship *Hartford* was in European waters when the *Chicago* arrived.

The two ships detached from the Asiatic Squadron did not reach the Mediterranean until September, and it was the twenty-fourth of that month before the squadron assembled at Naples for the first time as a unit. This rendezvous was brief, for within a week the squadron dispersed to begin its traditional port to port routine.[16] On 14 September, while the squadron's vessels were still under way for the rendezvous, President William McKinley died, victim of an anarchist's bullet. Within a few hours Vice President Theodore Roosevelt, summoned from a vacation in the Adirondacks, took the oath of office as the twenty-sixth president of the United States.

"So much of Theodore Roosevelt is comfortably familiar," John Blum wrote in *The Republican Roosevelt*. His colorful personality, flashing teeth, pince-nez, walrus mustache, bouncing vitality, physical courage, and moral fervor became well known to his contemporaries and later generations. The first decade of the twentieth century has been rightfully called the "first age of Roosevelt," for he shaped the foreign policy as well as much of the domestic history of the United States during that period.[17] A Renaissance man in his interests, Roosevelt was particularly attracted to the navy. He understood the relationship between a powerful navy and a vigorous foreign policy, considering worthless a policy not backed by the strength to maintain it. "The American people," he stated, "must either build and maintain an adequate navy or else make up their minds definitely to accept a secondary position in international affairs." He clearly would not tolerate a "secondary position," nor would the American people. As an outstanding "Realpolitiker," he considered a powerful navy to be the right arm or "Big Stick" of diplomacy.

Under the spur of Roosevelt's policy, the United States Navy truly came of age during the decade after the Spanish-American War. Admittedly fighting a badly outclassed navy, this conflict dramatically demonstrated America's potential naval power. The first lord of the Admiralty was keenly aware of this when he confided to a colleague, "I would never quarrel with the United States if I could possibly avoid it. It has not dawned on our countrymen yet . . . that, if the Americans choose to pay for what they can easily afford, they can gradually build up a navy, fully as large and then larger than ours and I am not sure they will not do it."[18]

Lord Lansdowne's statement proved prophetic, although the United States would not surpass Great Britain for decades. Nevertheless, in 1900 the American navy moved from sixth to fourth place, in 1906 to third place, and in 1907 to second place behind the British. This position was maintained until 1911, when Germany pushed ahead into second place. By the outbreak of World War I the United States had fallen to fourth place behind France. This drop in rank was not because the United States had deemphasized naval construction but a result of a gigantic naval race involving the European powers. Throughout these years emphasis was placed on capital ships. During Roosevelt's first term ten new battleships were laid down. Cruisers, torpedo-destroyer-boats, auxiliary vessels, and even submarines were added to the fleet, but the nation would be deficient in noncapital ships when we entered World War I.

The navy also attempted to reform its administrative structure during these years. The creation of the General Board in 1900 and the position of Chief of Naval Operations (CNO) in 1915 were the most important changes. Primarily an advisory body of professional officers, the General Board did not replace the bureau system but added a limited amount of centralized administration—not without some opposition from the bureaus. Nevertheless, under the leadership of Admiral George Dewey and the support of Roosevelt, the board gradually assumed a large role in policy determination.

Shortly after it was established, the General Board began to study the idea of acquiring naval bases outside the United States. Although the idea was certainly not new, the war and the acquisition of colonies added impulse to it. Rear Admiral Royal B. Bradford, the chief of the Bureau of Equipment whose responsibilities included supplying coal to American warships scattered over the globe, was an avid expansionist. He recommended a number of potential sites as naval stations. Priority was given to the Caribbean and the Far East, but he did not neglect Europe and Africa.[19]

The navy seriously considered establishing a base in the Canary Islands or along the Moroccan coast during the war with Spain. The Balearic Islands were even recommended and Bradford endorsed the idea, suggesting Port Mahon on the Island of Minorca. "It would be of immense value to any commercial nation," he emphasized.[20] The idea was dropped with the armistice. There is no evidence that the American negotiators at Paris approached the Spanish government about obtaining a site for a naval station in the Mediterranean or eastern Atlantic.[21]

Bradford, however, did not drop the idea. In 1899 the American consul at Marseilles suggested the establishment of a coal depot for American warships at that port, Gibraltar, or Bizerta. The chief of the Bureau of Equipment endorsed it, writing, "It is a simple matter to ship coal to the Mediterranean, but it is not so simple to obtain a place to store it." A month later the bureau reversed itself, voicing opposition to the acquisition of a coal depot in the Mediterranean, as "ordinary commercial coaling stations of the Mediterranean are sufficient . . . in time of peace." The bureau chief had not given up but simply shifted his attention to Africa. He urged the procurement of an African site "provided absolute sovereignty be obtained." Bradford was attracted to Liberia, but the State Department discouraged the idea.[22]

The General Board showed virtually no interest in establishing overseas bases and coaling stations in Europe or Africa. An undated and unsigned memorandum in the Admiral Dewey papers entitled "Government Coaling Depots in Order of Strategic Importance" listed eighteen potential sites. Algiers was the only site in European or African waters listed, and it was classified as "3rd importance." The General Board was primarily interested in the Caribbean and the Far East.[23]

One final episode occurred a few years later. In 1909 the government of the tiny Balkan kingdom of Montenegro apparently offered a bay and adjacent land to the United States for a naval base. The offer was not seriously considered. We no longer had a European Squadron, and warships visiting the Mediterranean could be coaled from commercial depots or from colliers.[24]

As a matter of fact, by that date colliers were being depended upon more and more to provide vessels operating in distant waters with their fuel supply. In 1901 the navy had nine colliers, and by 1904 the number had increased to thirteen. In June 1903, the Bureau of Navigation announced that colliers would be assigned as regular units of squadrons. The collier *Caesar* with a total capacity of 3,760 tons of coal was assigned to the European Squadron.[25] After the Spanish-American War, refrigerator or cold-storage ships began to shuttle back and forth to the various squadrons. The General Board did examine the problem of auxiliary vessels such as colliers, although it was much more concerned with combat vessels.

The concept of the "fleet in being" was probably the General Board's most important contribution to American naval policy. At the end of the Spanish-American War the navy returned to its traditional peacetime cruising policy of dispersing the vessels among the various stations and squadrons. Mahan, Dewey, and a few others opposed the policy, but Secretary Long and a majority of the senior officers led by Rear Admiral Arent B. Crowninshield, chief of the Bureau of Navigation, supported it. In 1900 the General Board went on record as favoring the concentration of all the major ships into one battle fleet. Its primary mission would be preparation for war—maneuvers and tactical training as a unit. Long refused to adopt the plan, stressing that it would have weakened the distant stations. However, in 1901 the board did persuade the secretary to agree to summer maneuvers by a reinforced North Atlantic Fleet.

In the following year two changes in naval bureacracy and one in executive leadership strengthened the board's powers and influence. Secretary Long resigned, and Crowninshield was replaced by Rear Admiral Henry C. Taylor, a naval progressive, as chief of the Bureau of Navigation. President McKinley's assassination elevated Roosevelt, an enthusiastic supporter of the Board, into the White House.[26]

Early in 1902, with Roosevelt's blessings, the board drew up plans for extended exercises in the Caribbean. The plan, as approved, included concentrating the units from the North Atlantic, South Atlantic, and European stations in one geographical area. The objective of this fleet mobilization was twofold: to test defense plans for the Caribbean drawn up by the Naval War College, which acted as the war planning agency of the General Board at that time, and to conduct general tactical maneuvers.[27]

Admiral Dewey agreed to assume personal command of the combined fleet, which was to assemble in the Caribbean late in the fall of 1902. The main battle force consisting of the Caribbean Squadron of four cruisers and two gunboats and four battleships of the North Atlantic Squadron was to rendezvous at Culebra, Puerto Rico. The South Atlantic and European squadrons were to join in the Gulf of Paria off Trinidad.

In the spring of 1902 Rear Admiral Crowninshield had assumed command of the European Squadron with his flag on the battleship *Illinois*. The recently commissioned *Illinois* along with her sister ships, the *Alabama* and the *Wisconsin*, were unique in the United States Navy. Their boilers were mounted fore and aft with the firerooms outboard of them to either side. This necessitated placing the vessels' two stacks side by side.[28] On 30 April, the *Illinois* steamed out of New York harbor and eighteen days later joined the remainder of the squadron, the cruisers *Chicago* and *Albany*, in Naples.[29]

This cruise was to be the finale for Arent Schuyler Crowninshield, scion of two prominent New York families. He had graduated from the naval academy shortly before the Battle of Gettysburg and had risen undramatically but steadily until 1897, when he was appointed to the most powerful bureaucratic position in the navy, chief of the Bureau of Navigation. His elevation to such a responsible position was due in no small part to the influence of an old friend, Thomas C. "Boss" Platt, a powerful political figure in New York. Crowninshield was ultraconservative as chief and frequently found himself at odds with the young assistant secretary of the navy, Roosevelt. He had opposed Roosevelt's nomination of Dewey to be commander-in-chief of the Asiatic Squadron, a fact that the victor of Manila Bay did not forget. In Dewey's *Autobiography*, Crowninshield is described as a "pronounced bureaucrat, with whose temperaments and methods I had little more sympathy than had the majority of the officers of the Navy. . . ."[30] Obviously, Crowninshield was uncomfortable with the former assistant naval secretary first as vice president and later president, and Dewey as president of the General Board and the most prestigious officer in the navy. He was nearing retirement age and had never commanded a squadron at sea. As his mentor Senator Platt said, in urging Crowninshield's appointment to the European Squadron, "Crowninshield is desirous of representing your administration at the Coronation [of Edward VII]. . . .[He] had no glory out of the late war."[31] Roosevelt, when he became president, was only happy to oblige.

From Naples the assembled squadron went to Southhampton for a naval review at Spithead in honor of Edward's coronation. After that the vessels made a summer cruise to the Baltic, where the *Illinois* was damaged by running aground on an artificial reef at the entrance to Christiana (later Oslo), Norway. The other vessels continued the cruise while the flagship went into drydock to repair the damage. Crowninshield was under orders to keep the squadron together and confine his cruising to the western Mediterranean until the winter maneuvers. After the flagship's repairs were completed, the squadron went to Villefranche and remained there until sailing for the West Indies early in November 1902.[32]

Crowninshield disapproved of the plan to concentrate the squadrons in the Caribbean, which would interfere with his European cruise. He also did not care to serve under Dewey. As he had done in the past, he used Platt as his mouthpiece. Roosevelt, obviously annoyed at the admiral's puerility, wrote the senator, "These maneuvers are undertaken for the benefit of the Navy as a whole. I could not possibly entertain . . . the idea of upsetting a scheme for the great benefit of our Navy because of any personal convenience of any Admiral whatsoever. . . . [The European Squadron] will be sent back doubtless as soon as the maneuvers are over, but it is a great deal more important for the Navy and therefore for the country that this Squadron should spend a couple of months in active work around Culebra . . . than that it should pass a year leisurely cruising around the Mediterranean."[33]

In late November the squadron arrived in the Caribbean. For nearly a month it joined with other naval units in various exercises before returning to the Mediterranean early in 1903. While in the Caribbean, Crowninshield received unconfirmed reports that after the conclusion of the maneuvers, the *Illinois* would be detached from the squadron and that the station might be abandoned.[34]

Although the department had no immediate plans to deactivate the European station, Admiral Taylor, the chief of the Bureau of Navigation, with the support of the General Board was determined to reorganize the fleet. He submitted a plan to the secretary of the navy recommending that the various cruising squadrons be "as nearly homogeneous as practicable." This would, he believed, result in better coordination when the squadrons were concentrated for maneuvers. As Admiral Dewey wrote in his report on the conclusion of the Caribbean exercises, "The naval force on any station in time of peace must hereafter compose a tactical unit, or portion of a fleet. It should not again occur that groups of vessels returning from foreign station to concentrate with others on the home station should have to be broken up and distributed to other divisions of the fleet because of the insignificant size of a group, or their lack of homogeneity."[35] Taylor also recommended that major units should be concentrated into two fleets, the North Atlantic and the Asiatic. The other squadrons, including the European, were to be substantially reduced in strength. The reorganization plan was approved.[36]

The European Squadron under this plan would consist of four cruisers. However, Crowninshield strongly objected to giving up the battleship *Illinois*, and Taylor was not inclined to push it. "It is unwise to treat a flag officer in a summary fashion, especially in matters concerning his flagship," Taylor wrote to the secretary of the navy. "I would like to have Crowninshield's consent to take the *Chicago* as the flagship of a handsome squadron of cruisers." He added, "My colleagues in the Bureau think I ought to force the matter in reference to the *Illinois*, but we are working not for months, but for years . . . and the delay of a few months in getting the *Illinois* into [the] . . . squadron of battleships will not affect the larger principle." Either the naval secretary or Roosevelt took a harder line, however, for Crowninshield returned to Europe in the *Chicago*.[37]

Within weeks after arriving back in Europe with the squadron, Crowninshield asked to be relieved of the command. Admiral Taylor approved the request but in some exasperation wrote, "Admiral Crowninshield seems to value his flagship more than his squadron." Crowninshield also recommended that the station be abandoned. "The inferior vessels *Chicago, Cincinnati*, and *Machias* selected for duty there . . . can reflect no credit upon the country," he protested to the naval secretary, "and in my judgment it would be unfortunate to show them there as a squadron." In another letter he approved the concept of "homogeneous squadrons" as long as the European Squadron was composed of battleships.[38] The Navy Department had no intention of deploying battleships in European waters and was actually giving some consideration to again abandoning the station.

Admirals Dewey and Taylor and the General Board, supported by Roosevelt, considered the traditional cruising policy of showing the flag as obsolete. Preparedness for war overrode everything else. "To this necessity," Dewey wrote, "peace cruising must yield as well as the old tradition of exhibiting our ships to foreign nations. The times have changed. Instant readiness for war has become indispensable and all other questions must bow before it."[39]

Not surprisingly the State Department strongly opposed abandoning the distant-station policy, emphasizing the responsibility of the navy in safekeeping American citizens and property abroad. The United States was at war infrequently; but the protection of this country's interests, especially commerce, was a persevering problem that could best be dealt with by naval forces stationed permanently in various parts of the world. Although Roosevelt, influenced by the General Board, still favored eliminating the foreign stations, he gave in. The stations would be retained for the present.[40]

In contrast to past policy, however, the Navy Department was to assume more direct control over the distant squadrons. They would be required to spend considerably more time in training and tactical exercises. The squadrons were to be kept intact as much as possible, rather than having the vessels cruising independently to various ports in the station; and they would be required to leave their stations for annual maneuvers in the West Indies.[41]

In December 1903, the Navy Department announced another change in its cruising policy. At the conclusion of the winter maneuvers, the various squadrons were to change stations. The European Squadron was to go to the South Atlantic station, the South Atlantic Squadron to the Caribbean Sea station, and the Caribbean Sea Squadron to the European station. This new policy would allow the personnel to become familiar with different parts of the world while the squadrons remained intact as tactical units.[42]

The winter maneuvers were delayed until the spring of 1904 because the European Squadron was in Turkish waters and could not be withdrawn. In February, the squadron sailed for the western hemisphere. It went first to Pensacola, Florida, for target practice. In early April, after the maneuvers were completed, the European Squadron, in accordance with the department's recently adopted policy, was assigned to the South Atlantic station. At the same time the Caribbean Sea Squadron under Rear Admiral Theodore Jewell was ordered to the European station. The squadron then consisted of the flagship *Olympia* and the cruisers *Baltimore* and *Cleveland*. The *Baltimore* was later replaced by the *Des Moines* for "homogeneity."[43] The squadron remained in European waters less than six months before sailing to the West Indies again for maneuvers. In January 1905, shortly after the squadron reached the fleet anchorage at Culebra, the Navy Department announced that the European station was to be abandoned. No squadron would return to European waters when the maneuvers were completed.[44]

There were two major reasons for this decision. Roosevelt was finally convinced that the squadron was useless for its primary responsibility of protecting American interests. For some time Admiral Dewey had been stressing this. From September 1903 through January 1904, the squadron was in Turkish waters providing support for the American minister who was attempting to negotiate difficulties with the Ottoman government. The squadron was withdrawn when it was realized that nothing was being accomplished. When the maneuvers of 1904 were completed, Roosevelt sent a powerful force of sixteen ships, including the battleships of the North Atlantic Squadron, into the Mediterranean. The presence of this powerful force in the eastern Mediterranean apparently persuaded the Turkish government to settle its differences with the United States. Roosevelt certainly thought so. He was convinced that the key to protecting American interests by sea power was not a permanent cruising squadron of relatively weak vessels but a powerful force exerting pressure. Such a force, however, could only remain abroad for a limited time, as its primary role was protecting the coastline of the United States.[45]

The second reason, and perhaps the more important one, was a continuation of the policy of reorganization. The South Atlantic and the European stations were to be abolished and their cruisers added to the North Atlantic Squadron, together forming the North Atlantic Fleet. This fleet was to be divided into four squadrons of two divisions each. During the following two years the reorganization reached its culmination with the designation of the Asiatic Squadron as the Asiatic Fleet, the creation of a Pacific Fleet out of all the naval forces in that ocean, and the concentration of all the battleships (some sixteen) in the Atlantic Fleet.[46] The secretary of the navy wrote in his annual report for 1905:

> The organization of the fleet . . . is very often interfered with by the demands . . . of divisions of the fleet or individual ships . . . for detached duty . . . the results of such detachment from the fleet and its work are more frequently injurious than beneficial to the public interests. The business of the fleet is to fight, and anything which interferes with the training for that purpose detracts from the attainment of that object.

This reorganization marked the end of the peacetime policy, established early in the nineteenth century, of permanent distant stations. The European station would not be revived until after World War I. In its place the department would detach units of the Atlantic Fleet to visit Europe periodically to show the flag. Provisional special squadrons would be formed and sent to areas where a show of naval power was needed to protect American citizens and property. From 1905 until our entry into World War I several special squadrons would be created and dispatched to the Mediterranean for this purpose. In this way the navy protected American interests while carrying out its primary responsibility of war preparation.[47]

During the years after the Spanish-American War international developments in Africa and Asia, as well as a series of dramatic realignments of the major European powers, convinced a large number of statesmen that war was inevitable in the near future. The growing awareness of American power persuaded many of them that the good will and diplomatic support of the United States should be cultivated. They assumed as a matter of course that the New World republic would play a stronger role in European affairs.

These convictions were not completely groundless. It is true that other parts of the world, particularly Asia and the Caribbean, received most of the attention during these years. There was little interest in European affairs either by the American people or their government, yet they were quite important. In 1900 Europe took three-fourths of American exports, and even though this would decline somewhat in the years preceding World War I, over 65 percent of our exports would continue to go there. Turko-American trade, negligible throughout the nineteenth century, began to grow rapidly during these years. In March 1911, an American chamber of commerce for the Levant, with a membership of 600, was organized in Constantinople. As early as that date American capital investments in the Near East were sufficiently large to worry the Russian Foreign Ministry. Although trade to Africa was still insignificant, it was expanding, particularly in the North African countries. Economic factors played an important role in American participation in Moroccan affairs. During the 1906 crisis Secretary of State Elihu Root demanded an acceptance of the Open Door principle for Morocco, a principle that inevitably led to economic rivalry between France and the United States in that country.[48]

For a number of years European governments had become more and more alarmed over what was frequently referred to as "the American peril," that is, the growing economic penetration of the Old World by the United States. Its acquisition of an overseas empire aroused apprehension in Berlin, St. Petersburg, Paris, and other capitals where there was concern that American expansion would continue even to the shores of Europe and Africa. This concern, first expressed during the Turkish crisis of the mid-1890s, gained momentum during and immediately after the war with Spain. Kaiser Wilhelm II speculated that "all this while America is getting bigger, will go on gathering strength and will gradually . . . found . . . an English-speaking world empire. . . ." British statesmen were slow to approve what they considered to be a new role in international affairs on the part of their American cousins. Although the first glimmer of rapprochement appeared in the latter part of the nineteenth century, they were still uneasy as to what direction American policy would go.[49]

The French were most sensitive to American activities in the Mediterranean. Their efforts to mediate during the Spanish-American War were at least partially related to their fears that the United States would take advantage of it to become a Mediterranean power. As early as May 1898, Cambon warned that the Washington government was interested in Tangiers, Morocco, and the Canary Islands as naval bases; and he later repeated his warnings. On 8 July, he wrote, "I know how these people are at present, and I cannot tell you how much I fear that they may approach Africa and become our neighbor." French newspapers reacted to the news of an American naval force being sent to bombard Spanish ports with demands for intervention. The Parisian paper *La Figara* asserted that "Europe can neither permit nor tolerate American naval action against the Spanish coast . . . or the meddling of the United States in European affairs."[50]

French uneasiness continued after the war. Cambon, even after he left Washington for another post, persevered in his concern over American expansion in the Mediterranean. Incidents such as the Perdiceras affair in Morocco and the enduring Turkish trouble distressed French officials, as did the American participation in the Algeciras Conference, even though this participation benefited France.[51]

Anxiety over American involvement in the Mediterranean was not confined to France. In Vienna the influential *Pester Lloyd* commented that "while [the Monroe Doctrine] . . . is still regarded as of binding force in the sense of excluding European influence from America, it does not appear in any way to prevent the Americans from establishing themselves in other continents." Spanish papers suspected American intervention in the Moroccan crisis of 1904 as preliminary to occupation of that country. The Rome paper

Nuova Antologia carried an article accusing the United States of imperialism not only in South America and Asia but also in Asia Minor, "and now in the Mediterranean—that is to say, in Europe itself." Russian papers also accused the United States of imperialistic designs but emphasized economic factors. "The necessity of finding scope for the development of her gigantic trade . . . has compelled the United States also to become a colony hunter," suggested one paper in St. Petersburg. In 1906 Czar Nicholas II questioned the American naval attaché about the contemplated visit of the fleet to the Mediterranean. "I suppose you are sending it into warm waters during the winter," he remarked in a not-so-subtle effort to discover the purpose.[52]

In 1900 Wilhelm II of Germany voiced his fear of an American fleet in the Mediterranean. German newspapers often were more virulent than their counterparts in neighboring France in attacking the United States. When warships were dispatched to Beirut in 1903 because of an alleged assassination of an American diplomatic official (later proven to be false), the Berlin press strongly condemned the action. The *National Zeitung* and the *Tageblatt* suggested that it was a pretext for American interference in Turkish affairs, and the *Neueste Nachrichten* noted in an editorial that "these are the same American chauvinists who want to forbid European intervention in American affairs on the ground of the Monroe Doctrine. . . ."[53]

German criticism of American involvement in the Mediterranean was only one example of increasing estrangement between the two countries. Germany's pro-Spanish position in the war of 1898, the Venezuelan crisis of 1902, her militarism and authoritarianism, convinced a growing number of Americans of that country's chauvinism, not only in upsetting the balance of power in Europe but also in seeking bases and colonies in the western hemisphere and Asia. Teddy Roosevelt, Secretaries of State John Hay and Root, and Admirals Mahan and Dewey, all agreed that Germany posed a serious threat. The deterioration of relations is reflected in the preparation of war plans by both countries against each other.[54]

While Germany became a potential enemy, Great Britain became a friend. Although somewhat an oversimplification, it is nevertheless true that the two English-speaking nations moved closer together in the years after 1898. Various factors contributed to what Bradford Perkins called the "Great Rapprochement." As noted earlier, in the 1890s leaders of both countries advocated stronger ties. During the Spanish-American War, Britain was the only major European power that aligned her sympathies with the United States. In the ensuing years, differences between the two countries were resolved with increasing harmony. Britain recognized American supremacy in the Caribbean by withdrawing her fleet and agreeing to a United States-controlled isthmian canal. One should also emphasize the fact that both countries found common interests in Asian problems and in the growing fear of German imperialism. During these years there was little concern on either side with seeking a formal alliance. The United States would not have discarded its traditional policy of nonentanglement, and Britain was primarily interested in preventing the United States from becoming an active enemy again and also in moving closer to Germany. "The only *one* thing in the World that England has to fear is Germany and the United States combining against England," warned Jackie Fisher, the first sea lord, in 1908.[55]

Yet the policy of the United States towards the powers was unclear at the beginning of the twentieth century. The European powers, having accepted America's "world power" status, became cautious bidders for its friendship. American representatives accredited to various European countries found that they were no longer on the fringe of the diplomatic colonies but recognized deputies of a "great power." For the first time courtesy visits by American men-of-war were considered to have important political implications. Although not so in many cases, the announced itinerary by an American warship or squadron frequently resulted in strong protests from countries not included. Charlemagne Tower, United States ambassador to Germany in 1903 wrote, "European politics are complicated and sensitive, and America is a very important factor in the movement of the world. Nobody wants to be disregarded or slighted by the United States, and not even to admit the appearance of it."[56]

Nevertheless, as Seward W. Livermore has pointed out, American naval policy after 1900 did tend to fall more and more into a pattern similar to traditional European practice in this respect. The appearance of American warships in European ports did have political objectives as well as the usual ones of promoting commerce and goodwill.[57] In 1911 the second division of the Atlantic Fleet under Rear Admiral Charles J. Badger visited various Baltic ports. The original purpose was to improve relations with Russia, which had been unsatisfactory for several years. Later Copenhagen, Stockholm, and Libau were added for diplomatic reasons.[58]

Even when the visits were strictly "courtesy" visits, Europeans frequently interpreted them overwise. When the North Atlantic Fleet under Admiral A. S. Barker visited Portugal in 1904, German papers accused the United States of intriguing for a naval station in the Azores. When the fleet later called at several ports in the Austrian Empire, including Fiume, Hungary, newspapers concluded that the playing of the Hungarian national songs by the ships' bands implied U.S. recognition of Hungarian national ambitions.[59]

The interrelationship of American naval policy with political affairs cannot be better illustrated than in the series of visits to French, British, and German ports in 1903. In March the European Squadron was ordered to participate in the ceremonies at Marseilles honoring the return of President Emile Loubet from Algiers. The French government made this request and Roosevelt agreed to it because the squadron was scheduled to be at Villefranche awaiting the arrival of a new commander-in-chief shortly before the ceremonies were to take place. Rear Admiral Charles S. Cotton hoisted his flag on the *Chicago* and, accompanied by the rest of the squadron, reached Marseilles on 30 April. There followed elaborate ceremonies and festivities, which climaxed when the admiral and his staff traveled to Paris in the presidential entourage.[60]

There was nothing unusual about American naval involvement in foreign ceremonies. In the 1890s U.S. warships participated in a number of such events, including the opening of the Kiel Canal in Germany and the Queen's Jubilee celebration in England, without attracting undue attention. However, this was before many European statesmen acknowledged the United States as a naval power. The participation by American warships in the French ceremonies occurred at a "sensitive" time in European politics. Admiral Cotton's visit to Paris coincided with the arrival of King Edward VII of Great Britain and was rightly considered to be symbolic of the two nations' moving closer together. A few months later the French president returned the visit, and diplomatic negotiations were initiated that ultimately led to the entente in 1904.

In this context it is easier to understand German reaction to the French visit by Admiral Cotton's squadron. For some time American diplomatic officials had urged Washington to include German ports in the European cruise itinerary of warships, but only training vessels made occasional calls. On one occasion Farragut's old flagship, the *Hartford*, was in Kiel when Wilhelm II arrived on board his yacht *Hohenzollern*. Hurrying on to Berlin the Kaiser sent word that he regretted not being able to inspect the "famous old ship." Shortly after that, the American chargé wrote the State Department, "I am of the opinion that it would be advantageous to have more modern ships visit German ports."[61]

To make matters worse, from the German point of view, the Kaiser had recently invited the North Atlantic Squadron to visit Kiel during the June (1903) regatta. Roosevelt had declined the invitation, but not to slight Germany; the squadron was conducting maneuvers in the Caribbean and would not make a European cruise that year. The German government was aware of this but nevertheless was annoyed at the French visit.

The German press demonstrated its displeasure for several days. The Frankfurter *Zeitung* blamed the whole matter on Secretary of State Hay and his dislike of Germany. The British press gleefully recorded German discomfort. The London *Times* emphasized on 20 April that the Emperor's invitation was refused and "that all this exchange of civilities results in a demonstration of closer sympathies with France."[62]

European papers then began to report that the American warships would go to Kiel after Marseilles. The Navy Department denied this, but the rumors persisted. On 11 May, Ambassador Tower in Berlin wrote Hay,

> I found in talking yesterday with Count Von Bulow that since the visit to Marseilles, this question has assumed a very serious importance and, to my surprise, I discovered an extreme sensitiveness upon the part of the Chancellor which evidently reflects the feeling of the Emperor himself. If

the American ships should not come to Kiel next June, it would be impossible to avoid the feeling in Germany that there had been a slight put upon the Empire by the American Government.

Von Bulow "in the strongest language" then requested that the European Squadron be sent to Kiel.[63]

Roosevelt, accompanied by the secretary of the navy and several other officials, was at that time on a speaking tour in the West. Hay consulted the Navy Department and recommended to the president that the squadron be ordered to Kiel. He also suggested reinforcing it with one vessel to "make a more respectable show." Roosevelt agreed. A battleship would be detached from the North Atlantic Squadron to serve as Cotton's temporary flagship. In telegraphing Hay of the decision, Roosevelt said, "As you say, the attitude of the German Government is puerile, but if we can save nice Speck's head by giving a battleship a voyage, I shall be delighted to do so."[64] One wonders if T. R. was more concerned about American-German relations or about trying to prevent the recall of Speck von Sternburg, the German ambassador to the United States and a good friend. Whatever the reason, Admiral Cotton was ordered to take his squadron to Kiel.

The British government followed with close attention the events leading to this decision. Hay received a personal note from the British ambassador inquiring whether the squadron would be sent to Kiel. The American ambassador in London, Henry White, wired the secretary of state that the King was "particularly interested in visit of American fleet to England." The ambassador was informed that the squadron would "touch" at a British port on the way to Kiel. He was informed that the battleship *Kearsarge* would rendezvous with the squadron at Southampton before departing for Germany. When another telegram arrived from White, stressing that the King wanted to "participate personally" in the squadron's reception, Roosevelt agreed to allow the squadron to take part in a naval review to be held at Portsmouth in July to commemorate the French president's official visit to Britain.[65]

"It must be owned that the naval love feast now going on at Kiel has an air of unreality," the New York *Times* remarked on 14 June. "While the host and the guest are exchanging civilities . . . each is preoccupied with the speculations to the figure he would be likely to cut if they met under different conditions." Even under the guise of diplomatic politeness, Admiral Cotton was startled when the Kaiser at a dinner on his yacht raised his glass and remarked, "I wish you to tell your President that if the United States is ever in difficulty, in a just cause, and needs the assistance of a friend, Germany's ships will be there."[66]

The squadron arrived in Kiel on 23 June. The emperor arrived from Berlin the following day and immediately received Admiral Cotton on board the *Hohenzollern*. The wining and dining, which lasted over a week, was interrupted by frequent courtesy calls and tours of the American ships by German dignitaries including the Kaiser, Prince Henry of Prussia, and Admiral Alfred von Tirpitz. Although the Germans were probably not very impressed with a squadron that included only one first-rate ship (Tirpitz certainly was not[67]), it was frequently stated in many American newspapers that the Kaiser invited himself on board the American ship in order to "spy" or inspect them. On the other hand German papers were astonished at the amount of money American sailors spent while on liberty. They were also fascinated by the ships' pets— "Mile," the *Kearsarge's* West Indian goat, "Georgia Ike," a razorback pig on the *Chicago*, and a parrot by the name of "Cursing Jim."[68]

As the squadron prepared to leave Kiel, one "tired" officer remarked to a reporter, "We have shot off more powder since being here than in all the time of the Spanish American War." Roosevelt, who rarely read newspapers, queried the naval secretary about press accounts of over a hundred deserters from the ships at Kiel. The secretary replied that only two "stragglers," not deserters, were left when the ships departed.[69]

Anglo-American affinity was certainly apparent when the squadron visited Portsmouth. Although the officers' and mens' social calendar was as full as at Kiel, there was less formality and more spontaneity. The American press lavished praise upon British hospitality. "Never was a more rousing reception tendered a visiting squadron in a foreign port than that given the American squadron . . . by British naval vessels, public officials, and the people," the *Army and Navy Journal* boasted. Five hundred enlisted men were guests of the mayor of Portsmouth at a luncheon. The officers attended a state ball at Buckingham Palace honoring the French president. Later King Edward entertained Admiral Cotton and a number of his officers at a royal banquet.[70] The visit lasted four days. The *Kearsarge* was then detached from the squadron and sailed for the United States, while the remainder of the vessels prepared to return to the Mediterranean and resume normal cruising duties.

Sixteen months later the European station was abolished, and the navy inaugurated its policy of sending units of the Atlantic Fleet and special squadrons to European waters. During these years preceding the outbreak of World War I, the navy continued to play an important diplomatic role in European affairs. Roosevelt, perhaps more than any other president, looked upon the navy as an instrument of diplomacy. The most dramatic illustration of this was the global cruise of the battleship fleet.

The Atlantic Fleet was the United States' most powerful force afloat, the nation's first line of defense at sea. In 1906, two years after the fleet was created, Roosevelt ordered the sixteen battleships that comprised the fighting line of this force to undertake a diplomatic tour of the globe.[71] Writers have suggested over the years that the motives for this cruise were training, friction with the Japanese, and the election of 1908. A recent authority, however, demonstrates that the major reason was simply publicity, for "Uncle Sam's Greatest Show on Earth."[72]

In December 1907, the fleet, under Rear Admiral Robley D. Evans, left

Hampton Roads on the first leg of its 46,000-mile, fourteen-month voyage. After rounding South America to the west coast of the United States, the fleet steamed across the Pacific, where it was warmly welcomed in Australia, New Zealand, the Philippines, China, and Japan. It then sailed for the Mediterranean by way of the Suez Canal.

The original schedule required the fleet to reach Hampton Roads by Washington's birthday, 1909. For that reason Rear Admiral Charles Sperry, who had taken Evans' place because of his ill health, was anxious to avoid lengthy stops in European ports. Roosevelt initially agreed, but diplomatic pressure persuaded the president to order the fleet to make several brief stops. Sperry met this obligation by dividing his force into small units: one division went to Italy and Villefranche, another to Marseilles and Tangiers, a third to ports in the eastern Mediterranean (Athens, Salonika, Smyrna, and Beirut), while the fourth went to ports along the northern coast of Africa. The battleship *Illinois* of the fourth division was diverted to Messina, Sicily, because of an earthquake that destroyed the city. The divisions then rendezvoused at Gibraltar for the Atlantic crossing.[73]

Roosevelt insisted that the world cruise had "immeasurably raised the prestige not only of our fleet but of the nation" and that it was an unqualified success. It was a remarkable performance from a technical point of view. Nevertheless, it is doubtful that it increased American prestige abroad. Many of the ships were obsolete, and the world powers for several years had witnessed American naval power.[74]

William Howard Taft, Roosevelt's successor in the White House, had little interest in or understanding of the use of naval power for diplomatic purposes. He was a pronounced pacifist, although not adverse to using gunboat diplomacy when convinced that American lives were threatened.[75] In the fall of 1910 a revolution occurred in Portugal, and the royal family fled the country on board their yacht. Taft immediately ordered the *Des Moines* to Lisbon to evacuate American subjects if necessary, "because I would like to have the country see that the Navy is useful."[76]

Taft also abandoned in large part the personal and private diplomacy for which his predecessor had been known. Instead, he relied heavily upon the advice of Philander C. Knox, his secretary of state. Knox, with Taft's blessings, tried to avoid becoming involved in European problems. When the Atlantic Fleet made a six-week cruise to European waters, it was stressed that the visits to British and French ports had no political significance.[77] The fleet was well received in both countries, and the British reception if anything surpassed that of 1903 in enthusiasm. At a Guildhall banquet, Commander William Sims, USN, promised his hosts that should Great Britain be threatened, "you may count upon every man, every dollar, every ship, and every drop of blood of your kindred across the seas."[78] Although Taft publicly rebuked the naval officer for these indiscreet remarks, it caused serious problems with Germany. Taft then tried to mollify German resentment by announcing that a training squadron would visit Kiel the following summer. This only made matters worse because the Navy Department had already announced that the battleship *Delaware*, the most recent addition to the navy's fighting line, was to take part in King George V's coronation naval review—the event was scheduled to take place at the same time that the training squadron was to visit Germany. Taft tried again in the spring of 1911 by sending the second division of the Atlantic Fleet to visit Kiel. A Russian port was added later for the specific purpose of improving relations with that country. It is doubtful, however, that the summer cruise improved relations with either Germany or Russia.[79] Taft's desire to avoid becoming involved in European affairs failed, and his hesitant use of naval forces to achieve diplomatic ends also was largely unsuccessful.

These episodes of naval diplomacy during the first decade of the twentieth century illustrate European sensitivity towards the United States and its potential relationships. These relationships began to assume a more definite pattern with growing sympathies towards the Anglo-French Entente in its rivalry with Germany. The United States considered Far Eastern and Caribbean affairs to be more important; yet American interests were involved in the Old World, particularly in North Africa and the Near East. These areas continued to be the most unstable and explosive with one crisis after the other in rapid succession—the Moroccan crisis, the Bosnian and Turkish crises of 1908–1909, the Agadir crisis, the Turko-Italian War, and finally two Balkan wars. The danger of a general conflict was ever present, and during most of this period American warships cruised the Mediterranean.

THE NEAR EAST AND AFRICA, 1899–1905

Historian generally agree that the Eastern Question and the intense rivalry among the European powers for control of Africa were major causes of World War I. The decay of the Ottoman Empire continued to generate crisis after crisis. Africa south of the Sahara had been progressively partitioned until by the beginning of the twentieth century very little remained that was not under the control of a European nation. In North Africa, Tripoli, later known as Libya, became the scene of conflict between Italy and Turkey; and Morocco, nominally independent under a sultan but long dominated by foreign interests, was the center of two serious international quarrels before French control was stabilized there in 1912.

The United States had no territorial ambitions in either Africa or the Near East. Nevertheless, as in the past, she found herself embroiled in both areas. The continued unrest made it necessary to protect American interests. In the Ottoman Empire the American concern was primarily humanitarian, but in North Africa it was economic.

At the beginning of the twentieth century it was not unusual for nations to employ warships to collect debts. However, this occurred only when the debtor was the weaker nation or in nonwestern areas where there was political and economic instability. Great Britain, France, and Germany resorted to this practice on a number of occasions in Latin America. At times this practice led to a diplomatic confrontation with the United States, which continued to insist on its rights of paternalism under the mantle of the Monroe Doctrine. The Venezuelan crisis of 1902 was a good example. Yet the United States was guilty of similar actions in other parts of the world. In the spring of 1899 the cruiser *Chicago* was ordered to Tangier to help collect debts owed to American merchants. The *Chicago*'s commanding officer demanded not only prompt payment of the debts but an official apology from the Moroccan government as well. The demands were supported by an ultimatum of twenty-four hours. There was a "probability," so the *Army and Navy Journal* said, "that she might have opened [fire] on the town had the money not been paid within the time limits." The demands were met, including the payment of some $8,850, and the cruiser departed.[1]

As the American minister later claimed that only a portion of the debts had been paid, a warship was again summoned and early in 1901 the battleship *New York* dropped anchor in Tangier. The warship's commanding officer understood what was expected of him. Upon clearing Gibraltar, the battleship had stripped for action. She fired the usual salute on entering Tangier's harbor but also trained her starboard battery on the city. The Moroccan officials also understood what was expected of them, and the remainder of the claimed debt was promptly paid. The ship's crew then held a funeral parade to bury a shipmate, and afterwards marched back to the ship led by the band playing, "In the Good Old Summer Time." Mission accomplished, the battleship left for Asiatic waters via the Suez Canal.[2]

The United States also utilized naval forces in Turkish waters to facilitate its efforts to collect "debts." Gunboat or battleship diplomacy had long been a part of American relations with the Ottoman Empire, yet many American diplomatic representatives in Turkey had instinctively opposed the threat of force, usually giving in, however, because of missionary pressure and their inability to accomplish anything through normal discourse. Even gunboat diplomacy had accomplished little, primarily because the Turkish government discounted American power, and the issues remained unsettled decade after decade. The major issue after the Spanish-American War was the settlement of American missionary claims growing out of the Armenian massacres.[3]

In the fall of 1898 Oscar Straus took up his residence in Constantinople as United States minister accredited to the Ottoman government. Straus hoped that he would be able to settle the claims question by tact and persuasion and not have to resort to threats of coercion as his predecessors had done. He was aware of the intense pressure that the missionary interests would exert on the president to use force, but McKinley had promised not to send warships into Turkish waters unless Straus requested them. For a year and a half, the minister diligently pursued his objectives apparently without any success. He attempted to direct the attention of the Sultan to his peaceful policy. In December 1898, he requested an audience with the Sultan, reminding him that there was "a strong popular sentiment in the United States to despatch her Navy to some Turkish port and to insist upon proper reparations."[4] However, this appeal and others went unheeded. In the winter of 1900 Straus returned to the United States, leaving Lloyd Griscom, the chargé d' affaires, in control of the legation.

Straus remained the American minister officially, but he did not return to Constantinople. In Washington he conferred with Secretary of State Hay and admitted his failure to persuade Turkish officials to settle the outstanding issues. Still reluctant to sanction the use of force, he recommended to Hay that rumors be "leaked" to the press implying that fleet would be sent to the eastern Mediterranean. Straus himself hinted to the Turkish minister in Washington that his return to the United States might herald the breaking off of diplomatic relations between the two countries.[5]

Newspapers duly reported such rumors, and Europe once again speculated as to American intent. Russian and Austrian papers were characteristically suspicious and suggested that the controversy with Turkey was a convenient subterfuge for American expansion in the Mediterranean.[6] Although a fleet was not sent, McKinley did agree to a single warship's making a visit to several Turkish ports. In May 1901, the protected cruiser *Albany* was ordered to the Mediterranean. However, her tour was brief; she hurried on to Asiatic waters with the outbreak of the Boxer Rebellion.[7]

In November the battleship *Kentucky* was ordered to stop at Smyrna for a brief visit on her way to the Orient. Griscom immediately set in motion a scheme designed to convince the Sultan that the warship was under orders to bombard the port if the claims were not paid. He sent an open cable to Captain Colby M. Chester of the *Kentucky* requesting that he "please take no action until hearing" from him. He also cabled the consul at Smyrna to "proceed on board and request Captain Chester to take no action without consulting" the legation. Fortunately for Griscom's plan, Chester was a reasonably intelligent officer and understood his ship's role. As he reported to the secretary of the navy, "arriving at Smyrna . . . I place[d] the ship as nearly in a war condition as our peaceful mission would allow." The ship was stripped for action, her guns uncovered, and she anchored within two hundred yards of the seawall.[8]

A few days later the matter was settled. Chester was invited to Constantinople, where he dined with the Sultan. The Ottoman government then signed a contract with the Cramp Shipyard in Philadelphia to build a cruiser for the Turkish navy. The contract included hidden funds to pay the missionary claims. The *Kentucky* then sailed to the east.

Apparently Griscom's bluff had worked, or so he, Chester, Straus, Hay, and others believed. However, it is doubtful that such an obvious subterfuge frightened Turkish officials into submission. It is more likely that pressure from Germany or Russia forced the Sultan into giving in, and the cruiser contract provided a convenient face-saving vehicle. Griscom, who was only twenty-eight at the time, later wrote in his memoirs, "Had I been older I would never have taken such a risk."

Although the claims issue was finally settled (actually it would be over two years before the money was finally paid by the Ottoman government), other problems continued to stir up American-Turkish relations. Inevitably they centered around the missionaries. Turkish officials harassed American missionaries in a variety of ways. Their institutions were not recognized by the

Sultan, preventing them from obtaining legalized exemption from certain taxes, and graduates of their schools, including those from the Beirut Medical College, were not recognized. They were not allowed to construct new buildings, not even orphanages. John G. A. Leishman, who succeeded Straus in Constantinople, like many of his predecessors developed an antipathy for the missionaries, blaming them for most of his work. One of Leishman's assistants wrote in his memoirs that his chief's "principle obsession was a violent hatred of the missionaries. . . ."[9] Leishman, who had made a fortune as an executive in Andrew Carnegie's steel companies, was mild mannered and preferred patience in trying to work with the Turkish government. He admitted that it was difficult to pursue such a policy. "I am sure even the lauded patience of Job would have been sorely taxed," he once wrote. As a matter of course he opposed gunboat diplomacy.[10]

Understandably, the missionaries were unhappy with the policy of "patience." They tried to persuade him to request a visit from a naval squadron. D. Stuart Dodge, a wealthy philanthropist and president of the board of the American Protestant College in Beirut, wrote the minister while he was in the United States, "We agree with you that no threats or display of force would be desirable or necessary; although it might be of advantage if our Mediterranean Squadron on its usual cruise, should happen to be in that general vicinity at this time."[11]

Perhaps inevitably, considering past experiences of American ministers in Turkey, even Leishman's patience began to wear thin. In the spring of 1903, he asked for the stationing of a small gunboat at Constantinople. The minister's complete turnabout, however, came in the following summer when he recommended breaking off diplomatic relations. Assistant Secretary of State Adee noted in a brief memo to the secretary, "what a whoop the Sultan would give if Leishman should suspend relations. His majesty could then have a breathing spell while our shop was closed, tranquilly relying on the six powers to see that we had no chance to pass the Dardanelles and blow him sky-high."[12]

Two incidents—one the supposed kidnapping of a missionary by Macedonian brigands, and the other the erroneous news of the assassination of an American diplomatic official—forced Leishman's hand and resulted in a return to gunboat diplomacy.

The kidnapping of the American missionary led to the normal demands for intervention. W. T. Stead, a well-known journalist, exclaimed, "Where is Dewey? Where is Sampson? Where are our invincible ironclads?" He went on to boast that if they were sent to the Mediterranean, "the Stars and Stripes would soon fly over the waters of the Sea of Marmora, and the thunder of the American guns would sound the death-knell of the Ottoman dynasty."[13] Warships were not sent because the missionary was released after a ransom was paid by the Turkish government.

On 27, August 1903, Leishman cabled the State Department that William C. Magelssen, the American vice-consul at Beirut, had been murdered. Roosevelt, vacationing with his family at Sagamore Hill, ordered the European Squadron to Beirut.

The squadron was at Villefranche, having been ordered to some "quiet port" in the Mediterranean for a brief period of rest and relaxation before leaving for winter maneuvers in the Caribbean. With the change in orders, liberty was cut short; and the squadron (flagship *Brooklyn*, cruisers *Machias* and *San Francisco*) sailed to Genoa to take on coal. Although coaling was done as rapidly as possible—bags of coal were even piled high on the vessel's decks—it was the 29th before the squadron got under way for the eastern Mediterranean.[14] Later the secretary of the navy reprimanded Admiral Cotton, in command of the squadron, for the delay in leaving for Beirut. He rejected the admiral's excuse that the orders arrived in the middle of the night and that the nearest coal depot was at Genoa.[15]

The squadron dropped anchor at Beirut six days after receiving the orders and then discovered that they had responded to a false alarm. The consul general was unharmed. According to Minister Leishman, the consul had used the wrong code to report an incident. Magelssen had been fired upon but had not been hit. Although the error was discovered within twenty-four hours, while the vessels were still coaling at Genoa, Roosevelt decided not to cancel the squadron's movement to the east.[16]

More than likely Roosevelt decided to use the Magelssen incident as a pretext to force the Ottoman government into settling the long-standing issues between the two countries. Certainly it was consistent with his advocacy of power as the determinant in world affairs. In a revealing letter to Roosevelt, Secretary of State Hay wrote on 3 September, "Leishman ought to be able to finish up our little chores with Turkey in a few days and report that the fleet is no longer needed. I have had two long talks with the Turkish minister and have told him if he does not want our ships in Turkish waters, it is very easy to cause them to depart. The Sultan has only to keep his word with us, and settle the two or three matters which have dragged too long." The British embassy in Washington informed Lord Lansdowne, the foreign secretary, that it was pressure from the American Board of Foreign Missions that had prompted the president to take such "energetic action." Leishman himself had requested warships shortly before the incident. Then on 30 August he reported that the decision to send a squadron to Beirut had caused "considerable excitement," that officials were worried, and that they would "make every effort to put the agreements which have been pending so long into execution."[17]

Roosevelt was no friend of the Turks. As assistant secretary of the navy he had urged a naval demonstration during the Armenian troubles. Four days after sending Cotton's squadron into Turkish waters, he confided in a letter, "If the chance comes when I say a word or do a deed for the oppressed people in Turkey, I shall do so. But I have a great horror of words that cannot be backed, or will not be backed by deeds."[18]

In spite of Roosevelt's bellicose words, he had no intention of going beyond sending a relatively weak naval force to Beirut. As he well knew the major powers, including the United States, frequently did this without any serious reaction from the Ottoman government. He ignored the assistant secretary of the navy's suggestion that Beirut be occupied until American demands were met and assured others that the vessels would be withdrawn if any complications should develop.[19]

Complications did develop. On Sunday, 6 September 1903, rioting broke out in Beirut between Christians and Moslems; before the day was over, some twelve people were dead and scores injured. That night the foreign consuls held a meeting and decided to request Admiral Cotton to land Marines to preserve order. The British and Austrian representatives conferred with the admiral on board his flagship, and the admiral at first refused their request without the Turkish governor's permission. The British consul, who sent a detailed account of the incident to his ambassador in Constantinople, pointed out that it was improbable that the governor would give his consent. "In reply to [the admiral's] quotations from the U.S. Naval Regulations respecting the inviolability of the soil of a 'civilized' and friendly power," the consul wrote, "I drew his attention to the fact that this country can only by courtesy be termed civilized, and moreover there were, I believe, precedents for the taking of such actions. . . ." Cotton finally agreed to land an armed force if the majority of foreign consuls requested it and "if the lives of Europeans were in imminent peril."[20]

The consuls, however, divided over this. The British, Italian, and Austrian consuls favored the idea while the Russian, French, and German consuls opposed it. The admiral had been reluctant to send an armed force ashore on his own responsibility, and the difference among the consuls convinced him not to do so. As he wrote the American consul,

> You will, of course, thoroughly understand that I cannot afford to make any mistake relative to landing an armed force on the soil of a nation with which the United States is at peace. The conditions for such an act upon my part must be clear-cut, and the consent of the Governor must be first obtained by you, *unless* an attack actually occurs, or or is about to occur, and without adequate attempt on the part of the Governor to give you instant and adequate protection.

Cotton did send his aide, a small marine detachment, and signalers to occupy the American consulate. Also, the ships' marine detachments with full field equipment, field guns, and the like were massed on the open decks in view of the shore. To further impress the governor, barges "under steam" were moored alongside the ships.[21]

When uneasy Turkish officials arrived on board the flagship, the admiral assured them that he would not land a force without first notifying the governor. Curiously, an American newspaper carried a caption that same day (7 September), "If the sick man of Europe forces Admiral Cotton to land the Marines his disease may take a fatal turn." This was a coincidence, for the news of a possible landing did not reach American papers until the following day.

The secretary of the navy later commended Cotton for his "discretion in treating the question of landing marines." Minister Leishman wrote Secretary Hay that Constantinople's foreign community highly approved Admiral Cotton's willingness to land marines, but the American minister admitted that he was relieved it was not necessary "as it would have . . . complicate[d] matter."[22]

Leishman predicted in a cable to the State Department that the Ottoman government would blame the riot on the presence of American warships, a prophecy that was quickly borne out. On the day after the riots, Chekib Bey, the Turkish minister in Washington, conferred with Secretary Hay and protested against the presence of the warships at Beirut, "as a cause of [the] excitement." Hay flatly denied the accusation. Both Hay and Adee in a later conversation with Chekib Bey admitted that the squadron had remained there because the long-standing issues between the two governments had not been settled.[23]

Hay departed on a two-week vacation feeling guilty, he told Roosevelt, for having "quit the field under fire." He wrote:

> I had cleared off my desk. . . . I had my tickets in my pocket and my carriage was at the door, when that abject Turk wriggled and squirmed into my library and almost made me miss my train by his piteous pleading that we should recall the ships. . . . I told him with an energy necessary by my hurry that he must not think they could fool with us indefinitely—that we must insist on our reasonable and moderate demands for things already promised, and that our ships would probably go or stay as the President thought our interest and dignity required.

Roosevelt had no intention of removing the vessels. "Under the circumstances it was out of the question for us not to send our squadron to Beirut, and out of the question for us to withdraw it afterwards," he wrote Hay.[24]

It is not possible to determine with the evidence now available that, as the Turkish government claimed, the presence of the American warships instigated the trouble in Beirut. The foreign consuls in that city did not think so, and as Hay reminded the Turkish minister, there was nothing new about foreign warships, including American ones, visiting Beirut. The State Department had been warned several weeks before that trouble could break out any moment between the Moslem minority and the Christian majority in the city. Furthermore, a serious uprising had occurred in Macedonia in August. Because of that crisis, the Ottoman government was understandably vexed by the possibility of unrest spreading into Syria. Leishman conjectured that the riots might have been caused by Macedonian sympathizers. More than likely what happened in

Beirut was simply another incident in the apparent perpetual chaos associated with the breakup of the old Ottoman Empire. Leishman, later supported by the Italian and French diplomatic representatives in Constantinople, blamed the rioting on the incompetency of the governor in Beirut. The American minister demanded the official's removal, which was promptly accomplished.[25] However, the British ambassador in Constantinople reported that "the French Ambassador . . . took alarm at the prospect of the representative of power other than France obtaining the dismissal of such an important functionary of Syria, sent his interpreter at the last moment to request the removal of the Vali [governor] and will no doubt claim a share in the credit of the success."[26]

Inevitably the ordering of American warships to Turkish waters again generated controversy both at home and abroad. The *Nation* called it an "unwelcomed illustration" of the president's "hot-headedness in all foreign negotiations." Dr. Albert Shaw, editor of the *Review of Reviews*, and Oscar Straus, former minister to Turkey, urged that the squadron be withdrawn, for fear that the United States would be drawn into the Eastern Question.[27] Straus evidently had forgotten his problems and recommendations while in Constantinople.

The British press generally supported the American action, while German papers were critical of it. The Cologne *Gazette*, considered a "semi-official" organ of the imperial government, agreed with the Turkish claim that the American squadron "directly precipitated" the riots. Undoubtedly, this paper reflected the views of the German government, which for economic reasons, particularly concerning the Bagdad Railroad, was involving itself more and more in Turkish affairs. The British government, on the other hand, feared the outbreak of war in the Near East over the Macedonian situation and considered the presence of the American squadron a deterrent to this.[28]

Leishman urged that the squadron be permitted to remain until the issues were resolved. "If the Turkish Government finds presence of fleet objectionable," he wrote, "they know an easy way of getting rid of it, and the more objectionable it proves the quicker they are likely to comply with our just demands." Admiral Cotton consulted with American diplomatic, business, and missionary interests in Syria and forwarded their opinions to the Navy Department, along with his recommendation that the squadron should remain until "definite satisfactory action is taken" by the Turkish government. Hay also preferred to keep the ships there for the time being or at least until "the settlement of two or three matters."[29]

The Ottoman government stubbornly refused to recognize officially the relationship between the presence of American warships and the other differences between the two nations. While the minister for foreign affairs in Constantinople publicly announced that the squadron was in Beirut on a "friendly visit," his representative in Washington was urging its withdrawal on the grounds that the trouble in Beirut was over. On 18 September, Adee scribbled a note to Hay, "Chekib was in again today to ask what news from Cotton. I said nothing today. To his good natured inquiry how we might expedite the withdrawal of the fleet I said that if it rested with him and me we could settle it in five minutes by ordering the fulfillment of the Sultan's promises. . . . He said, 'Naturellement' and dropped the subject."[30]

The new governor in Beirut attempted to persuade American officials that normalcy had returned to the city and that the vessels were no longer needed. He mentioned among other arguments that a number of arrests had been made, the police force had been reorganized, and other reforms would follow. The American consul in Beirut was enthusiastic in his reports to Leishman concerning the city's progress, and even Cotton was impressed with the new governor particularly after the admiral was offered a decoration.[31] Leishman cautioned the consul to say nothing to the Turkish governor that might suggest that the squadron would be withdrawn, "as other matters outside of the immediate question of Beirut must be considered."

The American government at every opportunity continued to make it clear that the warships would not depart until the issues were settled.[32] Early in October, the Turkish government yielded. Leishman was informed that certain specified claims would be immediately settled. Although these were minor claims concerning compensating missionaries for property damaged or destroyed, the American minister was convinced that the other, more general problems would be quickly settled. His optimism was ill-founded. Time and time again over the decades promises had been made, and nothing came from them. On 21 October, he wrote Hay, "Matters continue to drag along and my patience at times is sorely tried, but the adjustment of a few less important items encourages the hope that the daily promises of a prompt settlement of . . . other questions may be fulfilled." Three weeks later in some despondency, he admitted failure. The Ottoman government had not responded any further "and from the best information available not likely to. . . ." The usual cycle seemed complete when he wrote that "further delay would be worse than useless" and recommended that an ultimatum be presented to the Turkish government.[33]

Assistant Secretary of State Adee was probably not surprised at the minister's "drastic recommendation." During his many years in the State Department he had witnessed similar recommendations from the American representatives to the Ottoman government for the same reasons. He, of course, pooh-poohed it, writing to Hay:

I do not see how we can threaten or use force to compel compliance with such a demand, unless we are prepared to make virtual war against Turkey. If the question were of non payment of an indemnity or of reprisals for wrongs done to our citizens in violation of international rights, force—short of war—could be resorted to. . . . But to use force to compel

the granting of a favor would be an act of virtual war. . . . What we are
asking is that Turkey shall give our mission schools the same privileges
as are enjoyed by French, British, and other schools.[34]

Roosevelt had no intention of sending an ultimatum or going on any further
than he already had, and even the missionary pressure was brushed aside. The
squabble with Colombia over the Panama canal issue was occupying his attention, and at least for the time being the Turkish problem would be ignored.[35]

The problem could not be ignored in Beirut. After the rioting early in
September ended, the city slowly returned to its normal pace. The presence of
the American warships in the harbor, along with the arrests and trials of a
number of individuals accused of inciting the unrest, continued to excite the
local populace. Admiral Cotton, fearful of an incident, severely curtailed
liberty for the squadron. Only officers and a few chief petty officers were
allowed ashore, and for the latter liberty expired at 6:00 P.M., and for the
former two hours later.[36] The admiral recommended that the squadron be permitted to change anchorage to Smyrna, partly because it was a much better
harbor but also to allow liberty for the crews. Although his request was turned
down, the Navy Department did agree to rotate the ships to Port Said. The
Brooklyn was the first ship granted such permission; her crew spent the Christmas holidays there, the first time a majority of the men had been ashore in
nearly four months.[37]

On the whole the admiral's caution was wise. Only one major incident occurred. A warrant officer became intoxicated, failed to meet the liberty boat,
fired a revolver into a house, and took refuge in a house of ill repute. The Turkish police wisely informed American officials who apprehended him. His commanding officer formally apologized to the governor for the incident and
promised to punish the culprit.[38]

Admiral Cotton also tried to improve relations by having his squadron dress
ship for the Sultan's birthday. The ships were decked out with flags and pen-
nants during the day and strings of lights at night. Although the local press
lauded the American warships for this recognition, newspapers elsewhere in
the Empire remained critical of their presence.[39] A number of anti-American
incidents occurred. In the small port of Alexandretta members of the local
police allegedly broke into the American consulate, "insulted and threatened" the consul, and arrested a visitor. The consul then fled to Beirut. Admiral Cotton was ordered to escort the consul back to his post on one of his
cruisers and demand "proper reparation" from Turkish officials. "Proper reparation" consisted of a formal apology from the local governor and the return
of the arrested individual to the American consulate. As was frequently the
case in what was considered to be a minor post, the American representative in
Alexandretta was a local businessman, and more than likely his visitor (unidentified) was a Turkish subject. Nevertheless, the admiral's demands were
met and the cruiser returned to Beirut.[40]

Leishman, convinced that the Alexandretta incident occurred because of growing hostility aroused by the ships, was afraid that their presence might lead to more serious complications. He wrote Hay quite pessimistically on the last day of the year:

> The end of the year has been reached and . . . [the] question remains un-settled despite my unceasing efforts. . . . I can see no signs of an im-mediate settlement and have no confidence in the daily promises which are broken with as little compunction as they are lightly made. . . . the Imperial Ottoman Government continues to act . . . under the impression that the presence of the squadron need cause no particular uneasiness, having been informed by the Turkish Minister at Washington that its real influence cannot be exerted without express authority of Congress; and as long as this impression lasts the presence of the squadron is more of a hindrance than an assistance in securing a peaceful settlement.

The American minister was convinced that gunboat diplomacy had failed. In the middle of January 1904, in answer to an inquiry from the State Depart-ment concerning the need to keep the vessels in Turkish waters, he replied that "if the Department is not prepared to adopt more drastic measures," they should be immediately recalled.[41]

The Navy Department wanted the warships withdrawn from the Near East as soon as possible. The European Squadron was scheduled to participate in maneuvers in the Caribbean, but because of the Turkish problem, these had to be postponed until Cotton's ships were available.[42]

The squadron's preoccupation with the Turkish problem affected its training. Lieutenant Mark Bristol, the *Brooklyn*'s gunnery officer, confided in a letter to Lieutenant Commander William Sims, "[We] are getting a little dis-couraged by the prospect of not getting a chance at the target. . . . I have been trying to get [Admiral Cotton] . . . to cable the Department to ask permission to arrange to have target practice with two of the ships at a time leaving one here to stand guard. . . . But I cannot get him to do it so far. . . . The *Machias* has not had a target practice for over a year."

Cotton was very popular with the squadron's officers. He was willing to delegate responsibility, and as one officer wrote, "left us free from picayune interference." Bristol was one of Sim's protégés involved in gunnery experi-ments, and Cotton, unlike many senior officers, gave his support to them. As Bristol wrote, "this man would do anything to shove things along . . . and [has] backed us up right along the line." He added, "There is not much in being an Admiral these days when he cannot move his squadron once in six months of his own free will. If they would [only] take him into their confidence a little more."[43]

Actually Bristol was mistaken in presuming that the Navy Department was responsible for the delays in gunnery practice and training, because Admiral

Cotton was. The admiral was concerned about target practice, but he also considered the squadron's pressure on the Ottoman government to have priority over everything, including maneuvers. He stressed this to Leishman, to the Navy Department, and in a personal letter to the chief of the Bureau of Navigation.[44]

Admiral Taylor, the bureau's chief, was anxious to withdraw the squadron and reschedule the Caribbean maneuvers. It was at his recommendation that the secretary of the navy requested the State Department to release the squadron as soon as possible. Consequently, when Leishman agreed that the warships were no longer needed, the Navy Department was notified that they could be withdrawn from Turkish waters after January 1904. However, Secretary Hay decided to utilize the ships one last time in trying to persuade the Turkish government to give in. The squadron's removal would not be announced publicly until Leishman had an opportunity formally to inform the Sultan that the United States would withdraw the warships if the Turkish government met the American demands. The chance of such a "subterfuge" working was remote. The squadron's imminent departure was not a very well-kept secret; several days beforehand, Admiral Cotton was presented a going-away present by the American colony in Beirut.[45]

Promptly on 1 February, the squadron steamed out of Beirut, coaled at Naples, and left the Mediterranean for the Caribbean. Admiral Cotton, at his own request, was relieved of the European Squadron command at Gibraltar by Captain Harry Knox. When the squadron reached the Caribbean, Rear Admiral Joseph B. Coghlan was placed temporarily in command and then relieved by Rear Admiral Theodore F. Jewell in April 1904.[46]

Although the evidence is inconclusive, it seems only logical that Roosevelt was involved in the decision to remove the squadron. As a past master in the use of force to back up diplomacy, he reluctantly agreed with Leishman's assessment that Cotton's squadron was simply too weak. A more powerful force would not be available until the manuevers were completed. The battleships of the North Atlantic Fleet could then be used, for they were already scheduled to take a European cruise after the Caribbean exercises. The original schedule called for the battleships, accompanied by the European Squadron, to visit Lisbon, Trieste, and a French Mediterranean port before returning home. The European Squadron would be detached at Gibraltar. However, a schedule could be revised. On the day Cotton's ships sailed from Beirut, American newspapers reported that the Roosevelt administration had decided to send a powerful fleet to European waters, a "demonstration that will be sufficiently great to impress not only Turkey, but all Europe."[47]

Roosevelt later decided to strengthen the force by adding the South Atlantic Squadron. Altogether some sixteen vessels, including the most modern and powerful battleships in the American navy, were to make the cruise. On 24 May, Secretary Hay recorded in his diary, "I have written a private and confidential instruction to Leishman telling him to make all possible use of the approach of the . . . squadron to eastern waters. I must help him a little by indiscreet paragraphs in the news."[48] When Hay wrote this revealing statement in his diary, he knew that the South Atlantic Squadron, which was already under way for European waters ahead of the other units, was to be ordered to proceed immediately to Tangier, Morocco.

On the night of 18 May, Ion Perdicaris, a wealthy American, and his English stepson were kidnapped by Moroccan bandits from Perdicaris' summer home in the hills on the outskirts of Tangier.[49] Perdicaris was not only an intimate friend of Samuel R. Gummeré, the American consul-general in the city, but evidently was known to influential individuals in the United States as well.

The kidnapping created quite a furor in the United States and made headlines in the American press overnight. As Barbara Tuchman wrote in her colorful account of the incident, "a wealthy old gentlemen held for ransom by Mulai Ahmed Ben Raisuli, a cruel but romantic brigand out of the Arabian nights, could only but excite the American public."[50]

Gummeré, alarmed for the captives' safety, joined with Sir Arthur Nicolson, the British representative, in demanding that the Moroccan government obtain their release. They also wired their governments for naval support. Gummeré requested only one vessel, "large enough to be impressive." Roosevelt, however, decided to send the entire South Atlantic Squadron of four ships.[51] The president's decision to send an entire squadron rather than a single vessel may have been prompted by convenience; the South Atlantic Squadron was already under way for the Mediterranean. Also, Roosevelt was keenly aware of the impact such an action would have on public opinion, with the Republican convention only a month away.[52]

Early in May the South Atlantic Squadron under the Command of Rear Admiral French Chadwick had sailed from the Caribbean for Gibraltar. It was an ill-matched force consisting of the *Brooklyn*, a first-class cruiser that could make twenty knots, the *Boston*, a second-rate cruiser that was much slower, and two small schooner-rigged gunboats, the *Castine* and *Marietta*. The two gunboats had a great deal of difficulty in keeping up with the cruisers, and whenever the wind was fair, they would hoist their sails. The *Castine* even stepped the masts in her small boats and spread their small sails.[53] The squadron reached the Canary Islands where orders were received to leave immediately for Tangier. The ships sailed independently with the *Brooklyn*, carrying the flag of Admiral Chadwick, arriving in Tangier on 30 May, some twelve days after Perdicaris had been abducted.[54]

In the meantime efforts to secure the captives' release had not been successful. Gummeré was convinced that their lives were in danger unless the bandits' demands were met. Although Secretary of the State Hay considered this preposterous, he did request that the European Squadron be sent to strengthen the naval force at Tangier.[55]

The European Squadron, at that time under the command of Rear Admiral Jewell, consisted of Dewey's old flagship, the *Olympia*, and the cruisers *Baltimore* and *Cleveland*. The squadron had rendezvoused with the battleship squadron of the North Atlantic Fleet at Horta, Fayal, in the Azores on 28 May. Both squadrons were scheduled to depart for Lisbon later that day, and early in the afternoon they got under way, forming a long column upon leaving the anchorage. Still within sight of land, however, Admiral Jewell received a message (forwarded by the battleship *Iowa* from a signal station on shore) ordering his squadron to Tangier. The squadron arrived on the first day of June, raising to seven the number of American warships in the Moroccan port.[56] Admiral Chadwick assumed command of the combined force, a fortunate choice because he and Sir Arthur Nicolson had been friends for many years going back to the 1880's when the admiral was naval attaché in London.

Chadwick was closing out a long and distinguished career. He was an intelligent, learned scientific officer, one of the naval activists of the late nineteenth century. Through his writings and investigations of foreign navies, he played a prominent role in the development of the modern American navy. To junior officers, however, he was somewhat of a martinet; a very direct and forceful individual who frequently terrorized his subordinates by his penchant for punctuality and exactness. One young officer who spent a weekend in the Chadwick home was astonished at the regulations. He was told that "breakfast was eight o'clock and mind you *not* eight-one." He described how getting the admiral ready for church was as elaborate a proceeding as getting a ship under way: "Everyone . . . had his assigned duty. He stood in the hall by the front door calling out orders, while various members of the household fetched his hat, his gloves, his stick, his glasses. . . ."[57] Chadwick, however, was as well-qualified to handle the Perdicaris affair as any officer in the navy at that time. He had the confidence of Roosevelt, he was known to Nicolson, and he was tactful as well as intelligent.[58]

Immediately after the South Atlantic Squadron arrived in Tangier, Chadwick conferred with Gummeré and Nicolson and called on the Moroccan minister for foreign affairs. The two diplomats informed the admiral of their concern that local inhabitants (mostly Moslem) would use the Perdicaris incident as a pretext to riot against foreign influence. At their request, Chadwick agreed to land a force if the foreign colony was threatened.[59] As a precautionary measure, a few Marines were landed to guard Gummeré and Perdicaris's residences, the American consulate, and later the Belgian legation. Washington agreed with these measures but instructed the admiral not to use force without specific orders. Chadwick agreed that force should not be used; "an attack will cause [the captives'] . . . immediate murder," he wrote the secretary of the navy.

Roosevelt, however, was becoming increasingly impatient. The Republican Convention was nearing, and he was determined to settle the Moroccan problem in time to present a *fait accompli* to the delegates. He was aware that the American press was beginning to demand force to secure the captives' release. On 15 June, less than a week before the convention was to meet, Hay was told to approach England and France about a joint expedition.[60]

Neither the British nor the French considered a joint expedition practicable or desirable. A number of European countries, particularly France and Spain, viewed the concentration of American warships at Tangier with concern. According to Jules Cambon, French ambassador in Madrid, Spanish papers were stating that the United States was using the Perdicaris incident as an excuse to establish a naval base on that side of the Atlantic.[61] When the United States requested French assistance to rescue Perdicaris and his stepson, the French government was only too happy to oblige. France had been seeking to establish economic and political control in Morocco and resented American and British efforts to seek the captives' release without its help. French opinion was critical at first concerning the presence of the American warships; but later this changed, partly because of the participation by their representative in the negotiations with the bandits but primarily out of fear that violence might break out in the city. A large colony of French subjects lived in Tangier. The French representative told Nicolson after the prisoners had been released and all but two of the American warships had departed that he regretted their departure, as the possibility of violence remained.[62]

Sir Arthur Nicholson not only cooperated fully with the American consul in negotiating with the bandits but also considered the presence of Chadwick's force essential to "reassure the European population." The Moroccan government appealed to Nicolson to "encourage" the Americans to withdraw the naval force. The British minister responded that his government had also been asked to send a warship "owing to the inability of the local authorities to provide adequate means of protection." Nicolson expressed to his London superiors, however, the opinion that the vessels had little effect on the Moroccan officials, "who do not contemplate the possibility of any action being taken on shore by landing parties."[63]

Roosevelt gave up the idea of a joint expedition but continued to exert pressure on the Moroccan government through naval power. The battleship squadron under way for Lisbon was diverted to Gibraltar, within a few hours steaming from Tangier. The ships arrived on 20 June, and as Admiral Albert S. Barker, in command of the squadron, wrote in his memoirs, "had the [Perdicaris] case not been satisfactorily settled, I would had to go there myself with the battleships."[64]

By the time the battleships dropped anchor off Gibraltar, it appeared as if the crisis was easing and the captives would be released shortly. It was not all over, however. A confusing series of delays occurred, exasperating Gummeré to the point where he recommended an ultimatum and the landing of a force of Marines. Chadwick disagreed and so informed the Navy Department.

On 22 June, the day after the Republicans convened in Chicago, Hay cabled

Gummeré, "We want Perdicaris alive or Raisuli dead." Several sentences followed, however, clearly indicating that this was no ultimatum: "You will not arrange for landing Marines or seizing custom house without specific direction from the Department." It is generally accepted that the first line of the cable was for public consumption, particularly for the delegates at the convention.[65] The following day the captives were released.

Contemporary opinion, particularly American, credited Hay and Roosevelt with their release. Since then, opinion has divided. Some believe the French were responsible, others the British, and a few the Moroccan leaders. The evidence suggests, however, that the pressure of the American navy and the Moroccan government's belief that the United States would act if it did not, were major factors in the prisoners' release.[66]

With Perdicaris' freedom, the American naval force concentrated in Tangier and Gibraltar quickly dispersed. On 29 June, the European Squadron joined Barker's battleships at Gibraltar. Within a week they were steaming for Trieste. Shortly afterwards, the South Atlantic Squadron moved the few miles from Tangier to Gibraltar and remained there temporarily in case violence did break out in the Moroccan city. Roosevelt also considered sending Chadwick's squadron to join the other two in the Mediterranean and participate in a naval demonstration in Turkish waters. As mentioned earlier, such a demonstration had been planned but was delayed because of the Moroccan crisis.

Leishman, the American minister in Constantinople, had lost his earlier enthusiasm for gunboat diplomacy. When he was notified in late May that a naval force would be sent to the eastern Mediterranean, he replied that its presence would probably be more annoying than beneficial and that the Sultan would ignore it as he had previous demonstrations of this kind. Although Leishman had little confidence, he again tried to persuade the Ottoman government to come to terms. On 24 June he sent Hay an optimistic cable. That night Secretary of State Hay recorded in his diary, "The Sultan . . . seems to be alarmed about our fleet."[67] Their hopes were premature. In early July a depressed Leishman was again writing that he could get nothing out of the Ottoman government but meaningless promises.

As the American naval force made scheduled stops at Trieste, Fiume, and Corfu, the American minister's persistence and Turkish procrastination continued. Leishman demanded an audience with the Sultan that was granted only after the State Department announced that the squadrons would visit Smyrna. Hay then cabled Leishman that the warships would be held in readiness at Corfu to await the results of the conference with the Sultan.[68] Presumably, they would leave the eastern Mediterranean if the conference was a success, but go to Smyrna if it failed.

Considering the past history of American-Turkish relations, it is not surprising that the Sultan reneged on his promised audience. Hay, who had just returned from vacation, promptly requested the navy to order the warships to

Smyrna. However, only the European Squadron was sent to the Turkish port; the battleships instead left for Gibraltar. Obviously Roosevelt had abandoned the idea of a naval demonstration for he had earlier concluded that adequate pressure could be exerted on the Ottoman government only by the presence of a powerful naval force in Turkish waters. Yet, only the small cruisers of the European Squadron were ordered to Smyrna. One possible explanation for this decision was Secretary of State Hay's conviction that such a demonstration would fail and might lead to complications with one or more of the European powers. The secretary of state also persuaded Roosevelt to adopt another plan. Hay mentions in his diary that he recommended to the president that Leishman should demand an answer to the American claims and, if there were further delays, should leave on one of the warships at anchor in Smyrna harbor. Then the matter would be turned over to Congress. Roosevelt agreed, and the American minister in Constantinople was so informed.[69]

It seems clear that the Turkish government received intelligence of this threat and took it seriously. On 8 August, as the warships of the European Squadron were steaming towards the Turkish coast, Chekib Bey, the Ottoman representative in Washington, called on Hay in his office and later at his home, trying to persuade him to halt the "visit" by the warships. Hay wrote in his diary that night: "I declined to relieve his anxiety but told him things could not continue as they were." Leishman cabled from Constantinople during the day that an undersecretary of state for foreign affairs called on him "and begs me to use my influence to prevent the fleet from coming . . . assuring me that the promised reply will be given not later than Thursday." It is astonishing that the minister should have fallen for the same old subterfuge, but he did. He asked that the squadron's visit to Smyrna be delayed until after Thursday, and he repeated the request the following day.

John Hay, a cultivated gentlemen who at the start of his long illustrious career had been Abraham Lincoln's private secretary, was unusually forbearing with his subordinates abroad. Nevertheless, Leishman's acceptance of Turkish promises at face value were more than even he could endure. He sent off a sharply worded telegram (later getting Roosevelt's approval of what he had already done) to the minister in Constantinople pointing out that the warships could not be recalled and he was to be governed by the department's instructions. "The instructions," Hay wrote in his diary, ". . . [were those that Leishman] had been begging for a year past."[70]

On 10 August the British ambassador to the Ottoman Empire sent a long and accurate report to the Foreign Office concerning the controversy between the United States and Turkey. He concluded by predicting Turkish compliance with the American claims: "I have little doubt that in consequence of the movement of the American Fleet and the veiled threat of coercive measures most of the pending questions . . . will be speedily and promptly settled. . . ."[71] The British ambassador's information was accurate. Two days later Leishman informed the State Department that he had received an "informal memorandum" in which the Ottoman government agreed to most of the American demands. Although the American minister preferred a formal document rather than simply an informal memorandum, Hay and the president considered the informal note sufficient. Hay carried Leishman's message to a cabinet meeting and as the secretary described it in his diary, "fearing that Leishman might come away, he [Roosevelt] seized my despatch [answer to Leishman] and wrote it all over again, adding a peremptory veto to his breaking off diplomatic relations. . . ."[72]

On the same day that the cabinet meeting took place, the European Squadron arrived at Smyrna. Admiral Jewell found waiting for him a message from Leishman requesting the name of the ship that would be sent to Constantinople to remove him from the Turkish capital. Before the admiral could reply, Roosevelt's cable accepting the "informal memorandum" arrived. The following day the squadron left Smyrna.

Although Roosevelt included the Turkish settlement in his acceptance speech for the Republican nomination, many considered it premature. Hay confided in his diary, "I hope that question is closed for awhile—of course not forever, for the Sultan must grow wise and honest before we can be at peace with him altogether." A foreign correspondent for the London *Times* in Constantinople reported that all parties were pleased with the settlement but Leishman, who had little assurance that the agreement would be carried out. The British ambassador in Constantinople wrote, "There is reason to fear that fresh difficulties may arise later . . . in the execution of the verbal promises made by the Sublime Porte. The general impression seems to be that Mr. Leishman should have insisted upon the full and immediate execution of his demands . . . before . . . allowing the American fleet to leave Turkish waters."[73]

Leishman, of course, did want to get a stronger commitment while the warships were in Turkish waters, but Roosevelt ordered him to accept the unofficial note. One wonders if Roosevelt decided not to push his luck for fear of a failure that might hurt him politically. He all but admitted this to a friend. Adee, however, attributed the American minister's apparent disappointment to being "huffy because [Hay] . . . overrode his pet scheme of sailing away in a blaze of red fire and returning by way of apotheosis, as a star-crowned Ambassador."[74]

Five months after the three cruisers of the European Squadron sailed out of Smyrna harbor, they were deployed elsewhere, and the squadron was abolished. From 1905 until the United States declared war on Germany in April 1917, individual ships, detached units, and special squadrons were responsible for protecting American interests in the Old World.[75]

SPECIAL
SQUADRONS
AND THE
SCORPION

In December 1905, Roosevelt announced that, counting vessels under construction, the United States Navy would have an effective strength of forty armored ships—twenty-eight battleships and twelve armored cruisers. This number was impressive, but the actual strength at that time was approximately half. With the exception of the battleship squadron and cruisers in the Asiatic Fleet, the armored ships were concentrated in the North Atlantic Fleet. From this fleet, which would become more powerful each year, vessels would be detached and sent to European waters. Those ordered to the Old World during the decade preceding the outbreak of World War I were rarely sent to show the flag. Instead, they crossed the Atlantic for other specific purposes.

During the previous summer, a division of the North Atlantic Fleet, the cruisers *Brooklyn, Chattanooga, Galveston,* and *Tacoma*, under the command of Rear Admiral Charles P. Sigsbee went to France to bring back the remains of John Paul Jones. Sigsbee, who had commanded the ill-fated *Maine* when she was blown up in 1898, led a naval battalion selected from the four vessels to attend a ceremony in Paris. Early in July the *Brooklyn*, escorted by the other cruisers, carried the remains back to a splendid crypt at Annapolis.[1]

In August, a special squadron consisting of the cruiser *Minneapolis*, auxiliary cruiser *Dixie*, and collier *Caesar*, under the command of Rear Admiral Colby M. Chester proceeded to Spain and the northern coast of Africa to observe a solar eclipse that took place on the thirtieth of the month. The squadron was then ordered to the Baltic; but upon their reaching England, the cruise was cancelled, and the vessels returned to the United States.[2]

In 1906 Sigsbee returned with a squadron to European waters. One of the vessels carried Henry White, appointed by the president as a representative to the Algericas Conference, called to consider the explosive Moroccan question. The squadron remained at Gibraltar while the conference was held in the small Spanish port of Algericas. Newspapers, particularly European ones, speculated that the squadron was there in case England and France had trouble with Germany over the Moroccan question and that the vessels had swung at anchor a few miles from Morocco as a warning to the Kaiser. No documents have been found to substantiate this. However, the chief of the Bureau of Navigation informed Admiral Sigsbee that his squadron was being readied for emergency duty elsewhere:

> My original intention was that you should sail with your division about the 1st of the month on a trip to South America, then via Cape of Good Hope to Madagascar and Zanzibar and via the Red Sea to the eastern part of the Mediterranean. . . . Developments in Russia and Turkey have conspired to delay your departure, and make it advisable to hold your division in readiness for an emergency call. . . .[3]

The Turkish "development" concerned the decision by the United States government to raise the diplomatic post in Constantinople from a ministry to an embassy, in spite of the fact that the Ottoman government, as well as several of the European powers, were opposed to it. The Sultan at first refused to recognize Leishman as an ambassador and later declined to grant the American an audience. The Sultan's refusal to receive Leishman was more important than mere protocol, for every ambassador had the right to request and receive an audience with him. Diplomatic representatives below this rank had to negotiate for this privilege. In the spring and again in the fall of 1906, American naval vessels visited Turkish ports, apparently to pressure the Sultan into recognizing and receiving Leishman. His ambassadorial status was finally recognized, and an audience held by the Sultan, although what part the warships played in this is not known.[4]

The raising of the legation to an embassy made it only a matter of time before the question of stationing a small warship permanently in Constantinople was brought up again. Periodically during the years since the American Civil War, the American representatives in the Sultan's capital had petitioned for a stationnaire. Although the major European powers retained such a vessel, the Ottoman government had refused persistently to grant the United States permission on the grounds that that country was not a signatory of the Treaty of Paris of 1856. In July 1907, a bomb exploded in the garden of Leishman's summer residence. He used this as the justification to request a stationnaire. Although the State Department approved his request, it was never carried out. The navy reported that no suitable vessel was available.[5] An outbreak of violence in Turkey the following year resulted in the question being raised again, and this time a vessel was ordered to Constantinople.

Abdul Hamid had been Sultan since 1876. His long reign was characterized by conspiracy, revolt, the loss of large parts of his empire, repression and elimination of minorities, particulary Armenians, and constant foreign pressure and intervention. Discontent was widespread. In July 1908, a military revolt broke out in Macedonia and with extraordinary spontaneity spread throughout European Turkey. On 24 July, Abdul Hamid surrendered to the rebels' demands for a consitution and elections. As a result of the election that followed, a group generally called the "young Turks" came to power. The new regime faced enormous difficulties, and inevitably there was a great deal of unrest in the empire.

It was in this context that Leishman pleaded again for a stationnaire. He even recommended a particular vessel, the *Gloucester*, J. P. Morgan's former yacht that had been taken over during the Spanish-American War. The State Department agreed. As one official pointed out to Secretary of State Elihu Root, the new Ottoman regime was interested in establishing good relations with the United States and for this reason probably would not object to the idea. Root consulted with Roosevelt and the Navy Department and then cabled Leishman on 19 August, "Stationnaire will be sent promptly."[6] Nevertheless, a month would elapse before the navy decided on a suitable vessel, for the *Gloucester* was not available. However, another converted yacht, the *Scorpion*, was finally selected.[7]

The *Scorpion* was admirably equipped for this duty. She was formerly the steel twin-screw yacht *Sovereign* launched in 1896. Her overall length was 250 feet, with a 28-foot beam, displacing approximately 850 tons. She was fast for her day, with a maximum speed of approximately eighteen knots. Purchased shortly after the outbreak of hostilities between Spain and the United States, she was converted into a gunboat by removing her masts, bow sprit, and much of her interior furniture and furnishings. Steel plates were fitted to the outside of her engine and boiler rooms, and a battery of twelve small guns (later changed to four six-pounders) was installed. During the war, she spent most of her time on blockade duty off Santiago, Cuba. Afterwards, she was attached to the North Atlantic Fleet and was in the West Indies when ordered to Constantinople. Before crossing the Atlantic, the vessel entered the Philadelphia Navy Yard, where various modifications were carried out that included the removal of all but two of her guns and the enlarging of several compartments in order to carry a larger crew. However, this still did not enable her to carry the brass band requested by the State Department. Finally, a new complement of officers, all with some linguistic background, was assigned.[8]

While the *Scorpion* was in the yard fitting out for the cruise, diplomatic officials were working to obtain permission for the converted gunboat to pass through the Dardanelles. Assistant Secretary of State Adee, aware of past difficulties in obtaining Turkish approval, recommended informing the Ottoman government that the *Scorpion* was carrying a special envoy to convey the president's greeting to the Sultan. "The President's autograph letter could be friendly and expectant rather than congratulatory," Adee added. "The pudding is too hot yet for proof by degulition [?] and digestion—and it may be found indigestible. . . .''[9] The assistant secretary's forewarnings in this case were not needed, for on 15 October, permission was granted. One week later the *Scorpion* sailed for the Mediterranean, her open decks covered with bags of coal.[10] On 4 December 1908, six weeks after leaving Philadelphia, the small vessel arrived at Constantinople.

One of the *Scorpion's* officers would later denote her purposes for being in the Turkish capital as "prestige, protection, and pleasure." Although the last was not a purpose officially designated by the government, the other two were essentially correct. Lieutenant Commander George W. Logan, the ship's commanding officer, was told to investigate the responsibilities of the other nations' stationnaires and emulate them.[11]

The *Scorpion* was unique. The assignment of a station ship outside territorial waters was unprecedented in the United States Navy. There were no standing orders governing the relationship between the ambassador and the ship's commanding officer, and for this reason difficulties arose between Leishman and Logan. The ambassador assumed that since the vessel was assigned to the embassy, he had complete control over her. Leishman was correct in this to a point. Logan was ordered to assume the responsibilities of naval attaché as well as those of the *Scorpion's* captain and furthermore would be "under the direction and control of the ambassador." However, traditionally the captain of a naval vessel has a great deal of discretion in the operations of his vessel. This apparent contradiction in command responsibilities would create problems as long as the stationnaire was in service. For example, early in 1909 Leishman requested a decision on his authority to use the vessel for travel. The Navy Department agreed that the *Scorpion's* commanding officer had been ordered to comply with the wishes of the ambassador "whenever he desired to visit *Turkish ports* in that vessel on *official business* without obtaining the consent of the Navy Department."[12] It was up to the stationnaire's captain, however, to determine what was official business.

The *Scorpion's* sojourn in Constantinople was brief. Before the month of December was out, she was ordered to Messina, Sicily. On 28 December, an earthquake of appalling severity shook eastern Sicily, and completely destroyed Reggio, Messina, and a large number of villages, with loss of life estimated at 150,000. The *Scorpion* arrived in Messina harbor five days later and found a number of foreign ships already present and hundreds of Italian soldiers sifting through the smouldering ruins. The American gunboat sailed immediately to Naples to take on a cargo of relief supplies. By the middle of January 1909, she had been joined in the relief work by additional American vessels—the yacht of the ambassador to Italy, the supply ship *Culgoa*, and the battleship *Illinois*. The battleship divisions of the Great White Fleet in their spectacular around-the-world cruise were approaching the Mediterranean by way of the Red Sea when news of the disaster was received. The *Illinois* was immediately dispatched to the island to be followed later by an entire division.

The USS *Scorpion*, stationnaire at Constantinople, 1908–1927. *Courtesy of the United States Department of Navy.*

However, because of Italian disapproval of American aid, the division was sent elsewhere. Ambassador Lloyd C. Griscom said that it was a "matter of prestige, a distinctly manifest desire on the part of the Italians to handle the situation by themselves." The *Illinois* steamed on to Malta after a landing party of sailors located the bodies of the American consul and his wife. The *Scorpion* also departed, for Constantinople. Commander Logan reported that the vessel's presence benefited "in showing American sympathies and little else."[13]

Their departure was premature. Within days the Italian authorities were anxious for American aid. Lieutenant Commander Reginald R. Belknap, naval attaché in Rome, arrived and took charge of American relief operations. He chartered a ship at Genoa to bring in a cargo of medical and hospital supplies, food, and clothing. He also requested the return of the *Scorpion*, but in February she had entered a yard in Naples for extensive repairs to her boilers.[14]

Leishman was distressed over the absence of the *Scorpion*, which had been on station at Constantinople less than a month. He feared a renewal of turmoil in the empire because of political instability. The young Turk movement, in its efforts to establish parliamentary government, was running into difficulty. The first meeting of parliament in the middle of December 1908 had resulted in serious controversy between Turkish nationalists and representatives of the subject nationalities. Trouble continued into the new year and resulted in the forced resignation of the grand vizier. On 14 February, the day after his resignation, Leishman requested the immediate return of the *Scorpion*, but he was informed that it would take at least a month to complete repairs on the boilers.[15] Two months later rioting broke out in the Turkish capital that led to the collapse of the new government. Troops from outlying districts then marched into the city and deposed the Sultan. Civil war and violence spread into the interior, where early in April several thousand Armenians were massacred. In Adana two American missionaries were killed and several injured, and throughout Turkey American-sponsored churches, missions, and schools were destroyed.[16]

Leishman appealed for warships to protect American interests in the capital and along the coast of Asia Minor. "All feeling of security has in fact disappeared" in Constantinople, he wrote the secretary of state, and he blamed much of this on the absence of the *Scorpion*. When the troops began to occupy parts of the city, he cabled the State Department that serious trouble was imminent. Philander C. Knox, President William Howard Taft's recently appointed secretary of state, promptly replied that the armored cruisers *Montana* and *North Carolina* had been ordered to the eastern Mediterranean.[17] Leishman was unhappy with this decision. He wanted the stationnaire's return as quickly as possible but not additional warships that could offer no immediate protection to Americans in Constantinople. Warships from other nations were already concentrating in the Asia Minor ports. He continued urging that the cruisers should not be sent even after he was notified that they were en route to the Mediterranean. The vessels were no longer needed, he insisted, and their presence might antagonize the new regime. The orders, however, were not countermanded, and Leishman was advised that if the vessels were no longer required for emergency purposes, the Turkish government was to be notified that the visit was one of "friendly courtesy."[18]

Leishman's objections concerning the warships were ignored because of the recommendations of Francis M. Huntington Wilson, Secretary of the State Knox's first assistant. On 4 May, a State Department official noted the insecurity of Americans in Turkey and wrote Wilson, "It chimes in with your thought yesterday not to have the ships recalled just yet."[19] The State Department and President Taft received a large number of letters and telegrams urging strong action, including sending a fleet. Although the president did balk at a "fleet," he did approve dispatching the two cruisers.[20]

On 12 May, the cruisers dropped anchor at Mersin in Asia Minor. In the years before the United States became involved in war with Germany, the *North Carolina* and *Montana* along with their sister ships would spend considerable time in the eastern Mediterranean. Only four of this class were commissioned, the *Tennessee*, followed by the *Washington*, the *North Carolina*, and the *Montana*. Nicknamed the "Big Ten" because of their four 10-inch rifled guns in centerline turrets, these 14,500-ton vessels could make twenty-three knots at flank speed. Their armament (sixteen 6-inch rapid-fire guns in addition to the 10-inch guns) was equivalent to most battleships. They were initially organized into a cruiser squadron, but because of their speed, unusually long cruising range, and accommodations, they became the favorite type for special missions. Line officers admired them, but engineers considered their machinery unusually troublesome.[21]

The two armored cruisers were not the only vessels ordered to Turkish waters to protect American interests during the 1909 crisis. The revenue cutter *Tahoma*, a small sailing vessel en route to the Pacific via the Mediterranean and Suez Canal, was ordered to Alexandretta. Although apparently the nearest United States vessel, she arrived only the day before the cruisers dropped anchor at Mersin.[22]

On 14 May the *Montana* left Mersin and joined the *Tahoma* at Alexandretta. The revenue cutter had landed some food and her surgeon, but with the cruiser's arrival she resumed her interrupted cruise to the Pacific. The *North Carolina* sent a medical team to Adana, forty-two miles inland. There several thousand refugees were found, many encamped on property under the jurisdiction of American missionaries. Captain William A. Marshall, the *North Carolina*'s commanding officer, held a conference with the governor of Adana and threatened to land a force of Marines if order was not maintained. "I concluded that a decided statement, if not threats, would have much more

effect in spurring him to doing his duty towards protecting our citizens . . . than
. . . customary diplomatic language," he reported to the Navy Department. It
was, however, just another example of American bluff. "It is hardly necessary
for me to state," Marshall wrote, "that to land an armed force and send it a
distance of 42 miles from the protection of the guns of the vessel would be
unjustifiable from any standpoint." The *Montana's* captain also used rather
strong language in an interview with officials in Alexandretta: "I don't know
that it will have any effect, but it may. . . . It is the little drop of water that finally
wears away the stone."[23]

The attitude adopted by the cruisers' commanding officers towards the
Turks was essentially the same as Kirkland's in the 1890s or Worden's twenty
years before. It reflected their conviction that they were dealing with bar-
barians or at least inferior people who should be threatened as one threatens a
dog or a child to gain obedience. It was a racial attitude little different from that
expressed by Americans and other Caucasians toward nonwhite people
throughout the world, an attitude that has died slowly in the twentieth century.

For three months the U.S. vessels cruised along the coast of Turkish Asia
Minor, visiting various ports. Usually, the same format was followed. The captain or one of his officers would visit local officials and threaten the use of force
if American property and citizens were not respected and protected. They discovered no trouble, although the grim remains of violence were evident in a
number of localities. None of the intelligence gathered by the warships was
passed on to Leishman in Constantinople. In fact he was completely in the dark
concerning the vessels' movements. He received three brief messages from
Captain Marshall, the senior officer, during the weeks the cruisers were in
Turkish waters, in spite of the fact that Marshall had been ordered to cooperate with the ambassador and be "guided by his advice . . . as to points
where protection [was] . . . necessary."[24]

Leishman complained to Washington, and Marshall defended his actions by
outlining the cruisers' accomplishments (emergency medical relief, voluntary
contribution for relief by the ships' crews, visiting a large number of ports, and
the like). The *North Carolina's* captain also stated that he did not consider it
necessary to notify the ambassador, as the consuls were "in frequent correspondence with [him]." The Navy Department supported Marshall in spite of
the fact that, as the secretary of state wrote, "these statements suggest to this
Department . . . that no matter how satisfactory the conditions found at ports
visited may have appeared to Captain Marshall, this could not be known to the
Embassy unless communicated [to] it." The State Department also disapproved of the use of threats to land an armed force without consulting Washington beforehand. Marshall, however, was not reprimanded.[25]

Marshall clearly stretched to the limits his authority. He was certainly negli-
gent in failing to consult with Leishman or with Washington officials. Yet the
major problem was coordinating the efforts of two independent executive departments, "each with its own procedures and established ways." The Navy

Department defended Marshall with the customary argument that commanding officers should consult with civilian officials, but according to naval regulations "a commanding officer is solely and entirely responsible to the Navy Department for all official acts in the administration of his command." This appears to contradict the Navy Department's orders to Marshall dated 1 May. The policy, still generally accepted today, simply points up the dilemma over divided responsibility.[26]

Leishman had all along opposed the naval demonstration and continued to urge that the vessels be withdrawn. On 3 July, he got his wish. The two cruisers left Mersin for Naples, where they rendezvoused with the *Scorpion*. After transferring supplies, they sailed for the United States, and the stationnaire returned to Constantinople.[27]

Leishman's disapproval of the presence of American vessels in Turkish waters did not apply to the *Scorpion*, which was virtually unarmed and under his immediate control. The vessel was essential if the ambassador was to keep in touch with Americans throughout the empire. At that time transportation facilities in the Near East were quite primitive—a few short railroads or camel caravans. The station vessel provided the ambassador and his staff with the means of travelling beyond the Turkish capital. Leishman made trips to all parts of the empire in the months that followed, despite the fact that he found the stationnaire uncomfortable, especially in the stormy winter months. Oscar Straus, who replaced Leishman as ambassador in September 1909, recorded in his diary one rough trip from Constantinople to Salonica that took over three days. "At one time the roll was 42 degrees," he wrote.[28]

The *Scorpion* was also occasionally used to transport diplomatic, political, and business VIPs. President Taft's dollar diplomacy resulted in his administration taking a deep interest in the so-called Chester project, a gigantic railroad and investment venture by a group of American entrepreneurs in Turkey. The stationnaire served for a brief period as a floating headquarters for a special mission sent by Taft to investigate the project.[29]

When the *Scorpion* was not steaming around the eastern Mediterranean or the Black Sea, she was anchored at Constantinople. Along with the stationnaires of Germany, Italy, France, Great Britain, Russia, and Austria, she was moored to buoys off Topans, the Greek section of the city, during the winter months and at Therapia, fifteen miles up the Bosphorus, during the summer, when the ambassador had his residence there.

In the fall of 1911, the station vessel went to Trieste (then in Austria) for an extensive overhaul. While she was in the yard, war broke out between Italy and Turkey. The war, which began on 29 September and lasted over a year, was primarily a result of Italy's determination to acquire Tripoli, the last Ottoman possession in North Africa.[30] The United States, in spite of some support for intervention and mediation, followed its traditional policy of noninvolvement.[31]

Shortly before the war broke out, the cruiser *Chester* had been ordered to the

Mediterranean to support the State Department's demands for an investigation into the death of a member of an American archaeological expedition working in the ruins of Cyrene. The expedition had returned to Tripoli, and the *Chester* was instructed to "afford it such countanance as might be appropriate." The kind of assistance was not specified, but presumably it was to provide a place of refuge if needed. Refuge was not needed, and the cruiser, after a brief visit to Tripoli, went to Malta. Early in October she made a trip to Trieste to carry men and stores to the *Scorpion* and return to Malta when news of the war between Turkey and Italy was received. She was ordered to remain there in case U.S. nationals needed to be evacuated from Tripoli.[32]

On 5 November, the State Department was informed that the *Chester* would have to leave Malta because of a cholera outbreak. Secretary of State Knox was at Valley Forge, Pennsylvania; and in a telephone conversation with Adee, he decided to send the cruiser immediately to Tripoli and remove the consul and other Americans. It was an unfortunate decision, for the Italian government had already informed Washington that it assumed the responsibility of protecting Americans. The decision also came at a time when stories and editorials in European and American newspapers were accusing the Italians of atrocities in the war. Rome, convinced that the arrival of a warship to remove Americans would be interpreted as a response to the accusations, protested the cruiser's orders. Nevertheless the *Chester* went to Tripoli but found only two Americans to evacuate, the consul and Commander Andrew T. Long, naval attaché in Rome, in Tripoli as an observer. The members of the archaeological expedition had already left, although the State Department was not aware of this. The American warship remained in the African port only a few hours before sailing for Marseilles, but without the two Americans. Long later wrote that they decided to remain, as leaving might have jeopardized the friendly relations between Italy and the United States. Early in December the *Chester* left the Mediterranean for home.[33]

Italy's success in her war with Turkey acted as a stimulant to the Balkan States. While the war was in progress, these states concluded a series of alliances that prepared the way for an attack on the Ottoman Empire. In spite of efforts by the European powers, who feared that a Balkan war might spread into a general conflict, Montenegro declared war on Turkey on 7 October 1912, followed ten days later by Greece, Serbia, and Bulgaria. The Balkan allies were victorious from the beginning. By the end of October Bulgarian troops were approaching the final Turkish defenses before Constantinople. The fighting was so close that cannon fire could be heard in the Ottoman capital.

On 5 November, William W. Rockhill, who had replaced Oscar Straus at Constantinople, informed the State Department that the city's foreign colony was on the verge of panic. He had requested the assistance of neutral warships in the harbor, "as we have no ships coming here for the protection of our people." Yet, when Washington asked if warships were needed, the ambassador replied that adequate protection for foreigners, including Americans, was available.

Even before Rockhill's reply was received, the president had decided to dispatch a warship. For several days the State Department bickered with the Navy Department over the type of vessel needed. At first the navy recommended sending an unarmed transport to carry supplies and accommodate refugees. State Department officials, however, insisted that a warship was required, preferably "a speedy and roomy cruiser." The most suitable vessels were the armored cruisers, but they were in the reserve fleet; and vessels in the reserve fleet, although still in commission, were in an inactive status, stripped of crews, ammunition, fuel, and stores. At the State Department's insistence, the navy agreed to activate one for the emergency, and in a later cabinet meeting the decision was made to send not one but two of the armored cruisers. The *Tennessee* and *Montana* were ordered outfitted for this mission.[34]

As in the past, it was primarily missionary pressure that persuaded the president to order warships to Constantinople. In spite of Rockhill's confidence, not all Americans in Constantinople were reassured by the presence of foreign warships. They demanded American naval protection—protection which obviously could not be provided by the little *Scorpion*.[35]

The two cruisers were designated a "Special Service Squadron" and placed under the command of Rear Admiral Austin M. Knight. Admiral Knight was well known in the navy as the author of *Knight's Seamanship*, a manual that first appeared while he was in charge of the Department of Seamanship at the Naval Academy. He was in command of the reserve fleet when ordered to shift his flag to the Special Service Squadron.

The two cruisers were lying in the back channel at League Island Navy Yard in Philadelphia. The battleships *New Jersey* and *Louisiana* were nearly stripped of their crews to man these ships. The *Louisiana*, in drydock in Philadelphia, had her entire crew transferred to the *Tennessee*. The *New Jersey* had her orders to sail cancelled when she had to transfer a large part of her crew to the *Montana*. An entire train was chartered to transport them from New York to Philadelphia. Arriving on board the cruisers, the new crews had to prepare them for extended sea duty, an enormous undertaking; for everything had to be loaded by hand, including some 2,400 tons of coal for each vessel. While working parties struggled with stores piled up on the docks, coal was taken off canal boats on the channel side. On 11 November, three days after the orders were issued, the two vessels slipped their moorings, eased out into the channel, and steamed down the Delaware River into the Atlantic.[36]

While these vessels were being readied, the State Department sought assurances from the countries with naval forces already in Turkish waters that Americans would receive protection. The Coast Guard was also requested to hold the revenue cutter *Unalga* at Port Said.[37]

With a hostile army on her doorsteps Constantinople was the point of most danger. On 17 November, heavy firing could be heard all day. That night the foreign representatives and naval commanders conferred and agreed to land an international brigade of some 2,000 marines and sailors from the assembled vessels the following day. The *Scorpion*'s crew was so small that she could only provide twenty sailors to "protect" Roberts College. The gunboat dropped anchor in Bebek Bay within 200 yards of the college in order to land additional men if needed. The British cruiser *Weymouth* provided 120 men to guard the American embassy. There was no trouble in the city, however, and on 4 December, the day after an armistice was signed between Turkey, Bulgaria, and Serbia, the men were reembarked.[38]

The *Tennessee* reached Smyrna on 1 December, and the *Montana* arrived at Mersin the following day. Admiral Knight, carrying his flag on the *Tennessee*, found a dispatch from Rockhill informing him that negotiations for an armistice were under way and that the vessels were not needed. After consulting with local Americans, however, the admiral disagreed and strongly advised the Navy Department that the squadron be retained in Turkish waters for the present. "The tranquility," he wrote, "is in large degree due to the presence of foreign men of war. . . ."[39]

The foreign powers withdrew their vessels (other than the stationnaires) from Constantinople but retained those elsewhere in Turkish waters. There was concern that disturbances might break out after the peace treaty was signed, particularly if it was disastrous for Turkey. Even Rockhill had second thoughts and agreed that the American warships should remain. In February 1913, he requested that the Navy Department order one of the cruisers to Constantinople if trouble should break out there. The *Montana* went to Smyrna, where she was instructed "to coal and be ready to proceed to Constantinople." However, the vessel was never called for. In the meantime the *Tennessee* steamed up and down the coast, visiting various ports including Beirut, Mersin, Adana, Alexandretta, Tripoli, and Latakia.[40]

On 29 January 1913, Admiral Knight was detached from command of the squadron and ordered home. His replacement was Captain Frank F. Fletcher of the *Montana*. Upon arriving in Washington, Knight recommended that the squadron be withdrawn. The State Department disagreed, and President Woodrow Wilson, who had just been inaugurated, decided to keep the vessels in the eastern Mediterranean. His recently appointed secretary of the navy, Josephus Daniels, recorded in his diary the reason: "The Balkan War is not settled."[41]

A month later, however, a crisis developed on the opposite side of the globe that did bring the two cruisers home. Japanese-American relations had deteriorated sharply during Roosevelt's second administration. The United States' role in the Treaty of Portsmouth that ended the Russo-Japanese War was criticized by the Japanese people, who were also inflamed by the discrimination against Orientals in California. A possible crisis was averted with the signing of the so-called "Gentleman's Agreement" in 1907, but war talk continued on both sides of the Pacific. The General Board drew up a plan known as "Orange" based on possible war with Japan. Trouble brewed up again in April 1913, when the California legislature passed an act forbidding aliens ineligible for citizenship, like the Japanese, from owning agricultural land. The bill was passed on 15 April, and three days later there was a large anti-American demonstration in Tokyo. Tension mounted in both countries. On 29 April, the General Board sent a memo to Secretary Daniels recommending steps that should be taken immediately in "preparation for war against Orange." Among them was one ordering home the cruisers in Turkish waters. Although the Navy Department discounted the possibility of actual war breaking out, it was felt that a full-scale preparation for a conflict would be "of great benefit in the future."[42] The two warships in Turkish waters left for the United States.

Rockhill, who had earlier objected to the presence of the vessels, opposed their withdrawal. "Conditions," he wrote, ". . . do not appear as yet to have very materially changed for the better."[43] Nevertheless, both vessels reached the United States in late May 1913. Because the crisis with Japan had subsided by then, they returned to the reserve fleet. Once again the *Scorpion* was the only American vessel in Turkish waters.

The *Scorpion* remained in the vicinity of Constantinople during the months preceding the outbreak of World War I, venturing occasionally into the Black Sea but at anchor most of the time off the city or at Therapia. The ship's crew found the capital a delightful place for liberty. The sailors, upon leaving the ship, frequently went to the St. James Restaurant for dinner, then to Novotney's Beer Garden with its five-piece string orchestra playing Strauss waltzes, and finally to the Pera Palace with its vaudeville show or the Olympia Roller Skating Rink. They also enjoyed horseback riding on weekends, but this was stopped after two intoxicated crew members created an incident by galloping up and down the main street of a village. Other incidents persuaded the American colony to organize a service club. They leased a three-story building, hired a housekeeper, and called it the Scorpion Club. It became the hangout for the crew members while on liberty until the ship was interned in 1915.[44]

During the early weeks of World War I the *Scorpion* was moored in the harbor off the arsenal quay. The anchorage was unfortunate, both from strong winds which blew frequently out of the Sea of Marmara in the winter months and because of exposure to attack by Allied submarines. In January 1915, heavy weather pulled her stern into an interned Danish vessel anchored nearby. Damage was slight, but the *Scorpion*'s moorings were shifted some 150 yards further from land. Shortly after that the buoy chain parted, and she swung into midchannel, narrowly missing several vessels. In March 1915, a new commanding officer reported on board. Five days later he drowned along with three members of the crew while trying to return to the vessel during a storm. On 25 May, a British submarine, the E-11, came to periscope depth a few hundred yards from the *Scorpion*. According to the sub's captain, she nearly attacked a vessel carrying an American flag, which may have been the stationnaire. The submarine did blow up a barge and damage a freighter. One of the *Scorpion*'s officers described the incident:

> On the deck of the *Scorpion* we heard the quartermaster cry, "British Submarine!!" All hands scrambled up on deck in time to see the periscope . . . heading at full speed for the center of the harbor, regardless of buoy chains, numerous transports and sunken wrecks. Pandemonium broke loose in the harbor. Whistles shrieked, soldiers attempted to jump overboard from the transports, . . . all traffic on the bridge was stopped . . . even the shops up town began to close their doors.[45]

In the excitement, the *Scorpion* commanding officer, who had been drinking coffee, rushed out on deck, as did his mess boy. After they had gotten topside, the skipper turned to him and asked, "Jefferies, did you bring my cup?" "No, sir," the mess boy replied, "I didn't even have time to bring my own."[46]

The Turkish authorities then ordered the *Scorpion* moved to a less-exposed anchorage. She was finally moored off the Greek village of Arnaoutkeuy, halfway between Therapia and Constantinople. Roberts College and the American girls' school were close by, and the anchorage was protected by a spit of land jutting into the Bosphorus. The anchorage was isolated, however, and a coal barge and water lighter were purchased and moored alongside.[47]

With the *Scorpion* immobilized, anxious Americans throughout Turkey looked to additional naval vessels for support. Fortunately, American warships were available. Upon the outbreak of the war, Woodrow Wilson had ordered warships into European waters. They would remain until shortly before Congress declared war in April 1917.

11

WORLD WAR I: THE NAVY AND NEUTRALITY, 1914–1917

In March 1913, Woodrow Wilson entered the White House as the twenty-eighth president. A progressive and a social democrat absorbed in domestic issues, he had little interest or time for the military. His appointment of Josephus Daniels as secretary of the navy reflects this attitude. Daniels was a North Carolina newspaper editor, something of a pacifist, and as he later admitted himself, had had little knowledge of or contact with the navy.[1] Yet Wilson allowed him unreserved control of the navy and supported him to the end, in spite of Daniels' unpopularity with many naval officers, his controversial programs and reforms, and even the fact that the president's second wife considered the North Carolinian a political liability.[2] Wilson, unlike his two Republican predecessors, was not interested in the navy; but he was aware of Daniels' complete devotion to him and he reciprocated it.

William D. Leahy, the future admiral, wrote in his diary that Daniels was an able man, shrewd and intelligent, "a man of very superior energy, of calm judgment, devoted to his work."[3] Many of the reforms and policies that he championed, such as his plan to institute a basic educational and technical training program for enlisted men, his continued reorganization of naval administration, particularly the creation of the office of chief of naval operations, his determination to maintain civilian supremacy, even his general order prohibiting the use of any alcoholic beverage on board naval vessels, were sound. On the other hand he was suspicious of most naval officers and frequently ignored their recommendations. There is little doubt that his procrastination in advocating a "preparedness program" retarded the navy's readiness when the United States went to war in April 1917.

"It would be the irony of fate if my administration had to deal chiefly with foreign affairs," Wilson confided to a friend shortly before his inauguration. The remark not only acknowledged the inadequacy of his preparation to deal with foreign affairs, but also his absorbing concern with domestic issues.[4] Yet, foreign affairs dominated Wilson's administration, and his reputation to a large degree centered around his decisions concerning World War I and its aftermath.

The assassination of Archduke Francis Ferdinand and his wife on 28 June 1914 set off a chain reaction that ultimately plunged a large part of the world into war. The first explosion occurred on 28 July, when the Austrian-Hungarian government declared war on Serbia. Within a few days Germany, Russia, France, and Great Britain also entered the conflict. Gradually other nations in Europe, in the Far East, and finally in the Western Hemisphere would be drawn in.

Generally, Americans were mildly interested in the holocaust that began to consume Europe and were relieved that the United States was not involved. The majority strongly approved Wilson's proclamation of neutrality, although it quickly became apparent that the impartiality in speech and thought requested by the president was impossible to attain.

While Wilson was struggling with personal tragedy (his first wife died on 6 August), he was confronted with serious problems created by the war. It occurred at the peak of the summer tourist season, and some 30,000 Americans were caught unprepared in Europe. Banks and foreign exchanges were closed, steamship sailings were cancelled, and embassies and consulates were swamped by those stranded.

Wilson appointed a "Board of Relief" made up primarily of cabinet officials to make recommendations concerning the Americans stranded in Europe. Daniels at one time proposed sending the fleet to bring them back.[5] He was not on the board, however. His assistant, Franklin Delano Roosevelt, was appointed, and he strongly opposed his chief's suggestion. Roosevelt backed up the senior admirals who insisted that the fleet should be concentrated in American waters, not scattered all over the globe. Nevertheless, the board recommended using warships because of the need to get funds to Europe as quickly as possible. The navy agreed to this reluctantly, and once again the armored cruisers *Tennessee* and *North Carolina* were pressed into service.[6] On 3 August, and again two days later, the president sent special messages to Congress requesting funds for "the relief, protection and transportation of American citizens." Congress responded by quickly appropriating nearly three million dollars.[7]

The *Tennessee* sailed from New York on 6 August, carrying some three million in gold along with Henry Breckinridge, the assistant secretary of war, and a number of army officers to direct the relief work. Two days later the *North Carolina* followed. On board were a number of naval aviators who were apparently overlooked in the haste to get the vessel under way. For several months the cruiser had been engaged in aeronautical experiments, operating as a "mother" ship for flying boats. The pilots at first enjoyed the cruise, taking advantage of the opportunity to visit airfields and inspect the warplanes of the belligerent nations.[8]

Neither ship was in condition for an extended cruise. The *Tennessee*, which had been serving as a receiving ship, developed machinery problems crossing the Atlantic. Her crew had been obtained by "raiding" various ships in the Atlantic Fleet, and few of the "black gang" had any experience with coal burners. For days watches were frequently missed by confused bluejackets because, as one officer wrote, no one knew anyone else; "if a man did not report for his watch his petty officer had no way of locating him." Further, many of the enlisted personnel on both vessels were "short-timers," and within a few months more than 500 of them would have to be replaced.[9]

The *Tennessee* arrived at Falmouth, England, on 16 August, and the *North Carolina* slipped into port two days later. As soon as the latter vessel coaled ship the two cruisers left for continental ports under the protection of British patrol vessels. The *North Carolina* went to Le Havre, France, and the *Tennessee* to Rotterdam, Holland. After off-loading the relief funds, they returned to Falmouth. No unusual incidents occurred while they were in the war zone, although one British naval officer later claimed that a German light cruiser was able to escape a flotilla of destroyers because she was believed to be the *Tennessee*.[10] In Falmouth the *North Carolina* received orders to sail immediately for the eastern Mediterranean.

The Ottoman Empire did not immediately enter the war, but neither did she declare neutrality. Inevitably this situation produced speculations about her intentions. General mobilization of the armed forces and declaration of martial law throughout the empire, followed by rumors that the government was planning to abrogate the capitulations, alarmed foreigners. After mobilization the government seized houses, buildings, automobiles, wagons, and horses. Sailors from the *Scorpion* had to guard the American embassy's stables. One night the alarm was sounded by an uneasy sentry, and the unarmed bluejackets grabbed up pitchforks, shovels, and brooms, only to be confronted by the astonished ambassador.[11]

The ambassador called upon the *Scorpion* to provide protection not only for his stable but also for the embassy, other American property in Constantinople, and, after Turkey entered the war, the British embassy as well. Members of the ship's company escorted to the railway station French, Russian, and British nationals who were leaving the country. With her small crew of slightly over a hundred officers and men, the stationnaire could detach only about half for guard and escort duties. The vessel itself was virtually useless except as a place of refuge. She only carried two small naval guns, and because of the ambassador's insistence that the vessel was "essentially a yacht or despatch boat, rather than a gunboat," they had not been fired in years. A controversy developed with Turkish officials over their efforts to confiscate the ship's radio. After strong protests from the embassy, the Turks agreed to monitor it. Later the stationnaire was immobilized by Turkish authorities and placed under surveillance.[12]

Henry Morgenthau was the American ambassador to the Ottoman Empire at the outbreak of hostilities. On 15 August 1914, the ambassador cabled the State Department, "situation very critical. . . . Americans in all parts of the Empire fear for their safety." Two days later the American Tobacco Company, the MacAndrews and Forbes Company (which had a branch in Smyrna), several oil and licorice companies, and the American Board of Commissioners for Foreign Missions demanded naval ships not only for protection but also for transportation and communication. Normal commercial and banking operations had been disrupted, leaving American nationals and institutions in the country in dire need of funds and supplies. Although the State Department opposed it, President Wilson decided to use warships to assist American interests in the Near East. Undoubtedly he was under considerable political pressure. He also believed that naval vessels could reach Ottoman ports much faster and would be in less danger from attack by belligerent warships than commercial vessels.[13]

On 19 August, Washington officials began querying the European powers about sending American naval vessels into the eastern Mediterranean. Opposition was not expected. With the exception of Italy the major powers were involved in the war and were in no position to provide protection to their nationals in Turkey. The United States could do so. The State Department's assessment was not entirely correct. Although the German ambassador to the Ottoman Empire favored the presence of American warships, Berlin officials opposed it. On 1 August, Turkey had signed a secret agreement with Germany agreeing to declare war against Russia. The Ottoman government, however, delayed its entry into the conflict until military preparations were completed. According to one recent authority, if "any unusual naval activity off the coast of Syria" had occurred, Turkey would not have declared war on Russia.[14] Such activity presumably included American naval activity. Both Germany and her ally Austria pressured the Ottoman government into publicly denouncing the decision to send warships into the eastern Mediterranean, but because of the fear of straining relations with the United States, the protests were weak; at Morgenthau's advice, they were ignored.

Americans, in general, approved of the decision to send the warships. After all, such action had been taken numerous times in the past and, as they believed, was responsible for saving the lives of many people. Those who had reservations either kept them to themselves or were ignored. Oscar Straus, who had served as minister to the Ottoman Empire three times in twenty-six years, wrote Wilson that he feared such a decision might "project us into the European War." An officer on board the *North Carolina*, in a letter written after the vessel had arrived in Turkish waters, said that the principal American interest in Beirut was the Syrian College and "an American Comprador," a former chauffeur on an archaeological expedition who had become a partner in a firm that was engaged in supplying foreign ships. In a later letter to Captain Albert Gleaves the officer stressed the absence of danger to foreigners, suggesting that even the president of the local American college acted alarmed as a pretext to obtain funds. He was equally critical of the missionaries ("They live on the fat of the land"), Jews ("a great portion of those passing as American Christians are Jews"), Armenians, and the Allies ("Our presence . . . makes it unnecessary for the Allies to send ships here").[15]

On 4 September 1914, the *North Carolina* departed from Falmouth for the Mediterranean, carrying more than $150,000 in relief funds on board. She had been delayed until various private organizations in the United States could make arrangements with British banks to provide the money. Washington requested that the cruiser be allowed to take the funds directly to Constantinople, but the Ottoman government refused, citing the danger from mines. The Turkish foreign minister did agree to allow the *Scorpion* to meet the *North Carolina* at Smyrna. Evidently the stationnaire was immune to mines. Secretary of State William Jennings Bryan accepted the Turkish proposal, but the rendezvous had to be moved to the Dardanelles entrance because of an outbreak of bubonic plague in Smyrna.[16]

As the *North Carolina* sped through the Mediterranean, Turkish-American relations took a turn for the worse. Early in September, A. Rustin Bey, the Ottoman ambassador in the United States, wrote a statement published in the *New York Times* accusing American newspapers of prejudice towards Turkey. He said, among other things, that before criticizing his country, they should remember the numerous lynchings in the United States as well as the "water-cure" torture practiced by American soldiers in the Philippines several years before. When Secretary Bryan requested an explanation, Rustin Bey wrote what Professor Link had called "one of the most grossly insulting letters ever received by an American Secretary of State." The Turkish ambassador wrote that the American press had "poisoned public opinion" and that the sale of two warships to Greece as well as sending warships into Turkish waters (which he called a "naval demonstration") had strained relations between the two countries. Although Rustin Bey refused to retract his statement as requested by Bryan, he was not declared *persona non grata*. Wilson wanted to avoid increasing tension with Turkey. Nevertheless, Rustin Bey's usefulness was ended, and shortly afterward he departed for home.[17]

On 10 September, two days after Rustin Bey's accusation appeared in the *New York Times*, the Ottoman government notified the United States that it would consider the capitulations abrogated effective 1 October 1914. Although not unexpected nor entirely opposed by Morgenthau (who had been critical of economic capitulations, believing that they retarded economic growth), it brought outbursts of alarm from Americans throughout Turkey, as well as missionary and business interests in the United States with ties in Turkey. The American consul in Beirut cabled that a "state of uneasiness and anxiety" existed and added, "all the non-Moslems scanned the horizon, hoping to view the opportune arrival of the *North Carolina*." The consul at

Aleppo wrote that foreigners (and even prominent Turks) were evacuating the city and requested that warships be sent because of the presence of important American business interests.[18]

Although no outbreaks of violence against foreigners occurred when the capitulations were no longer recognized by the Ottoman government, Washington feared that trouble would sooner or later take place. On 3 October the *Tennessee* was ordered to join the *North Carolina* in the eastern Mediterranean.

After carrying gold to England and Holland, the *Tennessee* had transported some five hundred stranded American tourists from Le Havre to England. She had then returned to the French port to serve as headquarters ship for the relief work and was still there when ordered to Turkey.[19]

On 23 October, the *Tennessee* dropped anchor alongside the *North Carolina* in Beirut. A week later she left to carry medical supplies to Mitylene. While under way, the news was received by radio that Russia had declared war on Turkey. Turkish warships had deliberately bombarded the Russian Black Sea ports of Odessa and Novorossisk; the declaration of war followed. Within a week, Russia's allies, France and Great Britain, had joined in the war against the Ottoman Empire. On 7 November the Turkish government proclaimed a *jihad*, or holy war.

Turkey's final plunge into the abyss intensified the American warships' responsibilities. They would accept the burden of protecting and ultimately evacuating thousands of people—foreign nationals, Jews, and Armenians as well as Americans, from various parts of the empire. American sympathy with the Allied cause was a factor in this, but more important was the role of Henry Morgenthau. Morgenthau was a humanitarian, deeply concerned about the effects of the war upon Turkey. As the conflict went on, he became increasingly aggravated and disenchanted with the Ottoman government. As a Jew he was anxious about the fate of the Jewish people within the empire and interceded whenever necessary in their behalf. He later became equally troubled for the Armenians. Finally, as the representative of the most powerful neutral nation, he agreed to do anything that he could to aid belligerent nationals caught in Turkey by the outbreak of war. Aware that he had the confidence of President Wilson, he assumed the responsibility of directing American naval operations in Turkish waters. He had already received permission to use the naval vessels to transfer funds for the relief of Jews in Syria and Palestine. On 31 October, he ordered the consuls scattered throughout the empire to take charge of French and British interests. A week later Washington turned down a British request to increase the American naval force in Turkish waters, but did agree to protect British noncombatants. The British consul general at Smyrna urged that a landing force be provided from the American warships to aid British, French, and Russian subjects who had been refused permission to leave the country. In spite of a plea from Stanley Hollis, the zealous American consul at Beirut, Morgenthau rejected the British request.[20]

On 9 November, three days after Morgenthau had passed on the British request to Washington, American newspapers carried a story that marines and sailors from the *North Carolina* had landed in Beirut. The story was erroneous. On Sunday, 1 November, the cruiser had granted liberty to part of her crew, and the ship's band had given a public concert in the city's square. Apparently this sparked the rumor of a landing force.[21]

Turkish officials, as in the past, reluctantly tolerated the presence of the American warships. They were also quite concerned that the United States' assumption of the responsibility of protecting Allied subjects as well as their own nationals might lead to complications. Consul Hollis remarked that on the day the *North Carolina's* band gave the concert, a local official came to him "in great excitement" to protest American occupation of the city. Although there was no trouble in Beirut, a serious incident occurred near Smyrna two weeks later.

The entrance to Smyrna harbor was mined shortly after Turkey entered the war. Morgenthau agreed to keep American warships clear of the port, which angered American residents, who continued to demand that a warship be sent to the city. George Horton, the American consul, appealed to the ambassador, stating that the mine danger was exaggerated, that large steamers entered and departed from the port daily, and warned that, unless a naval vessel was sent, "American citizens, missionaries, and interests threatened immediate campaign American press for protection." Morgenthau did not change his decision, but he did send the *Tennessee* to Mitylene, some fifty miles from Smyrna, under orders to remain there to protect and provide refuge for any Americans desiring to leave Smyrna. Shortly after the cruiser reached Mitylene, the American, French, and British consuls arrived from Smyrna to confer with Captain Benton Decker, the *Tennessee's* commanding officer. He agreed that if it became necessary to evacuate the foreign residents, the ship would proceed to "Voulah Bay,"* approximately thirty miles from Smyrna. Small boats could then ferry the refugees out to the cruiser. Morgenthau approved this plan and decided to send the ship to Voulah Bay immediately.[22]

On 16 November, Captain Decker decided to confer with Horton. The cruiser steamed to within sight of Smyrna and anchored outside the mine field. Attempting to enter the harbor in his launch, Decker was fired upon by a coastal battery and forced to return to the ship. In his report he stated that shells straddled the launch. The Turks' report of the incident said that the first two shells were blanks and only a third one, fired when the boat refused to turn around, was explosive. The cruiser's executive officer, hearing firing and, as he later reported, being informed by the officer of the deck that heavy shells were striking near the launch, ordered the ship cleared for action and made preparations to get under way. He also informed the Turkish authorities by radio that if

---

*The name "Voulah Bay" could not be found in current gazetteers. A 1902 atlas mentions a town of "Vurla" on the Gulf of Symrna, approximately thirty miles from the city of Smyrna.

the firing continued, the *Tennessee* would bombard the fortifications. The exec's precautionary preparations were necessary and proper, but sending what amounted to an ultimatum was not. Upon being informed of the incident, Morgenthau immediately ordered the warship out of Turkish waters.

The following day a somewhat exaggerated account of the episode made headlines in American and European newspapers. The *Tennessee*'s chief engineer later recalled that the wardroom took up a collection to cable the story to New York. A Rueter's dispatch from Constantinople was the source of it in the English and French press.[23]

Morgenthau, as well as President Wilson and his advisers, feared that the incident might lead to more serious trouble. It had occurred only two days after the Sultan had proclaimed a holy war. American officials were particularly concerned for the missionaries scattered throughout the empire. After a cabinet session devoted to the "Smyrna incident," Morgenthau was advised not to send warships to any port unless Turkish officials clearly approved.[24]

On 24 November, Morgenthau telegraphed that an investigation convinced him that the Turks had fired in order to warn the launch of the mines. Wilson accepted this, and the United States formally apologized for the affair. Secretary of the Navy Daniels also reprimanded Decker: "Turkish government has perfect right to close any port it desires. . . . [The affair] was indiscreet and regrettable." He told Rear Admiral Bradley Fiske, his aide for operations, that if the launch had been hit, "he [Daniels] would have repudiated Decker's act altogether."[25] Captain Decker, however, continued to defend his action. He wrote Daniels that it was his understanding that the port was closed to warships and merchant ships but not to small boats. He later suggested a rather novel and totally indefensible theory that Turkey was not recognized in "civilized nations" and therefore did not have the right to close her ports. He also pointed out that recognizing the right of Turkey to close her ports weakened the U.S. policy concerning the capitulations.[26] Curiously, a court of inquiry was not asked for or called for, and Decker retained his command.

Decker's actions were defended by some newspapers. One British paper, the London *Morning Post*, even agreed with his assessment of Turkey: "The Turks, divorced from British naval guidance, have no clear appreciation of the law of nations. and the Germans, who prevail just now in Turkey's counsels, have no respect for it at all." This statement is understandable, considering British-Turkish relations. However, it was the German government that apparently persuaded its ally to accept the American apology. German-American relations were not especially strained in the fall of 1914 before unrestricted submarine warfare had become such a crucial issue, and it was feared that a Turkish-American confrontation more than likely would lead to war with the United States.[27]

For several days towards the end of November and the beginning of December 1914, the incident eclipsed the more pressing problems related to American neutrality. Assistant Secretary of State Robert Lansing's desk diary records almost daily conferences during this period with the president or Secretary Daniels and Admiral Fiske.[28]

The incident provided the Navy Department with an excuse to ask that the warships be withdrawn from the Mediterranean. Various officials warned the naval secretary of the danger of mistaken identity by belligerent vessels, especially submarines. Even the warring nations were concerned. The German government repeatedly requested that American naval vessels should be brightly lit at night while steaming near war zones.[29] They were particularly concerned about transports and colliers.

President Wilson had agreed to allow a naval vessel to transport Christmas toys to the children of war-torn Europe. The Chicago *Herald* initiated the project, which caught on throughout the country where it was endorsed by hundreds of newspapers, Sunday school classes, and community organizations. Its enormous popularity persuaded the president to sanction the use of the collier *Jason*, scheduled to carry fuel to the warships operating in Turkish waters. The "Christmas Ship," as she was called by the American press, departed from New York City on 13 November loaded with more than five million gifts valued at more than three million dollars. The *Jason* made several stops in England and continental ports distributing the presents before sailing for the eastern Mediterranean and routine duty as a collier for the American naval force there.[30]

On 24 November, and again three days later, Admiral Fiske conferred with State Department officials about withdrawing the naval vessels from the Mediterranean. Morgenthau strongly disapproved of the idea when he was first consulted, referring to the approaching period as "most critical." He later changed his mind and agreed that one of the cruisers should be withdrawn. "In my opinion," he wrote Secretary of State Bryan, "the chances of injuries that may result from misuse of [the] cruisers are far greater than protection they may render." At the same time he recommended evacuating American nationals from Turkey.[31] Secretary Bryan, who agreed with Morgenthau, persuaded Wilson that the presence of Americans in Turkey could seriously affect his efforts to maintain neutrality. The embassy in Constantinople sent out notices to American nationals advising them to leave the country, but on the whole the advice was ignored.[32]

Because of the evacuation decision, neither warship was withdrawn. The *North Carolina* remained in Beirut, while the *Tennessee*, which had withdrawn from Turkish waters after the Smyrna incident, remained close by, at Alexandria, Egypt. Although the Egyptian port was popular with the American sailors, liberty had to be curtailed because of a number of brawls with British bluejackets. One correspondent blamed the trouble on British unhappiness with American neutrality.[33]

Beirut was calm throughout these turbulent days, and one local Jewish resident later attributed this to the presence of the *North Carolina*. The cruiser granted liberty three times a week. On Christmas Day the ship's band gave a concert in front of the American consulate and later a successful benefit performance at the American Club to collect funds for destitute refugees in the city. The holiday's entertainment climaxed that night with a minstrel on board the warship, attended by invited guests from the city and an Italian cruiser also in the harbor.[34]

While Beirut was calm, much of Syria seethed with unrest. On 20 December, the Turkish government revoked permission for belligerent enemy nationals and neutrals to leave, apparently because of the presence of Allied naval craft off the coast, which the Turks believed presaged invasion. In late December a British warship appeared off the port of Alexandretta. An ultimatum was sent ashore threatening bombardment unless certain military supplies were destroyed. The Ottoman governor in Damascus retaliated by announcing that British refugees in his district would be executed if the city were fired upon. The naval vessel then withdrew without carrying out its threat, and no British subjects were harmed. Morgenthau angered Turkish officials in Constantinople by his declaration that U.S. warships would be sent to Alexandretta if any British nationals were executed. A few days after this, the *Askold*, a Russian cruiser, was involved in an incident at Tripoli and threatened to open fire on the city. No shots were fired, but the city remained tense as Allied vessels steamed in close at night and lit up the waterfront with flares and searchlights.[35]

On 28 December, the Ottoman government announced that the port of Jaffa would be closed to neutral ships and that any refugees in the city would be interned after that date. The port had become the focal point for hundreds of Allied nationals fleeing the country. Morgenthau interceded with Turkish officials and persuaded them to exempt the American warships from this order. They would be allowed to enter not only Jaffa but other ports as well. The Ottoman government was anxious to get rid of the refugees and considered the American vessels to be the most convenient means. German influence probably was a factor. The Kaiser's advisors in Turkey considered the Ottoman government in Constantinople to be weak and incompetent. They believed that the American warships might have a deterring effect on unrest that could lead to revolt and massacres. At any rate Morgenthau continued to receive verbal permission for the vessels to use Turkish ports.[36]

On 23 December, the *Tennessee*, carrying some $55,000 in gold, arrived in Jaffa. The American consul informed Captain Decker of the refugees' plight and appealed to him for assistance. Decker agreed to carry as many refugees as the cruiser could accommodate if Morgenthau agreed. On Christmas Day, the ambassador on his own authority cabled his approval, and the "compliments of the season."[37] Although the German consul reported that the cruiser left with approximately five hundred refugees on board, actually only half of that number, including a large number of Jews and several French nuns, were taken to Alexandria.

The *Tennessee* spent the following months transporting refugees, primarily Jewish, from various Turkish ports. There were nearly a hundred thousand Jews living in Asia Minor, the majority residing in Palestine. Most of them were not Ottoman subjects and had depended in the past on the protection provided by the western nations. The abolition of the capitulations abruptly changed this. On 17 December, the Jaffa governor ordered nearly six thousand Jews expelled. Similar expulsions occurred in other parts of the empire. The Ottoman government announced that "non-Ottoman" Jews remaining in the country would be interned. In the panic that followed, Jewish leaders advocated naturalization in order to prevent expulsion or internment. This plan had little effect primarily because the Turkish government preferred getting rid of what it considered a troublesome minority.[38]

The Jewish community in the United States was a powerful and influential body. Although admittedly divided over Zionism, it nevertheless was sensitive to the well-being of the Jewish settlements in Palestine. Ably led by Louis Brandeis and Jacob H. Schiff, effective pressure was exerted on the Wilson administration. The result was that naval vessels became the right arm of Jewish relief, not only in evacuating refugees but also in carrying funds and, more important, food, medical supplies, and even doctors.[39] Disease and famine ravaged Palestine. The Palestinian Jews suffered less than any other minority in the Ottoman Empire primarily because of the help from abroad, much of it carried on board American naval vessels.

By the middle of January 1915, the *Tennessee* had transported nearly six thousand Jewish refugees. On one trip over 1,200 were packed on board for the short voyage to Alexandria. The cruiser made her last trip in the middle of February, and when she docked at Alexandria, hundreds of members of the Jewish community in boats and on the breakwater cheered the vessel.[40]

In late January 1915, American newspapers reported that the Ottoman government planned to destroy all Zionist institutions and organizations in Palestine. Captain Decker was ordered to investigate, and his report convinced the State Department that the newspapers were substantially correct. On 18 February, Secretary Bryan instructed Morgenthau to warn the Turkish government that it would be held responsible for the lives and property of Jews and Christians.[41]

American Jewish leaders were particularly concerned for the Jewish Agricultural Station at Haifa. With American financial support it had played a significant role in improving the agricultural economy of Palestine. Although Decker was not allowed to visit the station, it remained intact until late in the war, in spite of the fact that it became the center of Jewish underground activities in Syria. Several members of the underground were even able to use the American warships as a means of contacting the Allies.[42]

The USS *Tennessee* off-loading refugees from Syria at Alexandria, Egypt, 1915. *Courtesy of the National Archives, Washington, D.C.*

The USS *Chicago*, flagship of the European Squadron, lying off Gravesend, England, summer 1894. *Courtesy of the National Maritime Museum, Greenwich, England.*

The Turkish threat against the Palestinian Jews was not carried out. Morgenthau and especially the representatives of the Central Powers exerted enough pressure that the repressive measures gradually ended in the spring of 1915.

During these months, American relief efforts continued. The collier *Vulcan* left the United States early in March loaded with coal for the cruisers and supplies for the Jewish people in Palestine. Protracted negotiations had to be conducted with the Allies before the vessel was allowed to land some nine hundred tons of food and medical supplies at Jaffa.[43]

The Allies had established a blockade early in the war, and by early 1915, it had closed all Ottoman ports in Asia Minor. The Turks had little time to devote to this problem, as they were being pressed hard elsewhere. In November 1914, a British force landed in Mesapotamia. By the late spring of the following year an enlarged force had advanced up the Tigris and Euphrates rivers in a movement designed to take Bagdad. In January 1915, the Allies agreed on a naval attack against the Dardanelles with Constantinople as the objective. Three months later a British naval force tried unsuccessfully to force the narrows, losing four vessels to mines. This was followed by an amphibious assault on the Gallapoli Peninsula, with several months of fierce fighting, as the Allied army tried to break through to the Ottoman capital.

In the spring of 1915 the Navy Department again requested that the vessels in the Mediterranean be permitted to withdraw. Lansing's desk diary notes that Admiral Fiske made frequent trips to his office to discuss the issue. The navy stressed that the cruisers needed overhauling badly because of their hasty departure at the outbreak of the war. High-ranking naval officers, including the cruiser squadron commander in the Atlantic Fleet and the chief of the Bureau of Navigation, recommended that the cruisers should be replaced by gunboats and chartered merchant ships as their primary responsibility appeared to be transporting refugees. The State Department, however, insisted that it was essential to maintain at least two "powerful" warships in Turkish waters. The navy gave in reluctantly but emphasized that the *Tennessee* and *North Carolina* needed to be relieved immediately. The *Des Moines* and the *Chester* were ordered to replace them and arrived early in the summer.[44]

The *Chester* (CL-1) launched in 1907 was utilized frequently for diplomatic missions in various parts of the world. The *Des Moines* was one of the *Denver*-class designated "peace cruisers" that were built in the first decade of the twentieth century. They were anachronistic when built, with a schooner rig and their steel hulls covered with wood and copper plate. Although often referred to as gunboats, they were sizable ships (3,200 tons and 309 feet long) with a relatively large bunker capacity and unusually roomy crew's quarters.[45]

The State Department's insistence on keeping two warships in Turkish waters reflected concern over the deterioration of American efforts to maintain neutrality. The sinking of the British transatlantic liner *Lusitania* off the

Irish coast with the loss of 1,198 lives including 124 Americans precipitated a crisis and controversy with Germany over unrestricted submarine warfare, a controversy that ultimately brought the United States into the conflict. It was also responsible for William Jennings Bryan's resignation as secretary of state and Robert Lansing's appointment in his place.

Although there was no immediate crisis with Turkey, relations between the two countries steadily got worse. Americans in the Ottoman Empire were subjected to harassments because the United States refused to modify its position concerning the capitulations. Morgenthau found it increasingly difficult to keep the various American educational and medical institutions from being taken over by the Ottoman government. In April 1915, the privilege of using cipher messages between the embassy and consulates was revoked, and censorship of mail was rigidly enforced. For a brief period even the use of the English ("enemy") language was forbidden.

The *Scorpion* also became the target of petty annoyances. A police boat circled the vessel twenty-four hours a day. Anything brought on board was carefully examined. Visits were curtailed; only individuals with passes provided by the local authorities were allowed to board the ship. In July 1915, an incident involving one of the officers photographing a German submarine was used as an excuse to moor the stationnaire below the bridges that crossed the Golden Horn. Morgenthau was able to delay the move by insisting that he liked to dine on board in hot weather, but she entered the Golden Horn in August and would remain there for the duration of the war. Morgenthau believed that the *Scorpion* was ordered moved by suspicious Turkish officials convinced that the vessel was in secret contact with British submarines. On one occasion they even accused the ship of signaling with a heliostat.[46]

The Golden Horn anchorage severely limited the crews' recreational opportunities. Swimming and boating were eliminated. The presence of a slaughterhouse and sewage that emptied nearby occasioned numerous complaints, especially during the hot months. Unfortunately, liberty had to be curtailed because brawls between the bluejackets and Germans became all too common. In order to occupy the crew, classes were started in history, spelling, and literature. Later, at the invitation of the president of Roberts College, the crew was housed in a dormitory during the summer months. There "*Scorpion* University" expanded its curriculum.[47]

The *Scorpion*'s anchorage in the Golden Horn increased the vessel's possible difficulties in case the United States became a belligerent. The ship's rather delicate situation was appreciated in both Constantinople and Washington. When Morgenthau asked her commanding officer what he would do if attacked, he replied, "defend it to the last." The Navy Department's instructions were scarcely more realistic. The commanding officer was told to withdraw through the Dardanelles if practicable; if not, "passage through the Bosphorus into the Black Sea should be considered," and as a last resort to remain in the Golden Horn. Later the embassy requested permission to send the vessel to a Romanian port, but the State Department refused.[48]

Turkish military strength in Syria was gradually weakened, as more and more troops were thrown into the intense fighting on the Gallipoli Peninsula. Morgenthau, concerned that the withdrawal of troops could result in an outbreak of internal trouble, urged Washington to keep the warships along the coast. The ambassador also redoubled his efforts to persuade Americans to leave. He held a conference with missionary and educational leaders, who agreed to support him in appealing for evacuation. Notices were sent into the interior urging Americans to move either to Constantinople where they could take the railway out of the country or to one of the ports in Asia Minor where they would be evacuated by naval vessels. If Morgenthau had requested Turkish permission to remove only American nationals, he would have had little difficulty, but he tried to gain permission to evacuate Italians as well as Americans.[49]

In May 1915, Italy had declared war on Austria-Hungary. There was little doubt that within a matter of time she would take similar action against Germany and Turkey. The final break with Turkey came three months after the declaration of war on Austria-Hungary. Although the Italian people were slow to recognize the need for another Turkish conflict, the major factor in the protracted delay was the determination by the Italian government to evacuate its nationals, including several hundred reservists, from Ottoman territory. The evacuation from Asia Minor would necessarily be by sea, and the only ships available were the American warships. Turkey, prompted by Germany, was able to drag out the negotiations, and only by the perseverance of Morgenthau was permission finally obtained.

On 28 May, three days after Italy declared war on Austria-Hungary, the Italian government through its representatives in Washington and Constantinople requested an American warship to evacuate Italian nationals in Asia Minor and carry them to Alexandria. With the State Department's approval Morgenthau approached the Ottoman government about removing Italians along with the Americans from Asia Minor ports. He obtained permission to evacuate the Americans but not the Italians.[50]

During the following weeks the American ambassador continued to press Ottoman officials about the Italians. In the meantime the warships evacuated others. On 25 June, the *Tennessee* left Beirut with some five hundred refugees, including Americans, Greeks, and Mehmed Vejihi Effendi, Moslem sheik of the Philippines, on board. The sheik was en route to the United States to confer with American officials about Philippine affairs. Apparently the State Department was unhappy about the sheik's visit, for instructions were sent to deny him passage on the American warships. However, the order arrived too late. After leaving Beirut, the *Tennessee* took on board 150 passengers at Jaffa and left for Alexandria. Two days later Morgenthau was informed that in the future the American vessels could remove refugees only from Beirut and Voulah Bay.[51]

The Italian government continued to exert pressure on the United States to evacuate its citizens from the Ottoman Empire. On 30 June, Thomas Nelson Page, the American ambassador to Italy, cabled President Wilson that Italy was on the point of declaring war against Turkey and "is waiting only until her consuls and her people can be got out." This together with appeals from the Italian diplomatic representatives had some influence. Morgenthau was instructed to try again, and this time he got a qualified yes from the Ottoman government. He was told that the Italians could be removed after all non-Ottoman Jews were taken out. In order to accomplish this, Morgenthau pressed into service not only the recently arrived *Des Moines*, but the collier *Caesar* as well. A number of Jews were removed, but they were still straggling into the ports after the American ships had started carrying out Italians. The Turkish government had agreed to allow the Italians to leave, but only from Beirut. The other ports were closed to the Italians.[52]

The Turkish position concerning the Italian nationals hinged on the realization that once they were gone Italy would probably declare war. As Sir Edward Grey, the British foreign secretary, noted, "They know well the value of [the] hostages they hold."[53] In reality, the Italian officials were not so much concerned about their nationals in Turkey as the hope that the issue of their removal would generate enthusiasm for war among the people. Italian newspapers tried to arouse public sentiment by playing up the Ottoman decision to permit evacuation only from Beirut. "Garroni [the Italian ambassador in Constantinople] seems anxious to create an incident," Morgenthau wrote in his diary. "He wants one by insisting that the authorities should permit our ships to go to Smyrna. I told him I would absolutely decline to send an American ship to a mined harbor."[54]

The British government was not particularly concerned as to the Italian justification for war with Turkey; the declaration was desired, however, as quickly as possible. The battles on the western front in the late spring and summer of 1915 had cost the British and French over 300,000 casualties. The initial landing on the Gallipoli Peninsula had failed to be followed by a break-out towards Constantinople. In the summer strong reinforcements were added to the Allied force, and a new landing at Suvla Bay was planned for early August. The sooner Italy was in, the better. Thomas Page wrote President Wilson that Italy "has not wanted to go to war with Turkey ... but her hand has been a little forced by her allies."[55]

On 12 July, Sir Rennell Rodd, the British ambassador in Rome, wrote Lord Grey, "I asked the [Italian] Minister for Foreign Affairs this afternoon whether his contemplated declaration of war on Turkey was any nearer to realisation. He said he had not been able to obtain an answer from the U.S. Government as to whether they would agree to send a ship of war to bring away the Italian subjects from Smyrna. . . . Once this was done he would be easier in his mind about taking the definite step."[56] "It is hoped," Lord Grey noted, "that the Turks will agree, as it is high time that Italy was officially at war. They are not likely to do so, however, except under strong U.S. pressure. . . ." Washington was assured that the Allied blockade along the Ottoman coast would be no problem. Jules Jusserand, the French ambassador to the United States, wrote Lansing, "that in case it were possible for the American Government to help in the removal of [Italian subjects] . . . to a place of safety, the Allied Governments would not fail to give to the ship entrusted with such a humanitarian mission all the necessary facilities." The British representative voiced similar assurances.[57] Allied pressure succeeded for Morgenthau was instructed to confer with Turkish officials about using Voulah Bay, which was not a port but was a good harbor. If they agreed, the *Des Moines* would be ordered to transport the Italians from there to the Island of Rhodes.

The Ottoman government agreed, probably because the Allied mine field in the bay would be discovered. Obviously the Allies would not allow the American warship to enter the bay unless a pass through the field had been cleared. The British navy strongly objected to this plan, and Morgenthau tried to persuade the Turks to let the *Des Moines* enter Mersin or Alexandretta.[58] The American ambassador was still negotiating when his Italian colleague informed him to "do nothing to facilitate departure of the Italians." The reason became clear a few days later when Italy broke off diplomatic relations with Turkey, using the refusal of the Ottoman government to allow the departure of Italian subjects as the major cause.[59] Italy declared war on 22 August 1915. On his own Morgenthau continued to press the Turkish government and eventually gained permission to evacuate by warship Italian women and children; however, less than a hundred were taken out.[60]

Throughout the fall of 1915 the two American cruisers *Chester* and *Des Moines* shuttled in and out of various Turkish ports transporting refugees. They carried out primarily neutrals and non-Ottoman Jews. The Ottoman government was still determined to remove all non-Ottoman Jews and insisted that they be carried out before the neutrals, including the Americans. The problem became complicated when Egyptian and British authorities refused to allow Jewish refugees to land in Alexandria without adequate funds for transportation elsewhere.[61]

Other restrictions hindered the warships in their mercy mission. Turkish permission had to be obtained to pick up a designated number of refugees in a particular port at a specified time. Permission from the Allied commander in charge of the blockade off the Syrian coast had to be obtained for each trip. All of this had to be coordinated by the ambassador, consuls, Turkish officials, and the commanding officers of the American naval vessels, usually by radio or telegraph. Cooperation between the ambassador and the naval commanders was satisfactory in the majority of cases. Captain Frank H. Schofield of the

Chester was an exception. In September 1915, he informed the ambassador that both ships would be withdrawn from the refugee transportation business for three weeks while target practice was carried out. On one occasion he flatly refused to enter a Syrian port because normal communications between himself and the local American representative were not possible. He also refused to carry Jewish males of military age until ordered to do so by the Navy Department. Although the naval officer had valid arguments for these decisions, they irritated the ambassador. In August 1915, Morgenthau wrote in his diary that "Schofield always tries to find some excuse for not doing things instead of endeavoring to be accommodating." On 15 September, he noted, "S is obstreperous again," and on 18 September he recorded, "*Chester* was going to Alexandretta.... This is a great relief as I had much trouble to persuade Schofield to do it."[62] The ambassador's problem with Schofield was solved in December when the *Chester* was ordered to Liberia. From there she returned to the United States.

The *Chester* was not replaced. Two factors were responsible for this decision: the closing of the Syrian ports to American warships and efforts by high-ranking naval officers to persuade President Wilson and his advisors to order the vessels home.

In December 1915, the Turkish foreign officer informed Morgenthau that no further visits by American warships to Syrian ports would be authorized. By this time most of the undesirable elements were out of Syria and Lebanon, and the Ottoman officials had lost their "humanitarian" zeal. With Italy in the war the Allies also decided that it was convenient to refuse the American vessels permission to pass through the blockade.[63] Admiral William S. Benson, the chief of Naval Operations, considered these valid reasons to urge that the vessels be withdrawn. Benson also pointed out that a number of incidents had occurred since Turkey entered the war; and although (at that time) the cruisers were allowed to pass through the Allied blockade, "there is more or less danger in our vessels visiting blockaded ports, due to misunderstanding, floating mines and even a wilful desire or intention to involve the United States by firing upon or injuring one of our Government vessels." Daniels, who tended at times to ignore advice from senior naval officers, did not pass the recommendation on to the State Department. Nevertheless, he did not order that a vessel be sent out to replace the *Chester*.

In September 1916, a rumor was passed on to the Navy Department that the *Des Moines* was to be blown up by German agents while the vessel was at anchor in Barcelona, Spain. Although the navy considered the bomb threat highly unlikely, the warship was ordered to another port. Admiral Benson also used the occasion to again urge that the naval vessels be withdrawn:

> This simply tends to confirm a feeling I have had since the European War began that the presence of our vessels in European waters was accom-

panied by great danger—a danger that to me seemed entirely unnecessary in view of the fact that the presence of our vessels in those waters could not possibly render adequate service to warrant the risk taken. I fully appreciate the desire to be of assistance to Americans in countries bordering on the Mediterranean and until the blockade of Syrian ports by the belligerents, this was not only a most merciful mission for our vessels to carry out in the Eastern Mediterranean, but one that we could not very well have withdrawn from with propriety. But now that their ports are blockaded and in view of the conditions that exist in that part of the world, it does seem that to continue any of our vessels in these waters is courting a possibility that might be embarrassing to say the least.[64]

Daniels agreed, but President Wilson continued to accept the State Department's position that the warships were needed in the Mediterranean. The worsening economic situation in the Ottoman Empire and its impact on American public opinion influenced this decision.

By the winter of 1916 famine was already widespread in Asia Minor. The Turkish government's callous confiscation of animals and foodstuffs, along with the Allied blockade, had brought on starvation. As the months went by, desperate pleas poured into the United States from missionaries and naturalized Americans of Syrian or Armenian descent residing in Turkey and their relatives in the United States. In turn, intense pressure was put on the Wilson administration through the news media, petitions, and direct appeals to government officials to provide relief or evacuation. During an election year Wilson could not afford to ignore these pleas.

During the winter of 1916 the U.S. government at the request of missionary organizations attempted to transport to Beirut and Jaffa badly needed medical supplies. The *Des Moines* was to carry them to Beirut and a collier to Jaffa. The Turks were willing, but the Allies, who considered medical stores war material, were not. In April, Lansing tried unsuccessfully to persuade the Allies to allow boats to offload the medical supplies from the American vessels outside the harbors.[65] A serious cholera outbreak in the summer finally moved the Allies to relax the blockade and allow the *Des Moines* to land medical supplies at Jaffa. The vessel's visit provided an opportunity to evacuate Americans still stranded in Syria. Secretary of State Lansing, rightly anticipating opposition by the belligerents, informed U.S. representatives in Constantinople, London, and Paris of the "widespread interest in this matter which [has] . . . been widely featured in newspapers. Any obstacle put in the way of rescue of these Americans from Syria," he warned, "will arouse deep and widespread indignation in this country against nation or nations blockading departure." He told the ambassadors to use their "strongest efforts . . . [as the] importance of this matter can be hardly overstated."[66]

Britain and France agreed to the evacuation, but Turkey did not. As the *Des Moines* waited, Abram Elkus, who replaced Morgenthau in Constantinople in the spring, made visit after visit to the office of the grand vizier, where he was turned away with the excuse that the Americans could leave as soon as certain unnamed military problems were worked out. After weeks of these fruitless negotiations, a frustrated Elkus wrote Lansing:

> There is little if any system in administration and great delay about everything. To get a positive answer quickly to anything is an impossibility. . . . [When] the Department requested the Embassy to obtain permission for American citizens . . . to leave Turkey on the *Des Moines* . . . I took it up with the Grand Vizier who was then acting as Minister of Foreign Affairs. . . . After considerable . . . discussion, the Grand Visier agreed to allow all American citizens to leave on the *Des Moines*. . . . I had been warned that the Grand Vizier sometimes made promises and then forgot them, so I wrote him a note the same day confirming . . . his promise. Then came the usual delay. . . . The Minister [of Foreign Affairs] returned and the matter must be taken up with him. He knew nothing about it. No records appear to have been kept and he would have to inquire. At last, after sending several notes, making several visits, an answer was received that the supplies on the *Des Moines* may be landed at Jaffa, but no one may leave on the *Des Moines*.

Elkus later wrote Lansing a "strictly confidential" letter that Djemal Pasha, the military governor of Syria, "does what he pleases and frequently declines to comply with wishes or decisions of the Sublime Porte. Porte says it only sends him recommendations not instructions."[67] The American ambassador was getting the runaround by Turkish officials reluctant to allow individuals to leave with knowledge of their country and its defenses.

While Elkus was displaying the frustration so common to American diplomatic representatives attempting to deal with Ottoman officials, he was under increasing pressure from Washington, including the White House. It seems clear that President Wilson was directly responsible for the major decisions concerning Turkish relations at this time. The controversy with Germany over unrestricted submarine warfare had eased considerably in the summer and fall of 1916 after the *Sussex* incident. As the election of 1916 approached, the president was obviously aware of the intense interest of a large and influential segment of the American people in the Turkish situation. Political considerations undoubtedly were involved in the increasingly hard line followed by the State Department.

The American government's growing concern over the Turkish problem was reflected in a note Elkus handed to the minister of foreign affairs in Constantinople on 22 November:

> The United States cannot longer acquiesce in delay in sending *Des Moines* to Jaffa and removal of American citizens from that place. . . . [This] attitude . . . constitutes such an infringement of American rights

and is so strong a manifestation of lack of friendliness towards the United States that the Department cannot believe that the Turkish Government... will any longer object to the only practical method by which they can leave Turkey now or in the near future.

In conclusion Secretary Lansing warned, "American citizens *must* be permitted to leave Turkey."[68]

Turkey's unbending stand on the issue spurred Lansing, apparently acting under presidential instructions, to threaten a break in diplomatic relations and possibly war. The Ottoman chargé was called in for a conference on 5 December, and informed that unless his government modified its position, the "matter" would be turned over to Congress. The German government was also approached to use its influence and persuade the Turks of the "gravity" of the situation. According to Professor May, Bethmann Hollweg, the German chancellor, was anxious for peace and welcomed President Wilson's efforts in this direction. The growing crisis between Turkey and the United States threatened to destroy these efforts.[69]

These negotiations had some effect, for the American ambassador in Berlin was informed by the German foreign office that the Ottoman government had agreed to allow the Americans to be evacuated. Two days after the Turkish chargé was given the ultimatum, Djemal Pasha arrived in Constantinople and conferred with Elkus. Shortly afterwards the ambassador was informed that naval vessels could be used for the evacuation, but only from Beirut, and only if the Americans agreed to remain in that city one month before departure "so that any information they had acquired would be useless."[70] This diplomatic victory was hollow, for the Americans in the Ottoman Empire were never evacuated.

In the middle of December the collier *Caesar* left the United States for Alexandria. She carried stores for the *Des Moines* and food, clothing, and medical supplies provided by the Armenian and Syrian Relief Committee and the Red Cross for the Syrians. The collier arrived at Alexandria on 23 January and was still there along with the *Des Moines* awaiting permission to carry the supplies to Syria and evacuate the Americans when the United States broke off diplomatic relations with Germany over the resumption of unrestricted submarine warfare. The uncertainties created by this crisis delayed the two vessels' departure for Syria. The State Department was not sure whether or not Turkey would join her ally in the break with the United States. Washington officials also feared an attack by German or Austrian submarines on the vessels and demanded "written guarantees" from these governments before allowing the ships to venture into Turkish waters.[71]

While negotiations were under way to obtain these "guarantees," Americans were arriving in Beirut. Elkus informed the State Department that "the order for the delay of the departure of the [vessels]... arrived just as Ameri-

cans were ready to leave Jerusalem, . . . many having sold household effects."
Nevertheless, the desired "guarantees" were not forthcoming. The Turkish
government said it could not give them, and Germany and Austria evidently
would not. The New York *Times* reported that the United States would not
directly approach these governments, because their submarine policies were
considered "illegal."[72] As the diplomats tried to solve this impasse, the naval
vessels remained at anchor in Alexandria, the refugees waited anxiously in
Beirut, and the Syrian people continued dying by the hundreds.

President Wilson was obviously distressed over the situation. On 6 February, he wrote Cleveland H. Dodge, an old friend and classmate at Princeton, "I
have thought more than once of your dear ones in Turkey with a pang of apprehension that was very deep. Fortunately, there is always one of our vessels
there, inadequate though it may be, and I hope with all my heart that we can
manage things so that there will be no real danger to the lives of our people
abroad. Still, I know how very anxious you must be and my heart is with
you."[73] From the U.S. point of view the evacuation was most important. The
tragedy was that others suffered because of it. In the words of one member of
the Red Cross, "The failure of the *Caesar* to reach Syria meant the loss of tens
of thousands [of lives]. . . . the greatest tragedy of the Syrian war."[74]

The Turkish problem, serious as it was, played only a minor role in American diplomacy during the early months of 1917. After the break with Germany
in February, Wilson sought desperately to avoid becoming a belligerent, but
the renewed attack by German submarines on American ships ultimately convinced him that there was no alternative to war. On 2 April, he asked Congress
for war; the request was granted by the Senate two days later, followed by the
House.

The Americans in Turkey, although not forgotten, were just pushed aside
during the final weeks of peace. In the middle of March, Elkus cabled the State
Department that Germany had agreed to allow the two naval vessels unrestricted passage to Beirut and Jaffa, provided they followed an exact time table
and route, which would of course be turned over to the German government in
advance. Unfortunately, Austria failed to give similar assurances. Apparently
Lansing then gave up. On the last day of March he told Representative Dow H.
Drukker that he "was unable at the present time to give any assurance that the
evacuation could take place in the near future." Admiral Benson again urged
that the ships be withdrawn but Daniels delayed: "[they] might save Americans and to withdraw now might cause [them] to be torpedoed." However,
shortly before war was declared on Germany, Daniels changed his mind. The
Des Moines was ordered to slip out of Alexandria as quietly as possible, take
on coal in Gibraltar, and return home. She reached New York on 25 April; the
collier *Caesar* arrived a few days later.[75]

The *Scorpion* was not so fortunate. Two days after the declaration of war,
the Ottoman government ordered the stationnaire to leave Constantinople

within twenty-four hours. This was an empty gesture to comply with international law; there was little chance that she would attempt to pass through waters sown with mines. Even discounting this threat, the vessel was in sight of a flotilla of German submarines.

The problem of what to do with the *Scorpion* in case of war had caused some anxiety in both Washington and Constantinople. Nevertheless, no explicit orders had been given to her commanding officer or the ambassador. "It is now six days since the United States broke off diplomatic relations with Germany, and I am without instructions as to how to proceed in case of a declaration of war," Commander Morton, the *Scorpion's* captain, informed Elkus. Morton went on to recommend that the crew be immediately evacuated. "Although we present the appearance of and are classed as an armed vessel, we have no ammunition for our guns." He later recommended "disabling the engines or sinking the ship, should the *Scorpion* and her crew not be permitted to leave."[76]

The ambassador opposed sinking or disabling the ship as "this would seriously jeopardize the lives and interests of American civilians." Finally, on 2 April, Morton was authorized to send members of the crew out of the country as quickly as possible. Before war was declared, thirty-six had left by train for Switzerland. On 11 April she was officially interned, her guns removed, and a guard stationed around the ship.[77] Even after internment the Navy and State departments continued efforts to evacuate the remainder of the crew. They were unsuccessful, and fifty-nine officers and men remained in Constantinople for the war's duration.[78]

The presence of American warships in European waters during the months the United States attempted to maintain its neutrality was a calculated risk. There was considerable danger from submarines, surface craft, and mines. An incident involving one of the belligerent nations could have had serious consequences, possibly precipitating an earlier entry into the war. Nevertheless, none occurred, and the vessels' relief work in the Near East was an impressive accomplishment. Clearly many lives were saved that would not have been saved without their work. Considering the circumstances, the attitude of the belligerent nations towards these neutral warships in war zones was surprisingly quite accommodating. In fact, Turkey's cooperation was a factor in the United States' decision not to declare war on that country.

The United States entered World War I in April 1917. Within two months the European station was reestablished with Vice Admiral William S. Sims in command. By November 1918, the U.S. had in European waters: eight battleships, five cruisers, five gunboats, sixty-eight destroyers, nine submarines, twenty-six converted yachts and other comparable patrol vessels, one hundred and twenty-one sub-chasers, thirty tugs and mine-sweepers, twelve auxiliary vessels, and seventy miscellaneous vessels, totaling altogether three hundred and fifty-four vessels of all classes—a far cry from the five wooden vessels that made up the European Squadron when it was established in 1865. More important, the basic purpose of the U.S. naval force operating in European waters was changed. For the first time since the Civil War the objective was combat.

ABBREVIATIONS

ABC Papers—American Board of Commissioners for Foreign Missions Archives, Houghton Library, Harvard University

T139—Records of the German Foreign Office Received by the Department of State from the University of California (Project I) National Archives Microfilm Number T139

T120—Records of the German Foreign Office Received by the Department of State, National Archives Microfilm Number T120

ADM—Admiralty, Public Records Office, London

PRO—Public Records Office, London

FO—Foreign Office, Public Records Office, London

RG24—Records of the Bureau of Personnel, United States National Archives

RG45—Naval Records Collection of the Office of Naval Records and Library, United States National Archives

RG52—Records of the Bureau of Medicine and Surgery, United States National Archives

RG59—General Records of the Department of State, United States National Archives

RG80—General Records of the Department of the Navy, 1798–1947, United States National Archives

RG313—Records of Naval Operating Forces, United States National Archives

M30—Despatches from United States Ministers to Great Britain, 1791–1906, National Archives Microfilm

M31—Despatches from United States Ministers to Spain, 1792–1906, National Archives Microfilm

M31—Despatches from United States Ministers to Russia, 1808–1906, National Archives Microfilm

M40—Domestic Letters of the Department of State, 1784–1906, National Archives Microfilm

M43—Despatches from United States Ministers to Portugal, 1790–1906, National Archives Microfilm

M46—Despatches from United States Ministers to Turkey, 1818–1906, National Archives Microfilm

M77—Diplomatic Instructions of the Department of State, 1801–1906, National Archives Microfilm

M89—Letters Received by the Secretary of the Navy from Commanding Officers of Squadrons, 1881–86, National Archives Microfilm

M125—Letters Received by the Secretary of the Navy: Captains' Letters, 1805–61, 1866–85, National Archives Microfilm

M353—Records of the Department of State Relating to Political Affairs of Turkey, 1910–29, National Archives Microfilm

M363—Records of the Department of State Relating to Internal Affairs of Turkey and Other States, 1910–29, National Archives Microfilm

M367—Records of the Department of State Relating to World War I and its Termination, 1914–29, National Archives Microfilm

M472—Letters Sent by the Secretary of the Navy to the President and Executive Agencies, 1837–86

M480—Letters Sent by the Secretary of the Navy to Chiefs of Navy Bureaus, 1842–85, National Archives Microfilm

M517—Letters Received by the Secretary of the Navy from the President and Executive Agencies, 1837–86, National Archives Microfilm

M518—Letters Received by the Secretary of the Navy from Chiefs of Navy Bureaus, 1842–85, National Archives Microfilm

M530—Records of the Department of State Relating to Political Relations Between Italy and Other States, 1910–29, National Archives Microfilm

M625—Area File of the Naval Records Collection, 1775–1910, National Archives Microfilm

T61—Despatches from United States Consuls in Tangier, Morocco, 1797–1906, National Archives Microfilm

T190—Despatches from United States Consuls in Canea, Crete, Greece, 1832–74, National Archives Microfilm

T815—Notes from the Turkish Legation in the United States to the Department of State, 1867–1906, National Archives Microfilm

NOTES

CHAPTER 1

1. For an outstanding study of the Mediterranean station before the Civil War *see* James A. Field, Jr., *America and the Mediterranean World, 1776–1882* (Princeton: Princeton University Press, 1969).

2. The African would be absorbed into the European Squadron; the West Indian into the Home Squadron. The Mediterranean would become, in order, the European Squadron, U.S. Naval Forces Operating in European Waters, Squadron 40-T, and the Sixth Fleet. The Eastern Squadron would become the Asiatic Squadron, and ultimately the Seventh Fleet. For a discussion of the distant station policy, *see* Robert G. Albion, "Distant Stations," *United States Naval Institute Proceedings* 80 (March, 1954): 265–71; Robert Johnson, *Thence Round Cape Horn* (Annapolis: United States Institute, 1963), pp. 1–16.

3. James Cable, *Gunboat Diplomacy: Political Applications of Limited Naval Force* (New York: Institute for Strategic Studies, 1971), p. 21.

4. *See* Milton Offutt, *The Protection of Citizens Abroad by the Armed Forces of the United States* (Baltimore: Johns Hopkins University Press, 1928), pp. ix–xi; Peter Karsten, *The Naval Aristocracy: The Golden Age of Annapolis and the Emergence of Modern American Navalism* (New York: The Free Press, 1972), p. 168.

5. William R. Braisted, *The United States Navy in the Pacific, 1897–1909* (Austin: University of Texas Press, 1958), p. 18.

6. Field, *America and the Mediterranean World*, p. 62.

7. *See*, for example, Karsten, *The Naval Aristocracy*, pp. 141–45, 164–66, 385; Lance Buhl, "The Smooth Water Navy: American Naval Policy and Politics, 1865–1878" (Ph.D. diss., Harvard University, 1968), pp. 129–31, 143, 146, 211–13; Kenneth J. Hagan, *American Gunboat Diplomacy and the Old Navy, 1877–1889* (Westport, Conn.: Greenwood Press, 1973), pp. 48–52; Field, *America and the Mediterranean World*, pp. 49, 63–64.

8. Quoted in Karsten, *The Naval Aristocracy*, pp. 143–44.

9. U.S., Congress, Senate, *Congressional Globe*, 42d Cong., 2d sess., 1872, 42, pt. 2: 1027; U.S., Congress, House, *Congressional Globe*, 41st Cong., 2d sess., 1870, 41, pt. 1: 345. *See also* U.S., Congress, House, *Congressional Globe*, 44th Cong., 2d sess., 1877, 44, pt. 2: 1577; Buhl, "The Smooth Water Navy," chap. 33 passim.

10. For Shufeldt, *see* Hagan's perceptive analysis in *American Gunboat Diplomacy*, pp. 35–41. Shufeldt's letter was reprinted and published in Hagan, *American Gunboat Diplomacy*, p. 249.

11. Karsten, *The Naval Aristocracy*, pp. 143–45; Hagan, *American Gunboat Diplomacy*, pp. 48–53. *See also* the *Annual Report of the Secretary of the Navy, 1865* (Washington, D.C.: Government Printing Office, 1866), pp. ix–xi; and Leland P. Lovette, "Why Should the Naval Officers Study American Foreign Policy," *United States Naval Institute Proceedings* 56 (May 1930): 426–34.

12. U.S., Congress, House, *Congressional Globe*, 41st Cong., 2d sess., 1870, p. 345; U.S., Congress, Senate, *Congressional Globe*, 40th Cong., 2d sess., 1869, 40, pt. 1: 165; Buhl, "The Smooth Water Navy," p. 165.

13. To Secretary of State, 29 June 1869, *Letters Received by the Secretary of the Navy from the President and Executive Agencies, 1837–86*, National Archives Microfilm Number M517, roll 32 (hereafter cited as M517).

14. George Dewey, *Autobiography* (New York: Charles Scribner's Sons, 1913), p. 158. For Shufeldt's quote *see* Hagan, *American Gunboat Diplomacy*, p. 37.

15. Robert L. Daniels, *American Philanthropy in the Near East, 1820–1960* (Athens: Ohio University Press, 1970), p. 121; Joseph L. Grabill, *Protestant Diplomacy and the Near East: Missionary Influence on American Policy, 1810–1927* (Minneapolis: University of Minnesota Press, 1971), p. 19.

16. For the missionary movement and American foreign policy *see* especially Grabill, *Protestant Diplomacy and the Near East. See also* Joseph L. Grabill, "The 'Invisible' Missionary: A Study in American Foreign Relations," *Church and State* 14 (Winter 1972): 96–106; Joseph L. Grabill, "Protestant Diplomacy: Bane and Boon," *Fide-Et-Historia* (Spring 1970): 53–62; Jeffery M. Dorwart, "The U.S. Navy and the Sino-Japanese War of 1894–1895," *American Neptune* 34 (July 1974): 214; Paul A. Varg, *Missionaries, Chinese, and Diplomats* (Princeton: Princeton University Press, 1958); Milton Plesur, *America's Outward Thrust: Approaches to Foreign Affairs, 1865–1890* (DeKalb: Northern Illinois University Press, 1971), pp. 174–85. Plesur denies that the U.S. government singled out missionaries for preferential treatment. *See* page 85 of his study.

17. Howard J. Kerner, "Turco-American Diplomatic Relations, 1860–1880" (Ph.D. diss., Georgetown University, 1948), p. 23.

18. Karsten, *The Naval Aristocracy*, p. 183.

19. 1 May 1871, *Letters Received by the Secretary of the Navy from Commanding Officers of Squadrons, 1881–1886*, National Archives Microfilm Number M89, roll 232 (hereafter cited as M89).

20. Rear Admiral William Radford to Rear Admiral Stephen Luce, 26 August 1870, Stephen Luce Papers, Library of Congress, Washington, D.C.; Buhl, "The Smooth Water Navy," pp. 44, 158; Walter R. Herrick, Jr., *The American Naval Revolution* (Baton Rouge: Louisiana State University Press, 1966), p. 148.

21. Alfred Vagts, *The Military Attache: A History* (Princeton: Princeton University Press, 1967), p. 32.

22. Sophie Radford de Meissner, *Old Navy Days: Sketches from the Life of Rear Admiral William Radford* (New York: H. Holt & Co., 1920), pp. 247–48; Hagan, *American Gunboat Diplomacy*, p. 205.

23. To Rear Admiral Samuel R. Franklin, 15 July 1885, Letters to Flag Officers, entry 16, National Archives Record Group 45 (hereafter cited as Letters to Flag Officers, RG45).

24. Theodore F. Jewell to commanding officer, European Squadron, 16 July 1904, Records of the European Squadron, 1869–1905, entries 23-24, Records of Naval Operating Forces, National Archives Record Group 313 (hereafter cited as Records of the European Squadron, RG313).

25. Rear Admiral Seaton Schroeder, *A Half Century of Naval Service* (New York: D. Appleton & Company, 1922), pp. 107–49; Rear Admiral Samuel R. Franklin, *Memories of a Rear Admiral* (New York: Harper & Brothers, 1898), pp. 259–60; Winfield Scott Schley, *Forty-Five Years under the Flag* (New York: D. Appleton & Company, 1904), p. 198; Thomas O. Selfridge,

Jr., to Secretary of the Navy, 24 August 1897, *Area File of the Naval Records Collection, 1775–1910*, National Archives Microfilm Number M625, roll 32 (hereafter cited as M625); James Bayard to Samuel Cox, 25 February 1886, *Diplomatic Instructions of the Department of State, 1801–1906*, National Archives Microfilm Number M77, roll 165 (hereafter cited as M77); Acting Secretary of the Navy to the Secretary of State, 11 October 1880, *Letters Sent by the Secretary of the Navy to the President and Executive Agencies, 1821–86*, National Archives Microfilm Number M472, roll 17 (hereafter cited as M472).

26. Francis Peabody, "An Episode in International Philanthropy," *New England Quarterly* 6 (March 1933): 85–97; Merli Curti, *American Philanthropy Abroad: A History* (New Brunswick, N.J.: Rutgers University Press, 1963), pp. 95–107.

27. For the Barcelona exposition *see* the unpublished autobiography of Rear Admiral Andrew T. Long in the Rear Admiral Andrew T. Long Papers, Southern Historical Collection, University of North Carolina, Chapel Hill. For the celebration of the discovery of America *see* Edith Benham Helm, *The Captains and the Kings* (New York: G. P. Putnam's Sons, 1954), pp. 21–26; H. Phelps to daughter, 7 January 1893, H. Phelps Papers, Division of Archives and History, Raleigh, North Carolina; Herrick, *American Naval Revolution*, pp. 147–48; various documents in M625, roll 25. For the Jubilee celebration, *see* Albert Gleaves, *The Life of An American Sailor: Rear Admiral William Hensley Emory* (New York: George H. Doran Company, 1923), p. 230. For the first decade of the twentieth century *see* Seward W. Livermore, "The American Navy as a Factor in World Politics, 1903–1913," *American Historical Review* 63 (July 1958): 863–80.

28. George T. Davis, *A Navy Second to None* (New York: Harcourt, Brace and Co., 1940), pp. 18–19. For the comments of two British officers *see* Vice Admiral Humphrey Hugh Smith, *A Yellow Admiral Remembers* (London: Edward Arnold & Co., 1932), pp. 86–87; Admiral Sir Charles Dundas, *An Admiral's Yarns* (London: Herbert Jenkins Limited, 1922), pp. 206–8.

29. *See*, for example, James A. Field, Jr., "A Scheme in Regard to Cyrenaica," *Mississippi Valley Historical Review* 64 (December 1957): 445–68; Commander Royal R. Bradford, "Coaling Stations for the Navy," *Forum* 26 (1899): 732–47. For French reaction to American interest in a Mediterranean base *see* Henry Blumenthal, *A Reappraisal of Franco-American Relations, 1830–1871* (Chapel Hill: University of North Carolina Press, 1959), pp. 69–70.

30. Rear Admiral Albert Gleaves to Secretary of the Navy, 27 August 1913, General Correspondence of the Secretary of the Navy, 1897–1915, Box 576, General Records of the Department of the Navy, 1798–1947, National Archives Record Group 80 (hereafter cited as General Correspondence of the Secretary of the Navy).

31. 13 October 1882, Henry Clay Cochrane Diary, Henry Clay Cochrane Papers, Marine Corps Museum, Washington Navy Yard, Washington, D.C.

32. It did not, of course, disappear. Pearl Harbor, Guantanamo Bay, Cuba, the Panama Canal, and later Subic Bay in the Philippines would be developed as overseas naval bases. Detente with Great Britain gave the United States potential naval bases in European waters. Richard D. Challener, *Admirals, Generals, and American Foreign Policy, 1898–1914* (Princeton: Princeton University Press, 1973), pp. 5, 36–41, 185, 193. Rear Admiral E. Bradford, chief of the Bureau of Equipment from 1897 to 1904, tried to kindle interest in such a base but without success. Seward W. Livermore, "American Naval Development, 1898–1914" (Ph.D. diss., Harvard University, 1943), pp. 24–25.

33. To Gustavus Fox, 21 June 1865, Gustavus Fox Papers, New York Historical Society, New York City.

34. To Secretary of the Navy, M89, roll 239. *See also* Robert G. Albion, "Communication and Remote Control," *United States Naval Institute Proceedings* 82 (August 1956): 834; Frank W. Gurney, "The U.S. Despatch Agency in London," *United States Naval Institute Proceedings* 62 (February 1936): 189–200; Plesur, *America's Outward Thrust*, p. 44.

35. Quoted in Albion, "Communication and Remote Control," p. 832.

36. This probably explains why communications between the Navy Department and squadron

commanders generally concerned logistical problems, personnel, and so on, and rarely anything about policy.

37. Secretary of the Navy to Mr. Irmaos, 18 June 1901, Operation of Fleets (OO), Box 12, Subject Files, Naval Records Collection of the Office of Naval Records and Library, National Archives Record Group Number 45 (hereafter cited as Operation of Fleets, RG45).

38. Luce to Admiral Radford, 21 April 1870, Stephen B. Luce Papers, Library of Congress, Washington, D.C. *See* Edward Mead Earle, "The Navy Influence on Foreign Relations," *Current History* 23 (February 1926): 648–55 for a critical review of naval officers as diplomatists.

39. Quoted in Karsten, *The Naval Aristocracy*, p. 172.

40. William L. Rodgers, "The Navy as an Aid in Carrying Out Diplomatic Policies," *United States Naval Institute Proceedings* 55 (February 1929): 99; Chester Colby, "Diplomacy of the Quarter Deck," *The American Journal of International Law* 8 (1914): 445. *See also* Challener, *Admirals, Generals, and American Foreign Policy*, pp. 56–57.

41. Blaine to the Secretary of the Navy, 22 November 1881, M517, roll 45.

42. Harvey to Seward, 29 October 1865, *Despatches from United States Ministers to Portugal, 1790–1906*, National Archives Microfilm Number M43, roll 21 (hereafter cited as M43).

43. John J. Leahey to author, 18 March 1972. For musicians in the European Squadron *see* Secretary of the Navy to Commanding Officer of the European Squadron, 14 December 1897, Records of the European Squadron, RG313.

44. *See*, for example, Rear Admiral J. C. Watson to Vice Admiral Sir John A. Fisher, 24 July 1900, M89, roll 235; Blumenthal, *Franco-American Relations*, pp. 84–85.

45. Henry Ballard to Commodore Daniel Patterson, 4 May 1834, *Letters Received by the Secretary of the Navy from Captains, 1807–61, 1866–85*, National Archives Microfilm Number M125, roll 194 (hereafter cited as *Captain's Letters*, M125). [unknown] to Hannah, 7 May 1840, Murrie Family Papers, Southern Historical Collection, University of North Carolina, Chapel Hill, N.C.

46. Caspar Goodrich, *Rope Yarns from the Old Navy* (New York: The Naval History Society, 1931), p. 131.

47. Allan R. Bosworth, *My Love Affair with the Navy* (New York: W. W. Norton & Company, Inc., 1969), p. 125.

48. Captain William E. Hopkins to Admiral Louis Goldsborough, 3 July 1866, Louis Goldsborough Papers, Duke University Library, Durham, N.C.

49. Charles I. Graves to Maggie, 27 December 1859, Charles I. Graves Papers, Southern Historical Collection, University of North Carolina, Chapel Hill, N.C.

50. Albert Gleaves, *The Life and Letters of Rear Admiral Stephen B. Luce* (New York: G. P. Putnam's Sons, 1925), p. 107.

51. Madeleine V. Dahlgren, *Memoir of John A. Dahlgren* (Boston: J. R. Osgood & Company, 1882), p. 42; Perry to William Graham, 3 December 1851, *The Papers of William Alexander Graham*, 6 vols., ed. J. G. De Roulhac Hamilton et al. (Raleigh, N.C.: State Department of Archives and History, 1957–1977), 4:221–22.

52. Quoted in Karsten, *The Naval Aristocracy*, p. 106. *See also* Holden A. Evans, *One Man's Fight for a Better Navy* (New York: Dodd, Mead & Company, 1940), p. 63.

53. Livermore, "American Naval Developments," p. 134. *See also* the *New York Herald*, 23 November 1910 and 11 January 1911.

54. Ingersoll to Secretary of the Navy, 30 September 1906, M625, roll 182. *See also New York Times*, 10 June 1894 and 17 November 1913.

55. *New York Times*, 29, 30 April, 7 May, 8, 21 June 1902; *Army and Navy Journal*, 10 May 1902; *Washington Post*, 5, 7 May 1902; M. A. DeWolfe Howe, *George von Lengerke Meyer: His Life and Public Services* (New York: Dodd, Mead and Co., 1920), p. 52.

56. *United States Naval Institute Proceedings* 99 (July 1974): 101–2.

57. Robert E. Coontz, *From the Mississippi to the Sea* (Philadelphia: Dorrance & Co., Inc., 1930), p. 66.

58. Admiral Sir Barry Donville, *By and Large* (London: Hutchinson, 1936), p. 26.

59. Karsten, *The Naval Aristocracy*, pp. 214–17.

60. An exception to this insensitivity can be found in a long letter written by an officer in the *North Carolina* in 1914. The writer and recipient of the letter are unknown. *See* letter dated 16 October 1914, Operation of Fleets (OO), Box 12, Subject Files, RG45.

61. Karsten, *The Naval Aristocracy*, pp. 224–25.

62. Schroeder, *A Half Century*, pp. 112–13, 122–24; Dundas, *An Admiral's Yarn*, pp. 120–21; Smith, *Yellow Admiral*, p. 89.

63. Ludlow Case to Secretary of the Navy, 9 June 1873, M89, roll 235.

64. Goodrich, *Rope Yarns*, p. 159. For the problem of enlisted personnel *see* Karsten, *The Naval Aristocracy*, p. 78; Charles Oscar Paullin, *Paullin's History of Naval Administration, 1775–1911* (Annapolis: U.S. Naval Institute Press, 1968), p. 12; Admiral David D. Porter, "Present Condition of the U.S. Navy," *International Review* 6 (June 1879): 377–79.

65. J. E. Craig, commanding officer of the *Albany*, to Secretary of the Navy, 1 May 1902, Records of the Euroepan Squadron, RG313. Karsten writes that efforts in the 1890s to enlist more native-born Americans was a result of the naval officers' racism, "a racism bred of social Darwinism." *The Naval Aristocracy*, p. 213. *See also* Frederick S. Harrod, *Manning the New Navy: The Development of a Modern Naval Enlisted Force, 1899–1940* (Westport, Conn.: Greenwood Press, 1978), pp. 16–17, 54–55.

CHAPTER 2

1. *Dictionary of American Biography*, s.v. "Goldsborough, Louis M."

2. M. C. Farenholt, "And There Were Giants in the Earth in Those Days," *United States Naval Institute Proceedings* 62 (April 1936): p. 521.

3. DuPont to his wife, 27 July 1862, *Samuel F. DuPont, A Selection from His Civil War Letters*, 3 vols., ed. John D. Hayes (Ithaca: Cornell University Press, 1969), 2: 169–70. *See also* Samuel R. Franklin, *Memories of a Rear Admiral* (New York: Harper Brothers, 1898), p. 143; and Caspar Goodrich, *Rope Yarns From the Old Navy* (New York: The Naval History Society, 1931), p. 30.

4. The station had officially been dissolved with the withdrawal of the Mediterranean Squadron in 1860, but throughout the war one or more American warships could be found cruising in European waters, showing the flag. *See*, for example, Captain Henry H. Thatcher, in command of the *Constellation*, to Gustavus Fox, 3 November 1862, Gustavus Fox Papers, New York Historical Society, New York City. Thatcher's letter describes the *Constitution's* port-to-port cruise in the Mediterranean.

5. William H. Merriam to Butler, 1 February 1865, Benjamin Butler Papers, Library of Congress; Seward to Charles Francis Adams, John Bigelow, etc., M77, roll 79.

6. For the *Rappahannock see* William J. Bray, Jr., "The Career of the *CSS Rappahannock*" (M.A. thesis, East Carolina University, 1975); Frank J. Merli, *Great Britain and the Confederate Navy, 1861–1865* (Bloomington: Indiana University Press, 1970), pp. 218–44; and Lynn M. Case and Warren F. Spencer, *The United States and France: Civil War Diplomacy* (Philadelphia: University of Pennsylvania Press, 1970), pp. 456, 469–70, 483, 492–93, 498, 500–9, 513, 550, 555.

7. Gideon Welles, *Diary of Gideon Welles, Secretary of the Navy under Lincoln and Johnson*, 3 vols., ed. Howard K. Beale (New York: W. W. Norton & Co., 1960), 2: 261.

8. Craven to Welles, *Official Records of the Union and Confederate Navies in the War of the Rebellion*, 30 vols. (Washington: U.S. Government Printing Office, 1894–1914), Ser. I, 3:415; John Bigelow, *Retrospections of an Active Life*, 3 vols. (New York: Baker and Taylor, 1909), 2: 331–34. For Craven's letter to Bigelow *see* ibid., 346–48.

9. Seward to Bigelow, 15 March 1865, M77, roll 57; Horatio Perry, U.S. chargé in Madrid,

to Craven, 18 March 1865, copy in the John Bigelow Papers, New York Public Library. *See also* Seward to Perry, 17 March 1865, M77, roll 143.

10. Quoted in George W. Dalzell, *The Flight from the Flag* (Chapel Hill: University of North Carolina Press, 1940), p. 16.

11. Welles to William Hunter, Acting Secretary of State, 29 April 1865, *Official Records, Navies*, Ser. I, 3:503–4. *See also* Welles, *Diary*, 2:261. For the "twenty-four-hour" rule *see* page 23.

12. Welles to Goldsborough, 3 June 1865, *Official Records, Navies*, Ser. I, 3:541–42; Goldsborough to Fox, 5 June 1865, Fox Papers. The chronology of Goldsborough's instructions is vague. He evidently was "officially" appointed to command the squadron in April 1865 (he acknowledged the appointment on 13 April). Goldsborough to Welles, 13 April 1865, M625, roll 18. He received some instructions, either verbal or written, in late April or early May and detailed instructions in June.

13. The State Department erred in its information about Portugal. That nation had never granted belligerent rights to the Confederacy, and Goldsborough's actions would be handicapped (with some embarrassment) before the mistake was corrected. Goldsborough to Welles, 9 August 1865, *Official Records, Navies*, Ser. I, 3:579; Welles to Goldsborough, 26 August 1865, 3:588. For the letter to Fox *see* the Fox Papers.

14. Seward to Bigelow, 15 March 1865, M77, roll 57.

15. Drouyn De Lhuys [French Foreign Minister] to Bigelow, 20 May 1865, in Bigelow, *Retrospections of an Active Life*, 2:572–74; Bigelow to Drouyn De Lhuys, 29 May 1865, ibid., 3:50–52; Seward to Bigelow, 17 June 1865, ibid., 3:76–77; Case and Spencer, *The United States and France*, pp. 580–81; Welles to Goldsborough, 18 June 1865, *Official Records, Navies*, Ser. I, 3:551.

16. Russell to Bruce, 2 June 1865, *Official Records, Navies*, Ser. I, 3:552–53; Ephraim D. Adams, *Great Britain and the American Civil War*, 2 vols. (New York: Longmans, Green & Co., 1925), 2: 267; Welles to Seward, 21 June 1865, *Official Records, Navies*, Ser. I, 3:555–56; Seward to Welles, 1 July 1865, ibid., 560–61; Welles to Goldsborough, 22 June, 15 August 1865, ibid., 558–59, 586; Seward to Adams, 7 June, 12 August 1865, M77, roll 79; Welles, *Diary*, 2: 319–22. The vessels in the European Squadron were ordered to avoid any port where awkward situations might arise. Goldsborough, for example, "boycotted" a French naval review held in Brest and Cherbourg in August because British naval vessels were present. Goldsborough to Craven, 23 July 1865, *Official Records, Navies*, Ser. I, 3:571; to Welles, ibid., 578; Bigelow to Seward, 22 August 1865, *Retrospections of an Active Life*, 2: 165–66; Goldsborough to Welles, 16 August 1865, M625, roll 18.

17. J. H. Upshur to Goldsborough, 25 November 1865, Louis Goldsborough Papers, New York Public Library, New York City. *See also* Fox to Charles Hale, U.S. consul in Alexandria, Egypt, 27 July 1865, Fox Papers; Goldsborough to wife, 21 October 1865, Louis Goldsborough Papers, Library of Congress, Washington, D.C.; William Nice to Goldsborough, 6 December 1865, ibid.

18. Goldsborough to Welles, 3 December 1865, M625, roll 18; Goldsborough to Welles, 6 December 1865, M89, roll 228.

19. Goldsborough to his wife, December 1865; Wheeler to Goldsborough, 6 December 1865, Goldsborough Papers, Library of Congress.

20. Harvey to Seward, 13 December 1864, 3, 24 February 1866, M43, roll 21.

21. 6 January 1865, Goldsborough Papers, Library of Congress.

22. Welles to Goldsborough, 28 October, 18 December 1865, Letters to Flag Officers, RG45. The depot at St. Paul de Loanda was abandoned in 1868.

23. John Niven, *Gideon Welles: Lincoln's Secretary of the Navy* (New York: Oxford University Press, 1973), pp. 506–7.

24. Charles O. Paullin, *Paullin's History of Naval Administration, 1775–1911* (Annapolis: United States Naval Institute, 1968), pp. 312–13.

25. 6 February 1866, Goldsborough Papers, Library of Congress.

26. *Annual Report of the Secretary of the Navy, 1866* (Washington, D.C.: Government Printing Office, 1967), p. 12. Welles to Goldsborough, 19 April 1866, Gideon Welles Papers, Library of Congress, Washington, D.C. The order not to go north of Denmark was probably issued because of Fox's visit to Russia.

27. 2 April 1866, Goldsborough Papers, Library of Congress.

28. Goldsborough to Harrell, 11 January 1866, Goldsborough Papers, New York Public Library; Goldsborough to his wife, 27 January 1866; John Hale, U.S. minister to Spain, to Goldsborough, 29 January 1866, Goldsborough Papers, Library of Congress; Hale to Goldsborough, 28 June 1866, Goldsborough Papers, William Perkins Library, Duke University, Durham, N.C.

29. Goldsborough to Fox, 3 July 1866, Fox Papers. *See also* Steedman to Goldsborough, 1 July 1866, Goldsborough Papers, Library of Congress. The *Swatara* was sent to Bremerhaven because of the removal of German subjects serving on American merchant vessels. *See* correspondence on this subject in the *Swatara* file, Goldsborough Papers, New York Public Library.

30. Goldsborough to the Secretary of the Navy, 26 November 1866, M89, roll 228; Seward to King, 26 November 1866, *Papers Relating to the Foreign Relations of the United States: 1866* (Washington, D.C.: Government Printing Office, 1861–), Pt. II, p. 147. Welles to Goldsborough, 24 December 1866, Letters to Flag Officers, RG45.

31. Goldsborough to Welles, 8 January 1867, M89, roll 228; Seward to King, 4 December 1866; Hale to Seward, 26 November 1866, *Foreign Relations: 1866*, Pt. II, pp. 149, 275–76; Osborn H. Oldroyd, *Assassination of Abraham Lincoln* (Rahway, N.J.: The Merchon Co. Press, 1901), p. 23.

32. Goldsborough to his wife, 21 April 1867, Goldsborough Papers, Library of Congress; Welles to Goldsborough, 24 December 1866, Letters to Flag Officers, RG45.

33. A court of inquiry held to investigate the epidemic placed the blame for it on the coal and "coal hulk" at Sierre Leone. For the court proceedings *see* the file on the *Kearsarge* in the Goldsborough papers, New York Public Library.

34. The best study of this subject is Harry N. Howard, *Turkey, the Straits and U.S. Policy* (Baltimore: The Johns Hopkins University Press, 1974). *See also* Howard, "The United States and the Problem of the Turkish Straits," *Middle East Journal* 1 (January 1947): 59–61; Howard, "The United States and the Problem of the Turkish Straits. The Foundations of American Policy (1830–1914)," *Balkan Studies* 3 (1962): 5–6; John B. Moore, *A Digest of International Law*, 8 vols. (Washington, D.C.: Government Printing Office, 1906), 1:664–65; Field, *America and the Mediterranean World, 1776–1882* (Princeton: Princeton University Press, 1969), pp. 255–56. The literature on the Straits question is voluminous. For a recent important study *see* Barbara Jelavich, *The Ottoman Empire, the Great Powers and the Straits Question, 1870–1887* (Bloomington: Indiana University Press, 1973).

35. For the *Ticonderoga's* visit *see* Morris to Secretary of State, 27 August, 7, 13 September 1866, M46, roll 20; Morris to Steedman, 1 September 1866; Steedman to Goldsborough, 1, 8 September 1866, Goldsborough Papers, Library of Congress; Seward to Morris, 29 September 1866, M77, roll 163.

36. Quoted in Glyndon G. Van Deusen, *William Henry Seward* (New York: Oxford University Press, 1967), pp. 514–15.

37. Field, *America and the Mediterranean World*, p. 247. *See also* Leland J. Gordon, *American Relations with Turkey: 1830–1930* (Philadelphia: University of Pennsylvania Press, 1932).

38. David Pletcher, *The Awkward Years: American Foreign Relations under Garfield and Arthur* (Columbia: University of Missouri Press, 1963), pp. 220–25.

39. *See also* Grabill, "The Invisible Missionary: A Study in American Foreign Relations," *Church and State* 14 (Winter 1972): 96–106; Field, *America and the Mediterranean World*; John H. Moore, "America Looks at Turkey, 1876–1909" (Ph.D. dissertation, University of Virginia, 1961), pp. 23, 90, 100; Rosaline Edwards, "Relations Between the United States and Turkey, 1893–1897" (Ph.D. thesis, Fordham University, 1952), pp. 52–53.

40. For incidents before the Civil War *see* Field, *America and the Mediterranean World*, pp. 285–297.

41. Ibid., p. 290.

42. Quoted in Peter Karsten, *The Naval Aristocracy: The Golden Age of Annapolis and the Emergence of Modern Navalism* (New York: Free Press, 1972), p. 224.

43. Oscar S. Straus, *Under Four Administrations: From Cleveland to Taft* (Boston: Houghton Mifflin Co., 1922), p. 224.

44. *See*, for example, James Brown to Fox, 6 July 1865, Fox Papers; J. A. Johnson to Secretary of State, 3 April 1867, M517, roll 30.

45. For U.S. involvement *see* the excellent article by Ernest R. May, "Crete and the United States, 1866–1869," *Journal of Modern History* 16 (December 1944): 286–93; William J. Stillman, *Autobiography of a Journalist*, 2 vols. (Boston: Houghton Mifflin Co., 1901), vol. 2; and Field, *America and the Mediterranean World*, pp. 317–19.

46. Goldsborough to consul at Piraeus, 1 December 1866, Goldsborough Papers, Library of Congress.

47. Stillman to Secretary of State, 12 February 1867, Goldsborough Papers, Library of Congress; Morris to Goldsborough, 23 January, 15 February 1867; Goldsborough to Morris, 9 February 1867, M89, roll 228.

48. 21 March 1867, M472, roll 11. *See also* Welles, *Diary*, 3:70–71.

49. Seward to Morris, 25 December 1866, M77, roll 163; Morris to Seward, 20 February 1867, M46, roll 20.

50. *Diary*, 3:71. Welles later wrote: "Seward said every man, woman, and child in the United States were against the Turks. I told him he would please except the Navy and the Navy Department." Ibid., p. 425.

51. Jeffers to Farragut, 19 August 1867, M89, roll 229.

52. Steedman to Goldsborough, 8 September 1866, Goldsborough Papers, Library of Congress.

53. John D. Hayes, "Captain Fox—He is the Navy Department," *United States Naval Institute Proceedings* 91 (September 1965): 70; Welles, *Diary*, 2: 509, 512.

54. Quoted in James A. Knowles, "Blue Water Monitor," *United States Naval Institute Proceedings* 99 (March 1973): 83.

55. For accounts of the Fox mission *see* Knowles, "Blue Water Monitor"; Field, *America in the Mediterranean World*, pp. 315–16; and J. F. Loubat, *Gustavus Fox's Mission to Russia* (New York: Arno Press, 1970). For official correspondence concerning the mission *see Foreign Relations: 1866* Pt. I, pp. 427–49; Pt. II, pp. 166–68, 178–81.

56. Goldsborough to his wife, 5 January 1867, Goldsborough Papers, Library of Congress.

57. On his birthday, February 18, he had a matinee on board the *Colorado* with "hundreds" of guests.

58. There is considerable correspondence in the Goldsborough Papers, Library of Congress, concerning the controversy. *See also* Welles, *Diary*, 3:85–86.

59. 30 June 1867, Goldsborough Papers, Library of Congress. *See also* Goldsborough to his wife, 7 July 1867, ibid.

60. In February 1866, Harvey had complained to the State Department that Goldsborough made no attempt to notify him of the movements of his ships. Seward passed it on to Welles, who wrote a mild reprimand to Goldsborough, pointing out that "there should be courteous cooperation between the diplomatic and naval representatives abroad." *See* Harvey to Seward, 24 February 1866, M43, roll 21; Seward to Welles, 30 March 1866, copy in Wirt Family Papers, Southern Historical Collection, University of North Carolina, Chapel Hill, N.C.; Welles to Goldsborough, 30 March 1866, Letters to Flag Oficers, RG45.

61. Arthur Otway, *Autobiography and Journals of Admiral Lord Clarence E. Paget* (London: Chapman & Hall, 1896), pp. 306–307.

62. Holmes to Motley, 10 October 1866, *The Correspondence of John Lathrop Motley*, 2 vols., ed. George W. Curtis (New York: Harper & Brothers, 1889), 2: 211.

63. Charles Lee Lewis, *David Glasgow Farragut: Our First Admiral*, 2 vols. (Annapolis: United States Naval Institute, 1943), 2: 336–37; Charles S. Foltz, *Surgeon of the Seas: The Adventurous Life of Surgeon General Jonathan M. Foltz in the Days of Wooden Ships* (Indianapolis: The Bobbs-Merrill Company, 1931), pp. 300–1.

64. For his European tour *see* James E. Montgomery, *Our Admiral's Flag Abroad: The Cruise of the Franklin* . . . (New York: G. P. Putnam & Son, 1869); Lewis, *Farragut*, 2: 336–365; Goodrich, *Rope Yarns*, pp. 46–61.

65. *Army and Navy Journal*, 26 October 1867.

66. *Foreign Relations: 1868*, pp. 114–15. For the official correspondence concerning Farragut's visit to Constantinople *see* ibid., pp. 114–19; Morris to Secretary of State, 21 August 1868, M43, roll 21; Seward to Morris, 14 September 1868, M77, roll 163.

67. May, "Crete and the United States, 1866–1869," p. 286; Field, *America and the Mediterranean World*, pp. 319–20; Montgomery, *Our Admiral's Flag Abroad*, pp. 252–53.

68. Cyrus Hamlin, *My Life and Times* (Boston: Congregational Sunday School and Publishing Society, 1893), pp. 471–73, 443–47. Historians have disagreed over Farragut's role in the establishment of Roberts College. *See* Field, *America and the Mediterranean World*, pp. 355–57; Kerner, "Turco-American Diplomatic Relations, 1860–1880" (Ph.D. diss., Georgetown University, 1948), pp. 178–81; Gordon, *American Relations with Turkey, 1830–1930*, pp. 225–26.

69. Quoted in May, "Crete and the United States, 1866–1869," p. 286.

70. Ibid., p. 291.

CHAPTER 3

1. Henry Erban to U.S. consul, Malta, 20 December 1894, Records of the European Squadron, RG313; W. Nice to Goldsborough, 6 December 1865, Louis M. Goldsborough Papers, Library of Congress, Washington, D.C.; Harvey to Seward, 10 February 1866, M43, roll 21; Pennock to Edgar Welles, 21 November 1868, Gideon Welles Papers, Library of Congress, Washington, D.C.

2. Charles Sperry to cousin, 7 April 1871, Charles Sperry Papers, Library of Congress, Washington, D.C. Sperry added in another letter, "I imagine [the Admiral] has a few casks of wine that he wants to send home, free of expense." *See also* Secretary of the Navy to Chief, Bureau of Provisions and Clothing, 22 June 1869, M480, roll 3.

3. *See*, for example, William G. Rice, consul at Spezia, to Admiral Goldsborough, 29 March 1866, M625, roll 19; Gideon Welles, *Diary of Gideon Welles, Secretary of the Navy under Lincoln and Johnson*, 3 vols., ed. Howard K. Beale (New York: W. W. Norton & Co., 1960), 3: 514.

4. Harvey to Secretary of State, 5 April 1867, M43, roll 21.

5. Welles to Seward, 21 June 1867, Welles Papers; Commodore A. N. Smith, Chief, Bureau of Equipment and Recruiting, to Welles, 15 June 1867, M518, roll 23. *See also* Harvey to Seward, 27 April, 5 May 1867, M43, roll 21. There is some discrepancy as to the amount of coal Abecassis was contracted to deliver. A letter from Abecassis to Goldsborough dated 27 June 1867 informed the admiral that he had received a contract to provide 2500 tons of coal. Goldsborough Papers, New York Public Library, New York.

6. Smith to Farragut, 18 December 1867, entry 299, Records of the Bureau of Personnel, RG24.

7. Welles to Seward, 26 January 1869, Welles Papers; Welles, *Diary* 3: 514; Smith to Welles, 11 December 1868, M518, roll 24.

8. Welles, *Diary*, 3: 525; Welles to Seward, 13 February 1869, Welles Papers; Harvey to Radford, 10 March 1869, M43, roll 22.

9. U.S., Congress, House, *Congressional Globe*, 41st Cong., 2d sess., 1870, 41, pt. 4: 2884–2885. Henry Neal, American consul in Lisbon, continued condemning the Abecassis contract. *See* letter to Fish, July 1869, and attached memo from Commodore Smith, M625, roll 21.

10. Smith to commander, European Squadron, 31 August 1869, 2 September 1870, entry 299, RG24.

11. Smith to Rear Admiral Charles Boggs, entry 299, RG24.

12. 8 August 1883 entry, Henry Clay Cochrane Diary, Henry Clay Cochrane Papers, Marine Corps Museum, Washington Navy Yard, Washington, D.C.; Rear Admiral Erban to Secretary of the Navy, 6 October 1893, Erban Papers, New York Historical Society, New York City.

13. General order dated 20 April 1869, RG45. *See also* Sophie Radford de Meissner, *Old Navy Days: Sketches from the Life of Rear Admiral William Radford* (New York: H. Holt & Co., 1920), p. 346.

14. 1 November 1869, M89, roll 230. For the "Red Ink" quote *see* Caspar Goodrich, *Rope Yarns from the Old Navy* (New York: The Naval Historical Society, 1921), p. 65.

15. Rear Admiral Augustus Case to Secretary of the Navy, 14 July 1874, M89, roll 236.

16. James A. Field, Jr., *America and the Mediterranean World, 1776–1882* (Princeton: Princeton University Press, 1969), p. 338; Lenoir Wright, *United States Policy Toward Egypt, 1830–1914* (New York: Exposition Press, 1969), p. 55; Howard R. Marraro, "Spezia: An American Naval Base, 1848–68," *Military Affairs* 7 (1943): 202–8.

17. David Lowenthal, *George Perkins Marsh: Versatile Vermonter* (New York: Columbia University Press, 1958), p. 287; Marraro, "Spezia: An American Naval Base, 1848–68," p. 208; W. G. Rice to Goldsborough, 29 March 1866, M625, roll 19.

18. Stillman to Steward, 14 May 1866, T190, roll 2.

19. Field, *America and the Mediterranean World*, pp. 319–20.

20. Ernest N. Paolino, *The Foundations of the American Empire: William Henry Seward and U.S. Foreign Policy* (Ithaca: Cornell University Press, 1973), pp. 30–32; Kenneth Bourne, *Britain and the Balance of Power in North America 1815–1908* (Berkeley: University of California Press, 1967), p. 304.

21. 28 July 1866, M472, roll 11. *See also* Seward to Welles, 11 June 1866, and Welles to Seward, 18 June 1866, M472, roll 11; and Buhl, "The Smooth Water Navy: American Naval Policy and Politics, 1865–1878" (Ph.D. diss., Harvard University, 1968), p. 148.

22. Smith to Goldsborough, 7 December 1866, Goldsborough Papers, Library of Congress; Welles to Seward, 15 March 1867, M472, roll 11.

23. Welles to Seward, 15 March, 8, 11 October 1867, M472, roll 11; Seward to Welles, 10 December 1868, M517, roll 32.

24. *La Turquie*, 15 December 1866; *La Patrie*, 4 December 1866, cited in Henry Blumenthal, *A Reappraisal of Franco-American Relations, 1830–1871* (Chapel Hill: University of North Carolina, 1959), p. 70.

25. Glyndon G. Van Deusen, *William Henry Seward* (New York: Oxford University Press, 1967), pp. 514–15.

26. For an interesting account *see* James A. Field, "A Scheme in Regard to Cyrenaica," *Mississippi Valley Historical Review* 44 (December 1957): 445–68. Alexandria, Egypt, was also recommended. *See Papers Relating to the Foreign Relations of the United States: 1873* (Washington, D.C.: Government Printing Office, 1974), Pt. II, p. 1125.

27. Victor Meslier to John M. Frances, 4 September 1873, M517, roll 36.

28. 10 August 1874, Hamilton Fish Papers, Library of Congress, Washington, D.C. *See also* Boker to Fish, 9 June 1874, Fish Papers, and Boker to Fish, 28 June 1874, M46, roll 27.

29. Henry Blumenthal, *France and the United States: Their Diplomatic Relations, 1789–1914* (Chapel Hill: University of North Carolina Press, 1969), p. 133.

30. Radford to Secretary of the Navy, 10 August 1869, M89, roll 230.

31. Quoted from Field, *America and the Mediterranean World*, p. 339. *See also* Radford to Secretary of the Navy, 19 August, 20 November, 13 December 1869, 7, 14 February and 22 April 1870, M89, roll 230; *Army and Navy Journal*, 16 July 1870; Italian Chargé d'Affaires to Secretary of State, 21 December 1869, M517, roll 32; Hamilton Fish Diary, entry dated 16 December 1869, Fish Papers; Robertson to Radford, 11 September 1869, RG45; Case to Secretary of State, 5 November 1873, M472, roll 13.

32. A. L. Gihon, Surgeon of the Fleet, to Joseph Beale, Surgeon General and Chief of the Bureau of Medicine, 24 August 1874, Letters received from all sources. Records of the Bureau of Medicine and Surgery, RG52.

33. Howell to Secretary of the Navy, 21 April 1881, M89, roll 244; Special Order of Rear Admiral S. R. Franklin, 20 May 1887, M625, roll 21; Samuel B. Franklin, *Memories of a Rear Admiral* (New York: Harper Brothers, 1898), p. 318.

34. Franklin, *Memories*, p. 260; *New York Times*, 17 December 1893. One officer mentioned that the French government did not use Villefranche for its naval vessels because of the closeness of Monaco and its gambling establishments. Schoonmaker to his father, 19 January 1881, Charles M. Schoonmaker Papers, Library of Congress, Washington, D.C.

35. Tilton to Mrs. Tilton, 16 March 1879, McLane Tilton Papers, Marine Corps Museum, Washington Navy Yard, Washington, D.C.; Schoonmaker to his father, 19 January 1881, Schoonmaker Papers.

36. *American Register*, 20 January 1883, copy in the Cochrane Papers; *Army and Navy Journal*, 24 February 1872.

37. Tilton to his wife, 14 January, 26 February 1879, Tilton Papers; *see also* Franklin, *Memories*, pp. 260–64; de Meissner, *Old Navy Days*, p. 352, and Edwin A. Falk, *Fighting Bob Evans* (New York: Jonathan Cape & Harrison Smith, 1931), p. 117.

38. Schoonmaker to his father, 19 January 1881, Schoonmaker Papers.

39. Tilton to his wife, 22 April 1878, Tilton Papers.

40. Franklin, *Memories*, pp. 179–80; *Army and Navy Journal*, 10 November 1877.

41. Worden to Thompson, 18 March 1877, Thompson to Worden, 6 April 1877, M89, roll 240.

42. Ammens to Robeson, M625, roll 21.

43. Robeson to Fish, 21 February 1877, M472, roll 15; Robeson to Worden, 26 February 1877, Letters to Flag Officers, Entry 16, RG45.

44. Worden to Thompson, 17 March 1877, M89, roll 240. For the negotiations with the Portuguese government *see* M517, roll 40.

45. Secretary of State to the Secretary of the Navy, 19 July 1877, M517, roll 40.

46. Kenneth J. Hagan, *American Gunboat Diplomacy and the Old Navy, 1877–1889* (Westport, Conn.: Greenwood Press, 1973), pp. 38–39.

47. Chandler to Captain Earl English, Chief of the Bureau of Equipment and Recruiting, 23 November 1882, Letters Received from the Secretary of the Navy, Entry 330, RG24; English to Secretary of the Navy, 24 November 1882, Captain Montgomery Sicard, Chief of the Bureau of Ordnance to Secretary of the Navy, 25 November 1882, Chief of the Bureau of Steam Engineering to Secretary of the Navy, 27 November 1882, Captain J. A. Smith, Chief of the Bureau of Provisions and Clothing to Secretary of the Navy, 27 November 1882, M518, roll 32. *See also* F. D. Wilson, Chief of the Bureau of Yards and Docks to Secretary of the Navy, 3 July 1883, M518, roll 32.

48. Smith to Chandler, 19 July 1883, William E. Chandler Papers, Library of Congress, Washington, D.C. In December 1883, Chandler in his annual report recommended the establishment of coal depots at Samana Bay or some harbor in Haiti and at points in Brazil, Chile, Central America, Liberia, East Africa, and Korea—none in European waters. David M. Pletcher, *The Awkward Years: American Foreign Relations Under Garfield and Arthur* (Columbia, Missouri: University of Missouri Press, 1963), p. 125.

49. Chandler to English, 20 July 1883, Entry 330, RG24; Baldwin to Secretary of the Navy,

20 July, 29 August, 1 September, 13 December 1883, Records of the European Squadron, RG313; Walker to Secretary of the Navy, 21 July 1883, M518, roll 32. *See also* William A. N. Allen's diary for 1883 in the William A. N. Allen Papers, Library of Congress, Washington, D.C.

50. Leon B. Richardson, *William E. Chandler, Republican* (New York: Dodd, Mead & Company, 1940), pp. 322–25.

51. For examples of this practice before the Civil War *see* Madeline V. Dahlgren, *Memoir of John A. Dahlgren* (Boston, Mass.: J. R. Osgood & Co., 1882), pp. 112–13; Benjamin F. Sands, *From Reefer to Rear Admiral: Reminiscences and Journal Jottings of Nearly Half a Century of Naval Life* (New York: Frederick A. Stokes Company, 1899), p. 143; Charles Graves to Cousin Maggie, 4 December 1859, Graves Papers, Southern Historical Collections, University of North Carolina, Chapel Hill, N.C.

52. For Goldsborough *see* letter to his wife, 17 August 1866, Goldsborough Papers, Library of Congress. For Farragut *see* Charles L. Lewis, *David Glasgow Farragut: Our First Admiral* (Annapolis: U.S. Naval Institute, 1943), p. 337, and Goodrich, *Rope Yarns*, pp. 48–49. For Welles's attitude *see* his *Diary*, 3: 93.

53. *Army and Navy Journal*, 25 June 1875, 4 September 1875.

54. Tilton to his wife, 4 August 1879, Tilton Papers; Charles Sperry to his wife, 23 February 1885, Sperry Papers.

55. Peter Karsten, *The Naval Aristocracy: The Golden Age of Annapolis and the Emergence of Modern American Navalism* (New York: The Free Press, 1972), pp. 116–17; Thomas O. Selfridge, *Memoirs of Thomas O. Selfridge, Jr., Rear Admiral, U.S. Navy* (New York: G. P. Putnam's sons, 1924), pp. 220–22.

56. Fairfax to Hunt, 24, 31 May 1881, William Hunt Papers, Reel 1, Library of Congress, Washington, D.C.; *New York Times*, 5, 11 August 1881.

57. Potter to English, 5 February 1885, M89, roll 245; *Army and Navy Journal*, 31 January 1885. Lieutenant Nathan Sargent, English's aide, kept a journal, but it does not mention the controversy. Nathan Sargent Papers, Library of Congress, Washington, D.C.

58. 3 March 1885, Letters of Flag Officers, Entry 16, RG45.

59. English to Whiting, 20 May 1885, James Siras (?) to Whiting, 18 March 1885, M89, roll 245.

60. *See* Captain Richard W. Meade to Chandler, 27 January 1885, Chandler Papers.

61. Whitney did detach three officers from the Asiatic Squadron shortly after taking office for violating the order. *Army and Navy Journal*, 11 April 1885. For the extensiveness of the custom in the 1890s *see* Robert McNeely to Fanny McNeely, 20 September 1896, Macay and McNeely Family Papers, Southern Historical Collection, University of North Carolina.

62. Franklin, *Memories*, p. 319.

63. Blaine to Harrison, 10 August 1891, *The Correspondence Between Benjamin Harrison and James G. Blaine*, ed. A. T. Volwiler (Philadelphia: The American Philosophical Society, 1940), pp. 170, 173–174; Walter Herrick, *The American Naval Revolution* (Baton Rouge: Louisiana State University Press, 1966), pp. 91–93. *See also* Admiral David D. Porter to Charles Boutelle, Chairman of the Naval Affairs Committee, 3 January 1890, David D. Porter Papers, Library of Congress, Washington, D.C. Porter was generally opposed to the acquisition of foreign coaling stations, considering them a liability in case of war. Hagan, *American Gunboat Diplomacy*, p. 19.

64. For a discussion of this theme *see* Karsten, *The Naval Aristocracy*, pp. 277–317.

CHAPTER 4

1. *Annual Report of the Secretary of the Navy: 1871* (Washington, D.C.: Government Printing Office, 1872), p. 5. *See also* "Report on Condition of Navy," 10 November 1870, Mss. in David D. Porter Papers, Library of Congress, Washington, D.C.

2. John R. Wadleigh, "1873—The Best Was Yet to Be," *United States Naval Institute Proceedings* 99 (November 1973): 58.

3. U.S., Congress, House, *Congressional Globe*, 40th Cong., 2d sess., 1867, 40, pt. 1: 213; *ibid.*, pt. 3, 2158; U.S., Congress, House, *Congressional Globe*, 41st Cong., 2d sess., 1870, 41, pt. 1: 345.

4. Rodgers to Shufeldt, 26 September 1872, Robert W. Shufeldt Papers, Library of Congress, Washington, D.C.

5. Neville T. Kirk, "Sentinel for a Century: The *Proceedings,* the Navy, and the Nation, 1873–1973," *United States Naval Institute Proceedings* 99 (October 1973): 97.

6. George Faulke to Chambers, 28 December 1883, W. I. Chambers Papers, Library of Congress, Washington, D.C.; Tilton to his wife, 19 April 1877, McClane Tilton Papers, Marine Corps Museum, Washington Navy Yard, Washington, D.C. For other remarks *see* Peter Karsten, *The Naval Aristocracy: The Golden Age of Annapolis and the Emergence of American Navalism* (New York: The Free Press, 1972), p. 279.

7. Porter to ———, 4 September 1868, Porter Papers; Gideon Welles, *Diary of Gideon Welles, Secretary of the Navy under Lincoln and Johnson*, 3 vols., ed. Howard K. Beale (New York W. W. Norton & Co., 1960), 3:563.

8. Guest to Porter, 25 November 1870, Porter Papers.

9. Jeffers to Commodore Alexander Pennock, 4 January 1869, Pennock to Welles, 15 January 1869, M89, roll 229. Pennock commanded the squadron for three months (December 1868–February 1869), until Radford arrived.

10. Quoted in the *Army and Navy Journal*, 23 October 1869.

11. Radford to Secretary of the Navy, 7 August, 25 October 1869, M89, roll 230.

12. Albert Gleaves, *Life and Letters of Rear Admiral Stephen B. Luce, U.S. Navy* (New York: G. P. Putnam's Sons, 1925), p. 114–15, 117–24. *See also* Case to Hamilton Fish, 30 August 1870, M472, roll 12.

13. The *Frolic* visited Stettin in 1867. *See* Caspar F. Goodrich, "The *Frolic* in the Baltic, 1867: A Reminiscence," *United States Naval Institute Proceedings* 41 (March–April 1915): 473–80, and D. B. Harmony to Farragut, 21 August 1876, M89, roll 229. *See also* Henry M. Adams, *Prussian-American Relations, 1775–1871* (Cleveland: The Press of Western Reserve University, 1960), p. 102.

14. Luce to Glisson, 14 October 1870, Stephen B. Luce Papers, Library of Congress, Washington, D.C.

15. Fish *Diary*, entry 26 September 1870, Hamilton Fish Papers, Library of Congress, Washington, D.C.. *See also* entry 20 January 1871. *See also* Elihu Washburne, *Recollections of a Minister to France, 1869–1877*, 2 vols. (New York: Charles Scribner's sons, 1887), 2: 26. For Washburne, *see* Dale Clifford, "Elihu Benjamin Washburne: An American Diplomat in Paris, 1870–71," *Prologue* 2 (Winter 1971): 161–74.

16. Boggs to Secretary of the Navy, 1 May 1871, M89, roll 232. *See also* Boggs to Secretary of the Navy, 14 February 1871, ibid.

17. Fish to Secretary of the Navy, 30 October 1870, M517, roll 33. Sickles to Glisson, 14 November 1870, M31, roll 50. *See also* Guest to Sickles, 13 November 1870, and Sickles to Glisson, 23 November 1870, M31, roll 50.

18. Secretary of the Navy to Glisson, 17 September 1870, Letters to Flag Officers, Entry 16, RG45; Mullany to Boggs, 18 February 1871, ibid.

19. Boggs to Mullany, 20 February 1871, M89, roll 232.

20. Boggs to his brother, 20 September 1871, M625, roll 21; *New York Times*, 22 August 1871. *See also Papers Relating to the Foreign Relations of the United States: 1872* (Washington, D.C.: Government Printing Office, 1873), Pt. II, pp. 314–315.

21. Robertson to Boggs, 21 January 1871, Letters to Flag Officers, Entry 16 RG45; Boggs to Secretary of the Navy, 1 May 1871, M89, roll 232.

22. Boggs was surprised that Alden was to relieve him. He had expected Rear Admiral T. A.

Jenkins, who was next in line on the seniority list. Boggs to his brother, September 1871, M625, roll 21. General Sherman sailed on the *Wabash* with Alden when she left New York in October 1882. For an account of the *Wabash*'s cruise *see* the unpublished memoir of Bowman McCalla, Navy Department Library, Washington Navy Yard, Washington, D.C.

23. Welles, *Diary*, 2: 362; Samuel R. Franklin, *Memories of a Rear Admiral* (New York: Harper Brothers, 1898) p. 215; Richard S. West, Jr., *The Second Admiral: A Life of David Dixon Porter, 1813–1891* (New York: Coward-McCann, Inc., 1937), p. 282; William H. Parker, *Recollections of a Naval Oficer, 1841–1865* (New York: Charles Scribner's Sons, 1883), p. 29.

24. Quoted in Kenneth Bourne, *Britain and the Balance of Power in North America, 1815–1908* (Berkeley: Univ. of California Press, 1967), p. 302. Adrian Cook in his recent study, *The Alabama Claims: American Politics and Anglo-American Relations, 1865–1872* (Ithaca: Cornell University Press, 1975), discounts the possibility of war (*see* p. 245).

25. 9 March 1872, Porter Papers; *Army and Navy Journal*, 20 April 1872.

26. Bourne, *Britain and the Balance of Power*, pp. 305–6. Spencer Childers, *The Life of the Right Honorable Hugh C. E. Childers*, 2 vols. (London: John Murray, 1901), 1: 173.

27. Alden to Robeson, 8 February 1872, M89, roll 234.

28. Sickles to Secretary of State, 22 June, Sickles to Alden, 17 June, Sickles to Martos, 20 June 1872, M31, roll 53.

29. Harry N. Howard, *Turkey, the Straits and U.S. Policy* (Baltimore: The John Hopkins University Press, 1974), p. 11; John B. Moore, *A Digest of International Law*, 8 vols. (Washington, D.C.: Government Printing Office, 1906), 1:665–66. Interestingly, the House of Representatives had recently passed a resolution urging the abolition of all restrictions upon the passage of vessels. No action was taken under this congressional resolution other than Seward's instructions to his representatives in Constantinople and St. Petersburg to gather information on the straits question.

30. Fish *Diary*, entry 1 July 1869. *See also* diary entry for 19 February 1870; Fish to Morris, 2 February 1870, M77, roll 163.

31. Allan Nevins, *Hamilton Fish: The Inner History of the Grant Administration* (New York: Dodd, Mead & Company, 1936), pp. 506–7; James T. Shotwell and Francis Deak, *Turkey at the Straits* (New York: Macmillan, 1940), pp. 51–52; Thomas A. Bailey, *America Faces Russia* (Ithaca: Cornell University Press, 1950), p. 116; Andrew Curtin to Fish, 19 December 1870, M35, roll 23.

32. Fish to Morris, 5 May 1871, to Boker, 3 January 1873, M77, roll 163.

33. Brown to Fish, 15, 29 June 1871, M77, roll 23; *Army and Navy Journal*, 19 August 1871.

34. Fish *Diary*, entry 4 December 1872; Boker to Fish, 30 November 1872, M46, roll 25; Secretary of the Navy to Alden, 4 December 1872, M89, roll 234.

35. Fish to Boker, 25 January 1873, M77, roll 163; Boker to Fish, 17 December 1872, M46, roll 25.

36. December 1872, M77, roll 25.

37. Hay to Secretary of State, 10 October, 19 November 1872, 30 May 1873, M517, roll 36.

38. Fish Papers, 10, 25 June 1873. The consul was J. Baldwin Hay.

39. Fish Papers, 21 August 1872; Boker to Fish, 20 March 1873, *Foreign Relations: 1873*, Pt. II, p. 1106; Edwards S. Bradley, *George Henry Boker: Poet and Patriot* (Philadelphia: University of Pennsylvania Press, 1927); Case to Robeson, 15 August 1873, M89, roll 235; Boker to Fish, 19 September 1873, Hamilton Fish Papers, Library of Congress, Washington, D.C.

40. Wells to Case, 31 July 1873, M89, roll 235.

41. Fish *Diary*, entry 5 August 1873; Case to Secretary of the Navy, 31 July 1873, to Sickles, 5 August 1873, M89, roll 235; Fish to Acting Secretary of the Navy, 5 August 1873, M517, roll 36; Reynolds, Acting Secretary of the Navy, to Secretary of State, 6 August 1873, M472, roll 13. *See also* documents from 31 July through 6 August 1873, M31, roll 58.

42. Case to Wells, 30 August 1873, Wells to Case, 17 September 1873, M89, roll 235.

43. Quoted in Joseph V. Fuller, "Hamilton Fish," in *The American Secretaries of State and*

Their Diplomacy, 10 vols., ed. Samuel F. Bemis (New York: Pageant Book Company, 1927–1929), 7:180–81.

44. Seaton Schroeder, *A Half Century of Naval Service* (New York: D. Appleton and Company, 1922), p. 73. *See also* Fish *Diary*, entry 14 November 1873; Robeson to Rear Admiral G. A. Scott, 12 December 1873, Letters to Flag Officers, Entry 16 RG45; Robley D. Evans, *A Sailor's Log* (New York: D. Appleton and Company, 1902), p. 168.

45. Nevis, *Fish*, pp. 673–75; John A. S. Grenville and George Young, *Politics, Strategy, and American Diplomacy: Studies in Foreign Policy, 1875–1917* (New Haven: Yale University Press, 1966), pp. 4–5.

46. Robeson to Case, 7 January, 16 March, 6 April 1874, Letters to Flag Officers, Entry 16 RG45; Case to secretary of the Navy, 6 May 1874, M89, roll 236; Franklin, *Memories*, p. 231; Schroeder *A Half Century*, pp. 70–74.

47. *Nation*, 20 November 1873; Grenville, *Politics, Strategy and American Diplomacy*, p. 5.

48. Schroeder, *A Half Century*, p. 74.

49. Fish to General Schenck in London, M77, roll 83. *See also* Worden to Secretary of the Navy, 11 November 1875, M89, roll 238; Franklin, *Memories*, pp. 232–36; and Nevins, *Fish*, pp. 878–79. Some thirty of the officers' wives and children were left for the winter at Villefranche when the ships sailed.

50. *La Correspondencia*, 25 November 1875, translation in M31, roll 75. *See also* Thomas A. Bailey, *A Diplomatic History of the American People*, 8th ed. (New York: Appleton-Century-Crofts, 1968), p. 389; Evans, *A Sailor's Log*, pp. 208–12; Franklin, *Memories*, pp. 265–67.

51. 29 January 1876.

52. Worden to Secretary of the Navy, 25 October 1876, M89, roll 239.

53. Thompson to Evarts, 6 July 1877, M472, roll 15. In August Worden requested that a three-month supply of stores for the squadron be sent to Smyrna. Worden to Thompson, 12 August 1877, M89, roll 240.

CHAPTER 5

1. Telegram dated 15 May 1876, M89, roll 239. *See also* Smithers, consul at Smyrna, to Maynard, 9 May 1876, Maynard to Worden, 10, 12, 20 May 1876, M46, roll 20; Maynard to Fish, 12 May 1876, M517, roll 39; Worden to Secretary of the Navy, 15 May 1876, M89, roll 239; S. R. Franklin, *Memories of a Rear Admiral* (New York: Harper Brothers, 1898), pp. 234–36; Fish *Diary*, entry 20 May 1876, Fish Papers, Library of Congress, Washington, D.C.; Fish to Maynard, 20 May 1876, M77, roll 164.

2. Seaton Schroeder, *A Half Century of Naval Service* (New York: D. Appleton & Co., 1922), p. 111; Worden to Secretary of the Navy, 25 October 1872, M89, roll 239.

3. 17 April 1875.

4. Worden to Secretary of the Navy, 26 April 1877, M89, roll 240; Everts to Secretary of the Navy, 30 March 1877, M517, roll 40.

5. Schroeder, *A Half Century*, p. 111; Worden to Secretary of the Navy, 8 March 1877, M89, roll 40; Maynard to Secretary of State, 19 March 1877, M517, roll 40; Thompson to Worden, 23 March 1877, Letters to Flag Officers, RG45.

6. Maynard to Secretary of State, 14 June 1877, M46, roll 33. *See also* the copy in M517, roll 40.

7. Journal of John Lowe, engineer on the *Dispatch*, entry 3 August 1877, Lowe Papers, Library of Congress, Washington, D.C.; Evelyn Schuyler Schaeffer, *Eugene Schuyler: Selected Essays with a Memoir* (New York: Charles Scribner's Sons, 1901), pp. 117, 120.

8. Henry Blumenthal, *France and the United States: Their Diplomatic Relations, 1789–1914* (Chapel Hill: University of North Carolina Press, 1969), p. 134; Thomas A. Bailey, *America Faces Russia: Russian-American Relations from Early Times to Our Day* (Ithaca: Cornell University Press, 1960), pp. 117–18; R. W. Seton-Watson, *Disraeli, Gladstone, and the*

Eastern Question (New York: W. W. Norton & Company, Inc., 1972), pp. 282–83.

9. D. W. Graply *Diary*, Historical Society of Pennsylvania, Philadelphia, Pennsylvania; Charles E. Clark, *My Fifty Years in the Navy* (Boston: Little, Brown and Company, 1917), pp. 91–93; Tilton to his wife, 22 December 1878, McClane Tilton Papers, Marine Corps Museum, Washington Navy Yard, Washington, D.C.

10. Tilton to his wife, 16 August 1877, Tilton Papers.

11. Tilton to his wife, 16 January 1878, ibid. *See also* Maynard to Le Roy, 14 January 1878, Le Roy to Maynard, 15 January 1878, M46, roll 34.

12. *Papers Relating to the Foreign Relations of the United States: 1878* (Washington, D.C.: Government Printing Office, 1878), pp. 364–72; Tilton to his wife, 13 March 1878, Tilton Papers.

13. Le Roy to Secretary of the Navy, 22 January 1878, M89, roll 241; Schaeffer, *Selected Essays*, p. 120; W. E. Woodward, *Meet General Grant* (New York: Premier Books, 1957), p. 266; John M. Mead, Minister to Greece, to Evarts, 9 March 1878, *Foreign Relations: 1878*, pp. 367–68.

14. James A. Field, Jr., *America and the Mediterranean World, 1776–1882* (Princeton: Princeton University Press, 1969), pp. 377–78.

15. Howell to John C. Watson, commanding the *Wyoming*, 6 March 1879, John C. Watson Papers, Library of Congress, Washington, D.C.; Le Roy to Secretary of the Navy, 16 January 1879, M89, roll 242; Howell to Secretary of the Navy, 14 February, 1 May, 8 August 1879, M89, roll 242; Heap to Secretary of State, 8 March 1879, M517, roll 42; Thompson to Secretary of State, 14 April 1879, M472, roll 16; Maynard to Secretary of State, 17 July 1879, M46, roll 35; Thomas O. Selfridge, Jr., *Memoirs of Thomas O. Selfridge, Jr.* (New York: G. P. Putnam's Sons, 1924), pp. 200–25; Field, *America and the Mediterranean World*, pp. 377–78.

16. Samuel S. Cox, *Diversions of a Diplomat in Turkey* (New York: C. L. Webster & Company, 1887), p. 154.

17. John H. Moore, "America Looks at Turkey, 1876–1909" (Ph.D. diss., University of Virginia, 1961), pp. 175–85.

18. Howell to Secretary of the Navy, 25 May 1880, M89, roll 243.

19. Albert Gleaves, *Life and Letters of Rear Admiral Stephen B. Luce, U.S. Navy* (New York: G. P. Putnam's Sons, 1925), p. 108.

20. Everts to Secretary of the Navy, 4 August 1880, John Hay to Secretary of the Navy, 30 August 1880, M517, roll 44; Howell to Secretary of the Navy, 19 August 1880, M89, roll 243; Thompson to Secretary of State, 31 August 1880, M472, roll 17; Hay to Maynard, 2 September 1880, M77, roll 164; C. M. Schoonmaker, commanding officer of the *Nipsic*, to Howell, 21 July 1880; to mother, 3, 4 September 1880, to father 10 September 1880, Charles M. Schoonmaker Papers, Library of Congress, Washington, D.C.; *Foreign Relations: 1880*, pp. 983–84.

21. Schoonmaker to Howell, 18 September; to mother, 19 September, 23 November, 5 December; to Harrison, 30 October; to father, 30 October; to sister, 22 November 1880; Schoonmaker Papers. *See also* Howell to Secretary of the Navy, 1 October 1880, M89, roll 243; Heap to Everts, 9 August, 15 September; Everts to Heap, 21 August; Hunter to Heap, 15 September 1880, *Foreign Relations: 1880*, pp. 986–88. Several years later when similar trouble in Turkey resulted in the dispatch of warships, the State Department sent an account of the "Parson incident" to President Grover Cleveland but concluded that it was questionable that the presence of the *Nipsic* pressured the Turkish government into a trial. Kennedy to Cleveland, 27 December 1895, reel 92, Grover Cleveland Papers, Library of Congress, Washington, D.C.

22. Fagan to Cochrane, 23 January 1877, Henry Clay Cochrane Papers, Marine Corps Museum, Washington Navy Yard, Washington, D.C. Commander Henry B. Robeson was in command of the *Vandalia*.

23. At least once a day the sultan travelled by caique to his mosque, and all foreign warships including American had to go through the irksome drill of manning the yards. For the engineers' incident *see* Farquhar, commanding officer of the *Quinnebaug*, to Maynard; 12 July 1879, M46, roll 35; Schroeder, *A Half Century*, p. 112.

24. Cox, *Diversions of a Diplomat in Turkey*, pp. 581–83.

25. Tilton to his wife, 1 February 1878, Tilton Papers. *See also* Fagan to Cochrane, n.d., Cochrane Papers; Franklin, *Memories*, p. 276.

26. Wallace to Blaine, 24 September, Blaine to Secretary of the Navy, 26 October 1881, M517, roll 45; Hunt to Secretary of State, 31 October 1881, M472, roll 17; Hunt to Nicholson, 31 October 1881, Letters to Flag Officers, Entry 16 RG45; Hunter to Wallace, 8 November 1881, M77, roll 164.

27. A. A. Adee to Olney, 2 August 1895, Richard Olney Papers, Library of Congress, Washington, D.C.; Irving McKee, *Ben-Hur Wallace* (Berkeley: University of California Press, 1947), pp. 210–11.

28. McKee, *Wallace*, p. 191. *See also* Chandler to Commanding Officer, European Squadron, 17 March 1884, Letters to Flag Officers, Entry 16 RG45; Wallace to Secretary of State, 8 April 1884, M517, roll 48; Baldwin to Secretary of the Navy, 23 April 1884, Records of the European Squadron, RG313. *See also* Frelinghuysen to Secretary of the Navy, 5 May 1884, M517, roll 48; Frelinghuysen to Wallace, 6 May 1884, M77, roll 165; Baldwin to Wallace, 11 April 1884, M46, roll 43; Cochrane to his sister, 11 May 1884, Cochrane Papers; *Army and Navy Journal*, 17 May 1884. The *Quinnebaug* had received permission to visit Constantinople in the spring of 1882, but the document misspelled the vessel's name. Admiral Nicholson refused to take her to the city until the mistake was corrected. The Turkish officials simply changed the document to read, "smaller ship." Cochrane *Diary*, entry for 9 March 1882, Cochrane Papers.

29. Charles Sperry to Mark Sperry, 3 March 1885, Charles Sperry Papers, Library of Congress, Washington, D.C.. *See also* Sperry to his wife, 23 February 1885, Sperry Papers; and English to Secretary of the Navy, 16 February 1885, M89, roll 245.

30. Charles Sperry to Mark Sperry, 21 April 1885, Sperry Papers; Lewis Wallace, *Lew Wallace: An Autobiography* (New York: Harper & Brothers, 1906), p. 971.

31. U.S. Bureau of the Census, *Historical Statistics of the United States: Colonial Times to 1957* (Washington, D.C.: Government Printing Office, 1960), pp. 550–57; Edward C. Kirkland, *Industry Comes of Age: Business, Labor and Public Policy, 1860–1897* (New York: Holt, Rinehart, and Winston, 1961), p. 282; Kenneth S. Latourette, *History of the Expansion of Christianity*, 7 vols. (New York: Harper & Brothers, 1937–45), 6:26.

32. G. H. Heap, consul, to Radford, 12 March 1870, William Radford Papers, Library of Congress, Washington, D.C.; Radford to Luce, 13 March 1870, Stephen B. Luce Papers, Library of Congress, Washington, D.C.; Gleaves, *Luce*, pp. 112–13; Fish to Secretary of the Navy, 14 March 1870, M517, roll 33; Robeson to Radford, 16 March 1870, Letters to Flag Officers, Entry 16 RG45; Luce to Radford, 21 April 1870, Luce Papers; Radford to Secretary of the Navy, 22 April 1870, M89, roll 230.

33. Alden to Secretary of the navy, 3 May 1872, M89, roll 235; Fish to Secretary of the Navy, 3 May 1872, M517, roll 36; *Foreign Relations: 1872*, Pt. II, pp. 1136–37.

34. For accounts of Vidal's diplomatic activities *see* Field, *America and the Mediterranean World*, pp. 339–42; Edwin A. Falk, *Fighting Bob Evans* (New York: Jonathan Cape & Harrison Smith, 1931), pp. 118–25. Evans was executive officer of the *Congress*.

35. Falk, *Evans*, p. 118.

36. Acting Secretary of State to Secretary of the Navy, 10 August 1875, M517, roll 38; Falk, *Evans*, pp. 119–20.

37. Callader to Secretary of the Navy, 17 August 1875, M517, roll 38.

38. Ibid., 29 August 1875.

39. Falk, *Evans*, pp. 123–24; Rohley Evans, *A Sailor's Log* (New York: D. Appleton & Co., 1902), pp. 203–4; J. Arthur to English, 18 August 1875, M89, roll 238. Vidal was clearly persona non grata but was not recalled for nearly a year. Fish *Diary*, entry 20 April 1875; Maynard to Secretary of State, 21 March 1876, M46, roll 30; Fish to Vidal, 22 April 1876, M77, roll 18.

40. Maynard to Secretary of State, 16 August 1875, M46, roll 28.

41. Graham H. Stuart, *The International City of Tangier* (Stanford: Stanford University Press, 1955), p. 39; Latourette, *History of the Expansion of Christianity*, 6:9.

42. Stuart, *The International City of Tangier*, pp. 19–20.

43. Luella J. Hall, *The United States and Morocco, 1776–1956* (Metuchen, N.J.: The Scarecrow Press, 1971), pp. 271–72. *See also* ibid., pp. 205–11, and Earl F. Cruickshank, *Morocco at the Parting of the Ways: The Story of Native Protection to 1885* (Philadelphia: University of Pennsylvania Press, 1935), p. 168.

44. Field, *America and the Mediterranean World*, p. 388; Latourette, *History of the Expansion of Christianity*, 6:26.

45. Silas Casey, commanding the *Wyoming*, to Howell, 21 April 1880, Silas Casey Papers, Library of Congress, Washington, D.C.; Field, *America and the Mediterranean World*, pp. 384–85.

46. Hunt to Nicholson, 25 November 1881, Letters to Flag Officers, RG45; Blaine to Hunt, 22 November 1881, M517, roll 45.

47. Nicholson had received the European command by default. It had been offered to Rear Admiral Donald M. Fairfax, but he turned it down for personal reasons. As no other rear admiral was available, Nicholson as senior commodore was offered the command and promoted to rear admiral. *New York Times*, 11 August 1881.

48. Caspar F. Goodrich, *Rope Yarns from the Old Navy* (New York: The Navy History Society, 1921), pp. 112–13; Robert E. Johnson, "A Cruise in the *U.S.S. Lancaster*," *The American Neptune* 33 (Fall 1973): 280–93; *Army and Navy Journal*, 28 September 1912.

49. For one officer's impressions *see* the diary of Lieutenant Cochrane, Cochrane Papers. Goodrich, who was on the *Lancaster* for the entire tour, says nothing in his memoirs about Nicholson. He does laud Gheradi and mentions that the ship was a happy one. *Rope Yarns*, pp. 112–16. *See also* Schaeffer, *Selected Essays*, pp. 161–62.

50. To Secretary of the Navy, Records of the European Squadron, RG313.

51. Whitehead to Watson, 22 July 1882, Watson Papers. *See also* Goodrich, *Rope Yarns*, pp. 118–19, and Henry H. Jessup, *Fifty-Three Years in Syria*, 2 vols. (New York: Fleming H. Revell, 1910), 2:472. Jessup, an American missionary, was on his way to the United States when caught in the maelstrom at Alexandria. Cochrane recorded in his diary on 10 July, "about 5 P.M. Mr. N. D. Cormanos, U.S. consul general at Cairo, came on board. . . . Neither the Admiral nor Captain invited him to eat or sleep, and at 9:30 at night I received word that he was hungry. Gave him a glass of wine and cold lunch and pay[master] Williams gave him his berth. *This is a most disgraceful Incident.*"

52. Elbert E. Farman, *Egypt and Its Betrayal* (New York: The Grafton Press, 1908), pp. 308–9.

53. Charles Chaille-Long, *My Life on Four Continents* (London: Hutchinson and Company, 1912), pp. 248–49; Nicholson to Secretary of the Navy, 5 July 1882, Records of the European Squadron, RG313. For the account by General Charles P. Stone, chief of the Egyptian General Staff, *see* letter of 4 April 1884, in the *Century Magazine* 28 (1884): 288–302. *See also* letter from Stone to General William T. Sherman, 30 October 1882, in the William T. Sherman Papers, Library of Congress, Washington, D.C. *See also* the *New York Times*, 11, 14, 16, 18, 20, 22, 25, 28 July 1882.

54. Field, *America and the Mediterranean World*, pp. 430–31; Lenoir Wright, *United States Policy Toward Egypt, 1830–1914* (New York: Exposition Press, 1969), pp. 117, 123–24.

55. *See* Cochrane diary, entry for 10 July 1882, Cochrane Papers; Charles Chaille-Long, "The Burning of Alexandria . . .", Washington *Evening Star*, 2 June 1907.

56. Cochrane diary, entry 12 July 1882, Cochrane Papers; Nicholson to the Secretary of the Navy, 14 July 1882, Records of the European Squadron, RG313.

57. Samuel S. de Kusel, *An Englishman's Recollections of Egypt, 1863–1887* (London: John Lane, 1915), p. 208. *See also* Wright, *United States Policy Toward Egypt*, p. 128.

58. Nicholson to Secretary of the Navy, 15 July 1882, Records of the European Squadron, RG313; Chaille-Long, *My Life on Four Continents*, p. 261, and idem, *Three Prophets: Chinese Gordon, Mohammed Ahmed (the Maahdi), Arabi-Pasha—Events before and after the Bombardment of Alexandria* (New York: D. Appleton & Company, 1884), pp. 180–81.

59. Cochrane diary, entry 15 July 1882, Cochrane Papers. For Goodrich's account *see Rope Yarns*, pp. 119–21. *See also* the diary of Albert Gleaves, who was a midshipman on the *Nipsic*, entries for 14–16 July 1882, Albert Gleaves Papers, Library of Congress, Washington, D.C.; *New York Herald*, 16 July 1882; U.S., Congress, House, "Report of the British Naval and Military Operations in Egypt," *Congressional Record*, 48th Cong., 2d sess., 1884–85, 48, House Misc. Document No. 29. Goodrich's official report is printed here. Robert D. Heinl, Jr., *Soldiers of the Sea* (Annapolis: United States Naval Institute, 1962), credits Cochrane with the command, but Goodrich was in overall command (see pages 91–93).

60. Chaillé-Long's diary, quoted in *Three Prophets*, pp. 185–86.

61. Heinl in *Soldiers of the Sea*, p. 92, writes that when news was received that an Egyptian relieving force was marching on the city, "French and Italian landing forces prudently reembarked. Not so Cochrane who announced that the Americans would 'stick by the British and take their chances.' " Cochrane's alleged statement is probably based on an article in Colburn's *United Service Magazine* for September 1882, but there is no supportive evidence. In fact, Admiral Nicholson decided to withdraw the landing force, leaving twenty-five men ashore to guard the American consulate.

62. Cormick to Chandler, 22 July 1882, in William Chandler Papers, Library of Congress, Washington, D.C. For the controversy *see* Charles M. Remey, ed., "Life and Letters of Rear Admiral George Collier Remey, U.S.N., 1841–1920," 10 vols. (typescript copy in the Library of Congress), 5, n.p.; *New York Herald*, 17 July 1882; *New York Times*, 22, 25, 28 July 1882; U.S., Congress, Senate, *Congressional Record*, 47th Cong. 1st sess., 1882, 47, pt. 2, p. 6146; *Foreign Relations: 1882*, p. 325. Lord Charles Beresford, in charge of the British forces landed to occupy the city, says nothing in his memoirs about the presence of the American force, other than that it was there. *The Memoirs of Admiral Lord Charles Beresford*, 2 vols. (London: Methuen & Company, Ltd., 1914), 1: 195.

63. Frelinghuysen to Secretary of the Navy, 15, 28 June, 2, 3 August 1882, M517, roll 46; Secretary of the Navy to Frelinghuysen, 19 June 1882, M472, roll 17.

64. *See*, for example, Frelinghuysen to Secretary of the Navy, 5 June, 18 September 1883, M517, roll 47; Felix Mathews, consul at Tangier, to Rear Admiral Earl English, 16 February 1885; English to Secretary of the Navy, 20 February 1885; Franklin to Secretary of the Navy, 22 June 1885, Letters to Flag Officers, Entry 16 RG45; Secretary of State to Secretary of the Navy, 11 March 1885, M517, roll 49; Secretary of State to Secretary of the Navy, 6 October 1887, M625, roll 21. Bowman McCalla in his memoirs mentions that while in command of the *Enterprise* in 1885, he was ordered to Tangier because of a dispute between the American consul and local officials over protection. McCalla said that he was instrumental in bringing about a negotiated settlement.

65. Goodrich, *Rope Yarns*, p. 128; Cochrane diary, entry for 10 March 1883, Cochrane Papers.

66. English to Chandler, 4 January, 28 July 1884, Chandler Papers; Evans, *A Sailor's Log*, p. 145; Earl English folder, ZB file, Office of Naval History, U.S. Navy Department, Washington, D.C.

67. Chandler to English, 2 December 1884, Letters to Flag Officers, Entry 16 RG45.

68. Quoted in Milton Plesur, *America's Outward Thrust: Approaches to Foreign Affairs, 1865–1890* (DeKalb: Northern Illinois University Press, 1971), p. 23. For an interesting account of the navy in the Congo region *see* Kenneth J. Hagen, *American Gunboat Diplomacy and the Old Navy, 1877–1889* (Westport, Conn.: Greenwood Press, 1970), pp. 59–77. *See also* William A. Williams, *The Roots of the Modern American Empire* (New York: Random House, Inc., 1969), pp. 261–63, and Walter LaFeber, *The New Empire: An Interpretation of American Expansion, 1860–1898* (Ithaca: Cornell University Press, 1963), pp. 52–53.

69. Edward Younger, *John A. Kasson: Politics and Diplomacy from Lincoln to McKinley* (Iowa City: University of Iowa Press, 1955), pp. 334–35.

70. Hagan, *American Gunboat Diplomacy*, pp. 76–77; Younger, *Kasson*, p. 336.

71. Dewey to Worthington, George Dewey Papers, New York Historical Society, New York

City. Dewey kept a diary of the cruise but records only such trivia as the weather and what he did. George Dewey Papers, Library of Congress, Washington, D.C. *See also* David Healy, *U.S. Expansionism: The Imperialist Urge in the 1890s* (Madison: the University of Wisconsin Press, 1963), p. 112.

72. *New York Times*, 18 June, 31 March, 19 November 1889.

73. George Dewey, *Autobiography of George Dewey: Admiral of the Navy* (New York: Charles Scribner's Sons, 1913), pp. 158–59; Hagan, *American Gunboat Diplomacy*, pp. 37–38, 52–55; Clayton R. Barrow, Jr., ed., *America Spreads Her Sails* (Annapolis: United States Naval Institute Press, 1973), pp. 160–61; U.S., Congress, Senate, *Congressional Record*, 48th Cong., 1st sess., 1884–85, 48, Report Number 161, p. 21.

CHAPTER 6

1. Robert Seager II, "Ten Years Before Mahan: The Unofficial Case for the New Navy, 1880–1890," *Mississippi Valley Historical Review* 40 (December 1953): 491–512; Kenneth E. Davidson, *The Presidency of Rutherford B. Hayes* (Westport, Conn.: Greenwood Press, 1972), p. 199.

2. Tracy to Walker, 29 December 1889, M625, roll 23; Walker to Tracy, 28 April, 30 May 1890; Tracy to Walker, 5 May 1890, Records of the Squadron of Evolution, entry 30, RG313. A very interesting account of the ABCD ships, including photographs, is found in John D. Alden, *The American Steel Navy* (Annapolis: United States Naval Institute, 1972), pp. 13–23. For an account of the squadron leaving the United States *see* Francis P. Thomas, *Career of John Grimes Walker, USN* (Boston: privately printed, 1959), pp. 64–66. There are two recent published scholarly studies of Tracy: Walter R. Herrick, Jr., *The American Naval Revolution* (Baton Rouge: Louisiana State University Press, 1966); and Benjamin Franklin Cooling, *Benjamin Franklin Tracy: Father of the Modern American Navy* (Hamden, Conn.: Archon Books, 1973).

3. Thomas, *Walker*, pp. 65–66. *See also* Walker to Tracy, 18 February 1890, Records of the Squadron of Evolution, RG313.

4. Winfield Scott Schley, *Forty-Five Years under the Flag* (New York: D. Appleton and Company, 1904), pp. 198–210.

5. Rear Admiral Andrew Benham to Tracy, 22 December 1892, M625, roll 25; Adee to Olney, 19 November 1895, Richard Olney Papers, Library of Congress, Washington, D.C.; *Papers Relating to the Foreign Relations of the United States: 1892* (Washington, D.C.: Government Printing Office, 1893), p. 609. General John A. Lejeune, later commandant of the Marine Corps and a young officer on the *Bennington* when she went to the Mediterranean in 1892, described the cruise in his memoirs. Major General John A. Lejeune, *Reminiscences of a Marine* (Philadelphia: Dorrance and Company, 1930), pp. 105–109. *See also* Herbert W. Bowen, *Recollections Diplomatic and Undiplomatic* (New York: Frederick H. Hitchcock, 1926), pp. 166–171.

6. For Herbert's administration *see* Hugh B. Hammett, *Hilary Abner Herbert: A Southerner Returns to the Union* (Philadelphia: The American Philosophical Society, 1976). According to Hammett, Herbert was not a territorial imperialist, but an "open door" imperialist. Herbert was appointed by Cleveland and became secretary in March 1893.

7. Walter LaFeber, *The New Empire: An Interpretation of American Expansion, 1860–1898* (Ithaca: Cornell University Press, 1963), pp. 151, 186; Mira Wilkins, *The Emergence of Multinational Enterprise: American Business Abroad from the Colonial Era to 1914* (Cambridge: Harvard University Press, 1970), pp. 70–71. As the Cleveland administration took control in 1893, agricultural exports, which consisted of three-fourths of all exports, had increased some 25 percent during the first two years of the 1890s, from $569,052,031 in 1890 to $754,489,843 in 1892. *See* U.S. Bureau of Statistics, *Foreign Commerce and Navigation for the Year Ending 1894* (Washington, D.C.: Government Printing Office, 1895), xxxiv–xxxv.

8. Bowen, *Recollections Diplomatic and Undiplomatic*, p. 185; Erban to Secretary of the Navy, 11 April 1894; Herbert to Erban, 20 May 1893, Henry Erban Papers, New York Historical Society, New York City; *New York Times*, 5 August 1893; *Foreign Relations: 1893*, p. 634.

9. Charles M. Remey, ed., "Life and Letters of Rear Admiral George Collier Remey, U.S.N., 1841–1920," 10 vols. (typescript copy in the Library of Congress), 6: n.p.; John M. Elliott, "Three Navy Cranks and What They Turned," *United States Naval Institute Proceedings* 49 (October 1924): 1625; Elliott, "With Erban and Mahan on the *Chicago*," *United States Naval Institute Proceedings* 62 (September 1941): 1234–40; Bowen, *Recollections Diplomatic and Undiplomatic*, pp. 180–81; Richard S. West, Jr., *Admirals of American Empire* (Indianapolis: The Bobbs-Merrill Company, 1938), p. 150; *New York Times*, 15 June 1893.

10. Mahan to his wife, 6 September 1893, Alfred T. Mahan Papers, Library of Congress, Washington, D.C.

11. Elliott, "Three Navy Cranks," p. 1623; Bowen, *Recollections Diplomatic and Undiplomatic*, p. 184.

12. A copy of the report is in the Mahan Papers. *See also* copy of letter dated 25 January 1894 demanding a court of inquiry. For details of the fitness report *see* William D. Puleston, *Life and Work of Captain Alfred A. Mahan* (London: Jonathan Cape, 1939), pp. 153–55. For Erban's letter of 11 November 1893 criticizing him, *see* the Erban Papers.

13. Quoted in a somewhat disrespectful manner from Mahan to Erban 19 February 1894, Erban Papers.

14. There is considerable correspondence concerning this problem in *Foreign Relations: 1893. See* under heading Turkey. *See also* Moore, *A Digest of International Law*, 8 vols. (Washington, D.C.: Government Printing Office, 1906), 3:679–711.

15. Bowen, *Recollections Diplomatic and Undiplomatic*, p. 225. *See also* Uhl to Secretary of the Navy, 29 November 1893; Terrell to Secretary of State, 21 December 1893, M625, roll 26; Terrell to Secretary of State, 29 January 1894, M46, roll 55.

16. 6 February 1894, M46, roll 55; Terrell to Erban, 5 February 1894, Erban Papers.

17. Erban to Secretary of the Navy, M625, roll 27; Erban to Terrell, 7 February 1894, Erban Papers; Gresham to Terrell, 12 February 1894, M77, roll 166.

18. Erban to Terrell, 19 March 1894, Records of the European Squadron, RG313; *Foreign Relations: 1894*, pp. 773–74.

19. *New York Times*, 20 July 1894.

20. Mahan to his wife, 6, 13 September 1894, Mahan Papers.

21. Charles H. Davis, *Life of Charles Henry Davis: Rear Admiral* (New York: Houghton Mifflin Company, 1899), pp. 321–22. Kirkland married the daughter of a prominent merchant in Montevideo, Uruguay. S. R. Franklin, *Memories of a Rear Admiral* (New York: Harper Brothers, 1898), p. 157.

22. Alexander Kirkland to Donald Lennon, 12 December 1973, William A. Kirkland Papers, East Carolina University Library, Greenville, N.C.; Yates Sterling, Jr., *Sea Duty: The Memoirs of a Fighting Admiral* (New York: G. P. Putnam's Sons, 1939), pp. 35–36; Mahan to his wife, 29 August 1894, Mahan Papers.

23. Memorandum dated 1 September 1894 and Kirkland letter to Secretary of the Navy dated 28 February, in Records of the European Squadron, RG313. Two different drafts of Kirkland's fitness report on Mahan are in the Kirkland Papers.

24. 29 December 1894. *See also* Gresham to Terrell, 15 December 1894, M77, roll 167.

25. Gibson to Terrell, 19 March 1895, Terrell to Secretary of State, 29 March 1895, M46, roll 59. Idem to Captain Charles O'Neil, 9 April 1895, Charles O'Neil Papers, Library of Congress, Washington, D.C.

26. For background to the Armenian massacres *see* M. S. Anderson, *The Eastern Question, 1774–1923* (New York: St. Martin's Press, 1966); William L. Langer, *The Diplomacy of Imperialism* (New York: Alfred A. Knopf, 1968); and Avedis K. Sanjian, *The American Communities in Syria under Ottoman Dominion* (Cambridge: Harvard University Press, 1965).

27. Langer, *The Diplomacy of Imperialism*, pp. 195–203.

28. L. Barlett to Judson Smith, 19 February 1895, American Board of Commissioners for Foreign Missions Archives, Houghton Library, Harvard University, hereafter cited as the ABC papers.

29. Erban's report does not mention a naval station at Smyrna nor at any other point in the Near East. More than likely the admiral was simply being agreeable, with no idea of carrying it beyond the conversation.

30. Gresham to Secretary of the Navy, 30 March 1895, Domestic Letters of the Department of State, 1784–1906, M40, roll 125. *See also* Uhl to Terrell, 8 April 1895, M77, roll 167, and the *New York Herald*, 5 April 1895.

31. Paul A. Varg, *Missionaries, Chinese, and Diplomats* (Princeton: Princeton University Press, 1958), pp. 52–54.

32. Lloyd C. Griscom, *Diplomatically Speaking* (Boston: Little, Brown and Company, 1940), p. 134. The best study on American missionaries in Turkey is John Grabill, *Protestant Diplomacy and the Near East: Missionary Influence on American Policy, 1810–1927* (Minneapolis: University of Minnesota Press, 1971), pp. 52–54. *See also* Rosaline de G. Edwards, "Relations Between the United States and Turkey, 1893–1897" (Ph.D. diss., Fordham University, 1952); George P. McDonough, "American Relations with Turkey, 1893–1901" (Ph.D. diss., Georgetown University, 1949); and John H. Moore, "America Looks at Turkey 1876–1909" (Ph.D. diss., University of Virginia, 1961). A recent study by Eugene W. Goll, "The Diplomacy of Walter Q. Gresham, Secretary of State, 1893–1895" (Ph.D. diss., The Pennsylvania State University, 1964), emphasizes the role of missionary diplomacy in the 1890s. He points out the embarrassment American officials were under "by the double standards that the United States practiced, for example, demanding admission of Americans to other nations while imposing immigration restrictions on orientals."

33. Description of an interview by the Reverend Joseph Greene, a missionary to Turkey, with Assistant Secretary of State Adee and Secretary Gresham, 29 March 1895, in a letter to Judson Smith, ABC Papers. *Foreign Relations: 1895*, pp. 1240–41; Uhl to Secretary of the Navy, 4 April 1895, M625, roll 28.

34. Von Radolin to Prince Von Hohenlohe, 17 April 1895, *German Diplomatic Documents, 1871–1914*, 4 vols., ed. E. T. S. Dugdale (New York: Barnes & Noble, Inc., 1969 reprint), 2:227–28.

35. Ralph E. Cook, "The United States and the Armenian Question, 1894–1924" (Ph.D. diss., Fletcher School of Diplomacy, 1957), p. 74. For the correspondence between Mavroyani Bey and the State Department *see Foreign Relations: 1895*, pp. 1248–51.

36. Bartlett to Smith, 10 June 1895, ABC Papers.

37. Frederick J. Bell, *Room to Swing a Cat* (New York: Longmans, Green and Company, 1938), pp. 237–240.

38. Gibson to State Department, 30 April 1895, copy in Kirkland Papers.

39. Kirkland to Herbert, 17 April 1895, M625, roll 28.

40. This manuscript, which O'Neil apparently wrote for publication, is in the O'Neil Papers and seems never to have been published.

41. 17 April 1895, FO 195, Turkey Embassy and Consular Archives. For O'Neil's report to Kirkland *see* 15 April 1895, M625, roll 28.

42. 29 April 1895, ABC Papers.

43. L. Bartlett to Judson Smith, 10 June 1895, ABC Papers. O'Neil made a more favorable impression.

44. *New York Times*, 18, 21 August 1895. *See* several letters in the *Boston Transcript*, 20 May 1895. *See also* the *New York Herald*, 22 August 1895, and the *New York Daily Tribune*, 12 October 1895.

45. Copies of Herbert's letter and Kirkland's reply are in the Kirkland Papers. *See also* the *Army and Navy Journal*, 21 September 1895. Terrell was also quite critical of the missionaries in his communications to the Department of State. *See* Goll, "Gresham," pp. 195–96.

46. Good accounts of the Kiel ceremonies can be found in Robley Evans, *A Sailor's Log* (New York: D. Appleton & Company, 1902), pp. 366–88; Edwin A. Falk, *Fighting Bob Evans* (New York: Jonathan Cape & Harrison Smith, 1931), pp. 197–209; Holden A. Evans, *One Man's Fight for a Better Navy* (New York: Dodd, Mead & Company, 1940), pp. 66–72; account in the O'Neil Papers, n.d. *See also* Kirkland to the Secretary of the Navy, 22 March, 6, 25, 27 May, 1, 7, 22 June 1895, M625, roll 28; Kirkland to Mahan, 4 April 1895, Mahan Papers.

47. A British officer mentioned in his memoirs that as the emperor left the *New York* the captain said: "Say, Emperor, next time you come on board my ship, I hope you'll give me time to button my trousers." Sir Charles Dundas, *An Admiral's Yarns* (London: Herbert Jenkins, Ltd., 1922), pp. 207–8. The *New York's* captain was Bob Evans, who does not mention the incident in his memoirs.

48. General order of Admiral Kirkland, 15 June 1895, Records of the European Squadron, RG313.

49. The Crown Prince presented Kirkland with a gold snuff box adorned with twenty-six diamonds surrounding a miniature of himself. Later the diamonds were divided among Kirkland's children and replaced by paste replicas. The snuff box was stolen in a house robbery. Letter from Alexander Kirkland to Don Lennon, 2 December 1973, Kirkland Papers. For Secretary of the Navy Herbert's approval of accepting the gift *see* letter dated 11 July 1895, Kirkland Papers.

50. Gresham died in May 1895, and Richard Olney was appointed in his place. For a recent excellent study *see* Gerald G. Eggert, *Richard Olney: Evolution of a Statesman* (University Park: The Pennsylvania State University Press, 1974).

51. Actually the arrests were made before the *Marblehead* sailed.

52. Adee to Secretary of the Navy, 10, 21, 22 August 1895, M40, roll 127; to Terrell, 12, 13 August 1895, M77, roll 167; Kirkland to O'Neil, 15 August 1895, M625, roll 29; Adee to Olney, 22 August 1895, Richard Olney Papers, Library of Congress, Washington D.C.; *New York Herald*, 11, 12 August 1895; Mavroyeni Bey to Secretary of State, 15, 24 August 1895, T815.

53. Christie to Gibson, 18 September; Gibson to Terrell, 19 September 1895, M46, roll 59.

54. For the European powers and the Armenian crisis *see* Langer, *Diplomacy of Imperialism*; Kenneth Bourne, *The Foreign Policy of Victorian England, 1830–1902* (New York: Oxford University Press, 1970), pp. 155–59; Cedric J. Lowe, *Salisbury and the Mediterranean, 1886–1896* (London: Routledge & K. Paul, 1965), pp. 98–100; idem, *The Reluctant Imperialist; British Foreign Policy, 1878–1902* (New York: Macmillan, 1969), pp. 196–203; Robert R. James, *Rosebery: A Biography of Archibald Philip, Fifth Earl of Rosebery* (New York: Macmillan, 1964), pp. 376–77; Paul J. Rolo, *Entente Cordiale: The Origin and Negotiations of the Anglo-French Agreement of 8 April 1904* (New York: St. Martin's Press, 1969), pp. 64–65; Anderson, *The Eastern Question*, pp. 255–59; J. A. S. Grenville, *Lord Salisbury and Foreign Policy: The Close of the Nineteenth Century* (London: Athlone Press, 1964), pp. 28–31, 44–47; Arthur J. Marder, *The Anatomy of British Seapower: A History of British Naval Policy in the Pre-Dreadnought Era, 1880–1905* (New York: Alfred A. Knopf, Inc., 1940), pp. 229–31, 241–51.

55. Terrell to Secretary of State, 8, 10 October, Olney to Terrell, 11 October 1895, M46, roll 59; *Foreign Relations: 1895*, pp. 1322–23; Resolution of the Evangelical Alliance of Boston, 1 October 1895, T815, roll 8; McAdoo to Kirkland, 11 October 1895, entry 19, Ciphers Sent, RG45.

56. O'Neil manuscript, n.d., O'Neil Papers; O'Neil diary, entry for 21 October 1895, O'Neil Papers; O'Neil to the governor of Mersin, 21 October 1895, O'Neil Papers; *Foreign Relations: 1895*, pp. 1352–54.

57. Emily Montgomery to O'Neil, 13 December 1895, O'Neil Papers; *Foreign Relations: 1895*, pp. 1288–89. There are several letters from missionaries to Judson Smith complimentary to O'Neil in M625, roll 30. For O'Neil and the *Marblehead's* activities during this month *see* copies of missionary letters, diaries, and the like in the O'Neil Papers. *See* especially Montgomery to O'Neil, 5 November; O'Neil to Vali of Adena, 1 November 1895, O'Neil Papers; and Webb to Montgomery, 29 October 1895, copy in O'Neil Papers.

58. *New York Times*, 22 October 1895; *New York Daily Tribune*, 22 October, 18 November 1895; *Army and Navy Journal*, 18 October 1895; Secretary of the Navy to Kirkland, 23 October 1895, M625, roll 29.

59. Kirkland letter to Mahan in the Mahan Papers. *See also* the *Army and Navy Journal*, 14 September 1895. For correspondence between Kirkland and Herbert concerning this controversy *see* the Kirkland Papers.

60. *New York Daily Tribune*, 2 October 1889; *Army and Navy Journal*, 5 October 1895.

61. *Army and Navy Journal*, 26 October 1895. For the memo *see* M625, roll 29.

CHAPTER 7

1. Selfridge received the command because no rear admirals were available and he was first in line for promotion to that rank.

2. Although the naval academy was founded in 1845, until the 1851 class the practice was to spend one year there and the remainder at sea. The class of 1851 was the first to remain at the academy for more than a year. Selfridge was confirmed as a rear admiral in January 1896.

3. William Keeler to his wife, 28 December 1862, Robert W. Daly, ed., *Aboard the USS Monitor: 1862: The Letters of Acting Paymaster William Frederick Keeler, U.S. Navy to His Wife Anna* (Annapolis: United States, Naval Institute, 1964), p. 252. For his early service *see* Edwin C. Bearss, *Hardluck Ironclad: The Sinking and Salvage of the Cairo* (Baton Rouge, Louisiana State University Press, 1966), pp. 80–81, *passim*; and Thomas O. Selfridge, Jr., *Memoirs of Thomas O. Selfridge, Jr.* (New York: G. P. Putnam's Sons, 1924).

4. Scattered through the flagships' letterbooks in Records of the European Squadron, RG313, are numerous examples of Selfridge's correspondence concerning his penchant for regulation and the like.

5. Herbert to Selfridge, 30 October 1895, M625, roll 229. Selfridge ignores the Turkish problem in his *Memoirs*. There is only one paragraph (mostly describing the unpleasantness of Smyrna) concerning the period from November 1895 through April 1896. *Memoirs*, pp. 251–52.

6. Lord Salisbury Papers, Christchurch College, Oxford, England.

7. Terrell to Cleveland, 2 July 1895, Grover Cleveland Papers, Library of Congress microfilm edition, Series II, roll 90, Washington, D.C.; Terrell to Olney, 27 October 1895, Richard Olney Papers, Library of Congress, Washington, D.C.

8. Ernest R. May, *Imperial Democracy: The Emergence of America as a Great Power* (New York: Harcourt, Brace & World, 1961), is the only study that includes a thorough examination of the Turkish crisis in the context of the Venezuelan and Cuban problems. Eggert in his study of Olney does recognize the relationship. None of the standard studies of the American navy in the 1890s recognizes its importance. *See* Walter Herrick, *American Naval Revolution* (Baton Rouge: Louisiana State University Press, 1966), and George T. Davis, *A Navy Second to None: The Development of Modern Naval Policy* (New York: Harcourt, Brace and Company, 1940), for example.

9. There is considerable correspondence in roll 92 of the Cleveland papers. *See also* Washburn to Kennedy, 16 December 1895; McClaughan to Kennedy, 5 November 1895; Kennedy to Cleveland, 18 November 1895, in the Cleveland Papers, roll 91. Kennedy offered to send his yacht to Constantinople to provide a place of refuge, but the missionaries insisted on a naval vessel. Washburn to Kennedy, 10 December 1895, copy in the Cleveland Papers, roll 91. *See also* Olney to Hamlin, 3 December 1895, M40, roll 128.

10. Memorandum of a conversation with the French ambassador, 9 November 1895, M46, roll 59.

11. Terrell to Secretary of State, 24, 27, 30 November; to Adee, 1, December 1895, M46, roll 59.

12. Terrell to Olney, 16 December 1895, 2 January 1896, M46, roll 59; *Papers Relating to*

the *Foreign Relations of the United States: 1895* (Washington, D.C.: Government Printing Office, 1866–1917), p. 1422; *New York Herald*, 20 December 1895.

13. Selfridge to Secretary of the Navy, 25, 30 November, 10, 19, 20 December 1895, Records of the European Squadron, RG313.

14. *Army and Navy Journal*, 2 November 1895; *New York Times*, 15 November 1895. *See* the penciled note of Adee attached to clipping of the above article in T815, roll 8. *See also* Terrell to Olney, 7 November 1895, M46, roll 59; Dwight to Smith, 22 November 1895, ABC Papers.

15. Olney to Cleveland, 20 November 1895, Cleveland Papers, roll 91; Terrell to Selfridge, 20, 21 November 1895, M625, roll 29; *Foreign Relations: 1895*, pp. 1344–45, 1380–83; Dwight to Terrell, 22 November 1895, Terrell to Olney, 4 December 1895 (includes the petition), M46, roll 60; Dwight to Smith, 22 November 1895, ABC Papers.

16. James D. Richardson, ed., *A Compilation of the Messages and Papers of the Presidents, 1789–1908*, 11 vols. (Washington, D.C.: Bureau of National Literature and Art, 1909), 9: 637–38.

17. *Foreign Relations: 1896*, pp. 1439–41; Terrell to Olney, 11 January 1896, M46, roll 60; Olney to Secretary of the Navy, 28 January 1896, M40, roll 128; Olney to Terrell, 24 January, 6 February 1896, M77, roll 167.

18. Olney to Secretary of the Navy, 9 December; to the president of the Stanford Manufacturing Company, 26 December 1895, M40, roll 128; Boutelle to Olney, 21 November 1895, Olney Papers; Olney to Boutelle, 23 November 1895, M40, roll 128; Robert L. Beisner, *Twelve Against Empire: The Anti-Imperialists, 1898–1900* (New York: McGraw-Hill Book Company, 1971), p. 146; Frederick H. Gillett, *George Frisbie Hoar* (Boston: Houghton Mifflin Company, 1934), p. 270; J.A.S. Grenville and George Young, *Politics, Strategy, and American Diplomacy: Studies in Foreign Policy, 1875–1917* (New Haven: Yale University Press, 1966), p. 223; Herbert to Selfridge, 11 December 1895, Entry 19, Ciphers Sent, RG45; Olney to Terrell, 13 December 1895; M77, roll 167; Cirre to Salisbury, 24 March 1896, FO195/1915.

19. Merli Curti, *American Philanthropy Abroad: A History* (New Brunswick: Rutgers University Press, 1963), pp. 131–32.

20. Herbert to Selfridge, 19 December 1895, Entry 19, Ciphers Sent, RG45; Selfridge to Secretary of the Navy, 21 December 1895, M625, roll 29; *New York Herald*, 20, 23 December 1895. Judson Smith had urged the landing of Marines. Selfridge to Olney, 3 December 1895, M40, roll 128.

21. 24 December 1895, Salisbury Papers; Earnest R. May, *Imperial Democracy* (New York: Harcourt, Brace & World, 1961), pp. 53–54.

22. Chamberlain to Goschen, 19 December 1895, Salisbury Papers.

23. 23 December 1895, Thomas Bayard Papers, Library of Congress, Washington, D.C.; Playfield to Bayard, 13 January 1896, Bayard Papers.

24. 11 January 1896. For newspaper articles *see* the *New York Herald*, 6, 7, 9, 12 January 1896; *New York Times*, 7, 13 January 1896; London *Times*, 6, 7 January 1896.

25. *Army and Navy Journal*, 11 January 1896; *New York Herald*, 7, 12 January 1896; *New York Times*, 13 January 1896; the *Nation* 62 (January, 1896): 88.

26. Selfridge to the Secretary of the Navy, 23 December 1895, Records of the European Squadron, RG313; Secretary of the Navy to Bunce, 21 December 1895; Bunce to commanding officers of vessels, 2 January 1896; Bunce to Lieutenant Fuller, 5 January 1896, Records of the North Atlantic Squadron, RG313. There is no evidence that the administration (including the secretary of the navy) considered the enormous logistical problems in maintaining a large naval force under wartime conditions in the eastern Mediterranean. The European Squadron purchased its coal in various ports from local companies. This supply would have been curtailed or cut off. Colliers could have been used, but the navy had not used them extensively at that time. Selfridge refused to contract for a coal lighter. Finally, there was the lack of a naval base. Gibraltar probably could have been used, but it was nearly 1500 miles from the eastern Mediterranean.

Secretary of the Navy Herbert is strangely silent on the Turkish situation in his unpublished memoirs. He concentrates on the Venezuelan crisis.

27. *Army and Navy Journal*, 8 February 1896.

28. May, *Imperial Democracy*, pp. 60–61, 74; Horace S. Merrill, *Bourbon Leader: Glover Cleveland and the Democratic Party* (Boston: Little, Brown, and Company, 1957), pp. 202–3; Gerald G. Eggert, *Richard Olney: Evolution of a Statesman* (University Park: The Pennsylvania State University Press, 1974), p. 242; Richard Hofstader, *The Paranoid Style in American Politics, and Other Essays* (New York: Knopf, 1966), p. 154; Grenville, *Politics, Strategy and American Diplomacy*, p. 162.

29. A memo dated 18 December 1897, attached to a letter from Angell to Sherman, M46, roll 64; minutes of a conversation, 23 January 1896, Olney Papers.

30. U.S., Congress, Senate, *Congressional Record*, 54th Cong., 1st sess., 1896, 54, Pt. I, pp. 144–145, 854–855, 959, 962–963, 1000–1002, 1007; Pt. II, pp. 1011, 1014–1016.

31. The *Nation* 52 (22 February 1896): 140; London *Times*, 27, 29 January, 4 February 1896; *New York Herald*, 28 January 1896; Hannotaux to Nelidov, 12 October 1896, Ministere des Affaires Etrangeres, *Documents diplomatiques Francais 1871–1914*, 41 vols., in various series (Paris: Imprimerie nationale, 1929–59), Ser. I:12.

32. Baynard to Cleveland, 28 January 1896, Cleveland Papers, roll 92. *See also* Tallmadge to Cleveland, 23 May 1896, Cleveland Papers, roll 94; Terrell to Secretary of State, 1 February 1896, M46, roll 60, and 21 February 1896, M625, roll 30.

33. Selfridge to Secretary of the Navy, 25 December 1895, Records of the European Squadron, RG313.

34. Herrick to Smith, 23 December; Dwight to Smith, 28 December 1895, ABC Papers; Terrell to Olney, 15, 29 December 1895, M46, roll 60; *Foreign Relations: 1895*, pp. 1427–34; copy of the "Constantinople Circular" (missionary paper) dated 25 January 1896, in Charles O'Neil Papers, Library of Congress, Washington, D.C.

35. McLaughlin to Dwight, 4 January 1896; Dwight to Judson Smith, 13 January 1896, ABC Papers; John Peters to Olney, 26 February 1896; Dwight to Terrell, 15 May 1896, copy in Olney Papers; Dwight to Smith, 5 March; Green to Smith, 10 March; E. Shadrock to Smith, 4 April 1896, ABC Papers; Dwight to Olney, 3 April; Peters to Olney, 21 March; Smith to Olney, 4 April; Dodge to Cleveland, 18 May 1896, Cleveland Papers, roll 94; Kennedy to Cleveland, 8 May 1896, copy in Olney Papers; *Harper's Weekly* 40 (5 December 1896): 40.

36. William L. Wilson, *The Cabinet Diary of William L. Wilson, 1896–1897*, Festus P. Summers, ed. (Chapel Hill: University of North Carolina Press, 1957), pp. 14, 25.

37. Uhl to Terrell, 4 January 1896, M77, roll 167; Sublime Porte to Terrell, 12 January 1896, M46, roll 60; *Foreign Relations: 1896*, p. 1461; Terrell to Olney, 14 January 1896, M46, roll 60; Currie to Salisbury, 29 January 1896, FO 195/1914; Terrell to Olney, 16 January 1896, M46, roll 60.

38. Currie to Salisbury, 5 February 1896, FO 195/1914; London *Times*, 3 February 1896; Terrell to Olney, 6 February 1896, M46, roll 61.

39. Selfridge to Secretary of the Navy, 25 December 1895, 29 January 1896; to Commanding officer, *Minneapolis*, 5 February 1896; Secretary of the Navy to Selfridge, 26 January 1896, Records of the European Squadron, RG313.

40. *The Cabinet Diary of William L. Wilson*, entry 14 April 1896, p. 65. Wilson wrote that Cleveland believed that the American minister to Russia should have been consulted before approving Selfridge. *See also* Selfridge to Terrell, 2 March 1896, M625, roll 30.

41. In his *Memoirs* Selfridge mentions the *Turkish* cruise in one paragraph and his visit to Russia in twenty-four pages (pp. 252–76).

42. Henry Harris Jessup, *Fifty-three Years in Syria*, 2 vols. (New York: Fleming H. Revell, 1910), 2: 621–22; *Foreign Relations: 1896*, pp. 911–13.

43. Dwight to Smith, 27 July 1896, ABC Papers; Dwight to Terrell, 27 July 1896; Terrell to Dwight, 31 July; Terrell to Olney, 31 July 1896, M46, roll 61.

44. Telegram from Navy Department to Selfridge, 25 August 1896; Selfridge to Commanding Officer, *Marblehead*, 25 August 1896, Records of the European Squadron, RG313; Terrell to

Olney, 24 August 1896, M46, roll 61; McAdoo to Selfridge, 24 August 1896, M625, roll 30; *Foreign Relations: 1896*, pp. 916–17.

45. Selfridge to Secretary of the Navy, 12 September 1896, Records of the European Squadron, RG313; Selfridge to Secretary of the Navy, 9 October 1896; Shepard to Terrell, 19 September 1896; Newell to Terrell, 15 September 1896, M625, roll 30; *Foreign Relations: 1896*, pp. 869–70.

46. Olney to Breckinridge, 22 May, 14 April 1896, Olney Papers; Breckinridge to Olney, 5 May 1896, quoted in McDonough, "American Relations with Turkey, 1893–1901" (Ph.D. diss., Georgetown University, 1949), pp. 226–27; Mavroyeni Bey to Secretary of State, 16 June 1896, T815, roll 8.

47. Mcadoo to Olney, 28 August; Adee to Olney, 30 August; Rockhill to Terrell, 31 August; Rockhill to Olney, 31 August 1896, Olney Papers. The *New York Times* on 30 August 1896 reported that her complement was reduced in order to carry more coal.

48. M46, roll 61, has a large number of clippings from European newspapers.

49. For background to Anglo-American cooperation *see* Marder, *The Anatomy of British Sea Power: A History of British Naval Policy in the Pre-Dreadnaught Era, 1880–1905* (New York: Alfred A. Knopf, 1940), pp. 252–55; Davis, *A Navy Second to None*, pp. 62–63; Peter Karsten, *The Naval Aristocracy: The Golden Age of Annapolis and the Emergence of Modern Navalism* (New York: The Free Press, 1972), pp. 107–16; May, *Imperial Democracy*, pp. 52–65; Alexander E. Campbell, *Great Britain and the United States, 1895–1903* (London: Longmans, 1960), pp. 192–96. Campbell suggests that the refusal of the United States to enter into joint action outside the Americas was a weakness in American diplomacy, "since it often implied a reluctance to act at all" (p. 192). He was referring particularly to the Far East, where trouble in China led to British efforts to persuade the United States to joint action.

50. Cleveland to Olney, 24 September 1896, Cleveland Papers, roll 95; Chamberlain to Olney, 19 September 1896, Olney Papers; J. L. Garvin, *The Life of Joseph Chamberlain*, 3 vols. (New York: The Macmillan Company, 1924), 3: 167; Charles C. Tansill, *The Foreign Policy of Thomas F. Bayard, 1885–1897* (New York: Fordham University Press, 1940), pp. 773–74; Eggert, *Olney*, pp. 241–42.

51. Kenneth Bourne, *Foreign Policy of Victorian England, 1830–1902* (New York: Oxford University Press, 1967), pp. 157–58; Grenville, *Salisbury and Foreign Policy*, pp. 82–87; William A. Langer, *Diplomacy of Imperialism* (New York: Alfred A. Knopf, 1968), p. 329.

52. Terrell to Olney, 5, 7 September, 8, 9, 22, 24, 27 October 1896, M46, roll 61; *New York Times*, 11 September, 8 October 1896; London *Times*, 6 October 1896; Breckinridge to Olney, 11 November 1896, copy in the Cleveland Papers, roll 95.

53. Rockhill to Olney, 9, 14 September 1896, Olney Papers; Selfridge to Terrell, 27 October 1896, Records of the European Squadron, RG313; Selfridge to Terrell, 28 October 1896, M46, roll 62; Selfridge to Secretary of the Navy, 7 October 1896, M625, roll 30; *New York Times*, 1 November 1896. *See also* John Barrows, *A World Pilgrimage* (Chicago: A. C. McClurg & Co., 1897), p. 247. The cruiser *Cincinnati* replaced the *Marblehead* in November.

54. *Foreign Relations: 1896*, pp. 926–29; Terrell to Olney, 6, 12 January 1897, M46, roll 62; Rockhill to Secretary of the Navy, 10 April 1897, M625, roll 31. *See also* Selfridge to Terrell, 29 April 1897, M46, roll 63.

55. Selfridge to Secretary of the Navy, 15 December 1896, M625, roll 30; Robert McNeely to "Fanny," 10 December 1896, Macay-McNeely Family Papers, Southern Historical Collection, University of North Carolina Library, Chapel Hill, N.C.; Jessup, *Fifty-three Years in Syria*, 2: 614–15; Thomas Christie to O'Neil, 14 November 1896, O'Neil Papers; Olney to Terrell, 30 December 1896, M77, roll 168.

56. Selfridge to Secretary of the Navy, 15 March 1897, M625, roll 31; McNeely to "Fanny," 15 March 1897, Macay-McNeely Family Papers.

57. George W. Allen, ed., *The Papers of John Davis Long, 1897–1904* (Boston: Massachusetts Historical Society, 1939), pp. 14–15; Rockhill to Secretary of the Navy, 31 March, 3, 12, 21

April 1897, M625, roll 31; U.S. Minister to Morocco to Secretary of State, 3, 12 April 1897, M46, roll 63.

58. Roosevelt to McKinley, 26 April 1897, Roosevelt to Long, 26 April 1897, Etling E. Morison, ed., *The Letters of Theodore Roosevelt*, 8 vols. (Cambridge: Harvard University Press, 1951–54), 1: 602–3 (hereafter cited as *Roosevelt Letters*). *See also* Roosevelt to Olney, 22 April 1897, Olney Papers. The American minister was pressing for reinforcements. *See* Terrell to Sherman, 24, 26 April; Madden to Terrell, 22 April; Washington to Short, 24 April 1897, M46, roll 63.

59. Selfridge to Secretary of the Navy, 23 April, 1, 8 May 1897, M625, roll 31; Long to Selfridge, 6 May 1897, Ciphers Sent, RG45. The admiral's reliance upon a major power to provide protection was not fulfilled. In June he ordered the *Bancroft* to Alexandretta because Turkish authorities had ordered out of the country Greek employees who worked for the Stanford Manufacturing Company, an American firm. Selfridge to Arnold, 16 June 1897, Records of the European Squadron, RG313.

60. Rockhill to Secretary of the Navy, 17 April; Secretary of the Navy to Rockhill, 23 April 1897, M625, roll 31; Selfridge to Secretary of the Navy, 8 May 1897, M625, roll 31. For the celebration *see* Albert Gleaves, *The Life of an American Sailor: Rear Admiral William Hemsley Emory, United States Navy* (New York: George H. Doran Company, 1923), pp. 230–33.

61. The news was unexpected. *See* McNeely to "Fanny," 7 June 1897, Macay-McNeely Family Papers. McNeely was a young officer on the *Minneapolis* at the time.

62. Day to Secretary of State, 28 June 1897, M625, roll 31; Selfridge to Sid Mahomet Torres, 10 July 1897, Records of the European Squadron, RG313; Long to Selfridge, 28 June 1897, Translations of Messages Sent, RG45; Selfridge to Secretary of the Navy, 9, 17 July 1897, M625, roll 32; Luella J. Hall, *The United States and Morocco, 1776–1956* (Metuchen, New Jersey: The Scarecrow Press, 1971), pp. 312, 364; *Army and Navy Journal*, 24 July 1897.

63. Selfridge to the Secretary of the Navy, 9 July 1897, M625, roll 31.

64. Selfridge to Secretary of the Navy, 8 December; Angell to Secretary of State, 20 December, and inclosures, International Relations and Politics (VI), Box 9, Subject Files, RG45; American Minister to Secretary of State, 21 December 1897, M625, roll 31.

65. Angell to Sherman, 18 December 1897; to Day, 14 August 1898, M46, roll 64, 65; James B. Angell, *The Reminiscences of James Burrill Angell* (New York: Longmans, Green and Co., 1912), pp. 210–11; Joseph L. Grabill, *Protestant Diplomacy and the Near East: Missionary Influence on American Policy* (Minneapolis: University of Minnesota Press, 1971), p. 44.

66. Oscar S. Straus, *Under Four Administrations, From Cleveland to Taft* (Boston: Houghton Mifflin Company, 1922), p. 124; John A. DeNovo, *American Interests and Policies in the Middle East, 1900–1939* (Minneapolis: University of Minnesota Press, 1965), pp. 5–6.

67. Straus, *Under Four Administrations*, pp. 128–29. McKinley, mindful of the political implications of the Turkish problem, told a visiting delegation from the board of the Presbyterian Missionary Society that he would be willing to employ coercive measures in Turkey but for the need to keep strong naval forces in home waters because of the Cuban situation. A. L. Tibawi, *American Interests in Syria, 1800–1901* (Oxford: Clarendon Press, 1966), pp. 296–97.

68. Hugo von Radolin to Holstein, 19 November 1895, *The Holstein Papers*, 4 vols., ed. Norman Rich and W. H. Fisher (Cambridge: Cambridge University Press, 1955–63), 3: 501–2; Robert L. Daniels, *American Philanthropy in the Near East, 1820–1960* (Athens: Ohio University Press, 1970), p. 120; interview of missionary with Olney, 23 January 1896, Olney Papers.

69. For example, *see* Herrick, *The American Naval Revolution*, pp. 185–86. Turkey is not even mentioned.

70. *See*, for example, U.S., Congress, House, *Congressional Record*, 54th Cong., 1st sess., 1896, 54, Pt. 4, pp. 3246–47.

CHAPTER 8

1. For a discussion of the evolution of war plans with Spain *see* John A. S. Grenville, "American Naval Preparation for War with Spain, 1896–1898," *Journal of American Studies* 2 (1968):

33–37; J.A.S. Grenville and George Young, *Politics, Strategy and American Diplomacy: Studies in Foreign Policy, 1875–1917* (New Haven: Yale University Press, 1966), pp. 269–77.

2. Roosevelt to Lodge, 21 September; to Kimball, 19 November 1897, Elting E. Morison, ed., *The Letters of Theodore Roosevelt*, 8 vols. (Cambridge: Harvard University Press, 1951–1954), I: 685–86, 716–17.

3. Howell to Chandler, 22 September 1897, William Chandler Papers, Library of Congress, Washington, D.C.; Margaret Leech, *In the Days of McKinley* (New York: Harper & Brothers, 1959), pp. 159–60; *Army and Navy Journal*, 7 August 1897.

4. Roosevelt to Chandler, 29 September; Chandler to Roosevelt, 13 October; Long to Chandler, 12, 16, 25 September; Chandler to Long, 14 October 1897, all in the Chandler Papers. *See also* Leech, *McKinley*, pp. 160–61, and Richard S. West, Jr., *Admirals of American Empire* (Indianapolis: Bobbs-Merrill Co., 1948), pp. 142–44.

5. Selfridge to the Secretary of the Navy, 20 August 1897, Operation of Fleets (OO), Box 12, Subject Files, RG45; Long to Selfridge, 18 January 1898, Entry 19, Ciphers Sent, RG45.

6. *New York Times*, 5 February 1898; Roosevelt to Howell, 25 February 1898, Ciphers Sent, RG45; Appendix to the *Report of the Chief of the Bureau of Navigation: 1898* (Washington, D.C.: Government Printing Office, 1898), p. 23.

7. Roosevelt to Long, 17 January 1898, *Roosevelt Letters*, 1: 759–60; Appendix to the *Report of the Chief of the Bureau of Navigation: 1898*, p. 25; John Long, *The New American Navy*, 2 vols. (New York: The Outlook Company, 1903), 1: 144–47. For information on the ammunition *see* correspondence between the Navy Department and Howell between 16 March and 24 March 1898, Records of the European Squadron, RG313.

8. 14 January 1898, *Roosevelt Letters* 1: 759–63. *See also* Roosevelt to Charles Henry Davis, 17 January 1898, ibid., 764–65.

9. President of the Board to Secretary of the Navy, 1, 18 June 1898, entry 371, War Board letterbook RG45. *See also* Rear Admiral French E. Chadwick, *The Relations Between the United States and Spain: The Spanish-American War*, 2 vols. (New York: Charles Scribner's Sons, 1911), pp. 11, 211.

10. For correspondence concerning the proposed operation *see* the War Board letterbook, RG45; William R. Braisted, *The United States Navy in the Pacific, 1897–1909* (Austin: University of Texas Press, 1958), pp. 40–41; Chadwick, *The Spanish-American War*, 2: 211–13, 280–81, 310–19. For the Spanish squadron's fuel problem *see* Lenoir Wright, *United States Policy Toward Egypt, 1830–1849* (New York: Exposition Press, 1909), pp. 181–85. Mahan, a member of the "Strategy Board," continued to urge sending the squadron even after Long cancelled the operation. Mahan to Long, 5 August 1898, George W. Allen, ed., *The Papers of John Davis Long, 1897–1904* (Boston: Massachusetts Historical Society, 1939), pp. 175–76.

11. The speech is quoted in a footnote in Norman Rich and M. H. Fisher, eds., *The Holstein Papers*, 4 vols. (Cambridge: Cambridge University Press, 1955–63), 4: 98. *See also* Holstein memorandum, 12 November 1898, ibid., pp. 98–99; editorial, *Blackwood Edinburgh Magazine* 163 (1898): 703; Thomas Bailey, *Essays Diplomatic and Undiplomatic of Thomas A. Bailey*, ed. Alexander DeConde and Armin Rappaport (New York: Appleton-Century-Crofts, 1969), pp. 45–46; Henry Blumenthal, *France and the United States: Their Diplomatic Relations, 1789–1914* (Chapel Hill: University of North Carolina Press, 1959), pp. 199–200, 216; Holger H. Herwig, *Politics of Frustration: The United States in German Naval Planning, 1889–1941* (Boston: Little, Brown and Company, 1976), pp. 26–27.

12. *Annual Report of the Secretary of the Navy, 1900* (Washington, D.C.: Government Printing Office, 1901), p. 6.

13. Robert Skinner to Secretary of State, 26 January; Secretary of the Navy to W. Beavis, Mayor, Turquay, England, 28 January 1899, M625, roll 35; Secretary of State to "editor," copy in file number 15245, General Correspondence of the Bureau of Navigation, 1889–1913, entry 88, RG24. For the cruises *see* M625, roll 39.

14. Crowninshield to Secretary of the Navy, 30 September 1902, Records of the European Squadron, RG313; Cromwell to Secretary of the Navy, 7, 8 July 1901, M625, roll 39; Winfield

Scott Schley, *Forty-Five Years Under the Flag* (New York: D. Appleton and Co., 1904), p. 406; *New York Times*, 7 July 1901. *See also* "An Oldtimer Recalls Ships of the European Squadron," *All Hands* (January 1960), pp. 38–39; and *Army and Navy Journal*, 13 July 1901.

15. M625, roll 39.

16. Spanish ports were avoided and would be avoided for many years. For an incident that occurred in 1913 when units of the Atlantic Fleet visited Cadiz *see* American consul to Secretary of State, 8 August 1913, and translation of Spanish newspapers inclosed; *see also* Josephus Daniels to Secretary of State, 3 November 1913, all in 811.3340/87, 89, 98, Decimal File, 1910–1944, entry 196, records of the Department of State, RG59 (hereafter cited by decimal file number). A British naval officer wrote in 1905 when his ship visited Spanish ports that on several occasions officers and men were stoned by boys because they were believed to be Americans. O. W. Andrews, *Seamarks and Landmarks* (London: Ernest Benn, Ltd., 1927), p. 239.

17. Eugene P. Trani, "Cautious Warrior: Theodore Roosevelt and the Diplomacy of Activism," in *Makers of American Diplomacy from Theodore Roosevelt to Henry Kissinger*, ed. Frank J. Merli and Theodore A. Wilson (New York: Charles Scribner's Sons, 1974), p. 25; and Grenville, *Politics, Strategy and American Diplomacy*, p. 310. *See also* Howard K. Beale, *Theodore Roosevelt and the Rise of America to World Power* (Baltimore: The Johns Hopkins Press, 1956), and Raymond A. Esthus, *Theodore Roosevelt and the International Rivalries* (Waltham, Massachusetts: Ginn-Blaisdell, 1970). For Roosevelt and the navy *see* Gordon C. O'Gara, *Theodore Roosevelt and the Rise of the Modern Navy* (Princeton: Princeton University Press, 1943); and Arthur M. Johnson, "Theodore Roosevelt and the Navy," *United States Naval Institute Proceedings* 84 (October 1958): 76–82.

18. Quoted in George Monger, *The End of Isolation: British Foreign Policy, 1900–1907* (London: T. Nelson, 1963), p. 72.

19. Seward W. Livermore, "American Naval Development, 1898–1914" (Ph.D. diss., Harvard University, 1943), pp. 19–25; Richard D. Challener, *Admirals, Generals, and American Foreign Policy, 1894–1914* (Princeton: Princeton University Press, 1973), p. 41.

20. E. G. Cushman to Secretary of the Navy, 13 June 1898, General Correspondence of the Secretary of the Navy, Box 187, RG80. *See also* Consul General, Tangier, to Secretary of State, 27 July 1898, M625, roll 34.

21. Commodore Bradford did inform Whitelaw Reid, a member of the American delegation at the Paris Peace Conference, that the "Canaries would be valuable." H. Wayne Morgan, ed., *Making Peace with Spain: The Diary of Whitelaw Reid* (Austin: University of Texas Press, 1965), p. 143.

22. Bradford to Secretary of the Navy, 12 April, 22 May 1899, General Correspondence of the Secretary of the Navy, Box 187, RG80; Bradford to Secretary of the Navy, 19 June 1899, General Correspondence of the Secretary of the Navy, Box 321, RG80; Challener, *Admirals, Generals and American Foreign Policy*, p. 38. The German government was informed of the United States' apparent interest in Liberia and was somewhat concerned. Alfred Vagts, *Deutschland Und Die Vereinigten Staaten In Der Weltpolitik*, 2 vols. (London: Lovat, Dickson & Thompson, Ltd., 1935), 2: 1994–95.

23. For the list of potential sites *see* file "General Board Papers," Box 56, George Dewey Papers, Library of Congress, Washington, D.C. *See also* Daniel J. Costello, "Planning for War: A History of the General Board of the Navy, 1900–1914" (Ph.D. diss., Fletcher School of International Law, 1969), p. 188; Challener, *Admirals, Generals and American Foreign Policy*, pp. 38–41; Alfred Vagts, "Hopes and Fears of an American German War, 1870–1915," *Political Science Quarterly* 55 (March 1940), p. 70.

24. Richard D. Challener, "Montenegro and the United States: A Balkan Fantasy," *Journal of Central European Affairs* 17 (October 1957), pp. 236–42.

25. Taylor to Moody, 23 June 1903, William H. Moody Papers, Library of Congress, Washington, D.C.; Challener, *Admirals, Generals and American Foreign Policy*, p. 193; Livermore, "American Naval Development, 1898–1914," pp. 146–47.

26. On 16 January 1902, Roosevelt wrote, "The most important position at present is Chief of

the Bureau of Navigation. Not to put Crowninshield on the European Squadron would mean that he would stay in the Bureau of Navigation, and I want Taylor in the Bureau." Letter to Dr. St. Clair McKelway, Theodore Roosevelt Papers, roll 327, Library of Congress, Washington, D.C. *See also* Costello, "The General Board," pp. 279–89.

27. Journal of Admiral George Dewey, entry 18 November 1902, Dewey Papers; Damond E. Cummings, *Admiral Richard Wainwright and the United States Fleet* (Washington, D.C.: Government Printing Office, 1962), pp. 143–44. These maneuvers have attracted a great deal of attention among historians because they coincided with the Venezuelan controversy of 1902. The role that Roosevelt played in this controversy, particularly whether or not he forced Germany to back down by a threat of naval action, has been the most discussed issue. *See* Beale, *Theodore Roosevelt and the Rise of America to World Power*, pp. 395–431; Steward W. Livermore, "Theodore Roosevelt, the American Navy, and the Venezuelan Crisis of 1902–1903," *American Historical Review* 51 (April 1946): 452–471; Edward B. Parsons, "The German-American Crisis of 1902–1903," *Historian* 33 (May 1971), pp. 346–52; Ronald Spector, "Roosevelt, the Navy, and the Venezuelan Controversy," 1902–1903," *American Neptune* 32 (October 1972), pp. 257–63; Paul S. Hobo, "Perilous Obscurity: Public Diplomacy and the Press in the Venezuelan Crisis, 1902–1903," *Historian* 32 (May 1970), pp. 428–48. For the European Squadron's role in the Carribbean Maneuvers *see* Ernest J. King and Walter Muir Whitehill, *Fleet Admiral King: A Naval Record* (New York: W. W. Norton & Company, 1952), pp. 41–43; Livermore, "Theodore Roosevelt, the American Navy, and the Venezuelan Crisis of 1902–1903," pp. 460–62; Costello, "The General Board," pp. 285–87; Records of Combined Squadrons, entries 93–95, RG313.

28. John D. Alden, *The American Steel Navy* (Annapolis: United States Naval Institute, 1972), pp. 135–36.

29. Ernest J. King and Walter Muir Whitehill, *Fleet Admiral King: A Naval Record* (New York: W. W. Norton & Company, 1952), pp. 37–38. King, Chief of Naval Operations in World War II, was flag midshipman on the *Illinois* during her tour as flagship of the European Squadron.

30. George Dewey, *Autobiography of George Dewey: Admiral of the Navy* (New York: Charles Scribner's Sons, 1913), p. 167. *See also* Walter Herrick, *The American Naval Revolution* (Baton Rouge: Louisiana State University Press, 1966), pp. 194–95; *Washington Post*, 4 May 1902.

31. Platt to McKinley, 29 July 1901, William McKinley Papers, reel 16, Library of Congress, Washington, D.C.

32. Moody to Crowninshield, 15 February 1902, Operations of Fleets (OO), Box 12, Subject Files, RG45; King, *Fleet Admiral King*, pp. 38–40. The naval review that Crowninshield fervently desired to attend was cancelled because King suffered from perityphitis. Crowninshield to Secretary of the Navy, 30 June 1902, Records of the European Squadron, RG313.

33. Roosevelt to Platt, 28 June 1902, *Roosevelt Letters*, 3: 283.

34. Crowninshield to Moody, 30 September; to Taylor, 30 September 1902, Records of the European Squadron, RG313.

35. Dewey to Secretary of the Navy, 15 January 1903, Dewey Papers.

36. Costello, "The General Board," pp. 285–88; Cummings, *Wainwright*, p. 144; *Annual Report of the Secretary of the Navy, 1903*, pp. 465–78, 649; Rear Admiral Henry C. Taylor, "The Fleet," *United States Naval Institute Proceedings* 29 (December, 1903), p. 805.

37. Taylor to Moody, 5, 14 December 1902, Moody Papers; Rear Admiral Bradley A. Fiske, *From Midshipman to Rear Admiral* (London: T. Werner Laurie, Ltd., 1919), pp. 350–51; Moody to Crowninshield, 5 February 1903, General Correspondence of the Bureau of Navigation, Box 20, RG24.

38. Crowninshield to Secretary of the Navy, 9 January 1903, General Correspondence of the Bureau of Navigation, Box 20, RG24; Crowninshield to Secretary of the Navy, 28 February 1903, Records of the European Squadron, RG313.

39. Dewey to Secretary of the Navy, 15 January 1903, Dewey Papers.

40. J. C. O'Laughlin, "The American Fighting Fleet, Its Strategic Disposition," *Cassier's*

Magazine 24 (1903): 381; Dewey to Secretary of the Navy, 5 December 1903, Series 420-1, Papers of the General Board of the United States Navy, Naval Operational Archives, Naval Historical Center, Washington Navy Yard, Washington, D.C.

41. Secretary of the Navy to Commander in Chief, European Squadron, 4 August 1903, M625, roll 43.

42. Unidentified clipping dated 12 December 1903 in the Rear Admiral Charles S. Cotton Papers, Library of Congress, Washington, D.C.; *Army and Navy Journal*, 19 December 1903.

43. The *Cleveland* and the *Des Moines* were the same class of cruisers. Jewell to Secretary of the Navy, 15 July 1904, M625, roll 43; *Army and Navy Journal*, 8 August 1903; *Annual Report of the Secretary of the Navy, 1904*, p. 18.

44. Secretary of the Navy to Jewell, 29 December 1904, General Correspondence of the Bureau of Navigation, Box 276, RG24; Colby to Secretary of the Navy, 12 January 1905, Operations of Fleets (OO), Box 12, Subject Files, RG45; Rear Admiral George Converse to Rear Admiral C. H. Davis, 22 November 1904, George Converse Papers, Library of Congress, Washington, D.C. Converse was Chief of the Bureau of Navigation. On 17 November he wrote Mrs. E. E. Chadwick, Rear Admiral French Chadwick's wife, that the European Squadron would not be reestablished until the following summer, "if then." Converse Papers.

45. For the Turkish controversy *see* pp. 156–64. Dewey wrote in his *Autobiography* a few years later that he considered the presence of a naval force in European waters to be "perfunctory."

46. Livermore, "American Naval Development, 1898–1914," pp. 125–26; *Army and Navy Journal*, 1 April 1905; Robert E. Johnson, *Thence Round Cape Horn* (Annapolis: United States Naval Institute, 1963), p. 164; Harold and Margaret Sprout, *The Rise of American Naval Power, 1776–1918* (Princeton: Princeton University Press, 1946), p. 282.

47. Converse to Sigsbee, 24 February 1905, Converse Papers.

48. Harold Underwood Faulkner, *The Decline of Laissez Faire, 1897–1917* (New York: Harper & Row, 1968), pp. 56–57; William C. Askew and J. Fred Rippy, "The United States and Europe's Strife, 1908–1913," *The Journal of Politics* 4 (1942): 708; Lloyd C. Gardner et al., *Creation of the American Empire: U.S. Diplomatic History* (Chicago: Rand McNally & Company, 1973), pp. 272–73; Wolfram W. Gottlieb, *Studies in Secret Diplomacy during the First World War* (London: Allen Unwin, 1957), p. 93; John A. DeNovo, *American Interests and Policies in the Middle East* (Minneapolis: University of Minnesota Press, 1963), pp. 60–61; Nasim Sousa, *Capitulatory Regime of Turkey: Its History, Origin, and Nature* (Baltimore: The Johns Hopkins Press, 1933), pp. 252–53.

49. Kenneth Bourne, *Britain and the Balance of Power, 1815–1908* (Berkeley: University of California Press, 1967), pp. 341–42; Michael Balfour, *The Kaiser and His Times* (New York: W. W. Norton & Company, 1972), p. 165.

50. Blumenthal, *France and the United States*, pp. 200–2; Christopher Andrew, *Theophile Delcasse and the Making of the Entente Cordiale* (London: The MacMillan Company, 1968), pp. 80–81; Ministere des Affaires Etangeres, *Documents diplomatiques Francais, 1871–1914*, 41 vols. (Paris: Imprimerie nationale), Ser. I, 14: 298, 354–55.

51. *Documents diplomatiques Francais*, Ser. II, 5: 193–94, 217; Andrew, *Delcasse*, p. 81; *New York Times*, 14 August 1904; Blumenthal, *France and the United States*, pp. 234–38; Eugene N. Anderson, *The First Moroccan Crisis, 1904–1906* (Hamden, Connecticut: Archon Books, 1966), p. 43.

52. Meyer to Roosevelt, 15 January 1906, Roosevelt Papers, roll 62. *See also* London *Times*, 14, 22 May 1900; *Documents diplomatiques Francais*, Ser. II, 5: 217; "The United States in the Mediterranean," *The American Monthly Review of Reviews* 30 (September 1904), pp. 358–59.

53. These and other German papers are quoted in the London *Times*, 31 August 1903; *Army and Navy Journal*, 5 September 1903. *See also* translation of a Berlin newspaper dated 3 September 1903 in the Cotton Papers. *See also* Bourne, *Britain and the Balance of Power*, p. 339; and L. B. Shippee, "Germany and the Spanish-American War," *American Historical Review* 30 (July 1925), pp. 754–77.

54. Vagts, "Hopes and Fears of an American War, 1870–1915," pp. 53–76, 514–35; Holger H. Herwig and David P. Trask, "Naval Operations Plans Between Germany and the United States of America 1898–1913: A Study of Strategic Planning in the Age of Imperialism," *Militargeschichtliche Mitteilungen* (2/1970):5–32; J. A. S. Grenville, "Diplomacy and War Plans in the United States, 1890–1917," *Transactions of the Royal Historical Society* 11 (1961): 1–21; Bradford Perkins, *The Great Rapprochement: England and the United States, 1895–1914* (New York: Atheneum, 1968), p. 245.

55. Quoted in Arthur J. Marder, ed., *Fear God and Dread Nought: The Correspondence of Admiral of the Fleet Lord Fisher*, 3 vols. (London: Fernhill, 1952–1959), 2: 142–43; *see also* Lionel M. Gelber, *The Rise of Anglo-American Friendship* (New York: Oxford University Press), pp. 134–35.

56. Livermore, "American Navy as a Factor in World Politics, 1903–1913," pp. 864–65.

57. 5 June 1903, John Hay Papers, Library of Congress, Washington, D.C.

58. Livermore, "American Navy as a Factor in World Politics, 1903–1913," pp. 875–77; William A. Williams, *American-Russian Relations, 1781–1947* (New York: Rinehart & Company, 1952), p. 75.

59. Livermore, "American Navy as a Factor in World Politics, 1903–1913," p. 870; Chester to Assistant Secretary of State, 8 August 1904, M625, roll 43.

60. Cotton to Secretary of the Navy, 19 May 1903, Records of the European Squadron, RG313; Darling to Secretary of State, 4 May 1903, copy in Roosevelt Papers, reel 33; Taylor to Captain James H. Dayton, 30 May 1903, M625, roll 42; *Papers Relating to the Foreign Relations of the United States: 1903* (Washington, D.C.: Government Printing Office, 1904), pp. 406–7; Livermore, "American Navy as a Factor in World Politics, 1903–1913," pp. 865–66. For an interesting account of the visit of Admiral Cotton's squadron to French, German, and British ports, *see* Francis X. Holbrook and John Nikol, "The Courting Season of 1903," *United States Naval Institute Proceedings* 101 (December 1975): 60–63.

61. John B. Hawley, commanding *Hartford*, to Secretary of the Navy, 12 August 1901; James B. Jackson to Secretary of State, M625, roll 40.

62. *See also New York Times*, 18 April 1903; *Army and Navy Journal*, 25 April 1903.

63. John Hay Papers, Library of Congress, Washington, D.C. *See also* Tower's official dispatch to Hay quoted in Livermore, "American Navy as a Factor in World Politics, 1903–1913," pp. 866–67; Baltimore *Sun*, 11 May 1903; *New York Herald*, 12 May 1903; and *Army and Navy Journal*, 16 May 1903.

64. Hay to Roosevelt, penciled undated copy in Hay Papers, Box 5; Moody to Admiral Taylor, 20 May 1903, Moody Papers; Roosevelt to Hay, 22, 26 May 1903, Roosevelt Papers, reel 416, reel 331; London *Times*, 23 May 1903.

65. White to Secretary of State, 3, 10, 14 June 1903, M30, roll 193; Moody to Hay, 8 June 1903; British Ambassador to Hay, 24 April 1903, Hay Papers; Hay to Moody, 8 June 1903, Moody Papers; Cotton to White, 13 June 1903, Records of the European Squadron, RG313; Livermore, "American Navy as a Factor in World Politics, 1903–1913," p. 868.

66. Cotton to the Secretary of the Navy, 6 July 1903, Cotton Papers. *See also* the *New York Times*, 14, 24, 25, 26, 28, 30 June 1903.

67. Grand Admiral A. von Tirpitz, *My Memoirs*, 2 vols. (London: Hurst & Blackett, 1919), 1: 186.

68. For the Kiel visit *see* the large number of newspaper clippings in the Cotton Papers; *Army and Navy Journal*, 4 July 1903; *Foreign Relations: 1903*, pp. 448–51; Admiral William Veszie Pratt's unpublished autobiography, Operational Archives, Naval Historical Center, Washington Navy Yard, Washington, D.C.

69. For the officer's remark *see* the *Paris Herald*, 29 June 1903. *See also* Roosevelt to Moody, 7 July, and Moody to Roosevelt, 8 July 1903, Roosevelt Papers, reel 34.

70. Cotton to Secretary of the Navy, 21 June 1903, Records of the European Squadron, RG313; assorted newspaper clippings in the Cotton Papers; The *Illustrated London News* had

pictures of the U.S. squadron on the front page of its 18 July 1903 issue.

71. Robert A. Hart, *The Great White Fleet* (Boston: Little, Brown and Company, 1965), is an excellent account of the round-the-world cruise.

72. Hart, *The Great White Fleet*, pp. 26–27.

73. Ibid., pp. 271–72. For an example of the kind of pressure exerted on Roosevelt *see* Henry H. Jessup, American Presbyterian Mission, Beirut, to Oscar Straus, 5 November 1908, copy in M625, roll 45. For an account of the *Illinois*'s cruise in the Mediterranean *see* Rear Admiral Long's unpublished autobiography. At Roosevelt's orders the Navy Department later sent the stationship *Scorpion* from Constantinople as well as two supply ships, the *Celtic* and *Culgeon* from the United States, to Messina. Commander Reginald R. Belknap, USN, commanded a large contingent of sailors from the vessels that were employed in rebuilding the city. *See* Ernest P. Bicknell, *Pioneering with the Red Cross* (New York: The MacMillan Company, 1935), pp. 120–23; General Correspondence of the Bureau of Navigation, Box 1082, RG24; Reginald R. Belknap Papers, Library of Congress, Washington, D.C.

74. Hart, *The Great White Fleet*, pp. 296–302.

75. *See* chapter 9.

76. Taft to Secretary of State Philander C. Knox, 7 October 1910, William Howard Taft Papers, Case File 9, Library of Congress, Washington, D.C. *See also* Acting Secretary of the Navy Winthrop to Taft, 7 October, Knox to Taft, 7 October 1910, Taft Papers, Case File 9.

77. S. Y. Smith to Secretary of State, 19 November 1910, Decimal File 811.3340/29, RG59. *See also* Livermore, "American Navy as a Factor in World Politics, 1903–1913," pp. 873–75.

78. Quoted in Perkins, *The Great Rapprochement*, p. 294. For Sims's explanation of the speech *see* Elting E. Morison, *Admiral Sims and the Modern American Navy* (Boston: Houghton Mifflin Company, 1942), pp. 277–85. For an account of the visit *see* Seaton Schroeder, *Half Century of Naval Service* (New York: D. Appleton & Company, 1922), pp. 409–24.

79. For the summer cruise *see* Decimal File 811.3340, RG59; Livermore, "American Navy as a Factor in World Politics, 1903–1913," pp. 874–75. Albert M. Cohen, a young officer on the *Louisiana*, kept a well-written diary of the cruise. *See* the Albert M. Cohen Papers, Library of Congress, Washington, D.C. For the German attitude *see* newspaper clippings in Decimal File 811.3340, RG59, and *Literary Digest* 41 (3 December 1910): 1030.

CHAPTER 9

1. *Army and Navy Journal*, 15 May 1899; Secretary of State to Secretary of the Navy, 2 May 1899, M625, roll 35; Consul General Tangier to Grand Vizier, 8 May 1899, copy in ibid., Rear Admiral Howell to Secretary of the Navy, 10 May 1899, ibid.; Hall, *The United States and Morocco, 1776–1956* (Metuchen, N.J.: Scarecrow Press, 1971), pp. 320–21.

2. William L. Adams, *Exploits and Adventures of a Soldier Ashore and Afloat* (New York: J. B. Lippincott Company, 1911), pp. 60–62. For correspondence concerning this incident *see* Despatches From United States Consuls in Tangier, Morocco, 1797–1906, National Archives Microfilm Number T61, rolls 23–25.

3. For these claims *see* p. 131. *See also* Naomi W. Cohen, *A Dual Heritage: The Public Career of Oscar S. Straus* (Philadelphia: Jewish Publishing Society of America, 1968), pp. 79–80.

4. Straus to Porte, 7 December 1898, Oscar Straus Papers, Library of Congress, Washington, D.C.

5. Straus to Hay, 17 May 1900, Straus Papers; Cohen, *Dual Heritage*, pp. 99–101.

6. London *Times*, 14, 22 May 1900; *Army and Navy Journal*, 2 June 1900, quoting the London *Spectator*.

7. Hay to Straus, 19 May 1900, Straus Papers.

8. Chester to the Secretary of the Navy, 14 December 1900, M625, roll 39. *See also* Griscom's vivid description of the negotiations in his memoirs, Lloyd C. Griscom, *Diplomati-*

cally Speaking (Boston: Little, Brown and Company, 1940), pp. 169–73. *See also Papers Relating to the Foreign Relations of the United States: 1901* (Washington, D.C.: Government Printing Office, 1902), pp. 514–15, for Griscom's report to the State Department.

9. Lewis Einstein, *A Diplomat Looks Back* (New Haven: Yale University Press, 1968), p. 31.

10. Leishman to Adee, 5 December 1902; to Dodge, 2 December 1902, M77, roll 70. *See also* Alfred L. Dennis, *Adventure in American Diplomacy, 1896–1906* (New York: E. P. Dutton & Company, 1928), pp. 453–59.

11. Dodge to Leishman, 27 November 1902, M77, roll 70. American consuls and other minor diplomatic officials in Turkey usually supported the missionaries' demands for warships. *See* Ravndal to Secretary of State, 22 July 1902, M625, roll 41; Eddy to Secretary of State, 11 December 1901, 1 November 1902, M77, roll 68, 70.

12. 5 August 1903, box 9, John Hay Papers, Library of Congress, Washington, D.C. *See also* Leishman to Secretary of State, 8 February, 8 May, 21 March 1903, M77, roll 71; Hay to Leishman, 3 June 1903, M77, roll 169; Coolidge to Hay, 2 July 1903, box 26, Hay Papers.

13. William T. Stead, *The Americanization of the World; or the Trend of the Twentieth Century* (New York: H. Marckley, 1902), p. 195. *See also* Urbain Gahier, "American Intervention in Turkey," *North American Review* 173 (November 1901): 618–26.

14. Telegram, Bureau of Navigation to Cotton, 27 August 1903, General Correspondence of the Bureau of Navigation, box 455, RG24; Cotton to the Navy Department, 4 September 1903, M625, roll 43; *Army and Navy Journal*, 8 August 1903; newspaper clippings dated 28 August 1903 in Charles Cotton Papers, Library of Congress, Washington, D.C.

15. Secretary of the Navy to Cotton, 25 September 1903, General Correspondence of the Bureau of Navigation, box 455, RG24; Cotton to the Secretary of the Navy, 22 October 1903, Records of the European Squadron, RG313.

16. Chief, Bureau of Navigation to Cotton, 29 August 1903, General Correspondence of the Bureau of Navigation, box 723, RG24; *Foreign Relations: 1903*, p. 771.

17. Rark to Lansdowne, 28 August 1903, FO5/2524. *See also* Rark to Lansdowne, 1 September 1903, FO5/2524. For Hay's letter to Roosevelt *see* 3 September 1903, box 4, Hay Papers. *See also Foreign Relations: 1903*, pp. 771–72. For Leishman *see* despatches to Secretary Hay, 29, 30 August, 4 September 1903, M46, roll 72.

18. Roosevelt to Paul Estournelles De Constant, 1 September 1903, Elting E. Morison, *The Letters of Theodore Roosevelt*, 8 vols. (Cambridge: Harvard University Press, 1952), 3: 584. *See also* Roosevelt to Olney, 22 April 1897, Richard Olney Papers, Library of Congress, Washington, D.C.

19. Roosevelt to Albert Shaw, 4 September 1903, *Roosevelt Letters*, 3: 588; Seward W. Livermore, "American Naval Development, 1898–1914" (Ph.D. diss., Harvard University, 1943), p. 122.

20. Richards to O'Conor, 8 September 1903, FO195/2140. *See also* letter dated 7 September, ibid.

21. Cotton to American consul, 7 September 1903; Ravndal to Cotton, 7 September 1903, Records of the European Squadron, RG313; *Foreign Relations: 1903*, p. 777; Log of *Brooklyn*, entries for 7, 8 September 1903, RG45; Ravndal to Secretary of State, 19 November 1903, M625, roll 43. Cotton's detailed report of the incident of 7 September dated 24 September 1903 in International Relations and Politics (VI), box 9, Subject Files, RG45.

22. Secretary of the Navy to Cotton, 20 October 1903, General Correspondence of the Bureau of Navigation, box 723, RG24; Leishman to Secretary of State, 8 September 1903, M46, roll 72.

23. 9 September 1903, Hay Papers; Leishman to Secretary of State, 8 September 1903, M46, roll 72; Hay to Roosevelt, 6 September 1903, Theodore Roosevelt Papers, reel 37, Library of Congress, Washington, D.C.; Leishman to American consul, Beirut, 14 September 1903, M46, roll 72; Dennis, *Adventures in American Diplomacy*, pp. 460–61; *Standard* (London) 9 September 1903.

24. Hay to Roosevelt, 10 September 1903; Roosevelt to Hay, 11 September 1903, Roosevelt

Papers, rolls 37, 332. *See also* Adee to Hay, 9, 10 September 1903, Hay Papers.

25. *Foreign Relations: 1903*, pp. 778–79; Leishman to Secretary of State, 9 September 1903; Hay to Leishman, 10 September 1903, M46, roll 72; Leishman to Hay, 16 September 1903, Hay Papers.

26. O'Conor to Lansdowne, 11 September 1903, FO78/5269. *See also* Henry Harris Jessup, *Fifty Years in Syria*, 2 vols. (New York: Fleming H. Revell, 1910), 2: 729.

27. *The Nation*, 17 September 1903; Shaw to Roosevelt, 3, 9 September 1903, Roosevelt Papers, reel 37. *See also* the *New York Times*, 30 August, 1 September 1903; unidentified clipping dated 30 August 1903, in the Roosevelt papers, reel 37. After the riots, the *New York Times* reversed itself and supported the presence of the warships. *See* the issue dated 10 September 1903. *See also Army and Navy Journal*, 12 September 1903.

28. Undated newspaper clipping in the Cotton Papers; *Army and Navy Journal*, 10 September 1903; London *Times*, 2, 25 September 1903; London *Morning Post*, 5 September 1903. The *Volksblatt*, a Vienna paper, wrote on 12 September that the American squadron was ordered to force the Straits. According to the *New York Times*, the French were also unhappy over the presence of American warships in Syria. *See* issue dated 13 September 1903. For Lord Lansdowne's policy during the Macedonian crisis *see* George Monger, *The End of Isolation: British Foreign Policy, 1900–1927* (London: T. Nelson, 1963), pp. 126–38.

29. Leishman to Hay, 9, 10, 16 September; Cotton to Leishman, 11 September 1903, M46, roll 72; Hay to Roosevelt, 7 September 1903, Hay Papers. Copies of the opinions of the Americans in Syria as given to Admiral Cotton are in the Cotton Papers. *See also* Roosevelt to Hay, 4 September 1903, Roosevelt Papers, reel 332.

30. Hay Papers.

31. Ravndal to Leishman, 11, 12, 13, 15 September; Leishman to Ravndal, 14 September; Leishman to Secretary of State, 15 September 1903, M46, roll 72; Ravndal to Cotton, 10 September 1903, Records of the European Squadron, RG313; Cotton to the Secretary of the Navy, 12 September 1903, General Correspondence of the Bureau of Navigation, box 723, RG24; Adee to Hay, 14, 16, 21 September 1903, Hay Papers.

32. The accusation by Turkish officials that the warships instigated the riots became a new issue. Leishman was instructed to demand a retraction.

33. Leishman to Secretary of State, 15 November 1903, M46, roll 73. *See also* Adee to Hay, 24 September 1903, Hay Papers; Adee to Leishman, 24 September; Leishman to American Consul, Beirut, 11 October; Leishman to Secretary of State, 21, 22 September, 6, 21 October, 6 November 1903, M46, rolls 72–73; *Army and Navy Journal*, 26 September, 10 October 1903 issues. Even the collaboration of the British representative had no effect. O'Conor to Lansdowne, 23 October 1903, FO78/15270.

34. He is referring to Turkish permission to allow the American school to construct new buildings when needed.

35. Hay to D. Stuart Dodge, 3 December 1903, Hay Papers; memo from Adee to Hay, 16 November 1903, M46, roll 73; letter from the American Board of Commissioners for Foreign Missions to Secretary of State, 17 October 1903, M77, roll 169.

36. According to a newspaper correspondent who reported from Beirut during this period, it was not all hardship, at least for the officers, as a large number of social events were given for them by the American colony. On 17 September, the officers attended a dinner given by the consul in their honor. A few days later they went to the Oaks, "the summer abode of the family of the Reverend Henry Harris. . . . Mrs. David Bliss gave a reception. . . . *Brooklyn* orchestra played for it." On Thanksgiving Day, hundreds of Syrians and Turks toured the ships. The day was also celebrated by boat races and the like. *See* the *New York Herald*, European edition, 17 January 1904, copy in the Cotton Papers.

37. Cotton to Leishman, 4 November; to Secretary of the Navy, 15 November 1903, Records of the European Squadron, RG313; Drummer Hay, British consul in Beirut, to Ambassador, 19 December 1903, FO195/2140.

38. He was court-martialed.

39. Translation of newspaper article dated 17 November 1903 and Leishman to Cotton, 19 November 1903, General Correspondence of the Bureau of Navigation, box 713, RG24; Cotton to Leishman, 4 November 1903, Records of the European Squadron, RG313.

40. Leishman to Secretary of State, 8, 15, 21, 22 December; Leishman to Cotton, 16, 20 December 1903, M46, roll 73; Cotton to Secretary of the Navy, 29 December 1903, M625, roll 43; *New York Times*, 17 December 1903.

41. Leishman to Hay, 31 December 1903, M46, roll 73; 17 January 1904, M625, roll 43.

42. *Army and Navy Journal*, 12 September, 3 October 1903 issues.

43. 14 October 1903, William Sims Papers, Library of Congress, Washington, D.C. *See also* Holden A. Evans, *One Man's Fight For a Better Navy* (New York: Dodd, Mead & Co., 1940), p. 130.

44. Cotton to Leishman, 13 October 1903, International Relations and Politics (VI), box 9, Subject Files, RG45; Cotton to Taylor, 31 October 1903, Cotton Papers; *Army and Navy Journal*, 19 December 1903.

45. Ravndal to State Department, 29 January 1904, M625, roll 43; Leishman to Hay, 21, 24, 30, 31 January, 6 February; Adee to Hay, 20 January 1904, M46, roll 73; Secretary of State to Leishman, 26, 30 January 1904, M77, roll 168. *See also* Secretary of State to Secretary of the Navy, 21 January 1904, M625, roll 43; Secretary of the Navy to Secretary of State, 22 January 1904, Confidential Letters Sent, September 1893–October, 1908, entry 20, RG45; letter from unnamed missionary to Leishman, 12 January 1904, copy in Hay Papers.

46. Secretary of the Navy to Secretary of State, 15 January; Secretary of State to Secretary of the Navy, 18 January 1904, M625, roll 43; Loomis to Leishman, 15 January 1904, M77, roll 168; Livermore, "American Navy as a Factor in World Politics, 1903–1913," p. 869.

47. 1 February 1904, clipping in the Cotton Papers. *See also* Secretary of the Navy to Secretary of State, 20 February 1904, M625, roll 43; Hay diary, entry for 23 February 1904, Hay Papers; *Foreign Relations: 1904*, p. 44.

48. Navy Department to Chadwick, 24 May 1904, General Correspondence of the Bureau of Navigation, Box 276, RG24; Hay diary, Hay Papers.

49. For the Perdicaris affair *see* George W. Collins, "United States-Moroccan Relations, 1904–1912" (Ph.D. diss., University of Colorado, 1965), pp. 6–36; Barbara Tuchman, "Perdicaris Alive or Raisuli Dead," *American Heritage* 10 (August 1959): 18–21, 98–101; Hall, *The United States and Morocco*, pp. 338–43.

50. Tuchman, "Perdicaris Alive or Raisuli Dead," p. 20.

51. Gummere to Secretary of State, 20 May 1904, T61, roll 27.

52. It is quite possible that the decision to send a powerful fleet into the Mediterranean was at least partly a result of the president's political ambitions.

53. Rufus Fairchild Zogbaum, *From Sail to Saratoga: A Naval Autobiography* (Rome: n.p.), pp. 103–4.

54. Chadwick to Secretary of the Navy, 30 May 1904, M625, roll 43.

55. Hay diary, entry for 28 May 1904, Hay Papers; Hay to Secretary of the Navy, 28 May 1904, M625, roll 43.

56. Barker to Secretary of the Navy, 29 May 1904, M625, roll 43; Jewell to Secretary of the Navy, 1 June 1904, Records of the European Squadron, RG313.

57. Zogbaum, *From Sail to Saratoga*, pp. 27–29.

58. The admiral's wife wrote Hay a letter in which she expounded on the theme that her husband was the right man in the right place at the right time. She feared that Admiral Jewell, who was senior to Chadwick, would take over when he arrived. There is no evidence that her letter had any effect on Hay. Chadwick continued to act for the navy even after Jewell arrived. *See* Cornelia Chadwick to Hay, 30 May 1904, Hay Papers.

59. Chadwick to Secretary of the Navy, 31 May 1904, M625, roll 43; Jewell to commanding officers of ships, 7 June 1904, Records of the European Squadron, RG313; Choates to Hay, 3 June 1904, M30, roll 196; *New York Times*, 9 June 1904.

60. Roosevelt to Hay, 13 June 1904, Hay Papers. *See also* Collins, "United States-Moroccan

Relations, 1904–1912," pp. 21–22, and *Harper's Weekly* 48 (June 18, 1904): 928–29.

61. Cambon to I. M. Delcassee, 29 May, 6 June 1904, Ministere des Affaires Etangères, *Documents Diplomatiques Francais 1871–1914*, 41 vols. (Paris: Imprimerie nationale), Ser. II, 5: 192–94, 217; *New York Times*, 3, 5 June 1904; London *Times*, 4 June 1904.

62. Chadwick to Hay, 24 June 1904, Hay Papers; Nicolson to Lansdowne, 30 June 1904, FO99/213.

63. Nicolson to Lansdowne, 4, 9 June 1904, FO99/413; Sid Ben Sliman to Nicolson, 3 June 1904, FO99/413; Nicolson to Sid Ben Sliman, 8 June 1904, FO99/413; London *Times*, 14 June 1904.

64. Albert S. Barker, *Everyday Life in the Navy: Autobiography of Rear Admiral Albert S. Barker* (Boston: R. G. Badger, 1928), pp. 401–2.

65. Tuchman, "Perdicaris Alive or Raisuli Dead," p. 100.

66. This is the opinion expressed in Collins, "United States-Moroccan Relations, 1904–1912," pp. 28–36.

67. Entry for 24 June 1904, Hay Papers. *See also* entry for 18 June in which he wrote, "Jusserand (the French ambassador to the United States) . . . was curious to know why we were sending a fleet to Turkey. I told him I hoped it would not be necessary." *See also* Leishman to Hay, 5 June 1904, Hay Papers.

68. *Foreign Relations: 1904*, pp. 822–24; Loomis to Leishman, 19 July 1904, M77, roll 168. For the visit to Adriatic and Greek ports *see Foreign Relations: 1904*, pp. 44–47, 344–45; *Annual Report of the Secretary of the Navy: 1904* (Washington, D.C.: Government Printing Office, 1905), pp. 455–57; Barker, *Everyday Life in the Navy*, pp. 404–5; Barker to Sims, 4 July 1904, Box 14, Sims Papers; Adee to Hay, 25 July 1904, Hay Papers.

69. Hay diary, entries for 5, 8 August 1904, Hay Papers; *Foreign Relations: 1904*, pp. 624–25; Roosevelt to Sickles, 8 August 1904, *Roosevelt Letters* 4:885; Jewell to Secretary of the Navy, 12 August 1904, M625, roll 44.

70. Diary entries for 9, 10 August 1904, Hay Papers; Leishman to Secretary of State, 9 August 1904, M46, roll 74; *Foreign Relations: 1904*, pp. 825–26; *New York Times*, 6 August 1904.

71. O'Conor to Lansdowne, 10 August 1904, FO78/5335. *See also* telegram from O'Conor to Lansdowne, 11 August 1904, ibid. The United States wanted to raise its representative in the Ottoman Empire to the rank of ambassador, but the Ottoman government opposed it primarily because of the expense involved in raising its representative in Washington to an ambassador. This change in rank would take place in 1906.

72. Diary entry for 12 August 1904, Hay Papers; *Foreign Relations: 1904*, p. 826; Leishman to Secretary of State, 12 August 1904, M46, roll 74; Roosevelt to Leishman, 12 August 1904, *Roosevelt Letters* 4: 891.

73. O'Conor to Lansdowne, 23 August 1904, FO78/5335. For Roosevelt's acceptance note *see* letter to Joseph Cannon, 12 September 1904, *Roosevelt Letters* 4: 921–42. *See also Foreign Relations: 1904*, p. 827. For the Turkish agreement *see* the *New York Times*, 10, 13 August 1904; London *Times*, 15 August 1904. A telegram from the British ambassador said that when the American naval squadron left Smyrna, it declined to exchange courtesies with the Turks. However, this is not mentioned in Admiral Jewell's report. O'Conor to Lansdowne, 13 August 1904, FO78/5339. For a German account of the controversy *see* the German ambassador in Constantinople to Von Bulow, 14 August 1904, T139, roll 139.

74. Roosevelt to John S. Kennedy, 22 August 1904, Roosevelt Papers, reel 335; Adee to Hay, 24 August 1904, Hay Papers.

75. In late September, the three cruisers made a northern cruise to the Baltic. The only excitement occurred when on returning south they blundered into the second squadron of the British Channel Fleet. This force was searching for the Russian Baltic fleet, which had fired on a number of fishing trawlers off Dogger Bank. The British ships cleared for action, and in order to avoid another mistake the American ships hoisted the largest flags that they had. Colby to Secretary of

the Navy, 12 January 1905, Operations of Fleets (OO), Box 12, Subject Files, RG45; O. W. Andrews, *Seamarks and Landmarks* (London: Ernest Benn, Ltd., 1927), p. 231.

CHAPTER 10

1. Sigsbee to Secretary of the Navy, 1 July 1905, M625, roll 44; Murray Wolffe, *Memoirs of a Gob* (New York: Exposition Press, 1949), pp. 48–50.

2. *Annual Report of the Secretary of the Navy: 1905* (Washington, D.C.: Government Printing Office, 1906), p. 387; Chester to Secretary of the Navy, 29 November 1905, M625, roll 44.

3. Converse to Sigsbee, 12 December 1905, George A. Converse Papers, Library of Congress, Washington, D.C. *See also* Allan Nevins, *Henry White, Thirty Years of American Diplomacy* (New York: Harper & Brothers, 1930), p. 268; *Outlook* 82 (13, 20 January 1906): 65, 103–4. Professor Livermore suggests that Roosevelt sent Sigsbee's squadron to Gibraltar in order to back up England and France. *See* Seward W. Livermore, "American Navy as a Factor in World Politics, 1903–1913," *American Historical Review* 63 (July 1958): 872. *See also* Tom T. Lewis, "Franco-American Relations During the First Moroccan Crisis," *Mid America* 55 (January 1973), pp. 21–36.

4. Henry Harris Jessup, *Fifty Years in Syria*, 2 vols. (New York: Fleming H. Revell, 1910), 2: 764; *The Nation* 83 (July 19, 1906), pp. 48–49; American minister to Root, 6 October 1906, M625, roll 44. The school problem was also generating controversy between the two governments again. *See Papers Relating to the Foreign Relations of the United States: 1906* (Washington, D.C.: Government Printing Office, 1907), pp. 1364–65.

5. Leishman to Secretary of State, 19 July 1907, M625, roll 45. *See also* the memorandum reviewing background to the question of a stationnaire, 6 August 1907, ibid.

6. Leishman to Secretary of State, 30 July 1908; Second Assistant Secretary of State to Root, 15 August 1908, Root to Leishman, 19 August 1908, General Records of the Department of State, Record Group 59, entry 186, Numerical File, 1906–1910, File 10044/80–82 (hereafter cited by numerical file number, RG59). Leishman provided the State Department with miscellaneous information concerning stationnaires belonging to other countries at Constantinople. He also warned that publicity was not desired; "it is necessary for us to take greater precaution to avoid slighting new government's susceptibilities." This included concealing the ship's armament below deck. Leishman to Secretary of State, 20 August 1908, M625, roll 45.

7. Adee to Roosevelt, 25 September; Roosevelt's secretary to Adee, 26 September 1908, 10044/80–82, RG59.

8. Vessel's data provided by the Ship's History Section, Naval History Division, Navy Yard, Washington, D.C. The ship has attracted considerable attention throughout the years, particularly by individuals who served on her. A number of letters concerning the *Scorpion* have appeared in *All Hands*. *See* especially the issues for April 1960, June 1960, August 1961, October 1959, and July 1959. *See also* the *New York Times*, 9 November 1936, pp. 3–4. For her service in the Spanish-American war *see* W. T. Claverius, "The *Scorpion* Passes," *United States Naval Institute Proceedings* 53 (September 1927): 969–73. *See also* Adee to Root, 21 August 1908, 10044/44, RG59, for the decision about carrying a band. For the *Scorpion* files, *see* General Correspondence of the Bureau of Navigation, 1903–1913, box 610, RG24.

9. Adee to Root, 21 August 1908, 10044/44, RG59.

10. Her bunkers were inadequate; they could not hold enough coal to reach the Azores. State Department to Leishman, 28 September 1908, 10044/68, RG59; *All Hands* (October 1959), 28–29; *Foreign Relations: 1908*, pp. 751–52; Leishman to Secretary of State, 15 October 1908, 10044/85, RG59.

11. Stewart Frederick Bryant, "The Tale of the Scorpion: A Story of the War Experiences of the American Sailors on the United States Ship *Scorpion* at Constantinople," unpublished manuscript in Naval Vessels (OS), *Scorpion* File, Box 278, Subject Files, RG45 (hereafter cited as

Bryant, "The Tale of the *Scorpion*," RG45). Bryant wrote this account while World War I was in progress, but he was never able to get it published.

12. Secretary of Navy to Secretary of State, 16 June 1909, 10044/281 RG59; 14 December 1909, 10044/378, RG59. *See also* Root to Secretary of the Navy, 28 October 1908, 10044/87, RG59; V. H. Metcalf to Logan, 20 October 1908, M625, roll 45; Newberry to Secretary of State, 21 October 1908, 10044/88, RG59; Secretary of State to Secretary of the Navy, 12 June 1909, M625, roll 46.

13. Quoted in Robert A. Hart, *The Great White Fleet* (Boston: Little, Brown and Company, 1965), p. 281. *See also* Logan to Secretary of the Navy, 13 January 1909; Admiral Sperry to Secretary of the Navy, 4 October 1909, M625, roll 46; Logan to Secretary of the Navy, 9 January 1909, General Correspondence of the Bureau of Navigation, 1903–1913, box 1082, RG24. British ships withdrew because of the Italian government's attitude.

14. Secretary of the Navy to Secretary of State, 18 January; Chief, Bureau of Navigation to ALUSNA, Rome, 2 February 1909, General Correspondence of the Bureau of Navigation, box 1082, RG24; Bacon to Leishman, 17 February 1909, 10044/138, RG59; Ernest P. Bicknell, *Pioneering With the Red Cross* (New York: The MacMillan Company, 1935), pp. 108–9; Reginald R. Belknap, "Earthquake Relief Work at Messina Reggio," *Survey* 32 (2 May 1914): 115–19.

15. She did not return to Constantinople until July 1909. Leishman to Secretary of the Navy, 23 May 1909, 10044/219, RG59.

16. *Foreign Relations: 1909*, pp. 562, 566–67; Bacon to Leishman, 17 February 1909, 10044/138, RG59; Ralph E. Cook, "The United States and the Armenian Question" (Ph.D. diss., Fletcher School of Diplomacy, 1957), p. 110; Joseph L. Grabill, *Protestant Diplomacy in the Near East: Missionary Influence on American Policy, 1810–1927* (Minneapolis: University of Minnesota Press, 1971), p. 50.

17. Taft had been in office approximately a month when the trouble broke out. Knox to Leishman, 15, 19, 21 April; State Department to Leishman, 18 April 1909, 10044/139, 145, 147, 151A, RG59.

18. *Foreign Relations: 1909*, pp. 568–73.

19. M. Harris to Wilson, 4, 24 May 1909, 10044/176–177, 218, RG59.

20. These letters and telegrams are in Numeral File 19274, RG59.

21. H. G. Bowen, *Ships, Machinery & Mossbacks: The Autobiography of a Naval Engineer* (Princeton: Princeton University Press, 1954), pp. 20–21. Bowen was engineering officer on the *Tennessee* in 1914. *See also* Edward L. Beach, *The Wreck of the Memphis* (New York: Holt, Rinehart & Winston, 1966), pp. 10–17. The *Tennessee* was renamed the *Memphis* in 1916. John D. Alden, *The American Steel Navy* (Annapolis: United States Naval Institute, 1972), p. 157.

22. The *Tahoma* arrived on 12 May. For the *Tahoma's* activities during this period *see* the daily log of J. H. Quinan, commanding officer of the *Tahoma*, J. H. Quinan Papers, Southern Historical Collection, University of North Carolina, Chapel Hill, N.C. *See also* State Department to Secretary of the Treasury, 22 April 1909, 10044/554, RG59.

23. Alfred Reynolds to J. H. Quinan, 18 May 1909; entries for 14–18 May 1909, Quinan Papers; Marshall to Secretary of the Navy, 14, 17 May 1909, M625, roll 46; Wolffe, *Memoirs of a Gob*, p. 77. The editor of *Outlook* asked Knox if Marines might be landed in Syria. The secretary replied that such an action "is very exceptional," but he admitted that it had been done in Haiti and "elsewhere." Baldwin to Knox, 6 May; Wilson to Secretary of State, 8 May 1909, 10044/184, RG59.

24. Secretary of State to Secretary of Navy, 29 April; Secretary of Navy to Secretary of State, 1 May 1909, M625, roll 46; Quinan to wife, 25 May 1909, Quinan Papers; Wolffe, *Memoirs of a Gob*, pp. 77–79; Leishman to Secretary of State, 27 April 1909, 10044/165, RG59.

25. Leishman to Secretary of State, 9 June; Knox to Secretary of State, 1 July; Adee to Secretary of Navy, 28 August 1909, 10044/289, 305, 356, RG59; Knox to Secretary of State, 30 June; Marshall to Secretary of Navy, 19 July 1909, M625, roll 46.

26. Richard D. Challener, *Admirals, Generals and American Foreign Policy, 1898–1914* (Princeton: Princeton University Press, 1973), pp. 269–70; Winthrop to Knox, 16 August 1909, 10044/351–356, RG59.

27. Leishman to Secretary of State, 5 June, 1 July; Secretary of Navy to Secretary of State, 14 July; Einstein to Marshall, 12 July; Wilson to Winthrop, 25 June 1909, 10044/291, 325, 338, 334A, 327, RG59; Secretary of the Navy to Marshall, 25 June 1909, M625, roll 46; Wolffe, *Memoirs of a Gob*, p. 79.

28. Diary entry, 7 March 1910, Oscar Straus diary, Oscar Straus Papers, Library of Congress, Washington, D.C.

29. F. M. Huntington Wilson, *Memoirs of an Ex-Diplomat* (Boston: Bruce Humphries, Inc., 1945), p. 224. On the Chester project *see* John A. DeNovo, *American Interests and Policies in the Middle East, 1900–1939* (Minneapolis: University of Minnesota Press, 1963).

30. M. S. Anderson, *The Eastern Question, 1774–1923* (New York: St. Martin's Press, 1966), pp. 287–88.

31. For interest in intervention *see* William C. Askew and J. Fred Rippy, "The United States and Europe's Strife," *Journal of Politics* 4 (February 1942): 72–74.

32. Memorandum of Adee to Knox, 30 September; Adee to Leishman, 6 October 1911, Philander C. Knox Papers, Library of Congress, Washington, D.C.; Taft to Lodge, 12 April 1911, William H. Taft Papers, Library of Congress, Washington, D.C.; Wilson to Secretary of State, 10 October 1911, M530, roll 3; C. W. F. to Adee, 11 October; Adee to Secretary of the Navy, 11 October 1911, M530, roll 3.

33. Unfinished autobiography of Admiral Long, Andrew Long Papers, Southern Historical Collection, University of North Carolina Library, Chapel Hill, N.C.; Wood to Secretary of State, 9 November; Adee to Knox, n.d.; O'Brien to Secretary of State, 8 November 11, M530, roll 4; Adee to Wood, 5 November; Wilson to Knox, 6 November; Decker to Secretary of the Navy, 7 November 1911, Knox Papers. *See also* Secretary of the Navy to Knox, 15 November; Knox to Secretary of the Navy, 18 November 1911, M530, roll 4.

34. Chief of the Division of Near Eastern Affairs to Adee, 6 November; Adee to Chief of the Division of Near Eastern Affairs, 7 November; Chief of the Division of Near Eastern Affairs, to Wilson, 7 November 1912, Decimal File 367.11/8, RG59. On 3 November the Turkish government granted permission for foreign warships to pass through the Dardanelles, and within days an international fleet had assembled at Constantinople. Warships were also dispatched to Salonica. Paul G. Halpern, *The Mediterranean Naval Situation, 1908–1914* (Cambridge: Harvard University Press, 1970), pp. 100–5. *See also* Sir Telford Waugh, *Turkey Yesterday, Today and Tomorrow* (London: Chapman and Hall, 1930), p. 136.

35. R. H. Dodge to Secretary of State, 4 November; Adee to Dodge, 5 November; Rockhill to Secretary of State, 5, 7 November; Adee to Rockhill, 4 November 1912, Decimal File 367.11/3, 6, 7b, 8, 12, RG59; Knox to Taft, 16 November 1912, series 6, file 40, Taft Papers. *See also* R. M. Sommerville, corresponding secretary of the Board of Foreign Missions of the Reformed Presbyterian Church to Secretary of the Navy, 6 November; Secretary of the Navy to Secretary of State, 8 November 1912, Decimal File 367.11/11, 29, RG59; *Army and Navy Journal*, 9 November 1912.

36. Unpublished biographical memoir of Admiral Aaron S. Merrill, Aaron S. Merrill Papers, Southern Historical Collection, University of North Carolina, Chapel Hill; *All Hands* (January 1959): 28.

37. Wilson to Rockhill, 8 November; "M" to Adee, 11 November 1912, Decimal File 367.11/15a, 39a–40, RG59. *See also* the correspondence with U.S. embassies in capitals of Germany, Great Britain, Russia, France, and Austria in Decimal File 367.11/16–20, 74, 79, RG59.

38. Rockhill to Secretary of State, 12, 20, 21 November 1912, Decimal File 367.11/60, 75–76, RG59; Secretary of the Navy to Secretary of State, 25 November 1912, Decimal File 367.11/66, RG59; Rockhill to Secretary of State, 27 November 1912, M363, roll 26. During the

war the *Scorpion's* medical officer and hospital steward served voluntarily in a Turkish hospital under the Red Cross for a week. The vessel's enlisted men cut out hundreds of pajamas and hospital sheets. The ship's carpenter helped construct a temporary hospital. McCauley to Secretary of the Navy, 14 July, 4 December 1913, file 26742/62, RG80. Waugh, *Turkey*, p. 136; Lynn A. Scipio, *My Thirty Years in Turkey* (Rindge, New Hampshire: Richard R. Smith, Publisher, 1955), p. 67.

39. Memoir, Merrill Papers, telegram from commanding officer, *Montana*, to Secretary of the Navy, 14 December 1912, copy in Franklin Delano Roosevelt Papers, Group 10, Box 48. *See also* Rockhill to Knight, 3 December, to Secretary of State, 14 December, 12 April; Knight to Rockhill, 16 December, Decimal File 367.11/99, 91, 139, 114, RG59. All are dated 1912 but the one for 12 April.

40. Knight to Secretary of the Navy, 8 December 1912; Fletcher to Knight, 14 December 1912; Fletcher to Secretary of the Navy, 28 February 1913; Rockhill to State Department, 8 January, 13 February 1913, M353, roll 4. *See also* Consul, Beirut, to Secretary of State, 2 December 1912, M363, roll 26; Rockhill to Secretary of State, 10 January 1913, General Correspondence of the Secretary of the Navy, Box 1702, RG80.

41. Entry 8 March 1913, Josephus Daniels, *The Cabinet Diaries of Josephus Daniels, 1913-1921*, ed. E. David Cronin (Lincoln: University of Nebraska Press, 1963), p. 5. *See also* Knight to Secretary of the Navy, 13 March 1913, Decimal File 367.11/133, RG59; Daniels to Chief, Bureau of Supplies and Accounts, 1 April 1913, General Correspondence of the Secretary of the Navy, file 27673, RG80. Fletcher agreed with Knight. Fletcher to Daniels, 16 March 1913, M353, roll 5.

42. General Board Proceedings, 29 April 1913, 5:83–84, Papers of the General Board of the United States Navy, Navy History Division, Washington Navy Yard, Washington, D.C.; William R. Braisted, *The United States Navy in the Pacific, 1897–1909* (Austin: University of Texas Press, 1971), pp. 125–27, 130; Newton Jones to Albert Gleaves, 12 May 1913, Albert Gleaves Papers, Library of Congress, Washington, D.C.

43. Moore, Acting Secretary of State to Rockhill, 5 May; Rockhill to State Department, 6 May 1913, Decimal File 367.11/139, 143, RG59.

44. *All Hands* (July 1959; August 1961); note from Turkish officials to the American consul, 1 October 1909; Chester to Straus, 11 July 1910; Straus to Secretary of State, 8 July 1910, file 124.6718a, RG59; Straus diary, entry for 4 July 1910, Straus Papers.

45. McCauley to Secretary of the Navy, 15 March 1915, file 124.6718a/29, RG59; Bryant, "The Tale of the *Scorpion*," RG45; Henry Morgenthau diary, entries for 17, 21 March 1915, Henry Morgenthau Papers, Library of Congress, Washington, D.C.; Morgenthau to Secretary of State, 24 March 1915, Decimal File 811.321/49, RG59. *See also* Lewis Einstein, *Inside Constantinople: A Diplomatist's Diary During The Dardanelles Expedition, April-September, 1915* (London: John Murray, 1927), pp. 66–67; Morgenthau to Secretary of State, 25 May 1915, M367, roll 21; Morgenthau diary, entry for 25 May 1915, Morgenthau papers. For the exploits of the E-11 *see* Peter Shankland and Anthony Hunter, *Dardanelles Patrol* (London: Fontana Books, 1965).

46. *All Hands* (August 1961), pp. 26–27.

47. H. S. Babbitt to Morgenthau, 3 April 1915, copy in General Correspondence of the Secretary of Navy, file 27642/99, RG80; McCauley to Secretary of Navy, 7 November 1914, Correspondence of the Secretary of Navy, file 27642/99, RG80.

CHAPTER 11

1. Josephus Daniels, *The Wilson Era: Years of Peace, 1910–1917* (Chapel Hill: University of North Carolina Press, 1944), pp. 122–23.

2. Arthur S. Link, *Wilson: The New Freedom* (Princeton: Princeton University Press, 1956), pp. 124–25.

3. William D. Leahy Papers, Library of Congress, Washington, D.C.

4. Arthur S. Link, *Wilson the Diplomatist: A Look at His Major Foreign Policies* (Baltimore: The Johns Hopkins Press, 1957), pp. 5, 11.

5. Daniels to commanding officer, Atlantic Fleet, 3 October 1913, General Correspondence of the Secretary of the Navy, Box 674, RG80; Rufus Furchild Zogbaum, *From Sail to Saratoga: An Autobiography* (Rome: n.p.), pp. 182–87; Seward W. Livermore, "American Navy as a Factor in World Politics, 1903–1913," *The American Historical Review* 63 (July 1958): 878.

6. Frank Freidel, *Franklin D. Roosevelt: The Apprenticeship* (Boston: Little, Brown & Company, 1952), pp. 238–39.

7. American ambassador, Berlin, to Secretary of State, 31 July 1914, M367, roll 1. *See also* Wilson to Fitzgerald, 3 August 1914, Series IV, case 1645, Woodrow Wilson Papers, Library of Congress, Washington, D.C.; memo of conference of heads of departments concerning emergency relief for Europe, 5 August 1914, Series IV, case 1645, Wilson Papers; circular dated 4 August 1914, Decimal File 840.48, RG59; *New York Times*, 3, 5 August 1914; commanding officer, *North Carolina*, to Secretary of the Navy, 29 August 1914, Area 4 File, 1910–27, National Archives, RG45; Arthur S. Link, *The Struggle for Neutrality, 1914–1915* (Princeton: Princeton University Press, 1960), pp. 74–76. The assistant secretary of the navy (Roosevelt) was given the task of informing the public that the vessels were not ordered to Europe in order to carry the refugees home. Roosevelt to D. A. Newhall, 7 August 1914, Group 10, Franklin D. Roosevelt Papers, Franklin D. Roosevelt Library, Hyde Park, New York.

8. Theodore Roscoe, *On the Seas and in the Skies: A History of the U.S. Navy's Air Power* (New York: Hawthorn Books, Inc., 1970), pp. 48–49; Rear Admiral George van Deurs, *Wings for the Fleet, A Narrative of Naval Aviation's Early Development, 1910–1916* (Annapolis: United State's Naval Institute, 1966), pp. 116–17; Edward Blakelee to Albert Gleaves, 24 October, 16 November 1914, Albert Gleaves Papers, Library of Congress, Washington, D.C.

9. Victor Blue to Operations, 16 April 1915, General Correspondence of the Secretary of the Navy, file 27673/284, RG80; H. G. Bowen, *Ships, Machinery & Mossbacks: The Autobiography of a Naval Engineer* (Princeton: Princeton University Press, 1954), pp. 20–27; George Horton, *Recollections Grave and Gay: The Story of a Mediterranean Consul* (Indianapolis: Bobbs-Merrill, 1927), pp. 210–11.

10. Sir Roger Keyes, *The Naval Memoirs of Admiral of the Fleet Sir Roger Keyes: Scapa Flow to the Dover Straits, 1916–1918* (London: Thornton Butterworth, Ltd., 1935), p. 76. *See also* commanding officer, *Tennessee*, to Secretary of the Navy, 22 August 1914, Area 4 File, RG45.

11. Stewart Frederick Bryant, "The Tale of the *Scorpion*: A Story of the War Experiences of the American Sailors on the United States Ship *Scorpion*," unpublished manuscript in Naval Vessels (OS), *Scorpion* File, Box 278, RG45. *See also Foreign Relations of the United States, Supplement: 1914* (Washington, D.C.: Government Printing Office, 1928), pp. 757, 762–63; Hollis to State Department, 7 August 1914, M353, roll 5; Morgenthau Diary, entry of 5 August 1914, Henry Morgenthau Papers, Library of Congress, Washington, D.C.; George W. Stinagle, "Ambassador Henry Morgenthau to Turkey, 1913–1916: Protection of American Rights" (M.A. thesis, East Carolina University, 1973), pp. 54–58; Henry Morgenthau, *Ambassador Morgenthau's Story* (Garden City: Doubleday, Page and Company, 1918), p. 65.

12. *Foreign Relations: 1914, Supplement*, pp. 756–57; Morgenthau to Secretary of the Navy, 7 May 1914, General Records of the Secretary of the Navy, File 27642/67, RG80; Morgenthau diary, entries for 21, 22 August 1914, Morgenthau Papers; Lewis Einstein, *A Diplomat Looks Back* (New Haven: Yale University Press, 1968), p. 129. *See also* McCauley to Secretary of the Navy, Decimal File 124.671a/20, RG59. For the *Scorpion's* activities up to being immobilized *see* pp. 183–84.

13. Parker to Bryan, 17 August; Barton to Bryan, 17 August 1914, Decimal File 367.11/188, 179, RG59; Morgenthau to Secretary of State, 15 August 1914, M367, roll 12; *Foreign Relations: 1914, Supplement*, pp. 62, 66–67, 756–67; C. Cook to Davis, 4 January 1915,

Decimal File 840.48/1146, RG59. For demands from American diplomatic representatives in Turkey *see* Horton (Beirut) to Secretary of State, 4, 7, 15, 17, 19 August 1914; Morris to Morgenthau, n.d.; Morgenthau to Secretary of State, 6 August 1914, M353, roll 5; Morgenthau to Secretary of State, 5, 10, 11 August; Bryan to Morgenthau, 8 August 1914, Decimal File 367.11/233, 172, 174, 165, RG59. *See also* Morgenthau diary, entries for 5, 10, 15 August 1914, Morgenthau Papers.

14. Frank E. Weber, *Eagle on the Crescent: Germany, Austria, and the Diplomacy of the Turkish Alliance, 1914–1918* (Ithaca: Cornell University Press, 1970), pp. 76–78; *Foreign Relations: 1914, Supplement*, pp. 759–61, 961. *See also* Bryan to American ambassador, Paris, 19 August; Gerald (Berlin) to Bryan, 22 August; American ambassador, Paris, to Bryan, 22 August 1914, Decimal File 367.11/185a, 186, 194, RG59; *New York Times*, 28 August, 6 September 1914; Gray to Secretary of State, 5 September 1914, Robert Lansing Papers, Library of Congress, Washington, D.C.

15. Straus to Wilson, 8 October 1914, Series IV, case 128, Wilson Papers; Blakelee to Gleaves, 16 November 1914, Gleaves Papers. A letter with almost identical words and phrases as the Blakelee letter but with no name attached was sent to the Navy Department. *See* Naval Vessels (OS), *North Carolina* File, Subject Files, 1911–27, RG45.

16. Roosevelt to Secretary of State, 11 September 1918, Decimal File 840.48/703, RG59; Daniels to commanding officer, *North Carolina*, 12 September 1914, Area 4 File, RG45; Morgenthau to Bryan, 28 August, 2 September 1914, Decimal File 367.11/199, 209, RG59; Morgenthau diary, entries for 28, 29 August, 1 September 1914, Morgenthau Papers; *Army and Navy Journal*, 27 August 1914. Bryan cabled Louis Marshal of the American Jewish Committee and suggested that additional funds could be taken to the Near East by the *North Carolina*. He suggested that a London bank be contacted to provide the funds. 28 August 1914, Decimal File 367.11/196, RG59. *See also* Lansing to Boroughs (lawyer representing MacAndrews and Forbes), 3 September 1914, Lansing Papers.

17. *New York Times*, 8 September 1914; Link, *Wilson and the Struggle for Neutrality*, pp. 68–69. The two warships were sold to Greece in May 1914. Turkey vigorously protested the deal at the time. *See Paul G. Halpern, The Mediterranean Naval Situation, 1908–1914* (Cambridge: Harvard University Press, 1970), pp. 351–52. The head of the British naval mission to Greece considered the vessels worthless. Mark Kerr, *Land, Sea, and Air: Reminiscences of Mark Kerr* (London: Longmans, 1927), p. 196.

18. American consul at Beirut to Bryan, 18 September; Jackson (Aleppo) to State Department, 8 October; Morris to Morgenthau, n.d., 1914, M353, roll 5–6; Reynolds to Wilson, 17 September 1914, Series II, box 116, Wilson Papers. *See also The Independent* 79 (21 September 1914): 403.

19. Secretary of the Navy to commanding officer, *Tennessee*, 3 October 1914, General Correspondence of the Secretary of the Navy, file 27673, RG80; Stinagle, "Ambassador Henry Morgenthau to Turkey," pp. 61–64; Decker, commanding the *Tennessee*, to Daniels, 1 September 1914, Area 4 File, RG45; Osborne, American consul in Le Havre, to Bryan, 3 September; Herrick, American ambassador to France, to Bryan, 8 October 1914, Decimal File 840.48/510, 506, RG59.

20. Hollis to Bryan, 8 October 1914, copy in General Correspondence of the Secretary of the Navy, file 27592, RG80; Morgenthau diary, entries for 17, 18 October 1914, Morgenthau Papers; Hollis to Morgenthau, 30 October, and Morgenthau's endorsement of the cable forwarded to Bryan, 30 October 1914, M353, roll 6; Page to Grey, 6 November; and British consul general at Smyrna to Grey, 6 November 1914, FO 371/2145; Nelson Page, American ambassador, Rome, to Bryan, 21 November 1914, M367, roll 18. Hollis had also requested additional warships as the U.S. is "alone . . . in a position to act as international policeman," to Bryan, 16 November 1914, M353, roll 6.

21. Hollis to Bryan, 2 November 1914, M353, roll 6; Daniels to Bryan, 11 November; Decker to Daniels, 13 November; Morgenthau to Bryan, 14, 17 November 1914, M367, roll 8.

22. Morgenthau to Bryan, 21 September 1914, Decimal File 840.48/652, RG59; Horton to Morgenthau, 23 September; Morgenthau to Horton, 23 September; Morgenthau to Bryan, 23 September, 10 October 1914, Decimal File 367.11, RG59; C. Reed to Rev. Charles Riggs, copy in Morgenthau Papers; Morgenthau to Bryan, 1 October 1914, M365, roll 8; C. R. Love to Bryan, 10 October; Horton to Morgenthau, 14 November 1914, M353, roll 5, 6; Decker to Daniels, 7, 14 November 1914, General Correspondence of the Secretary of the Navy, file 27673, RG80; Morgenthau to Horton, 13 November 1914, M367, roll 19.

23. *New York Times*, 19 November 1914; London *Daily News*, 18 November 1914; Bowen, *Ships, Machinery & Mossbacks*, pp. 25–27.

24. Lansing to Morgenthau, 20 November; Morgenthau to Bryan, 21 November 1914, M367, roll 18; *New York Times*, 20 November 1914; memo dated 21 November 1914, Series IV, case 128, Wilson Papers. *See also* the Bradley Fiske diary, entry for 23 November 1914, Bradley Fiske Papers, Library of Congress, Washington, D.C.; Daniels to Wilson, 17 November 1914, Series II, box 120, Wilson Papers.

25. Fiske diary, entry 25 November 1914, Fiske Papers; Daniels to Decker, 19 November 1914, General Correspondence of the Secretary of the Navy, File 27673, RG80.

26. Horton in his memoirs agrees with Decker's account. *Recollections Grave and Gay*, pp. 231–33. *See also* Decker to Daniels, 17, 18, 25 November 1914, General Correspondence of the Secretary of the Navy, File 27673, RG80; Fiske diary, entry 24 December 1914, Fiske Papers; *Army and Navy Journal*, 28 November 1914; *New York Times*, 24 November 1914; Enver to Morgenthau, 24 November 1914, M367, roll 18.

27. Morgenthau diary, entry 22 November 1914; Wagenhein to A. A., 22 November 1914, T139, roll 472.

28. *See* entries for 21, 24, 27, 28 November and 12 December 1914, especially. Lansing diary, Lansing Papers. On 21 November Lansing wrote that a fifty-minute conference was held at the White House on the Smyrna incident. Daniels also attended.

29. For German warnings *see* Bernstaff to Secretary of State, 3 October, 17 February 1915, M367, roll 14, 1.

30. For the background to the "Christmas Ship" *see* Series IV, case 1643E, Wilson Papers. *See also* Lansing to various American diplomatic representatives in Europe, 28 October 1914, Decimal File 840.48/987, RG59. The *Jason* brought back from Europe treasure from art galleries to be stored in the United States for the duration. *Annual Report of the Secretary of the Navy: 1915* (Washington, D.C.: Government Printing Office, 1916), p. 66.

31. Morgenthau to Bryan, 12 December; Daniels to Bryan, 27 November 1914, M353, roll 6; Lansing diary, entries for 12, 14 December 1914, Lansing papers; Morgenthau to Secretary of State, 4 December 1914, M367, roll 19; *New York Times*, 21 November 1914.

32. *Foreign Relations: 1914, Supplement*, pp. 776–81; Bryan to Wilson, 16 December 1914, Series II, box 125, Wilson Papers; Morgenthau diary, entry for 22 December 1914, Morgenthau Papers.

33. *New York Times*, 19 June 1916: Lewen Francis B. Weldon, *"Hard Lying": Eastern Mediterranean, 1914–1919* (London: H. Jenkins, Ltd., 1926), pp. 85–86.

34. J. Oman to Daniels, 29 December 1915, General Correspondence of the Secretary of the Navy, file 27592, RG80; Alexander Aaronsohn, *With the Turks in Palestine* (New York: Houghton Mifflin Company, 1916), pp. 30, 63–64. In February, liberty was granted daily, including overnight for some crew members. Oman to Daniels, 6 March 1915, M353, roll 6.

35. Oman to Daniels, 29 December 1914, General Correspondence of the Secretary of the Navy, file 27592/238, RG80; Morgenthau diary, entry for 15 January 1915, Morgenthau Papers; *Foreign Relations: 1915, Supplement*, p. 961; *New York Times*, 28 December 1914. A press dispatch from Athens said that it was an American warship that threatened to bombard Tripoli, Daniels to Commanding Officer, *North Carolina*, 28 December 1914, M367, roll 19. The commanding officer of the British cruiser *Dora* disbelieved Decker's reports that Jaffa would be mined. *See* Commanding Officer, *Dora*, to Commanding Officer, East India Squadron, 6

February 1915. For use of searchlights *see* Commanding Officer, *Dora*, to Commanding Officer, East India Squadron, 21 January 1915, both in ADM 137/1091.

36. Morgenthau diary, entry for 27 December 1914, Morgenthau Papers; Morgenthau to Secretary of State, 27, 28 December 1914, M353, roll 19.

37. Morgenthau to Secretary of State, 25 December 1914, Decimal File 840.48/1091, RG59; Decker to Daniels, 30 December 1914, General Correspondence of the Secretary of the Navy, file 27673/264, RG80; Imperial Consul, Jaffa, to Bethmann Hollweg, 2 January 1915, T120, roll 4331.

38. For the best account *see* Frank E. Manuel, *The Realities of American Palestine Relations* (Washington, D.C.: Public Affairs Press, 1949), pp. 119–54. *See also* Howard M. Sachar, *The Emergence of the Middle East, 1914–1924* (New York: Knopf, 1970), pp. 191–93; Egmont Zechlin, *Die deutsche Politik und die Juden in Ersten Weltkrieg* (Gottingen: Vandenhoeck u. Ruprecht, 1969), pp. 319–20; Morgenthau to Secretary of State, M353, roll 43; memo entitled "expulsion of Russian Jews of Jaffa," probably sent to the Secretary of the Navy by the commanding officer, *Tennessee*, in General Correspondence of the Secretary of the Navy, file 27673/264, RG80.

39. Cyrus Adler, *Jacob H. Schiff: His Life and Letters*, 2 vols. (New York: Doubleday, Doran and Company, Inc., 1928) 2: 277–78.

40. A cameraman recorded the event, which was shown in movie houses in the United States. *See* Decker to Daniels, 7 February 1915, M353, roll 43. *See also* Manuel, *The Realities of American Palestine Relations*, p. 124; Decker to Daniels, 18 February 1915, General Correspondence of the Secretary of the Navy, file 27673/280, RG80. The German ambassador in the United States apparently had a good source of information in the Navy Department, for his cables to Berlin frequently contained Decker's reports to the Navy Department, usually on the same day that they were received. For example, *see* Bernstoff to A.A., 18 January 1915 and 2 March 1915, T120, roll 4331. Cecil Spring Rice, British ambassador to the United States, wrote to Lord Balfour, the foreign secretary, "The U.S. Navy Department is full of German spies. So be careful what information gets to them." 25 October 1915, file 19740, Arthur James Balfour Mss., British Museum, London.

41. Bryan to American consul, Alexandria, 30 Janaury 1915, M353, roll 43; Decker's report on Zionism (over twenty pages in length), dated 10 February 1915, copy in Morgenthau Papers. *See also* Decker to Daniels, 16 February 1915, Decimal File 367.116/294, RG59; Turkish Foreign Office to Morgenthau, 1 March 1915, M353, roll 43. Decker prepared long detailed intelligence reports on Syria, Jewish, and Turkish officials and on military affairs in general. For the reports *see* General Correspondence of the Secretary of the Navy, file 27673, RG80; *See also Foreign Relations: 1915, Supplement*, p. 979.

42. Anita Engle, *The Nili Spies* (London: the Hogarth Press, 1959), pp. 44, 52–53.

43. *See* Morgenthau Papers, box 4, for correspondence concerning the *Vulcan*. *See also* Manuel, *The Realities of American Palestine Relations*, pp. 140–42; *New York Times*, 15 February 1915; Bernstoff to A.A., 19 March 1915, T120, roll 4331. According to Daniels' biographer, the naval secretary was sympathetic to the relief efforts. Joseph L. Morrison, *Josephus Daniels: The Small-d Democrat* (Chapel Hill: University of North Carolina Press, 1966), p. 141. American naval vessels strictly observed neutrality by refusing to communicate directly with Allied blockading vessels. On one occasion a British warship carried a message from the American consul general in Cairo to one of the American cruisers, but the cruiser's commanding officer refused to accept it. Weldon, *"Hard Lying,"* p. 92; Commanding officer, *Dora*, to senior officer, Egypt, 13 April 1915, ADM 137/1091.

44. Commanding officer, *Des Moines*, to Daniels, 14 April 1915, Decimal File 840.48/1584, RG59; Blue to Operations, 16 April 1915, including Fletcher to Daniels, 7 April 1915; and Caperton to commanding officer, Atlantic Fleet, 11 March 1915, General Correspondence of the Secretary of the Navy, file 27673/284, RG80; Lansing desk diary, entries for 1, 11 March, 19 April 1915; Secretary of State to Secretary of the Navy, 25 February 1915, Decimal File 840.48/1318, RG59.

45. Commanding Officer, *Des Moines*, to Daniels, 24 June 1915, Decimal File 840.48/1584. *See also* John D. Alden, *American Steel Navy* (Annapolis: United States Naval Institute, 1972), p. 161; John M. Kennaday, "Fine Sea Boats . . . of No Fighting Value," *United States Naval Institute Proceedings* 104 (January 1978): 92–94.

46. Lewis Einstein, *Inside Constantinople: A Diplomatist's Diary During the Dardanelles Expedition, April-September, 1915* (London: John Murray, 1917), pp. 204–5. Morgenthau diary, entries for 24, 26 July, 6, 7 August 1915, Morgenthau Papers; Bryant, "The Tale of the *Scorpion*."

47. Morgenthau diary, 16 September 1915, Morgenthau Papers; *New York Times*, 9 March 1916; Bryant, "The tale of the *Scorpion*." In the Bryant manuscript *see* especially the chapter entitled, "Life in the Golden Horn." *See also* Morton, commanding the *Scorpion*, to Secretary of the Navy, 15 September 1915, 27 January 1917, General Correspondence of the Secretary of the Navy, file 27642/109, RG80. When Turkish officials requested three hundred tons of coal from the *Chester* and were refused, they retaliated by stopping all liberty for the *Scorpion's* crew. Only the commanding officer was allowed to go ashore. Scofield to Daniels, 31 July 1915, Decimal File 840.48/1599, RG59; Hollis to Secretary of State, 6, 20 August 1915, Decimal File 367.11/748, 796, RG59. *See also* Decker to Daniels, 27 May 1915, for another example of harassment. General Correspondence of the Secretary of the Navy, Box 1505, RG80.

48. Morgenthau *Diary*, 10 June 1915, Morgenthau Papers; Daniels to commanding officer, *Scorpion*, 15 September 1915, General Corresepondence of the Secretary of the Navy, file 27642/108, RG80; Philip to Secretary of State, 3 April 1916, Decimal File 124.6718a/37, RG59.

49. Elliott to Foreign Office, 6 March 1915, FO 371/2484; Stinagle, "Ambassador Henry Morgenthau to Turkey," pp. 97–98; William N. Chambers, *Yoljuluk:/Random Thoughts on a Life in Imperial Turkey* (London: Simpkins, Marshall, Ltd., 1928), pp. 82–84.

50. Wolfram W. Gottlieb, *Studies in Secret Diplomacy during the First World War* (London: Allen & Unwin, 1957), pp. 314–18, 358. *See also Foreign Relations: 1915, Supplement*, p. 972; Einstein, *Inside Constantinople*, pp. 85–86, 117; Daniels to Lansing, 10 June 1915, General Correspondence of the Secretary of the Navy, box 1505, RG80; Morgenthau diary, entries for 13, 22 June 1915, Morgenthau Papers.

51. Morgenthau to Secretary of State, 27 July 1915, Decimal File 840.48/613, RG59; Lansing to Morgenthau, 21 June 1915, Decimal File 367.1 i/625, RG59. This was the *Tennessee's* last trip. She left immediately for the United States, and Decker in his final report wrote that the ship carried some 5,700 passengers during the year without even "a complaint of loss of baggage." 9 July 1815, General Correspondence of the Secretary of the Navy, box 1505, RG80. *See* additional correspondence on this in the same box.

52. Page to Wilson, 30 June 1915, Thomas Nelson Page Papers, William Perkins Library, Duke University, Durham, N.C.; Lansing to Morgenthau, 7 July 1915, Decimal File 840.48/1510, RG59. *See also* Morgenthau to Lansing, 2 July 1915, Decimal File 367.65/2, RG59; and 27 July 1915, Decimal File 840.48/1613, RG59. For the *Caesar's* voyage in the Mediterranean including the evacuation of Jews *see* Zogbaum, *From Sail to Saratoga*, pp. 225–30.

53. Memorandum, 17 July 1915, FO 371/2376.

54. Entry for 26 July 1915, Morgenthau diary, Morgenthau Papers. *See also* Rodd to Grey, 17 July 1915, FO 371/2376, and 27 July 1915, FO 800/65.

55. 30 June 1915, Page Papers.

56. FO 371/2376. In his published memoirs Rodd completely ignores the role the Italian subjects in Turkey played in Italy's delay in declaring war. Sir James R. Rodd, *Social and Diplomatic Memoirs, 1902–1919* (London: Edward Arnold & Company, 1925).

57. Jusserand to Lansing, 26 July 1915, Decimal File 367.65/6, RG59. *See also* Foreign Office to Bertie (British ambassador in Paris), 20 July 1915, FO 371/2366, and Bertie to Sir Edward Grey, 28 July 1915, FO 371/2376. For British pressure on the United States *see* Rodd to Grey, 12, 17 July 1915, FO 371/2376.

58. Vice Admiral, Eastern Mediterranean, to Admiralty, 28 July 1915; Grey to Spring Rice,

29 July; Spring Rice to Grey, 31 July 1915, FO 371/2376; Daniels to Lansing, 29 July 1915, Decimal File 840.48/1716, RG59; Morgenthau to Lansing, 30 July 1915; Lansing to Morgenthau, 30 July; Lansing to Daniels, 30 July; Daniels to Lansing, 2 August 1915, in Decimal File 367.65/7–8, RG59; Lansing desk diary, entry for 4 August 1915, Lansing Papers.

59. Morgenthau *Diary*, 10, 20 August 1915, Morgenthau Papers; Rodd to Grey, 6 August 1915, FO 371/2376.

60. Morgenthau to Lansing, 10, 11 August 1915, Decimal File 367.65/9–10, RG59; Page to House, 15 August 1915, Page Papers; *New York Times*, 19 August 1915; *Foreign Relations: 1915, Supplement*, pp. 976–77; Scofield, commanding officer of the *Chester*, to Daniels, 5 September 1915, Decimal File 840.48/1734, RG59.

61. Morgenthau to Lansing, 30 July 1915, M353, roll 43; Scofield to Daniels, 20 September 1915, M353, roll 44.

62. *See* Morgenthau to Lansing, 30 July, 21 September 1915, M353, roll 43; Scofield to Daniels, 5 September 1915, Decimal File 840.48/1734, RG59.

63. U.S. consul, Alexandria, to Lansing, January 1916, Decimal File 840.48/1723, RG59; Commanding officer, *Caesar*, to Daniels, 6 April 1916, copy in Decimal File 811.33/99, RG59; *Foreign Relations: 1916, Supplement*, p. 832; Morgenthau diary, 21 September 1915, Morgenthau Papers; American consul, Mersin, to Morgenthau, 24 September 1915, M367, roll 24.

64. Benson to Frank Polk, 4 October 1916, copy in the Edward M. House Papers, Yale University, New Haven, Ct. *See also* memorandum from Benson to Daniels, 10 September 1915, in the William S. Benson Papers, Library of Congress, Washington, D.C.; Daniels to Lansing, 2 August 1916, Decimal File 811.33/107, RG59; American consul general, Barcelona, to Secretary of State, 4 September 1916, Decimal File 811.3352/2, RG59.

65. *Foreign Relations: 1916, Supplement*, pp. 924–29; American chargé at Cairo to Lansing, 26 January 1916, Decimal File 840.48/1746, RG59; Morgenthau to commanding officer, *Des Moines*, 2 March 1916, 840.48/1838, RG59; commanding officer, *Des Moines*, to Benson, 16 April 1916, and inclosures, Benson Papers.

66. Lansing to American embassy, Paris, 25 September 1916, Decimal File 367.11/1288, RG59. *See also Foreign Relations: 1916, Supplement*, p. 937; Lansing to American embassy, Constantinople, 30 September; Daniels to Lansing, 28 September 1916, Decimal File 367.11/1301, 1309, RG59.

67. Elkus to Lansing, 17 November 1916, M353, roll 6. *See also* Elkus to Lansing, 20, 23 October, 13, 27 November 1916, Decimal File 367.11/1381, 1404, 1447, 1470, RG59; Barton to Lansing, 7 November; and Adee to Barton, 7 November 1916, Decimal File 367.11/527, RG59; Lansing to Elkus, 10 November; Bliss (Paris) to Lansing, 1 October; Lansing to Bliss, 1 October 1916, Decimal File 367.11/1404, 1408, 1369b, RG59.

68. Lansing to American embassy, 22 November 1916, Decimal File 367.11/1447, RG59.

69. Ernest R. May, *The World War & American Isolation, 1914–1917* (Cambridge: Harvard University Press, 1959), pp. 392–95; Lansing to Elkus, 11 December; to American ambassador (Berlin), 14 December; Grew to Lansing, 19 December 1916, Decimal File 367.11/470, 1524a, 1525, RG59.

70. Elkus to Lansing, 10 December 1916, Decimal File 367.11/1518, RG59. The Turks also agreed to allow the American vessels to take out one load of Palestinian wine for transshipment to the United States.

71. Lansing to Elkus, 3 January 1917, Decimal File 367.11/1571, RG59; *Foreign Relations: 1916, Supplement*, pp. 938–40; ibid, *1917, Supplement* 1: 113, 134–35; ibid., *1918, Supplement* 2: 538–40. *See also* Daniels to Lansing, 23 January 1917, Decimal File 367.11/1676, RG59; *New York Times*, 3, 4 February 1917; John A. DeNovo, *American Interests and Policies in the Middle East, 1900–1939* (Minneapolis: University of Minnesota Press, 1963), p. 106.

72. *New York Times*, 21 February 1917. *See also Foreign Relations: 1918, Supplement*, pp. 540–41; Elkus to Lansing, 20 February 1917, Decimal File 367.11/1889, RG59. On 28 February, the *New York Times*'s headline on p. 1 read, "Won't Guarantee Cruisers' Safety."

73. Quoted in DeNovo, *American Interests and Policies in the Middle East*, p. 106.

74. Margaret McGilvary, *The Dawn of a New Era in Syria* (New York: Fleming H. Revell, 1920), pp. 92–95.

75. The naval secretary had resisted pressure from the professional officers in the department to recall the vessels and, in fact, had designated a replacement for the *Des Moines* if a warship were to be maintained in the Mediterranean. *See* Benson to all bureau, 22 January 1917, Series 420–1, Papers of the General Board of the Navy, Naval History Division, Washington Navy Yard, Washington, D.C.; Daniels, *Diaries*, p. 118, Daniels Papers; *Foreign Relations: 1918, Supplement* 2: 542–44.

76. Morton to ambassador, 11 February 1917, Naval Vessels (OS), *Scorpion* File, Subject Files, RG45; Polk to Daniels, 17 February 1917, M367, roll 32. On 3 February, the *Scorpion* was ordered to burn all code and signal books and confidential publications. Lansing to Elkus, Decimal File 124.6718a/57c, RG59. An Italian newspaper reported the ship sunk on 15 February. *See* the *New York Times*, 18 February 1917.

77. *Foreign Relations: 1917, Supplement* 1: 601; Morton to Daniels, 2 March 1917, Naval vessels (OS), *Scorpion* File, Subject Files, RG45; Elkus to Lansing, 2 April 1917, M367, roll 33; Morton to Daniels, via ambassador, 7 April 1917, Decimal File 124.6718a/63a–65, RG59; Daniels to Lansing, 23 February 1917, Naval Vessels (OS), *Scorpion* File, Subject Files, RG45; Lansing desk diary, 2 March 1917, Lansing Papers.

78. Stovall to Lansing, 12 May; Daniels to Lansing, 18 April 1917, Decimal File 124.6718a/73, 66, RG59. *See also* Daniels, *Diaries*, p. 134; Lansing to Senator Fletcher, 23 April; to American Legation, Stockholm, 28 April; Elkus to Lansing, 17 June 1917, Decimal File 124.7618a/67a, 72, 81, RG59.

BIBLIOGRAPHY

PRIMARY SOURCES

Manuscripts and Microfilm, by Collection and by Country

COLLECTIONS

In Library of Congress:

Allen, William A. H.	Luce, Stephen B.
Bayard, Thomas	McKinley, William
Benson, William S.	Moody, William H.
Bristol, Mark L.	Morgenthau, Henry
Bryan, William J.	Olney, Richard
Butler, Benjamin	O'Neil, Charles
Casey, Silas	Porter, David D.
Chandler, William E.	Radford, William
Cleveland, Grover	Remey, George C.
Cohen, Albert M.	Rodgers, William
Converse, George A.	Roosevelt, Theodore
Cotton, Charles S.	Root, Elihu
Daniels, Josephus	Sargent, Nathan
Dewey, George	Schoonmaker, Charles M.
Fish, Hamilton	Sherman, William T.
Fiske, Bradley	Shufeldt, Robert W.
Gleaves, Albert	Sims, William S.
Goldsborough, Louis	Sperry, Charles S.
Gresham, Walter Q.	Straus, Oscar
Hay, John	Taft, William H.
Hunt, William	Taylor, Henry
Knox, Philander	Tracy, Benjamin
Lansing, Robert	Watson, John C.
Leahy, William D.	Welles, Gideon
Lowe, John	Wilson, Woodrow

In North Carolina Division of Archives and History (Raleigh):

Phelps, H., papers

In New York Historical Society:

Dewey, George
Erban, Henry
Franklin, S. R.
Goodrich, Caspar F.
Greene, Samuel Dana

In New York City Public Library:

Bigelow, John
Goldsborough, Louis

In Historical Society of Pennsylvania, Philadelphia:

Grapley, D. W., diary

In Yale University:

House, Edward M.

In Harvard University, Houghton Library:

Papers of the American Board of Commissioners for Foreign Missions

In Franklin D. Roosevelt Library, Hyde Park:

Franklin D. Roosevelt papers

In East Carolina University Library:

Kirkland, William A.

In William Perkins Library, Duke University:

Goldsborough, Louis
Page, Thomas Nelson

In Southern Historical Collection, University of North Carolina Library:

Long, Andrew T.
Macay and McNeely family
Merrill, Aaron S.
Murrie family
Quinan, J. H.
Wirt family

COUNTRY

Germany:

Records of the German Foreign Office Received by the Department of State from the University of California (Project I), National Archives Microfilm Number T139

Records of the German Foreign Office Received by the Department of State, National Archives Microfilm Number T120

Great Britain:
Public Records Office

In Christchurch College, Oxford University, England:

Admiralty (ADM) 137 (1914–1915 War Histories)
Foreign Office (FO) 5 (United States) 78 (Turkey), 195 (Turkey embassy and consular archives), 371 (political), 99 (Morocco), 800 (Grey papers)

　　Lord Salisbury papers

In British Museum, London:

　　Arthur James Balfour Papers

United States: National Archives:

Record Group 24 (Records of the Bureau of Naval Personnel):
　　Entry 88 (General Correspondence, 1889–1913, Bureau of Navigation)
　　Entry 299 (Letters Sent to the Commanders of Squadrons and Other Units in European Waters, 15 June 1866–18 November 1881)
　　Entry 330 (Letters Received from the Secretary of the Navy, 1862–1885)
　　Entry 382 (General Records of the Bureau of Navigation, 1891–1918)

Record Group 45 (Naval Records Collection of the Office of Naval Records and Library):
　　Entry 16 ("Letters to Flag Officers," 1861–1888)
　　Entry 19 (Translations of Messages Sent in Cipher, October 1888–January 1910)
　　Entry 20 (Confidential Letters Sent, September 1893–October 1908)
　　Entry 40 (Translations of Messages Received in Cipher, November 1888–August 1910)
　　Entry 371 (Letters and Telegrams Sent by the Naval War Board, 20 April–11 August 1898)
　　Area 4 Files, 1910–1927
　　Subject File, 1775–1910
　　Subject File, 1910–1927

Record Group 52 (Records of the Bureau of Medicine and Surgery)

Record Group 59 (General Records of the Department of State):
　　Entry 186 (Numerical File, 1906–1910)
　　Entry 196 (Decimal File, 1910–1944)

Record Group 80 (General Records of the Department of the Navy, 1798–1947):
　　General Correspondence of the Secretary of the Navy

Record Group 313 (Records of Naval Operating Forces):
　　Entry 23–24 (Records of the European Squadron, 1869–1905)
　　Entry 30 (Records of the Squadron of Evolution)
　　Entry 31–57 (Records of the North Atlantic Squadron)
　　Entry 93–95 (Records of Combined Squadrons)

Microfilm Number M30 (Despatches from United States Ministers to Great Britain, 1791–1906)
Microfilm Number M31 (Despatches from United States Ministers to Spain, 1792–1906)

Microfilm Number M35 (Despatches from United States Ministers to Russia, 1808–1906)
Microfilm Number M40 (Domestic Letters of the Department of State, 1784–1906)
Microfilm Number M43 (Despatches from United States Ministers to Portugal, 1790–1906)
Microfilm Number M46 (Despatches from United States Ministers to Turkey, 1818–1906)
Microfilm Number M77 (Diplomatic Instructions of the Department of State, 1801–1906)
Microfilm Number M89 (Letters Received by the Secretary of the Navy from Commanding Officers of Squadrons, 1881–86)
Microfilm Number 125 (Letters Received by the Secretary of the Navy: Captains' Letters, 1805–61, 1866–85)
Microfilm Number M353 (Records of the Department of State Relating to Internal Affairs of Turkey, 1910–29)
Microfilm Number M363 (Records of the Department of State Relating to Political Relations Between Turkey and Other States, 1910–29)
Microfilm Number M365 (Records of the Department of State Relating to Political Relations Between the United States and Turkey, 1910–29)
Microfilm Number M367 (Records of the Department of State Relating to World War I and Its Termination, 1914–29)
Microfilm Number M472 (Letters Sent by the Secretary of the Navy to the President and Executive Agencies, 1821–86)
Microfilm Number M480 (Letters Sent by the Secretary of the Navy to Chiefs of Navy Bureaus, 1842–86)
Microfilm Number M517 (Letters Received by the Secretary of the Navy from the President and Executive Agencies, 1837–86)
Microfilm Number M518 (Letters Received by the Secretary of the Navy from Chiefs of Navy Bureaus, 1842–85)
Microfilm Number M530 (Records of the Department of State Relating to Political Relations Between Italy and Other States, 1910–29)
Microfilm Number M625 (Area File of the Naval Records Collection, 1775–1910)
Microfilm Number T61 (Despatches from United States Consuls in Tangier, Morocco, 1797–1906)
Microfilm Number T190 (Despatches from United States Consuls in Canea, Crete, Greece, 1832–74)
Microfilm Number T815 (Notes from the Turkish Legation in the United States to the Department of State, 1867–1906)

United States: Department of the Navy (Naval History Division, Navy Yard, Washington, D.C.)
English, Earl, folder, ZB file
Papers of the General Board of the United States Navy
Pratt, Admiral William V., autobiography
Scorpion File (Ship's History Section)

United States: Department of the Navy (Navy Department Library):
McCalla, Bowman, Memoirs

United States: Department of the Navy (Marine Corps Museum, Navy Yard, Washington, D.C.):
Cochrane, Henry Clay Papers
Tilton, McClane Papers

Official Printed Documents by Country

France:

Ministère des Affaires Etrangeres. *Documents diplomatiques Francais 1871–1914*. 14 vols. Paris: Imprimerie nationale.

Germany:

Dugdale, E.T.S., ed. *German Diplomatic Documents, 1871–1914*. 4 vols. Reprint. New York: Barnes & Noble, Inc., 1969.

Spain:

Spanish Diplomatic Correspondence and Documents. Trans. Washington, D.C.: Government Printing Office, 1905.

United States:

Bureau of the Census. *Historical Statistics of the United States: Colonial Time to 1957*. Washington, D.C.: Government Printing Office, 1960.
Bureau of Statistics. *Foreign Commerce and Navigation for the Year Ending 1894*. Washington, D.C.: Government Printing Office, 1895.
Department of the Navy. *Annual Reports of the Secretary of the Navy: 1866–1917*. Washington, D.C.: Government Printing Office, 1867–1918.
———. *Report of the Chief of the Bureau of Navigation: 1898*. Washington, D.C.: Government Printing Office, 1898.
———. *The United States Navy in Peacetime*. Washington, D.C.: Government Printing Office, 1931.
Department of State. *Papers Relating to the Foreign Relations of the United States: 1861–1917*. Washington, D.C.: Government Printing Office, 1862–1919.
Right to Protect Citizens in Foreign Countries By Landing Forces. 3rd rev. ed. Washington, D.C.: Government Printing Office, 1934.
U.S., Congress, House, *Congressional Globe*, 41st Cong., 2d sess., 1870, 41, pt. 1.
U.S., Congress, House, *Congressional Globe*, 44th Cong., 2d sess., 1877, 44, pt. 2.
U.S., Congress, House, *Congressional Record*, 48th Cong., 2d sess., 1884–1885, 48, House Miscellaneous Document Number 29.
U.S., Congress, House, *Congressional Record*, 54th Cong., 1st sess., 1896, 54, pt. 4.
U.S., Congress, Senate, *Congressional Globe*, 40th Cong., 2d sess., 1869, 40, pt. 1.
U.S., Congress, Senate, *Congressional Globe*, 42d Cong., 2d sess., 1872, 42, pt. 2.
U.S., Congress, Senate, *Congressional Globe*, 44th Cong., 1st sess., 1876, 44, Executive Document Number 170.
U.S., Congress, Senate, *Congressional Record*, 47th Cong., 1st sess., 1882, 47, pt. 2.

Books

Aaronsohn, Alexander. *With the Turks in Palestine*. New York: Houghton Mifflin Company, 1916.
Adams, William L. *Exploits and Adventures of a Soldier Ashore and Afloat*. New York: J. B. Lippincott Company, 1911.
Allen, George W., ed., *The Papers of John Davis Long, 1897–1904*. Boston: Massachusetts Historical Society, 1939.
Andrews, O. W. *Seamarks and Landmarks*. London: Ernest Benn, Ltd., 1927.
Angell, James B. *The Reminiscences of James Burrill Angell*. New York: Longmans, Green and Company, 1912.
Barker, Albert S. *Everyday Life in the Navy: Autobiography of Rear Admiral Albert S. Barker*. Boston: R. G. Badger, 1928.
Barrows, John. *A World Pilgrimage*. Chicago: A. C. McClurg & Company, 1897.
Beresford, Admiral Lord Charles. *The Memoirs of Admiral Lord Charles Beresford*. 2 vols. London: Methuen & Company, Ltd., 1914.
Bicknell, Ernest P. *Pioneering with the Red Cross*. New York: The Macmillan Company, 1935.

Bosworth, Allan R. *My Love Affair with the Navy*. New York: W. W. Norton & Company, Inc., 1969.

Bowen, H. G. *Ships, Machinery & Mossbacks: The Autobiography of a Naval Engineer*. Princeton University Press, 1954.

Bowen, Herbert W. *Recollections Diplomatic and Undiplomatic*. New York: Frederick W. Hitchcock, 1926.

Chaille-Long, Charles. *My Life in Four Continents*. London: Hutchinson and Company, 1912.

Chambers, William N. *Yoljuluk: Random Thoughts on a Life in Imperial Turkey*. London: Simpkins, Marshall, Ltd., 1928.

Clark, Charles E. *My Fifty Years in the Navy*. Boston: Little, Brown & Company, 1917.

Collum, R. S. *The History of the United States Marine Corps*. New York: L. R. Hamersly Company, 1903.

Coontz, Robert E. *True Anecdotes of an Admiral*. Philadelphia: Dorrance and Company, 1935.

Cox, Samuel S. *Diversions of a Diplomat in Turkey*. New York: C. L. Webster & Company, 1887.

Cronin, E. David., ed. *The Cabinet Diaries of Josephus Daniels, 1913–1921*. Lincoln: University of Nebraska Press, 1963.

Curtis, George W., ed. *The Correspondence of John Lathrop Motley*. 2 vols. New York: Harper & Brothers, 1889.

Dahlgren, Madeleine V. *Memoir of John A. Dahlgren*. Boston: J. R. Osgood & Company, 1882.

Daly, Robert W., ed. *Aboard the USS Monitor: 1862; The Letters of Acting Paymaster William Frederick Keeler, U.S. Navy, To His Wife, Anna*. Annapolis: United States Naval Institute, 1964.

de Kusel, Samuel S. *An Englishman's Recollections of Egypt, 1863–1887*. London: John Lane, 1915.

Dewey, George. *Autobiography of George Dewey: Admiral of the Navy*. New York: Charles Scribner's Sons, 1913.

Donville, Admiral Sir Barry. *By and Large*. London: Hutchinson, 1936.

Dundas, Sir Charles. *An Admiral's Yarns*. London: Herbert Jenkins, Ltd., 1922.

Einstein, Lewis. *Inside Constantinople: A Diplomatist's Diary During the Dardanelles Expedition, April-September, 1915*. London: John Murray, 1917.

———. *A Diplomat Looks Back*. New Haven: Yale University Press, 1968.

Evans, Holden A. *One Man's Fight for a Better Navy*. New York: Dodd, Mead & Company, 1940.

Evans, Robley D. *A Sailor's Log*. New York: D. Appleton & Company, 1902.

Fiske, Rear Admiral Bradley A. *From Midshipman to Rear Admiral*. London: T. Werner Laurie, Ltd., 1919.

Franklin, S. R. *Memories of a Rear Admiral*. New York: Harper & Brothers Publishers, 1898.

Gibbons, Helen Davenport. *The Red Rugs of Tarsus: A Woman's Story of the Armenian Massacres*. Paris: Hagop Turabian, 1919.

Goodrich, Rear Admiral Caspar F. *Rope Yarns From The Old Navy*. New York: The Naval History Society, 1921.

Griscom, Lloyd C. *Diplomatically Speaking*. Boston: Little, Brown and Company, 1940.

Hamilton, J., G. De Roulhac, et al., eds. *The Papers of William Alexander Graham*. 6 vols. Raleigh, North Carolina: State Department of Archives and History, 1957–1977.

Hamlin, Cyrus. *My Life and Times*. Boston: Congregational Sunday School and Publishing Society, 1893.

Hayes, John D., ed. *Samuel F. DuPont, A Selection from his Civil War Letters*. 3 vols. Ithaca: Cornell University Press, 1969.

Hepworth, George P. *Through Armenia on Horseback*. New York: E. P. Dutton Company, 1898.

Horton, George. *Recollections Grave and Gay: The Story of a Mediterranean Consul*. Indianapolis: The Bobbs-Merrill Company, 1927.

Jessup, Henry Harris. *Fifty-three Years in Syria*. 2 vols. New York: Fleming H. Revell, 1910.

Kerr, Mark. *Land, Sea, and Air: Reminiscences of Mark Kerr*. London: Longmans, Green and Company, 1927.

Keyes, Sir Roger. *The Naval Memoirs of Sir Roger Keyes*. 2 vols. London: Thornton Butterworth, Ltd., 1935.

King, Ernest J., and Walter Muir Whitehill. *Fleet Admiral King: A Naval Record*. New York: W. W. Norton & Company, Inc., 1952.

Lejeune, Major General John A. *The Reminiscences of a Marine*. Philadelphia: Dorrance and Company, 1930.

Marder, Arthur J., ed., *Fear God and Dread Nought: The Correspondence of Admiral of the Fleet Lord Fisher*. 3 vols. London: Fernhill, 1952–59.

Mayo, L. S., ed., *America of Yesterday as Reflected in the Journal of John Davis Long*. Boston: Atlantic Monthly Press, 1923.

McGilvary, Margaret. *The Dawn of a New Era in Syria*, New York: Fleming H. Revell, 1920.

Montgomery, James E. *Our Admiral's Flag Abroad: The Cruise of Admiral D. G. Farragut, Commanding the European Squadron in 1867–68 in the Flag Ship Franklin*. New York: G. P. Putnam & Son, 1869.

Morgan, H. Wayne, ed. *Making Peace with Spain: The Diary of Whitelaw Reid*. Austin: University of Texas Press, 1965.

Morgenthau, Henry. *All in a Life-Time*. Garden City: Doubleday, Page & Company, 1923.

———. *Ambassador Morgenthau's Story*. Garden City: Doubleday, Page & Company, 1918.

Morison, Elting E., ed., *The Letters of Theodore Roosevelt*. 8 vols. Cambridge: Harvard University Press, 1951–1954.

Otway, Arthur. *Autobiography and Journals of Admiral Lord Clarence E. Paget*. London: Chapman & Hall, 1896.

Parker, William H. *Recollections of a Naval Officer, 1841–1865*. New York: Charles Scribner's Sons, 1883.

Rich, Norman, and M. H. Fisher, eds. *The Holstein Papers*. 4 vols. Cambridge: Cambridge University Press, 1955–63.

Rodd, Sir James R. *Social and Diplomatic Memoirs, 1902–1919*. London: Edward Arnold and Company, 1925.

Sands, Benjamin F. *From Reefer to Rear-admiral: Reminiscences and Journal Jottings of Nearly Half a Century of Naval Life*. New York: Frederick A. Stokes, 1899.

Schley, Winfield Scott. *Forty-Five Years Under the Flag*. New York: D. Appleton and Company, 1904.

Schroeder, Seaton. *A Half Century of Naval Service*. New York: D. Appleton and Company, 1922.

Scipio, Lynn A. *My Thirty Years in Turkey*. Rindge, New Hampshire: Richard R. Smith, Publisher, 1955.

Selfridge, Thomas O., Jr. *Memoirs of Thomas O. Selfridge, Jr.* New York: G. P. Putnam's Sons, 1924.

Smith, Vice Admiral Humphrey Hugh. *A Yellow Admiral Remembers*. London: Edward Arnold & Company, 1932.

Stillman, William J. *The Autobiography of a Journalist*. 2 vols. Boston & New York: Houghton, Mifflin and Company, 1901.

Stirling, Rear Admiral Yates, Jr., U.S.N. *Sea Duty: The Memoirs of a Fighting Admiral*. New York: G. P. Putnam's Sons, 1939.

Straus, Oscar S. *Under Four Administrations: From Cleveland to Taft*. Boston: Houghton Mifflin Company, 1922.

Stuermer, Harry. *Two War Years in Constantinople*. New York: George H. Doran & Company, 1917.

Summers, Festus P., ed. *The Cabinet Diary of William L. Wilson, 1896–1897*. Chapel Hill: University of North Carolina Press, 1957.

Tirpitz, Grand Admiral A. von. *My Memoirs*. 2 vols. London: Hurst & Blackett, 1919.
Twain, Mark [Samuel L. Clemens]. *The Innocents Abroad.* New York: Harper & Brothers, 1911.
Volwiler, A. T., ed. *The Correspondence between Benjamin Harrison and James G. Blaine, 1882–1893.* Philadelphia: The American Philosophical Society, 1940.
Wallace, Lewis. *Lew Wallace: An Autobiography.* New York: Harper & Brothers, 1906.
Washburn, George. *Fifty Years in Constantinople and Recollections of Roberts College.* Boston & New York: Houghton Mifflin Company, 1909.
Washburne, Elihu E. B. *Recollections of a Minister to France, 1869–1877.* 2 vols. New York: Charles Scribner's Sons, 1887.
Weldon, Lewen Francis B. *"Hard Lying": Eastern Mediterranean, 1914–1919.* London: H. Jenkins, Ltd., 1926.
Welles, Gideon. *Diary of Gideon Welles, Secretary of the Navy Under Lincoln and Johnson.* 3 vols. Edited by Howard K. Beale. New York: W. W. Norton & Company, Inc., 1960.
Wilson, F. M. Huntington. *Memoirs of an Ex-Diplomat.* Boston: Bruce Humphries, Inc., 1945.
Wolffe, Murray. *Memoirs of a Gob.* New York: Exposition Press, 1949.
Young, John R. *Around the World with General Grant.* 2 vols. New York: The American News Company, 1879.
Zogbaum, Rufus Fairchild. *From Sail To Saratoga: A Naval Autobiography.* Rome: n.p.

Articles

"American Diplomacy on the Bosphorus." *The Outlook* 55 (17 April 1899): 1028–31.
Belknap, Reginald R. "Earthquake Relief Work at Messina and Reggio." *Survey* 32 (2 May 1914): 115–19.
Ellicott, John M. "With Erben and Mahan on the *Chicago*." *United States Naval Institute Proceedings* 62 (September 1941): 1234–40.
Goodrich, Caspar F. "The *Frolic* in the Baltic: A Reminiscence." *United States Naval Institute Proceedings* 41 (March-April 1915): 473–80.
Hamlin, Cyrus. "America's Duty to Americans in Turkey." *North American Review* 163 (September 1896): 276–81.
"The United States and the Porte," *The Outlook* 55 (27 February 1897): 593–99.
"The United States in the Mediterranean." *The American Monthly Review of Reviews* 30 (September 1904): 358–59.
Zogbaum, Rufus F. "With Yankee Cruisers in French Harbors." *Illustrated Scribner's* 8 (November 1890): 625–43.

Periodicals

All Hands, 1959–1960
Army and Navy Journal
Blackwood Edinburgh Magazine, 1898
Boston Transcript, 1895
Century Magazine, 1884
Harper's Weekly
Illustrated London News, 1903
Literary Digest, 1910
Morning Post (London), 1903
New York Daily Tribune
New York Herald
New York Times
Outlook, 1906
Paris Herald, 1903

Standard (London), 1903
The Nation
Times (London)
Washington Evening Star, June 2, 1907
Washington Post

SECONDARY SOURCES

Books

Adams, Ephraim D. *Great Britain and the American Civil War*. New York: Longmans, 1925.

Adams, Henry M. *Prussian-American Relations, 1775–1871*. Cleveland: The Press of Western Reserve University, 1960.

Adler, Cyrus. *With Firmness in the Right: American Diplomatic Action Affecting Jews, 1840–1945*. New York: The American Jewish Committee, 1946.

———. *Jacob H. Schiff: His Life and Letters*. 2 vols. New York: Doubleday, Doran and Co., Inc., 1928.

Alden, John D. *American Steel Navy*. Annapolis: United States Naval Institute, 1972.

Anderson, Eugene N. *The First Moroccan Crisis, 1904–1906*. Hamden, Connecticut: Archon Books, 1966.

Anderson, M. S. *The Eastern Question, 1774–1923*. New York: St. Martin's Press, 1966.

Andrew, Christopher. *Theophile Delcasse and the Making of the Entente Cordiale*. London: The MacMillan Company, 1968.

Askew, William C. *Europe and Italy's Acquisition of Libya*. Durham: Duke University Press, 1942.

Bailey, Thomas A. *The Policy of the United States Toward the Neutrals, 1917–1918*. Baltimore: The Johns Hopkins Press, 1942.

———. *America Faces Russia: Russian-American Relations from Early Times to Our Day*. Ithaca: Cornell University Press, 1960.

———. *A Diplomatic History of the American People*. 8th ed. New York: Appleton-Century-Crofts, 1969.

———. *Essays Diplomatic and Undiplomatic of Thomas A. Bailey*. Edited by Alexander DeConde and Armin Rappaport. New York: Appleton-Century-Crofts, 1969.

Balfour, Michael. *The Kaiser and His Times*. New York: W. W. Norton, 1972.

Barrow, Clayton R., Jr., ed. *America Spreads Her Sails*. Annapolis: United States Naval Institute, 1973.

Beach, Edward L. *The Wreck of the Memphis*. New York: Holt, Rinehart & Winston, 1966.

Beale, Howard K. *Theodore Roosevelt and the Rise of America to World Power*. Baltimore: The Johns Hopkins Press, 1956.

Beisner, Robert L. *Twelve Against Empire: The Anti-Imperialists, 1898–1900*. New York: McGraw-Hill Book Company, 1968.

Bemis, Samuel F., ed. *The American Secretaries of State and Their Diplomacy*. 10 vols. New York: Pageant Book Company, 1927–1929.

Bill, Frederick J. *Room to Swing a Cat*. New York: Longmans, Green and Company, 1938.

Blumenthal, Henry. *A Reappraisal of Franco-American Relations, 1830–1871*. Chapel Hill: University of North Carolina Press, 1959.

———. *France and the United States: Their Diplomatic Relations, 1789–1914*. Chapel Hill: University of North Carolina Press, 1969.

Bourne, Kenneth. *The Foreign Policy of Victorian England, 1830–1902*. New York: Oxford University Press, 1970.

———. *Britain and the Balance of Power in North America, 1815–1908*. Berkeley: University of California Press, 1967.

Bradley, Edward S. *George Henry Boker: Poet and Patriot.* Philadelphia: University of Penn-
    sylvania Press, 1927.
Braisted, William R. *The United States Navy in the Pacific, 1897–1909.* Austin: University of
    Texas Press, 1958.
———. *The United States Navy in the Pacific, 1909–1922.* Austin: University of Texas Press,
    1971.
Cable, James. *Gunboat Diplomacy: Political Application of Limited Naval Force.* New York:
    Institute of Strategic Studies, 1971.
Campbell, Alexander E. *Great Britain and the United States, 1895–1903.* London: Longmans,
    1960.
Campbell, Charles S. *Anglo-American Understanding, 1898–1903.* Baltimore: The Johns
    Hopkins Press, 1957.
Case, Lynn M., and Warren F. Spencer. *The United States & France: Civil War Diplomacy.*
    Philadelphia: University of Pennsylvania Press, 1970.
Chadwick, Rear Admiral French E., U.S.N. *The Relations Between the United States and
    Spain: The Spanish-American War.* 2 vols. New York: Charles Scribner's Sons, 1911.
Chaille-Long, Charles. *Three Prophets: Chinese Gordon, Mohammed Ahmed (the Maahdi),
    Arabi-Pasha—Events before and after the Bombardment of Alexandria.* New York: D.
    Appleton & Company, 1884.
Challener, Richard D. *Admirals, Generals, and American Foreign Policy 1898–1914.* Prince-
    ton: Princeton University Press, 1973.
Chatterton, Edward K. *Dardanelles Dilemma.* London: Rich & Cowan, Ltd., 1935.
Childers, Spencer. *The Life of the Right Honorable Hugh C. E. Childers.* 2 vols. London: John
    Murray, 1901.
Clymer, Kenton J. *John Hay: The Gentleman as Diplomat.* Ann Arbor: University of Michigan
    Press, 1974.
Cohen, Naomi W. *A Dual Heritage: The Public Career of Oscar S. Straus.* Philadelphia: Jewish
    Publishing Society of America, 1969.
Cook, Adrian. *The Alabama Claims: American Politics & Anglo-American Relations, 1865–
    1872.* Ithaca: Cornell University Press, 1975.
Cooling, B. Franklin. *Benjamin Franklin Tracy: Father of the Modern American Navy.*
    Hamden, Connecticut, Archon Books, 1973.
Cruickshank, Earl F. *Morocco at the Parting of the Ways: The Story of Native Protection to
    1885.* Philadelphia: University of Pennsylvania Press, 1935.
Cummings, Captain Damon E., USN (Retired). *Admiral Richard Wainwright and the United
    States Fleet.* Washington, D.C.: Government Printing Office, 1962.
Curti, Merli. *American Philanthropy Abroad: A History.* New Brunswick: Rutgers University
    Press, 1963.
Dalzell, George W. *The Flight From the Flag.* Chapel Hill: University of North Carolina Press,
    1940.
Daniels, Josephus. *The Wilson Era: Years of Peace—1910–1917.* Chapel Hill: University of
    North Carolina Press, 1944.
Daniels, Robert L. *American Philanthropy in the Near East, 1820–1960.* Athens: Ohio Uni-
    versity Press, 1970.
Davis, Charles H. *Life of Charles Henry Davis, Rear Admiral 1807–1877.* Boston and New
    York: Houghton, Mifflin and Company, 1899.
Davis, George T. *A Navy Second to None: The Development of Modern American Naval Policy.*
    New York: Harcourt, Brace and Company, 1940.
Davison, Kenneth E. *The Presidency of Rutherford B. Hayes.* Westport, Connecticut: Green-
    wood Press, 1972.
Deak, Francis, and James T. Shotwell. *Turkey at the Straits: A Short History.* New York: The
    Macmillan Company, 1940.

Dennis, Alfred L. *Adventures in American Diplomacy, 1896–1906*. New York: E. P. Dutton & Company, 1928.

De Novo, John A. *American Interests and Policies in the Middle East, 1900–1939*. Minneapolis: University of Minnesota Press, 1963.

Earle, Edward M. *Turkey, the Great Powers and the Bagdad Railway: A Study in Imperialism*. New York: The Macmillan Company, 1923.

Eggert, Gerald G. *Richard Olney: Evolution of a Statesman*. University Park: The Pennsylvania State University Press, 1974.

Engle, Anita. *The Nili Spies*. London: The Hogarth Press, 1959.

Esthus, Raymond A. *Theodore Roosevelt and the International Rivalries*. Walthan: Ginn-Blaisdell, 1970.

Falk, Edwin A. *Fighting Bob Evans*. New York: Jonathan Cape & Harrison Smith, 1931.

Farman, Elbert E. *Egypt and its Betrayal*. New York: The Grafton Press, 1908.

Farragut, Loyall. *David G. Farragut*. New York: D. Appleton & Company, 1879.

Faulkner, Harold U. *The Decline of Laissez Faire, 1897–1917*. New York: Harper & Row, 1968.

Field, James A., Jr. *America and the Mediterranean World, 1776–1882*. Princeton: Princeton University Press, 1969.

Gardner, Lloyd C., Walter F. LaFeber, and Thomas J. McCormick. *Creation of the American Empire: U.S. Diplomatic History*. Chicago: Rand McNally & Company, 1973.

Garvin, J. L. *The Life of Joseph Chamberlain*. 3 vols. New York: The Macmillan Company, 1924.

Gelber, Lionel M. *The Rise of Anglo-American Friendship*. New York: Oxford University Press, 1938.

Gibbons, Herbert. *The Blacklist Page of Modern History: Events in Armenia in 1915*. New York: G. P. Putnam, 1916.

Gillett, Frederick H. *George Frisbie Hoar*. Boston: Houghton Mifflin Company, 1934.

Gleaves, Rear Admiral Albert. *The Life of an American Sailor: Rear Admiral William Hemsley Emory, United States Navy*. New York: George H. Doran Company, 1923.

———. *Life and Letters of Rear Admiral Stephen B. Luce, U.S. Navy*. New York: G. P. Putnam's Sons, 1925.

Gordon, Leland J. *American Relations with Turkey, 1830–1930: An Economic Interpretation*. Philadelphia: University of Pennsylvania Press, 1932.

Gottlieb, Wolfram W. *Studies in Secret Diplomacy during the First World War*. London: Allen & Unwin, 1957.

Grabill, Joseph L. *Protestant Diplomacy and the Near East: Missionary Influence on American Policy, 1810–1927*. Minneapolis: University of Minnesota Press, 1971.

Grenville, J.A.S. *Lord Salisbury and Foreign Policy: The Close of the Nineteenth Century*. London: Athlone Press, 1964.

———, and George Young. *Politics, Strategy, and American Diplomacy: Studies in Foreign Policy, 1875–1917*. New Haven: Yale University Press, 1966.

Hagan, Kenneth J. *American Gunboat Diplomacy and the Old Navy, 1877–1889*. Westport, Connecticut: Greenwood Press, 1970.

Hall, Luella J. *The United States and Morocco, 1776–1956*. Metuchen, N.J.: The Scarecrow Press, Inc., 1971.

Halpern, Paul G. *The Mediterranean Naval Situation, 1908–1914*. Cambridge: Harvard University Press, 1970.

Hammett, Hugh B. *Hilary Abner Herbert: A Southerner Returns to the Union*. Philadelphia: The American Philosophical Society, 1976.

Hart, Robert A. *The Great White Fleet*. Boston: Little, Brown and Company, 1965.

Healy, David. *U.S. Expansionism: The Imperialist Urge in the 1890s*. Madison: The University of Wisconsin Press, 1963.

Healy, Laurin H., and Luis Kutner. *The Admiral*. Chicago: Ziff-Davis Publishing Company, 1944.

Heinl, Robert D., Jr. *Soldiers of the Sea*. Annapolis: United States Naval Institute, 1962.

Herrick, Walter. *The American Naval Revolution*. Baton Rouge: Louisiana State University Press, 1966.

Herwig, Holger H. *Politics of Frustration: The United States in German Naval Planning, 1889–1941*. Boston: Little, Brown and Company, 1976.

Hinckley, Frank E. *American Consular Jurisdiction in the Orient*. Washington: W. A. L. Lowdermilk, 1906.

Hirsch, Mark D. *William C. Whitney: Modern Warwick*. New York: Dodd, Mead & Co., 1948.

Hofstader, Richard. *The Paranoid Style in American Politics, and Other Essays*. New York: Knopf, 1966.

Howard, Harry N. *Turkey, The Straits and U.S. Policy*. Baltimore: The Johns Hopkins University Press, 1974.

Howe, M. A. De Wolfe. *George von Lengerke Meyer: His Life and Public Services*. New York: Dodd, Mead and Company, 1920.

Hyman, Joseph C. *Twenty-Five Years of American Aid to Jews Overseas*. New York: Jewish Publication Society of America, 1930.

Iiams, Thomas M., Jr. *Dreyfus, Diplomatists and the Dual Alliance: Gabriel Hanotaux at the Quai D'orsay (1894–1898)*. Genève: Librairie E. Droz, 1962

James, Henry. *Richard Olney and His Public Service*. Boston: Houghton Mifflin Company, 1923.

James, Robert R. *Rosebery: A Biography of Archibald Philip, Fifth Earl of Rosebery*. New York: Macmillan, 1964.

Jelavich, Barbara. *The Ottoman Empire, the Great Powers and the Straits Question, 1870–1887*. Bloomington: Indiana University Press, 1973.

Jessup, Henry H. *The Setting of the Crescent and the Rising of the Cross*. Philadelphia: The Westminster Press, 1898.

Johnson, Robert E. *Thence Round Cape Horn*. Annapolis: United States Naval Institute, 1963.

Karsten, Peter. *The Naval Aristocracy: The Golden Age of Annapolis and the Emergence of Modern American Navalism*. New York: The Free Press, 1972.

Kirkland, Edward C. *Industry Comes of Age: Business, Labor and Public Policy, 1860–1897*. Chicago: Quadrangle Books, Inc., 1967.

LaFeber, Walter. *The New Empire: An Interpretation of American Expansion, 1860–1898*. Ithaca: Cornell University Press, 1963.

Langer, William L. *The Diplomacy of Imperialism*. New York: Alfred A. Knopf, 1968.

Langley, Lester D. *The Cuban Policy of the United States: A Brief History*. New York: John Wiley, 1968.

Latourette, Kenneth S. *History of the Expansion of Christianity*. 7 vols. New York: Harper & Brothers, 1937–45.

Leech, Margaret. *In the Days of McKinley*. New York: Harper & Brothers, 1959.

Lewis, Charles L. *David Glasgow Farragut: Our First Admiral*. Annapolis: United States Naval Institute, 1943.

Lief, Alfred. *Brandeis: The Personal History of an American Ideal*. New York: Stackpole Sons, 1936.

Link, Arthur S. *Wilson: The New Freedom*. Princeton: Princeton University Press, 1956.

——. *Wilson the Diplomatist: A Look at His Major Foreign Policies*. Baltimore: The Johns Hopkins Press, 1957.

——. *Wilson: The Struggle for Neutrality, 1914–1915*. Princeton: Princeton University Press, 1960.

——. *Wilson: Confusions and Crises, 1915–1916*. Princeton: Princeton University Press, 1964.

————. *Wilson: Campaigns for Progressivism and Peace, 1916–1917*. Princeton: Princeton University Press, 1965.

Long, John D. *The New American Navy*. 2 vols. New York: The Outlook Company, 1903.

Loubat, J. F. *Gustavus Fox's Mission to Russia*. New York: Arno Press, 1970.

Lowe, Cedric J. *Salisbury and the Mediterranean, 1886–1896*. London: Routledge & K. Paul, 1965.

————. *The Reluctant Imperialist: British Foreign Policy, 1878–1902*. New York: Macmillan, 1969.

Lowenthal, David. *George Perkins Marsh: Versatile Vermonter*. New York: Columbia University Press, 1958.

McKee, Irving. *Ben-Hur Wallace*. Berkeley: University of California Press, 1947.

Manuel, Frank E. *The Realities of American-Palestine Relations*. Washington, D.C.: Public Affairs Press, 1949.

Marder, Arthur J. *The Anatomy of British Seapower: A History of British Naval Policy in the Pre-Dreadnought Era, 1880–1905*. New York: Alfred A. Knopf, 1940.

May, Ernest R. *The World War and American Isolation, 1914–1917*. Cambridge: Harvard University Press, 1959.

————. *Imperial Democracy*. New York: Harcourt, Brace & World, 1961.

Merli, Frank J. *Great Britain and the Confederate Navy, 1861–1865*. Bloomington: Indiana University Press, 1970.

————, and Theodore A. Wilson, eds. *Makers of American Diplomacy from Theodore Roosevelt to Henry Kissinger*. New York: Charles Scribner's Sons, 1974.

Merrill, Horace S. *Bourbon Leader: Grover Cleveland and the Democrat Party*. Boston: Little, Brown and Company, 1957.

Monger, George. *The End of Isolation: British Foreign Policy, 1900–1907*. London: T. Nelson, 1963.

Moore, John B. *A Digest of International Law*. 8 vols. Washington, D.C.: Government Printing Office, 1906.

Morison, Elting E. *Admiral Sims and the Modern American Navy*. Boston: Houghton Mifflin Company, 1942.

Morrison, Joseph L. *Josephus Daniels: The Small-d Democrat*. Chapel Hill: University of North Carolina Press, 1966.

Neale, R. G. *Great Britain and the United States Expansion, 1898–1900*. East Lansing, Michigan: Michigan State University Press, 1966.

Nearing, Scott, and Joseph Freeman. *Dollar Diplomacy: A Study in American Imperialism*. New York: The Viking Press, 1925.

Nevins, Allan. *Henry White: Thirty Years of American Diplomacy*. New York: Harper & Brothers Publishers, 1930.

————. *Hamilton Fish: The Inner History of the Grant Administration*. New York: Dodd, Mead & Company, 1936.

Nicolson, Harold C. *Portrait of a Diplomatist: Being the Life of Sir Arthur Nicolson, First Lord Carnock, and a Study of the Great War*. Boston: Houghton Mifflin Company, 1930.

Niven, John. *Gideon Welles: Lincoln's Secretary of the Navy*. New York: Oxford University Press, 1973.

Offutt, Milton. *The Protection of Citizens Abroad by the Armed Forces of the United States*. Johns Hopkins University Studies in Historical and Political Science, vol. 46, no. 4. Baltimore: The Johns Hopkins Press, 1928.

O'Gara, Gordon C. *Theodore Roosevelt and the Rise of the Modern Navy*. Princeton: Princeton University Press, 1943.

Oldroyd, Osborn H. *The Assassination of Abraham Lincoln*. Rahway, N.J.: The Merchon Company Press, 1901.

Paolino, Ernest N. *The Foundation of the American Empire: William Henry Seward and U.S.*

Foreign Policy. Ithaca: Cornell University Press, 1973.

Paullin, Charles O. *Paullin's History of Naval Administration, 1775–1911*. Annapolis: U.S. Naval Institute, 1968.

Perkins, Bradford. *The Great Rapprochement: England and the United States, 1898–1914*. New York: Atheneum, 1968.

Petrie, Sir Charles. *The Life and Letters of Sir Austen Chamberlain*. 2 vols. London: Cassell & Company, 1939.

Plesur, Milton. *America's Outward Thrust: Approaches to Foreign Affairs, 1865–1890*. DeKalb, Illinois: Northern Illinois University Press, 1971.

Pletcher, David M. *The Awkward Years: American Foreign Relations under Garfield and Arthur*. Columbia, Missouri: University of Missouri Press, 1963.

Pringle, Henry F. *The Life and Times of William Howard Taft*. 2 vols. New York: Farrar & Rinehart, Inc., 1939.

Puleston, William D. *The Life and Work of Captain Alfred Thayer Mahan*. New Haven: Yale University Press, 1939.

Richardson, James D., ed. *A Compilation of the Messages and Papers of the Presidents, 1789–1908*. 11 vols. Washington, D.C.: Bureau of National Literature and Art, 1909.

Richardson, Leon B. *William E. Chandler, Republican*. New York: Dodd, Mead & Company, 1940.

Rolo, Paul J. *Entente Cordiale: The Origin and Negotiations of the Anglo-French Agreement of 8 April, 1904*. New York: St. Martin's Press, 1969.

Roscoe, Theodore. *On the Seas and in the Skies: A History of the U.S. Navy's Air Power*. New York: Hawthorn Books, Inc., 1970.

Sachar, Howard M. *The Emergence of the Middle East, 1914–1924*. New York: Knopf, 1970.

Sanjian, Avedis K. *The Armenian Communities in Syria under Ottoman Dominion*. Cambridge: Harvard University Press, 1965.

Sarkissian, Arshag. *History of the Armenian Question to 1885*. Urbana: University of Illinois Press, 1938.

Schaeffer, Evelyn Schuyler. *Eugene Schuyler: Selected Essays with a Memoir*. New York: Charles Scribner's Sons, 1901.

Scholes, Walter V., and Marie V. Scholes. *The Foreign Policy of the Taft Administration*. Columbia: University of Missouri Press, 1970.

Seton-Watson, R. W. *Disraeli, Gladstone, and the Eastern Question*. New York: W. W. Norton & Company, Inc., 1972.

Smith, Daniel M. *Robert Lansing and American Neutrality, 1914–1917*. Berkeley: University of California Press, 1958.

Sousa, Nasim. *Capitulatory Regime of Turkey: Its History, Origin, and Nature*. Baltimore: The Johns Hopkins Press, 1933.

Sprout, Harold, and Margaret Sprout. *The Rise of American Naval Power, 1776–1918*. Princeton: Princeton University Press, 1946.

Stead, William T. *The Americanization of the World; or the Trend of the Twentieth Century*. New York: H. Marckley, 1902.

Stuart, Graham H. *The International City of Tangier*. Stanford: Stanford University Press, 1955.

Tansill, Charles C. *The Foreign Policy of Thomas F. Bayard, 1885–1897*. New York: Fordham University Press, 1940.

Thomas, Francis P. *Career of John Grimes Walker, USN, 1835–1907*. Boston: privately printed, 1959.

Thompson, Arthur W., and Robert A. Hart. *The Uncertain Crusade: America and the Russian Revolution of 1905*. Amherst: University of Massachusetts Press, 1970.

Tibawi, A. L. *American Interests in Syria, 1800–1901*. Oxford, England: Clarendon Press, 1966.

Trumpener, U. *Germany & the Ottoman Empire, 1914–18*. Princeton: Princeton University Press, 1968.

Trauth, Sister Mary P. *Italo-American Diplomatic Relations, 1861–1882*. Washington, D.C.: The American University, 1958.

Tyler, Alice F. *The Foreign Policy of James G. Blaine*. Minneapolis: University of Minnesota Press, 1927.

Vagts, Alfred. *Deutschland und die Vereinigten Staaten in der Weltpolitik*. 2 vols. London: Lovat Dickson & Thompson, Ltd., 1935.

——. *Defense & Diplomacy: The Soldier and the Conduct of Foreign Relations*. New York: King's Crown Press, 1956.

——. *The Military Attache: A History*. Princeton: Princeton University Press, 1967.

Van Deusen, Glyndon G. *William Henry Seward*. New York: Oxford University Press, 1967.

Varg, Paul A. *Open Door Diplomat: The Life of W. W. Rockhill*. Urbana: University of Illinois Press, 1952.

——. *Missionaries, Chinese, and Diplomats*. Princeton: Princeton University Press, 1958.

Waugh, Sir Telford. *Turkey, Yesterday, Today and Tomorrow*. London: Chapman and Hall, 1930.

Weber, Frank E. *Eagle on the Crescent: Germany, Austria, and the Diplomacy of the Turkish Alliance, 1914–1918*. Ithaca: Cornell University Press, 1970.

West, Richard S., Jr. *The Second Admiral*. New York: Coward-McCann, Inc., 1937.

——. *Admirals of American Empire*. Indianapolis: The Bobbs-Merrill Company, 1948.

Wilkins, Mira. *The Emergence of Multinational Enterprise: American Business Abroad from the Colonial Era to 1914*. Cambridge: Harvard University Press, 1970.

Williams, William A. *American Russian Relations, 1781–1947*. New York: Rinehart & Company, 1952.

——. *The Roots of the Modern American Empire*. New York: Random House, Inc., 1969.

Williamson, Samuel R., Jr. *The Politics of Grand Strategy: Britain and France Prepare for War, 1904–1914*. Boston: Harvard University Press, 1969.

Woodward, William E. *Meet General Grant*. New York: Premier Books, 1957.

Wright, Lenoir. *United States Policy Toward Egypt, 1830–1914*. New York: Exposition Press, 1969.

Younger, Edward. *John A. Kesson: Politics and Diplomacy from Lincoln to McKinley*. Iowa City: University of Iowa Press, 1955.

Zechlin, Egmont. *Die deutsche Politik und die Juden in Ersten Weltkrieg*. Gottingen: Vandenhoeck u. Ruprecht, 1969.

Articles

Askew, William C., and J. Fred Rippy. "The United States and Europe's Strife." *Journal of Politics* 4 (February 1942): 68–79.

Blumenthal, Henry. "George Bancroft in Berlin, 1867–1874." *The New England Quarterly* 37 (June 1964): 224–41.

Bradford, Commander Royal R. "Coaling Stations for the Navy." *Forum* 26 (1899): 732–47.

Challener, Richard D. "Montenegro and the United States: A Balkan Fantasy." *Journal of Central European Affairs* 17 (October 1957): 236–42.

Clifford, Dale. "Elihu Benjamin Washburn: An American Diplomat in Paris, 1870–71." *Prologue* 2 (Winter 1970): 161–74.

Cloverius, W. T. "The *Scorpion* Passes." *United States Naval Institute Proceedings* 53 (September 1927): 969–73.

Colby, Chester. "Diplomacy of the Quarter Deck." *The American Journal of International Law* 8 (1914): 443–76.

Coontz, Robert E. "The Navy as a Protective Investment." *Current History* 17 (December

1922): 403–10.

Cox, Frederick J. "The American Naval Mission in Egypt." *Journal of Modern History* 26 (June 1954): 173–78.

Ellicott, J. M. "Three Navy Cranks and What They Turned." *United States Naval Institute Proceedings* 49 (October 1924): 1615–28.

Farenholt, A. "And There Were Giants on the Earth in Those Days." *United States Naval Institute Proceedings* 62 (April 1936): 519–21.

Field, James A., Jr. "A Scheme in Regard to Cyrenaica." *Mississippi Valley Historical Review* 44 (December 1957): 445–68.

Gahier, Urbain. "American Intervention in Turkey." *North American Review* 173 (November 1901): 618–626.

Grabill, Joseph L. "Missionary Influence on American Relations with the Near East." *Muslim World* 58 (January & April 1968): 43–56, 141–54.

———. "Cleveland H. Dodge, Woodrow Wilson, and the Near East." *Journal of Presbyterian History* 48 (Winter 1970): 249–64.

———. "The Invisible Missionary: A Study in American Foreign Relations." *Journal of Church & State* 14 (Winter 1972): 96–106.

Greene, Fred. "The Military View of American National Policy, 1904–1940." *American Historical Review* 66 (January 1961): 354–77.

Grenville, J.A.S. "Goluchowski, Salisbury and the Mediterranean Agreement." *Slavonic Review* 36 (1958): 340–69.

———. "Diplomacy and War Plans in the United States, 1890–1917." *Transactions of the Royal Historical Society* 11 (1961): 1–21.

———. "American Naval Preparation for War with Spain, 1896–1898." *Journal of American Studies* 2 (1968): 33–47.

Herwig, Holger H., and David F. Trask. "Naval Operations Plans Between Germany and the United States of America, 1898–1913: A Study of Strategic Planning in the Age of Imperialism." *Militargeschichtliche Mitteilungen* 2/1970: 5–32.

Hobo, Paul S. "Perilous Obscurity: Public Diplomacy and the Press in the Venezuelan Crisis, 1902–1903." *The Historian* 32 (May 1970): 428–48.

Howard, Harry N. "The United States and the Problem of the Turkish Straits." *Middle East Journal* I (January 1947): 59–72.

———. "The United States and the Problem of the Turkish Straits: The Foundations of American Policy (1830–1914)." *Balkan Studies* 3 (1962): 1–28; 4 (1963): 225–50.

———. "President Lincoln's Minister Resident to the Sublime Porte: Edward Joy Morris (1861–1870)." *Balkan Studies* 5 (1964): 205–20.

Jefferson, Margaret M. "Lord Salisbury and the Eastern Question, 1890–1898." *Slavonic and East European Review* 39 (1960–61): 44–60.

Johnson, Arthur N. "Theodore Roosevelt and the Navy." *United States Naval Institute Proceedings* 86 (October 1958): 76–82.

Lewis, Charles Lee. "The Old Navy at Constantinople." *The United States Naval Institute Proceedings* 59 (October 1933): 1442–48.

Livermore, Seward W. "Theodore Roosevelt, the American Navy and the Venezuelan Crisis of 1902–1903." *The American Historical Review* 51 (April 1946): 452–71.

———. "American Navy as a Factor in World Politics, 1903–1913." *The American Historical Review* 63 (July 1958): 863–79.

Luzzatti, Luigi. "The economic relations of the United States with Italy." *North American Review* 177 (August 1903): 247–59.

May, Arthur J. "Crete and the United States, 1866–1869." *Journal of Modern History* 16 (December 1944): 286–93.

O'Laughlin, J. C. "The American Fighting Fleet: Its Strategic Disposition." *Cassier's Magazine* 24 (1903): 375–86.

Parsons, Edward B. "The German-American Crisis of 1902–1903." *Historian* 33 (May 1971): 436–52.
Peabody, Francis. "An Episode in International Philanthropy." *New England Quarterly* 6 (March 1933): 85–97.
Porter, Admiral David E. "Present Condition of the U.S. Navy." *International Review* 6 (June 1879): 369–85.
"The Right Arm of Diplomacy." *Public Opinion* 7 (July 1889): 271.
Shippee, L. B. "Germany and the Spanish-American War." *American Historical Review* 30 (July 1925): 754–77.
Smith, Daniel. "Robert Lansing and the Formation of American Neutrality Policies, 1914– 1915." *Mississippi Valley Historical Review* 43 (June 1956): 59–81.
Smith, Harold F. "Bread for the Russians: William C. Edgar and the Relief Campaign of 1892." *Minnesota History* 42 (Summer 1970): 54–62.
Spector, Ronald. "Roosevelt, the Navy and the Venezuelan Controversy: 1902–1903." *American Neptune* 32 (October 1972): 257–63.
Taylor, Henry C. "The Fleet." *United States Naval Institute Proceedings* 29 (December 1903): 805.
Tuchman, Barbara. "Perdicaris Alive or Raisuli Dead." *American Heritage* 10 (August 1959): 18–21.
Vagts, Alfred. "Hopes and Fears of an American German War, 1870–1915." *Political Science Quarterly* 54 (December 1939): 514–35; 55 (March 1940): 53–76.
Xydis, Stephen G. "Diplomatic Relations between the United States and Greece, 1868–1878." *Balkan Studies* 5 (1964): 47–62.

Supplemental Articles

Gurney, Frank W. "The U.S. Despatch Agency in London." *United States Naval Institute Proceedings* 62 (February 1936): 189–200.
Holbrook, Francis X., and John Nikol. "The Courting Season of 1903." *United States Naval Institute Proceedings* 101 (December 1975): 60–63.
Johnson, Robert E. "A Cruise in the *U.S.S. Lancaster*." *The American Neptune* 33 (Fall 1973): 280–92.
Lewis, Tom T. "Franco-American Relations During the First Moroccan Crisis." *Mid-America* 55 (January 1973): 21–36.
Marroro, Howard R. "Spezia: An American Naval Base, 1848–68." *Military Affairs* 7 (1943): 202–8.
Rodgers, William L. "The Navy as an Aid in Carrying Out Diplomatic Policies." *United States Naval Institute Proceedings* 55 (February 1929).
Seager, Robert, II. "Ten Years Before Mahan: The Unofficial Case for the New Navy, 1880– 1890." *Mississippi Valley Historical Review* 40 (December 1953): 491–512.

Unpublished Works

Bray, William J., Jr. "The Career of the *CSS Rappahannock*." Master's thesis, East Carolina University, 1975.
Buhl, Lance C. "The Smooth-Water Navy: American Naval Policy and Politics, 1865–1876." Ph.D diss., Harvard University, 1968.
Collins, George W. "United States-Moroccan Relations, 1904–1912." Ph.D. diss., University of Colorado, 1965.
Conrad, Roberick H. "Spanish-United States Relations, 1868–1874." Ph.D. diss., University of Georgia, 1969.
Cook, Ralph E. "The United States and the Armenian Question." Ph.D. diss., Fletcher School of Diplomacy, 1957.

Costello, Daniel J. "Planning for War: A History of the General Board of the Navy." Ph.D. diss.,
    Fletcher School of Diplomacy, 1969.
Edwards, Rosaline de G. "Relations Between the United States and Turkey, 1893–1897." Ph.D.
    diss., Fordham University, 1952.
Ellsworth, H. A. "One Hundred Eighty Landings of the United States Marines," Marine Corps
    Historical Section, Department of the Navy Library, 1934.
Goll, Eugene W. "The Diplomacy of Walter Q. Gresham, Secretary of State, 1893–1895."
    Ph.D. diss., Pennsylvania State University, 1974.
Jackson, Shirley F. "The United States and Spain, 1898–1918." Ph.D. diss., Florida State
    University, 1967.
Kerner, Howard J. "Turco-American Diplomatic Relations, 1860–1880." Ph.D. diss., George-
    town University, 1948.
Livermore, Seward W. "American Naval Developments, 1898–1914." Ph.D. diss., Harvard
    University, 1943.
McDonough, George P. "American Relations with Turkey, 1893–1901." Ph.D. diss., George-
    town University, 1949.
Moore, John H. "America Looks at Turkey, 1876–1909." Ph.D. diss., University of Virginia,
    1961.
Schilling, Warner R. "Admirals and Foreign Policy, 1913–1919." Ph.D. diss., Yale University,
    1953.
Stinagle, George W. "Ambassador Henry Morgenthau to Turkey, 1913–1916: Protection of
    American Rights." Master's thesis, East Carolina University, 1973.

INDEX

About the Author

William N. Still, Jr. is professor of history at East Carolina University, Greenville, North Carolina. He is the author of *Confederate Shipbuilding* and *Iron Afloat: The Story of the Confederate Armorclads*, among many other works.